PHP & MySQL

Second Edition

the missing manual®

The book that should have been in the box®

Brett McLaughlin

O'REILLY®

Beijing | Cambridge | Farnham | Köln | Sebastopol | Tokyo

PHP & MySQL: The Missing Manual, Second Edition

by Brett McLaughlin

Published by O'Reilly Media, Inc.,
1005 Gravenstein Highway North, Sebastopol, CA 95472.

O'Reilly books may be purchased for educational, business, or sales promotional use. Online editions are also available for most titles (*http://my.safaribooksonline.com*). For more information, contact our corporate/institutional sales department: (800) 998-9938 or *corporate@oreilly.com*.

November 2011:   First Edition.
November 2012:   Second Edition.

Revision History for the Second Edition:

   2012-11-5   First release

See *http://oreilly.com/catalog/errata.csp?isbn=0636920024927* for release details.

[LSI]

ISBN: 978-1-449-32557-2

Contents

Part One: **PHP and MySQL Basics**

Part Two: **Dynamic Web Pages**

Part Three: From Web Pages to Web Applications

The Missing Credits

ABOUT THE AUTHOR

 **Brett McLaughlin** is a senior-level technologist and strategist, active especially in web programming and data-driven, customer-facing systems. Rarely focused on only one component of a system, he architects, designs, manages, and implements large-scale applications from start to finish with mission-critical implementations and deadlines.

Of course, that's all fancy-talk for saying that Brett's a geek, spending most of his day in front of a computer with his hands flying across a keyboard. Currently, he spends most of his time working on NASA projects, which sounds much cooler than it actually is. But hey, maybe that satellite overhead really is controlled by PHP and MySQL...

ABOUT THE CREATIVE TEAM

Nan Barber (editor) has been working on the Missing Manual series since its inception. She lives in Boston with her husband and various electronic devices. Email: *nanbarber@oreilly.com.*

Holly Bauer (production editor) lives in Ye Olde Cambridge, Massachusetts, where she is an avid home cook, prolific DIYer, and mid-century modern furniture design enthusiast. Email: *holly@oreilly.com.*

Bob Russell (copyeditor) is a documentation specialist and President of Octal Publishing, Inc., in Salem, New Hampshire (*www.octalpub.com*). Email: *bob.russell@ octalpub.com.*

Bob Pfahler (indexer) is a freelance indexer. For the past five years, he has indexed many computer books as well as biographies, history, and business books. When he is not working, he likes to take bike rides in the foothills outside of Denver. He indexed this book as an associate for Potomac Indexing (*www.potomacindexing.com*).

Roger House (technical reviewer) is a freelance software developer living in northern California. He has written code in many languages for various kinds of applications. He enjoys algorithm design, use of data structures, and applications of mathematics. Web: *www.rogerfhouse.com.* Email: *rhouse@sonic.net.*

Steve Suehring (technical reviewer) is a technical architect with an extensive background finding simple solutions to complex problems. Steve plays several musical instruments (not at the same time) and can be reached through his website *www .braingia.org.*

ACKNOWLEDGMENTS

Acknowledgments are nearly impossible to do well. Before you can thank anyone of substance, the music swells and they're shuffling you off stage. Seriously, apart from the writing, there's my wife, Leigh, and my kids, Dean, Robbie, and Addie. Any energy or joy or relaxation that happens during the long writing process filters through those four, and there are never enough royalties to cover the time lost with them. I suppose it's a reflection of their love and support for me that they're OK with me writing anyway.

There's certainly the writing. Brian Sawyer was the first guy to call me when I became available to write, and he called when I was really in need of just what he gave me: excitement about me writing and encouragement that I could write for the Missing Manual series. I won't forget that call anytime soon. And, there's Nan Barber, who IM'ed and emailed me throughout the entire process. She showed a really unhealthy level of trust that wasn't earned, and I'm quite thankful...especially in the dark days of early August, when I had hundreds of pages left to write, in just a few short weeks.

Roger House and Steve Suehring, my technical reviewers, were both picky and gentle. That's about all you can ask. And Steve filled out my PHP holes. He caught one particularly nasty issue that I think vastly improved the book. You don't realize this, but you owe him a real debt of thanks if this book helps you.

— Brett McLaughlin

THE MISSING MANUAL SERIES

Missing Manuals are witty, superbly written guides to computer products that don't come with printed manuals (which is just about all of them). Each book features a handcrafted index and cross-references to specific pages (not just chapters).

Recent and upcoming titles include:

Access 2010: The Missing Manual by Matthew MacDonald

Adobe Edge Animate: The Missing Manual by Chris Grover

Buying a Home: The Missing Manual by Nancy Conner

CSS3: The Missing Manual, Third Edition, by David Sawyer McFarland

Creating a Website: The Missing Manual, Third Edition, by Matthew MacDonald

David Pogue's Digital Photography: The Missing Manual by David Pogue

Dreamweaver CS5.5: The Missing Manual by David Sawyer McFarland

Droid 2: The Missing Manual by Preston Gralla

Droid X2: The Missing Manual by Preston Gralla

Excel 2010: The Missing Manual by Matthew MacDonald

Facebook: The Missing Manual, Third Edition by E.A. Vander Veer

FileMaker Pro 12: The Missing Manual by Susan Prosser and Stuart Gripman

Flash CS5.5: The Missing Manual by Chris Grover

Galaxy S II: The Missing Manual by Preston Gralla

Galaxy Tab: The Missing Manual by Preston Gralla

Google Apps: The Missing Manual by Nancy Conner

Google SketchUp: The Missing Manual by Chris Grover

HTML5: The Missing Manual by Matthew MacDonald

iMovie '11 & iDVD: The Missing Manual by David Pogue and Aaron Miller

iPad: The Missing Manual, Fifth Edition by J.D. Biersdorfer

iPhone: The Missing Manual, Sixth Edition by David Pogue

iPhone App Development: The Missing Manual by Craig Hockenberry

iPhoto '11: The Missing Manual by David Pogue and Lesa Snider

iPod: The Missing Manual, Eleventh Edition by J.D. Biersdorfer and David Pogue

JavaScript & jQuery: The Missing Manual by David Sawyer McFarland

Kindle Fire: The Missing Manual, Second Edition by Peter Meyers

Living Green: The Missing Manual by Nancy Conner

Mac OS X Snow Leopard: The Missing Manual by David Pogue

Mac OS X Lion: The Missing Manual by David Pogue

Microsoft Project 2010: The Missing Manual by Bonnie Biafore

Motorola Xoom: The Missing Manual by Preston Gralla

Netbooks: The Missing Manual by J.D. Biersdorfer

NOOK Tablet: The Missing Manual by Preston Gralla

Office 2010: The Missing Manual by Nancy Connor, Chris Grover, and Matthew MacDonald

Office 2011 for Macintosh: The Missing Manual by Chris Grover

Palm Pre: The Missing Manual by Ed Baig

Personal Investing: The Missing Manual by Bonnie Biafore

Photoshop CS6: The Missing Manual by Lesa Snider

Photoshop Elements 11: The Missing Manual by Barbara Brundage

PowerPoint 2007: The Missing Manual by E.A. Vander Veer

Premiere Elements 8: The Missing Manual by Chris Grover

QuickBase: The Missing Manual by Nancy Conner

QuickBooks 2013: The Missing Manual by Bonnie Biafore

Quicken 2009: The Missing Manual by Bonnie Biafore

Switching to the Mac: The Missing Manual, Snow Leopard Edition by David Pogue

Switching to the Mac: The Missing Manual, Lion Edition by David Pogue

Wikipedia: The Missing Manual by John Broughton

Windows Vista: The Missing Manual by David Pogue

Windows 7: The Missing Manual by David Pogue

Windows 8: The Missing Manual by David Pogue

Word 2007: The Missing Manual by Chris Grover

WordPress: The Missing Manual by Matthew MacDonald

Your Body: The Missing Manual by Matthew MacDonald

Your Brain: The Missing Manual by Matthew MacDonald

Your Money: The Missing Manual by J.D. Roth

Introduction

Given that you're reading this book, the chances are good that you've built a web page in HTML. You've styled it by using Cascading Style Sheets (CSS) and maybe written a little JavaScript to validate your custom-built web forms. If that wasn't enough, you've learned a lot more JavaScript, threw in some jQuery, and constructed a whole lot of web pages. Maybe you've even moved your JavaScript into external files, shared your CSS across your entire site, and validated your HTML with the latest standards.

But now you want more.

Perhaps you've become frustrated with your website's inability to store user information in anything beyond cookies. Maybe you want a full-blown online store, complete with PayPal integration and details about what items are in stock. Or maybe you've simply caught the programming bug and want to go beyond what HTML, CSS, and JavaScript can easily give you.

If any of these are the case—and you may find that *all* of these are the case—learning PHP and MySQL is a great way to take a giant programming step forward. Even if you've never heard of PHP, you'll find it's the best way to go from building web pages to creating full-fledged web applications that store all sorts of information in databases. This book shows you how to do just that.

■ What PHP and MySQL Can Do

PHP can handle payment processing on its own, and it can connect with services like PayPal and Google Checkout. PHP can store and load images from a database or a file system and give you the ability to log users in and out as well as control what they see throughout your application.

Add in MySQL, and you can store your users' names, addresses, billing data, and even their preferences regarding the color of their own personal landing page. MySQL can store just a few bits of data, a few thousand lines of data, or every page access by every user who ever logs into your application.

And, of course, PHP can easily connect to MySQL. PHP can do everything from grabbing a user name based on a user ID to storing the details about financial transactions to actually creating tables and updating their structures, and MySQL can back-end all that work and store that data. Ultimately, this is the stuff of web applications; it's what a web application *is*.

Obviously, web applications like this aren't simple. They have a lot of complexity, and that complexity has to be managed and ultimately tamed into a usable, sensible web application that you can maintain and your users can enjoy. That's what this book is about: building web applications, and doing it with an understanding of what you're doing, and why you're doing it.

■ What Is PHP?

PHP started out as a set of tools for doing simple web-related tasks. It appeared on the Web scene way back in 1994. Initially, PHP did nothing more than just track visits to a particular web page (the online resume of Rasmus Lerdorf—the inventor of PHP). It was then expanded to interact with databases, as well as provide a tool set for online guest books and HTML form processing. The next thing you know, it was hugely popular as an alternative to less web-friendly languages like C.

New versions of PHP started coming out, and an increasing number of web programmers adopted it as their scripting language of choice for web tasks. PHP 3, 4, and now 5 are now mainstays on the Web. PHP has become fast while remaining lightweight. And, of course, its ability to easily interact with databases such as MySQL remains one of its most attractive features.

What Is PHP Like?

PHP is a programming language. It's like JavaScript in that you spend most of your time dealing with values and making decisions about which path through your code should be followed at any given time. But it's like HTML in that you deal with output—tags that your users view through the lens of their web browsers. In fact, PHP in the context of web programming is a bit of a mutt; it does lots of things pretty well, rather than just doing one single thing. (And, if you've ever wondered *why* it's called PHP, see the box on the following page.)

Personal Home Page, Indeed

What does PHP stand for?

PHP is an acronym. Originally, it stood for *Personal Home Page Construction Kit*, because lots of programmers used it to build their websites, going much further than what was possible with HTML, CSS, and JavaScript. But in the last few years, "personal home page" tends to sound more like something that happens on one of those really cheap hosting sites, rather than a high-powered programming language.

So now, PHP stands for *PHP: Hypertext Preprocessor*. If that sounds geeky, it is. In fact, it's a bit of a programmer joke: PHP stands for something that actually contains PHP within itself. That makes it a *recursive* acronym, meaning that it references itself. You don't have to know what a recursive acronym is; that won't be on the quiz. Just be warned that PHP's recursive acronym won't be the last weird and slightly funny thing you'll run across in the PHP language.

PHP Is All About the Web

If you came here for web programming, you're in the right place. Although you can write PHP programs that run from a command line (check out Figure I-1 for an example), that's not really where it excels. The PHP programs you write run within your website, part and parcel with your HTML forms, web sessions, and browser cookies. For example, PHP is great at integrating with your website's existing authentication system, or letting you create one of your own.

```
Untitled
<?php

echo "Hello there. So I hear you're learning to be a PHP programmer!\n";
echo "Why don't you type in your name for me:\n";
$name = trim(fgets(STDIN));

echo "\nThanks, " . $name . ", it's really nice to meet you.\n\n";

?>
```

FIGURE I-1

Sure, you can run PHP programs from a Terminal window or a command shell in Windows. But most of the time, you won't. PHP is perfectly suited to the Web, and that's where you'll spend most of your time.

You'll spend a lot of time not just handing off control to an HTML page, but actually writing the HTML you're already familiar with right into your PHP scripts. Lots of times, you'll actually write some PHP and then write some HTML, all in the same PHP file, as in the following example:

```
<?php
require '../../scripts/database_connection.php';
// Get the user ID of the user to show
$user_id = $_REQUEST['user_id'];

// Build the SELECT statement
$select_query = "SELECT * FROM users WHERE user_id = " . $user_id;
```

```
// Run the query
$result = mysql_query($select_query);

// Assign values to variables
?>

<html>
  <head>
    <link href="../css/phpMM.css" rel="stylesheet" type="text/css" />
  </head>
  <body>
    <div id="header"><h1>PHP & MySQL: The Missing Manual</h1></div>
    <div id="example">User Profile</div>
    <div id="content">
      <div class="user_profile">
        <h1><?php echo "{$first_name} {$last_name}"; ?></h1>
        <p><img src="show_image.php?image_id=<?php echo $image_id; ?>"
class="user_pic" />
          <?php echo $bio; ?></p>
        <p class="contact_info">Get in touch with <?php echo $first_name; ?>:</
p>
        <ul>
    <!-- And so on... lots more HTML here. -->
</html>
```

This script references another script, *database_connection.php,* and then extracts a user's ID from the request parameters sent by a web browser. The script uses that ID to search a database for the rest of the user's information. Then, it builds the data into a web page that's created on the fly.

The result? Pages that are both full of HTML and have dynamic content, like Figure I-2.

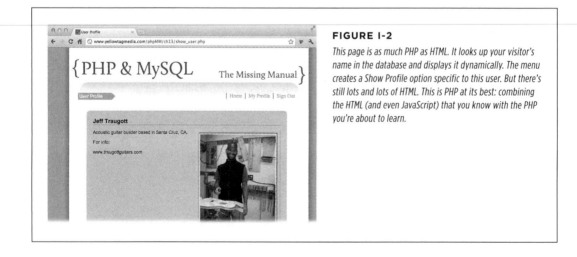

FIGURE I-2

This page is as much PHP as HTML. It looks up your visitor's name in the database and displays it dynamically. The menu creates a Show Profile option specific to this user. But there's still lots and lots of HTML. This is PHP at its best: combining the HTML (and even JavaScript) that you know with the PHP you're about to learn.

JavaScript Is Loose, PHP Is...Less So

If you've written some JavaScript—and if you're checking out this book, that's probably the case—you know that JavaScript lets you get away with just about anything. You can occasionally leave out semicolons; you can use brackets, or not; you can use the *var* keyword, or not. That sort of looseness is great for getting things working quickly, but at the same time, it's frustrating. It makes finding bugs tricky at times, and working across browsers can be a nightmare.

PHP is not quite as loose as JavaScript, so it makes you learn a little more structure and tighten up your understanding of what's going on as your program is constructed and then run. That's a good thing, because it will end up making you tighten up your JavaScript skills, too. And, perhaps best of all, PHP's stodgy consistency makes it easier to learn. It gives you firm rules to hang on to, rather than lots of "You can do this...or this...or this..."

So get ready. There is a lot to learn, but everything you learn gives you something on which to build. And PHP, lets you know right away when there's a problem. You won't need to pop open an error console or keep an eye out for the tiny yellow warning triangle in Internet Explorer as you do with JavaScript. More often, you'll get a nasty error that stops you in your tracks and screams, "Fix me!" And, over the next couple of hundred pages, you'll be able to do just that: fix the problems you'll run across in typical PHP programs, whether you've written those programs or someone else has.

PHP Is Interpreted

PHP code comes in the form of *scripts*, which are plain-text files that you create and fill with code. Whereas HTML uses lots of angle brackets and keywords like html, head, and ul, PHP uses lots of dollar signs ($) and keywords like mysql_query and echo. So, HTML and PHP don't look at all alike. But where they are alike is in the basic underlying format: they're both just text. You can open up an HTML document not just in a web browser, but in Notepad or an integrated development environment (IDE) like Eclipse or even a command-line editor like vi or emacs. The same is true for PHP: it's just text. So, get ready; throughout this book, you'll be typing words—albeit strange ones, with lots of underscores—and saving those words into text files called scripts.

Once you've got a script, you let a PHP program interpret that script. The PHP *interpreter* is a piece of software on your web server that reads your script and makes sense of it, giving the web server output and directions about where to go next or how to handle a user's form field entries. Your script—remember, just a text file—is interpreted, one line at a time, every time it is accessed.

This is a bit different from languages like Java or C++, which are *compiled*. In those languages, you also write your code in text files, but then run a command that turns those text files into something else: class files, binary files, pieces of unreadable code that your computer uses.

The beauty of an interpreted language like PHP—and JavaScript, for that matter—is that you write your code and go. You don't need a bunch of tools or subsequent steps. You write PHP, test it out in the browser, and then write some more. It's fast, and that usually means it's pretty fun.

PHP Doesn't Run in the Browser

There's one other big difference between PHP and what you may be used to with HTML, CSS, and JavaScript. It's a big difference, too; in fact, this difference is such a big deal that it's going to affect everything you do when it comes to writing PHP scripts, getting those PHP scripts to run, and checking them out in a web browser.

So what's the difference? It's this: PHP, unlike HTML or CSS or JavaScript, doesn't run entirely in a browser.

What does that mean? Chapter 1 begins to get into the details, but for now, you just need to know that HTML, JavaScript, and CSS are entirely handled by your web browser software. Whether you use Internet Explorer, Apple Safari, Google Chrome, Mozilla Firefox, or Opera, once you have a browser, you have everything you need. That's why you can write an HTML document, save it with an extension like .html, double-click that file, and voilà: your browser opens (assuming you've got things set up on your computer the right way) and you're looking at HTML. You can reference CSS in that HTML file as well as JavaScript, and the same thing happens. Write code, save, and open. Pretty easy stuff.

With PHP, you'll need a bit more than that. The PHP interpreter interacts with your browser but doesn't run in the browser automatically. In other words, you cannot simply double-click a PHP script and expect a browser to pop up and handle things. HTML forms that submit to a PHP script won't "just work" the way that HTML and JavaScript do.

Right now, then, you just need to know two things:

- It's going to take a little more work to get your PHP programs working. You can't just write and save a script and then open it the way you can HTML. Don't worry; you'll learn exactly how to get PHP working both locally—on your computer—and remotely—on a web hosting company's servers. But it's going to take a little more effort.

- It's not trivial to set up everything you need to run PHP programs on your own computer—especially once you involve MySQL, too (more on this in just a moment). That's why Internet Service Providers (ISPs) and web hosting companies exist! They take care of that sort of thing. So, although it's possible to do all your PHP coding on your own machine, it's a lot more common to write your scripts and then send them to a remote web server. Sound scary? It's not...but it's important. You'll spend a good bit of time in this book writing code and uploading it to a server.

PHP is different from JavaScript and HTML in some important ways. You'll get used to those differences, but you'll be a lot less frustrated and confused if you go in knowing that you'll have to do some things differently when it comes to PHP.

What Is MySQL?

MySQL is a database. It stores your information, your users' information, and anything else you want to stuff into it. But, beyond its ability to store information, MySQL is popular. In fact, it's the most popular open-source database system in the world. It has literally millions of users working with it, finding and reporting problems, and testing its limits. And, it has thousands of developers that at some point have helped improved its code base.

MySQL is essentially a warehouse in which you can store things to be looked up later. Not only that, MySQL provides you with a really fast mechanism to find all that stuff you stuck in the warehouse whenever it's needed. By the time you're through this book, you'll love MySQL. It will do work that you could never do on your own, and it will do that work tirelessly and quickly.

It's also the perfect companion to PHP. It's easy to install on any system; it doesn't take up huge resources like larger commercial offerings such as Oracle's or IBM's products; and its easy to connect to. In fact, you'll find that PHP and MySQL are perfectly matched, with a ton of easy-to-use functions that let PHP scripts to do just about anything you can imagine with a MySQL database.

> **NOTE** There's actually a lot more nuance to MySQL—and SQL, the language in which you'll interact with MySQL—but it's better to save that for Chapter 4, when you've got a little PHP under your belt.

About This Book

PHP is a web-based language, not a program that comes in a box. Tens of thousands (maybe even hundreds of thousands) of websites have bits of PHP tutorial or instruction on them. That's great, right? Well, not so much. Those websites aren't all current. Some are full of bugs. Some have more information in the comment trails—scattered amongst gripes, complaints, and lambasting from other programmers—as they do in the main page. It's no easy matter to find what you're looking for.

The purpose of this book, therefore, is to serve as the manual that should have been included when you download PHP. It's the missing PDF, if you will (or maybe the missing eBook, if you're a Kindle or Nook or iPad person). In this book's pages, you'll find step-by-step instructions for getting PHP running, writing your first program... and your second program...and eventually building a web application from scratch. In addition, you'll find clear evaluations of the absolutely critical parts of PHP that you'll use every day, whether you're building a personal blog or a corporate intranet.

NOTE This book periodically recommends *other* books, covering topics that are too specialized or tangential for a manual about PHP and MySQL. Careful readers may notice that not every one of these titles is published by Missing Manual parent company O'Reilly Media. If there's a great book out there that doesn't happen to be published by O'Reilly, this book will still let you know about it.

PHP & MySQL: The Missing Manual is designed to accommodate readers at every technical level. The primary discussions are written for advanced-beginner or intermediate web authors and programmers. Hopefully, you're comfortable with HTML and CSS, and maybe even know a bit of JavaScript. But, if you're new to all this Web stuff, take heart: special boxes called "Up to Speed" provide the introductory information you need to understand the topic at hand. If you're an advanced user, on the other hand, keep your eye out for similar boxes called "Power Users' Clinic." They offer more technical tips, tricks, and shortcuts for the experienced computer fan.

Macintosh and Windows

PHP and MySQL work almost precisely the same in their Macintosh and Windows versions. Even more important, you'll do most of your work by uploading your scripts and running your database code against a web server. That means that your hosting provider has to deal with operating system issues; you get to focus on your code and information.

In the first few chapters, you get your system set up to write code and deal with PHP scripts. Thereafter, you will soon forget about whether you're on a Macintosh or using a Windows-based computer. You'll just be writing code, the same way you write HTML and CSS. And remember, you'll soon be uploading your scripts to remote web servers, so your own computer is only part of the solution.

FTP: It's Critical

One piece of software that's absolutely critical is a good FTP client. No matter how awesome your scripting skills become—and they're gonna be formidable!—you have to actually get your scripts to your web hosting server. That's where FTP comes in: it's the means by which a file on your computer gets placed in just the right location on a remote server.

NOTE **From the author:** Typing in a command-line editor is actually exactly how I work. But then, I'm a dinosaur, a throwback to days when you had to watch commercials to see primetime TV, and you'd miss emails because your pocket didn't buzz every time your boss whisked you a command through the ether.

Today, for most of you, a good text editor and a good graphical FTP client are much better choices. Seriously, my addiction owns me, and I so badly want to :*wq!* it.

Chapter 1 points you to several great editors, and the fancier ones will have FTP built right in. If you don't opt for an integrated solution, a dedicated FTP program like Cyberduck (*www.cyberduck.ch*) is great, too. You can write a script, throw it online, and test it all with a few mouse clicks. So, go ahead and get that FTP program downloaded, configured for your web hosting service (which might also be called your ISP), and fired up. You're gonna need it.

About the Outline

PHP & MySQL: The Missing Manual is divided into five parts, each containing several chapters:

- **Part 1: PHP and MySQL Basics**. In the first four chapters, you install PHP, get it running on your computer, write your first few PHP programs, and learn to do a few basic things like collect user information via a web form and work with text. You also install MySQL and become thoroughly acquainted with the structure of a database.

- **Part 2: Dynamic Web Pages**. These are the chapters in which you start to build the basics of a solid web application. You add a table in which you can store users and their information, and get a grasp of how easily you can manipulate text. From URLs and emails to Twitter handles, you use regular expressions and string handling to bend letters, numbers, and slashes to your will.

- **Part 3: From Web Pages to Web Applications**. With a solid foundation, you're ready to connect your web pages into a more cohesive unit. You add custom error handling so that your users won't become confused when things go wrong. You also add your own debugging to help you find problems. You also learn how to store references to users' images of themselves, store the images themselves in a database, and learn which approach is best in which situations.

- **Part 4: Security and the Real World**. In even the simplest of applications, logging in and logging out is critical. In this section, you build an authentication system and then deal with passwords (which are important, but a bit of a pain). You then work with cookies and sessions, and use both to create a group-based authorization system for your web application.

- **Part 5: Appendixes**. Although the first several chapters show you how to get PHP and MySQL onto your own Macintosh or Windows-based computer the easy way, using the WampServer software package or the Mac's built-in installation, the two appendixes in this section show you how to install the software manually for full control of all the details.

At the Missing Manual website (*www.missingmanuals.com/cds/phpmysqlmm2e*), you can find every single code example, from every chapter, in the state it is shown for that chapter.

■ About the Online Resources

As the owner of a Missing Manual, you've got more than just a book to read. Online, you can find example files so that you can get some hands-on experience, as well as tips, articles, and maybe even a video or two. You can also communicate with the Missing Manual team and tell us what you love (or hate) about the book. Head over to *www.missingmanuals.com*, or go directly to one of the following sections.

Missing CD

This book doesn't have a CD pasted inside the back cover, but you're not missing out on anything. Go to *www.missingmanuals.com/cds/phpmysqlmm2e* to download code samples, code samples, and also, some code samples. Yup, there are a lot of them. Every chapter has a section of code for that chapter. And, you don't just get completed versions of the book's scripts: You get a version that matches up with each chapter, so you'll never get too confused about exactly how your version of a script or web page should look.

And so you don't wear down your fingers typing long web addresses, the Missing CD page also offers a list of links that you can click to bring you to the websites mentioned in this book.

Registration

If you register this book at Oreilly.com (*http://oreilly.com*), you'll be eligible for special offers—like discounts on future editions of *PHP & MySQL: The Missing Manual*. Registering takes only a few clicks. To get started, type *www.oreilly.com/register* into your browser to hop directly to the Registration page.

Feedback

Got questions? Need more information? Fancy yourself a book reviewer? On the Feedback page, you can get expert answers to questions that come to you while reading, share your thoughts on this Missing Manual, and find groups for folks who share your interest in PHP, MySQL, and web applications in general. To have your say, go to *www.missingmanuals.com/feedback*.

Errata

In an effort to keep this book as up-to-date and accurate as possible, each time we print more copies, we'll make any confirmed corrections you've suggested. We also note such changes on the book's website, so you can mark important corrections into your own copy of the book, if you like. Go to *http://tinyurl.com/phpmysql2e-mm* to report an error and view existing corrections.

■ Safari® Books Online

PHP and MySQL Basics

PHP: What, Why, and Where?

P HP is ultimately just text that is taken by your web server and turned into a set of commands and information for your web browser. And because you're just working in text, there's not a lot you have to do to get going as a PHP programmer. You need to become familiar with PHP itself, and the best way to do that is to install PHP on your own computer as well as becoming familiar with how PHP runs on a remote web server.

Then, you need to run an actual script. Don't worry; it's amazingly easy to write your first program in PHP. Not only that, you'll run your script, upload it to your web server, and access your script with a web browser...and that's all in the first two chapters!

Throughout the process, you'll begin taking control. With PHP, you become an active participant in your web pages. PHP lets you listen carefully to your users and say something back. So get going; there's no reason to leave your users with passive HTML pages any longer.

■ PHP Comes in Two Flavors: Local and Remote

One of the most difficult things to get a handle on when it comes to PHP programming doesn't have much to do with programming at all. It's figuring out just how PHP runs, how it interacts with your web browser and web server, and why it's not possible to just double-click a PHP file on your hard drive and see the script in that file run.

HTML and CSS Run Within a Web Browser

First, it's worth thinking back to when you were a wee programmer, writing your first HTML page. You could save that page in a file, name that file with a *.html* extension, and boom—you had a web page. Double-click that file, and on most computers, you see that page open up in a web browser. That's because just as a *.doc* file is connected to the Microsoft Word program, a *.html* file is connected to a web browser (specifically, the browser you've chosen as the default on your computer). Figure 1-1 should give you an idea.

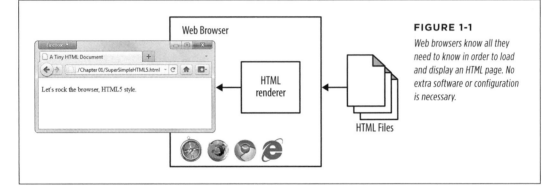

FIGURE 1-1

Web browsers know all they need to know in order to load and display an HTML page. No extra software or configuration is necessary.

If you keep thinking back, you probably added some styling to your HTML pages. Using the style attribute and <style></style> tags in your HTML document, you could change fonts, add striping to your table rows, and generally spice up otherwise boring text.

Then, at some point, some well-meaning web designer slapped your hand and insisted that you start writing all your CSS in external style sheets, and referencing those files in the head of your HTML, like this:

```
<link rel="stylesheet" href="styles/mysite.css" type="text/css" />
```

You might even have a few style sheets for the benefit of people viewing your website on mobile devices or printing out a page:

```
<link rel="stylesheet" href="styles/mysite.css" type="text/css" media="all" />
<link rel="stylesheet" href="styles/print.css" type="text/css" media="print" />
```

But you can still double-click that HTML file, and your browser knows what to do (see Figure 1-2). That's because, once again, the web browser is completely capable of not just rendering HTML, but applying all those CSS styles to the page, too. Again, no extra software needed.

At this point, even though you're using only two technologies—HTML and CSS—you need only a single program to handle those technologies: the web browser.

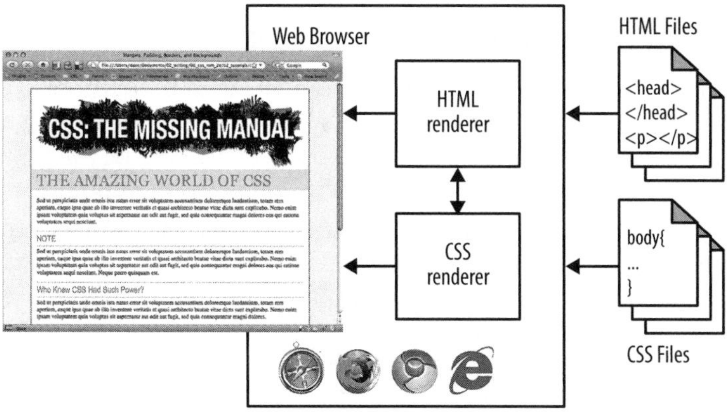

FIGURE 1-2

As was the case with HTML, web browsers don't need any extra help or plug-ins to turn your textual CSS descriptions into styles and apply those styles to your HTML elements.

JavaScript Adds Complexity, but Not Software

Next up in the pantheon of web technologies that every designer and fledgling programmer needs to learn: JavaScript. Suddenly, you weren't limited to elements that never moved and text that never changed. Whether it was simple phone number validation, more advanced jQuery functions that turned boring gray boxes into animated buttons and <div> elements into tabs, or even the new HTML5 canvas object, within which you could build entire JavaScript-based 3D games, your pages suddenly had new life with JavaScript.

But just as with HTML and CSS, JavaScript is at heart a web technology, and even more specifically, a *browser-based technology*. In other words, support for JavaScript is part and parcel of your web browser. In fact, if a new version of JavaScript were to appear—something that rarely happens these days—you'd need to download a new version of your *browser* to get that version of JavaScript. Just as you can't upgrade your HTML installation outside of your browser, you can't upgrade your JavaScript installation outside of your browser.

You Probably Have Multiple Versions of JavaScript Already!

Think about it: if JavaScript is built in to your browser, and you have more than one browser, you actually have multiple installations of JavaScript on your computer. Suppose that you have Internet Explorer and Firefox; you've got the JavaScript installation that came with Internet Explorer *and* the one that came with Firefox. Add Chrome or Opera to the mix, and you've got a few more installations. And, if you have multiple versions of a single browser—like Firefox 3.6.3 for testing with older Linux-based systems and the most current version (14 something-or-other as of late), they each have a different JavaScript installation.

Even though JavaScript doesn't get updated very often, those multiple installations usually translate into multiple versions of JavaScript, because JavaScript isn't a product that is distributed by a central organization to browser developers. Rather, it's a *specification*: a document that defines how things should work to be considered as JavaScript. That means that each browser has to write code that matches that specification so that they can say, "Yes, you can run JavaScript in our browser!"

Furthermore, each browser does things a bit differently, and that's why a website feature that works perfectly in Firefox might not quite work perfectly in Internet Explorer, and vice versa. So, even if you have two browsers that implement the same version of the JavaScript specification, the code in that implementation isn't identical; there are usually differences.

What does all this mean to you? Test your code—JavaScript, PHP, or otherwise—in as many browsers as you can. Things aren't always the same in every browser, and it's up to you—not your users—to handle inconsistencies.

Figure 1-3 shows you how JavaScript fits in (hint: just as HTML and CSS do).

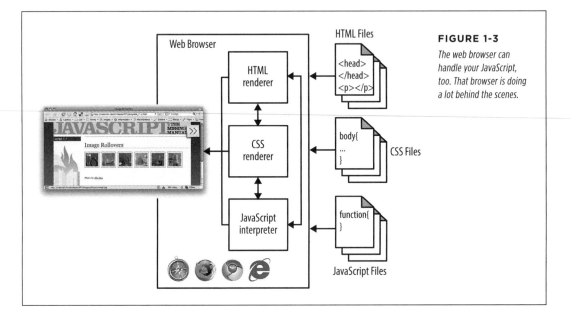

FIGURE 1-3

The web browser can handle your JavaScript, too. That browser is doing a lot behind the scenes.

NOTE The code that handles your HTML and CSS isn't quite as disconnected as it might appear from Figure 1-2 and Figure 1-3. In other words, there are no individual components in your web browser that render HTML or CSS. But you get the idea; your browser can handle all these different tasks and technologies and turn them into a web page.

PHP Is Not Part of Your Browser

And here's where things change from the easy, browser-centric view of the world. When you download a web browser, you get HTML, CSS, and JavaScript, but you do *not* get PHP. PHP scripts—which you'll soon be writing—have to be interpreted by the PHP interpreter program, called *php*. And, you can't just add a PHP interpreter to your browser. It doesn't know what to do with scripts and isn't built to interpret PHP.

Instead, you need PHP on a web server. It's the web *server*—not the web *browser*—that can interact with a PHP interpreter. Your browser can handle HTML on its own, but it has to make a request to a web server to deal with PHP scripts. That server can take your PHP scripts and run them, and then take the response and send it back to your browser. Your browser can then understand and handle the response.

So, Figure 1-4 adds a couple of new wrinkles: the PHP interpreter, the magical thing that takes the PHP scripts you'll be writing and does something useful with them; and a web server to communicate with that interpreter. These both live outside of your web browser. In this scenario, the browser now makes a request to the server and then takes the response and shows it to you.

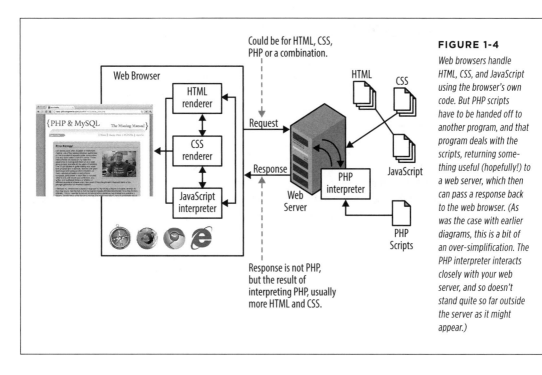

FIGURE 1-4

Web browsers handle HTML, CSS, and JavaScript using the browser's own code. But PHP scripts have to be handed off to another program, and that program deals with the scripts, returning something useful (hopefully!) to a web server, which then can pass a response back to the web browser. (As was the case with earlier diagrams, this is a bit of an over-simplification. The PHP interpreter interacts closely with your web server, and so doesn't stand quite so far outside the server as it might appear.)

Here's the basic process:

1. **A web browser makes a request for some page.** That page might be a URL on a remote web server, or a local file on your computer.

WARNING Right away, there's potential for trouble here. If the browser requests a local HTML, CSS, or JavaScript file, there's no problem. That's because, as you now know, browsers can handle those file types. But if it requests a PHP file without going through a web server you're not going to get a response that the browser can handle on its own.

---

2. **Assuming that the request goes to a web server, the web server returns HTML (and CSS and JavaScript) or, in the case of PHP, passes the PHP request on to the PHP interpreter.**

3. **The PHP interpreter does what it's supposed to: it interprets, or runs, the PHP.** The result of that should be something that a browser *can* understand, like HTML. It passes this result, or response, back to the web server.

4. **The web server gives the browser back something that the browser can understand: the HTML result of interpreting a PHP script, or CSS, or JavaScript, or a combination of all of the above.**

Understanding this difference in how PHP works, as opposed to HTML, CSS, and JavaScript, is important because it determines the approach you'll take to writing PHP scripts and getting those scripts to run.

Write Anywhere, Run Where There's PHP

The cool thing about HTML, CSS, and JavaScript is that because they're built in to browsers and you can download browsers so easily, those technologies become instantly available. It's tough to even find a computer *without* a browser preinstalled. So, you turn on your computer for the first time, and boom, you can start creating web pages immediately. Double-click the HTML file, your browser fires up, and you're good to go.

But PHP *isn't* part of that browser. It's *not* always preinstalled. If you write a PHP script and then double-click it, you'll probably see a code editor launch, but not something that will actually run that script. Even worse, if your browser does open up your PHP script, it's not a web server. It doesn't have a PHP interpreter. It will just show you your code, rather than run it, and what good is that to anyone?

This long prelude is just a big warning: although it's easy enough to start writing PHP scripts, you can't just open them in Dreamweaver or Firefox and expect them to run. You'll end up frustrated and annoyed, and that's no good for anyone.

The bottom line is this: You can write PHP on your own local computer, but you've got two choices for actually *running* that PHP:

1. **You can go through the lengthy process detailed in the next section and install PHP on your local computer.** This process will take some time, and you'll have to monkey around a bit with your computer at a system and network level. You'll also need a local web server to handle the PHP interpreting part of the gig. This way, you'll not only have a browser that can handle HTML, CSS, and JavaScript, but a complete setup that can take on PHP without a problem, too—right on your own computer.

2. **You can write your scripts locally and always upload them to an Internet Service Provider (ISP) or web hosting company.** Every ISP and web hosting company supports PHP, and you usually don't have to do anything more than name your scripts with a *.php* extension. This option involves less initial setup, but it means that every time you edit your script, you need to upload it again to your ISP. It also means that double-clicking your PHP script won't do anything more than, at best, open your editor. You can't test your scripts on your own computer.

Both choices are equally good, and which one you choose depends largely on your circumstances. Even though it might seem perfectly natural to jump right into up-loading your scripts, you aren't always going to have a network connection. (The sound you just heard was the cheering of all the programmers who have an hour-long commute into work on their local metro or subway!) For those unwired situations, it's nice to be able to keep developing on your own computer without the need to access your hosting provider. Note only that, installing PHP on your own computer is great for understanding what the PHP interpreter actually does.

So, before you start writing scripts that you can't even run, it's time to get PHP working on your own computer (if you want to), and then talk about getting scripts running out there in the wild, as well.

NOTE In the long run, you probably want to have both a way to use of PHP and MySQL without an Internet connection and a hosting provider or ISP set up. That way, you can work on your own computer whenever you want, and then upload your scripts when they're ready to see the light of day.

■ PHP: Going Local

It's not difficult to install PHP on your own computer. This is typically called a *local installation*, which just means that all your programs are running on your own local machine. (For more detail on how the whole thing works, see the box on page 22.)

Although PHP isn't preloaded on every computer like web browsers are, it's still easy to download PHP from the Internet, get it working on your computer, and get up and running fast...all without spending a dime. On top of that, most of the easiest and best tools for writing PHP code are also free. You just have to know where to find them.

POWER USERS' CLINIC

Local Software Runs on *localhost*

The term *local* has a lot of meanings in computer programming, especially when you start interacting with networks. Every computer is capable of sending information to itself, through a *loopback* network interface. This interface usually has the IP address 127.0.0.1 and a hostname of *localhost*.

This scenario becomes pretty handy when you want to run a web server on your own computer, and that's what you'll be

doing later when you get a local installation of PHP up and going. When you want to access that web server, you need to type something into your browser, and that's where *localhost* comes in. You can enter either the IP address *http://127.0.0.1*, or *http://localhost*, and your computer will send your request to itself...and any software you've got installed and running that's capable of receiving that request.

> **NOTE** The next section explains how to install PHP on computers running Microsoft Windows. If you have a Macintosh, flip to page 28.

PHP on the Windows-Based Computers (WampServer Installation)

Open your favorite web browser and head to *www.wampserver.com*. This is the online home of WAMP, which stands for Windows, Apache, MySQL, PHP. The site is shown in Figure 1-5.

> **NOTE** Although the website is called WampServer—and describes the grouping of software "Apache, PHP, MySQL on Windows"—the WAMP acronym lives on.

Select the relevant Download link for your version of Windows. If you're not sure, you can go to your Control Panel, select System, and then poke around. You'll see either "32-bit Operating System" or "64-bit Operating System," and that tells you what you want. Just select the first link on the top-left of the page that matches your system.

When downloading starts, you see a warning—actually, a couple of them—about needing some C++ extensions. Click the link for your system (see Figure 1-6), download the extensions (see Figure 1-7), and then run the downloaded file. You'll need to allow the downloaded program to update your system, accept a license agreement, and install the extensions. When that's complete, a screen appears like the one in Figure 1-8.

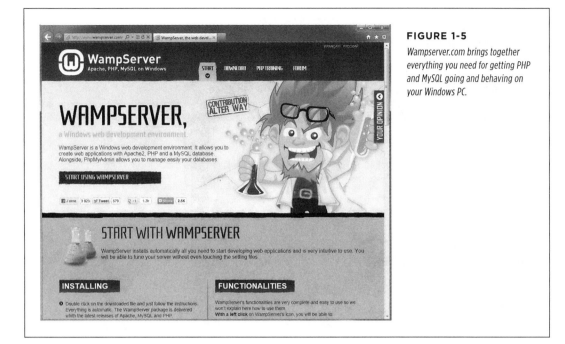

FIGURE 1-5

Wampserver.com brings together everything you need for getting PHP and MySQL going and behaving on your Windows PC.

FIGURE 1-6

WampServer requires some extra work on your part before it can install, most notably, you need to download some C++ extensions to get everything in the PHP interpreter behaving.

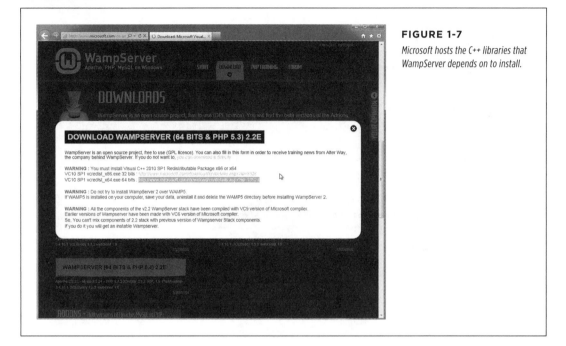

FIGURE 1-7

Microsoft hosts the C++ libraries that WampServer depends on to install.

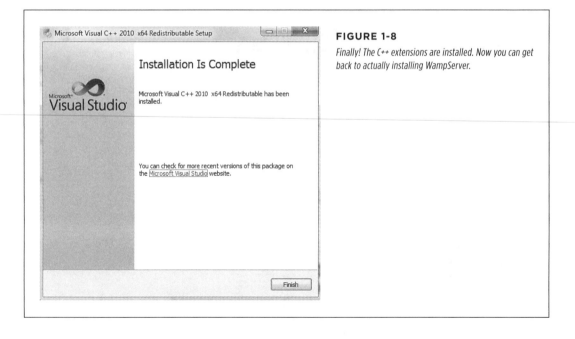

FIGURE 1-8

Finally! The C++ extensions are installed. Now you can get back to actually installing WampServer.

Once you've installed the C++ extensions, go back to Wampserver.com, select Downloads again, and then click the download link. This time, you can ignore the warning. Click the words "you can download it directly."

The ad-heavy site you're taken to will trigger a download in a few seconds. Then, save and run that file; you're *finally* installing WampServer. Figure 1-9 is what you're aiming for.

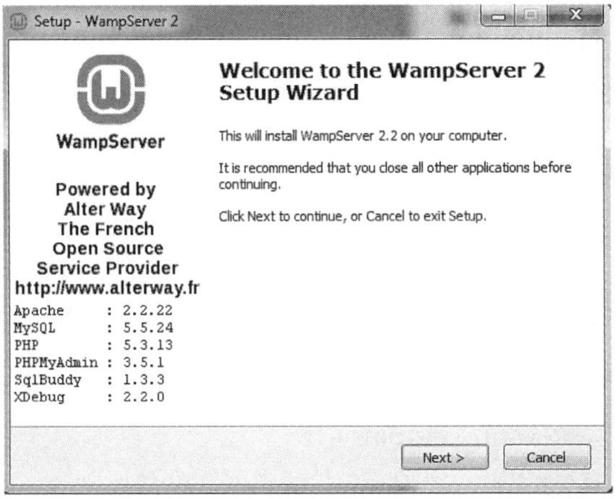

FIGURE 1-9

All that work for the little pink "W" logo. It's worth it, though. Installing PHP manually (as detailed in the appendixes) makes this look like a walk in the park.

Accept the license and default installation directory (typically *C:\wamp*). You might want to create a quick link icon, or at least a desktop shortcut, and then let installation take off. Select your default browser. You'll then be asked about allowing Apache to access public networks (Figure 1-10). The best option here is usually the default supplied by the WampServer installer.

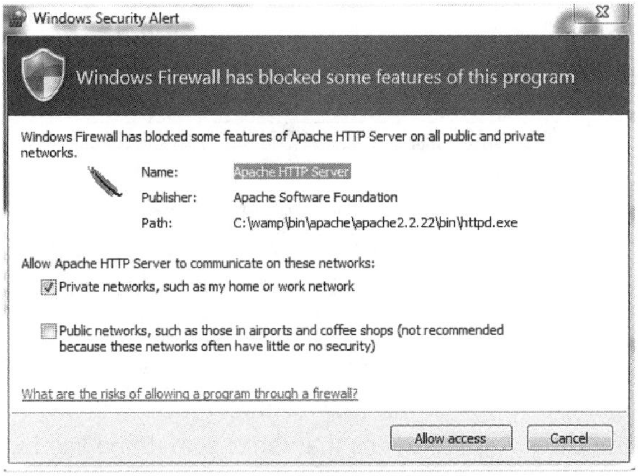

FIGURE 1-10

Unless your computer is directly connected to the Internet and has its own dedicated, publicly available IP address, the default options are just fine here.

You then have a few other options for PHP mail, and then you're finished. Launch WampServer, and you should see...nothing! Well, almost nothing. On the right side of the taskbar, notice there is now a little green "W" (check out Figure 1-11).

FIGURE 1-11

Now you've got WampServer running happily in the background. For your troubles, though, it appears you've only got this little green "W" icon.

Click the green W icon to see all of the things you've been reading about, like PHP, MySQL, and Localhost, as shown in Figure 1-12.

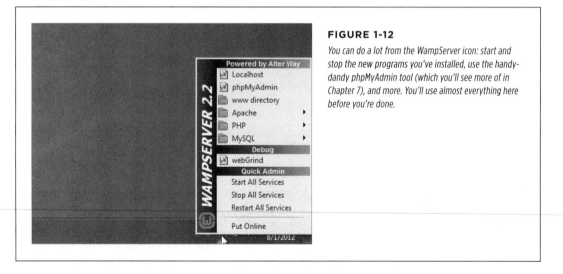

FIGURE 1-12

You can do a lot from the WampServer icon: start and stop the new programs you've installed, use the handy-dandy phpMyAdmin tool (which you'll see more of in Chapter 7), and more. You'll use almost everything here before you're done.

You're almost done. Select the top option, Localhost. (If you don't remember what localhost means, see the box on page 22.) A new web browser window or tab opens with an address that references your own locally installed web server. This Server Configuration page presents information about your own web server setup (see Figure 1-13). It isn't particularly impressive to look at, but it's proof that your Windows computer can now serve up web pages.

While on the Server Configuration page, in the Tools section (about halfway down the page), click the *phpinfo()* link. A page opens that looks something like Figure 1-14, which is everything you'll ever need to know about your local PHP installation.

More important, it means that your browser made a request to a web server, and that web server processed some PHP (the `phpinfo` function) and handed back a response to your browser. Not only *can* you run PHP on your computer, you just did.

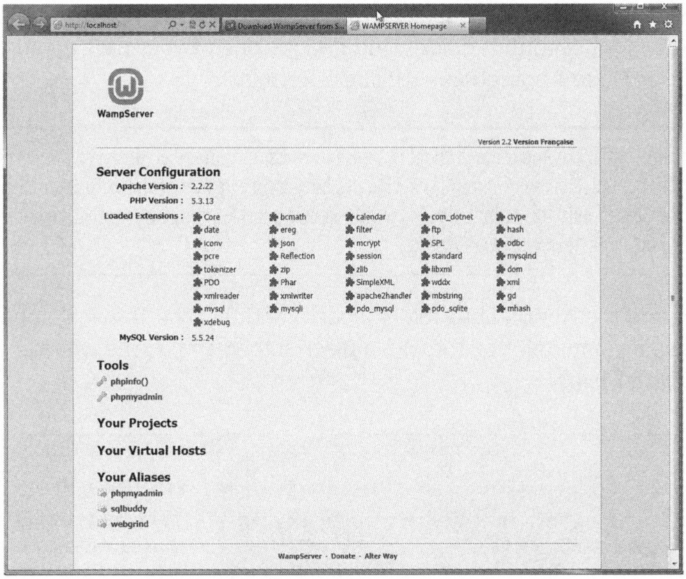

FIGURE 1-13

Having a web server running on your local computer isn't necessary for developing HTML, CSS, or most JavaScript applications. But because a browser can't interpret PHP, a local web server is essential if you want to write PHP scripts on that computer and run them without uploading them to a server somewhere.

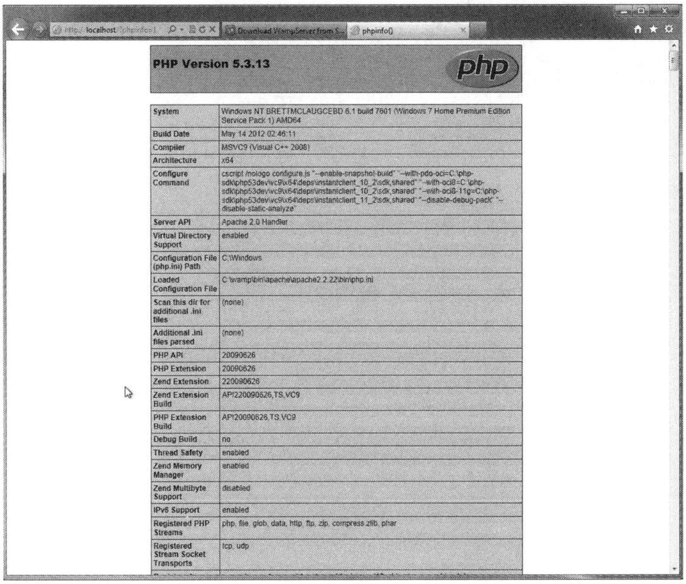

FIGURE 1-14

And the big win: PHP is running! Actually, your browser made a request to your local web server, your local web server executed some PHP, and then it responded to your browser with the response from that PHP command.

You've got PHP! Now it's time to get scripting.

PHP on the Mac (Default Installation)

If you've got a Mac, you've got more than just a sleek, shiny machine and way too many ways to spend even more money with Apple, you've already got PHP installed. To prove it, open the Terminal application on your Mac. If you've never used Terminal, don't worry; you'll get used to it quickly and find it's one of your best friends for working with PHP. Go to Applications→Utilities→Terminal.

> **NOTE** You can also get to the Applications folder in a flash by pressing Shift-⌘-A. However, this keyboard shortcut works only in the Finder. If you're currently viewing this book in an e-reader or online, for example, click your desktop and *then* press Shift-⌘-A. Shift-⌘-A is a little-known shortcut, but if you're the programming type, you're probably all about keyboard shortcuts.

Once you've found the Applications folder, open it and find the Terminal application. It looks like a computer monitor with a black screen and a little white arrow, as shown in Figure 1-15.

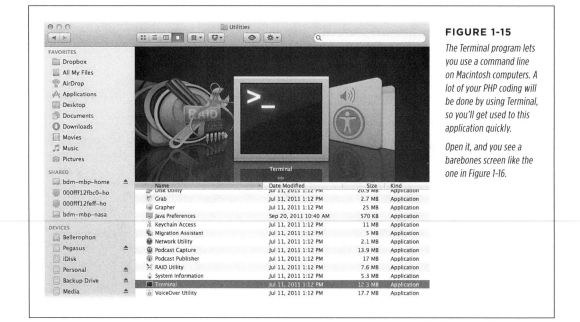

FIGURE 1-15

The Terminal program lets you use a command line on Macintosh computers. A lot of your PHP coding will be done by using Terminal, so you'll get used to this application quickly.

Open it, and you see a barebones screen like the one in Figure 1-16.

> **TIP** You'll often use Terminal for testing your PHP programs before you upload them to your server. To make it easier to launch Terminal, drag the icon onto your dock.

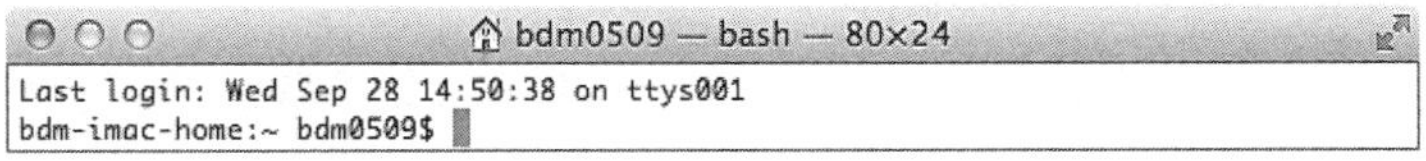

```
  ○ ○ ○              ⌂ bdm0509 — bash — 80×24              ⤢
Last login: Wed Sep 28 14:50:38 on ttys001
bdm-imac-home:~ bdm0509$ ▮
```

FIGURE 1-16

When you first open Terminal, you won't be too impressed. You'll get a line that probably matches your computer's name and then a weird dollar sign. Don't worry...this will all soon be old hat.

To ensure that PHP is installed on your system, type php (all in lowercase letters) and press Enter. Unfortunately, the way to know things are working is if you *don't* see anything but that blank cursor, a little further down in Terminal. It won't even blink at you anymore; it's just a boring, dark gray square.

Press Control-C to stop that single eye from hanging around and to display the blinking cursor again. This time, type which php. The which command lets you know where on your computer the program you type is located. In this case, you're asking where the php program is located. You'll probably get something back that looks like Figure 1-17; for the computer in this example, php is in the */usr/bin* directory. You'll probably get a similar result.

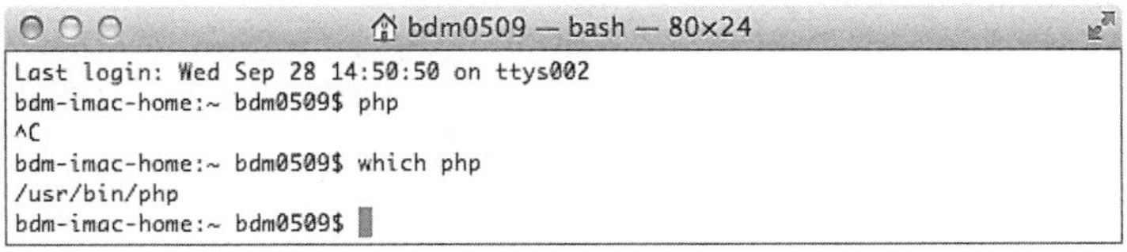

```
  ○ ○ ○              ⌂ bdm0509 — bash — 80×24              ⤢
Last login: Wed Sep 28 14:50:50 on ttys002
bdm-imac-home:~ bdm0509$ php
^C
bdm-imac-home:~ bdm0509$ which php
/usr/bin/php
bdm-imac-home:~ bdm0509$ ▮
```

FIGURE 1-17

Lots of the programs you'll use in Terminal are scattered around your Mac's hard drive. The which command lets you know exactly where a program resides on your machine.

Once you've seen where php is, you're ready to go. It was installed all along.

Take Control of Your PHP Installation

Like most of the programs on your computer, the PHP software package (which includes the php program you've been running) is updated fairly often. Most of the time, if you're keeping your computer updated with Apple's Software Update, this isn't something to worry about. But if you want to see what version of PHP you're running, you can type php -version into your Terminal window. You'll get back something like this:

```
Bretts-MacBook-Pro:~ bdm0509$ php -version
PHP 5.3.4 (cli) (built: Dec 15 2010
12:15:07)
Copyright (c) 1997-2010 The PHP Group
Zend Engine v2.3.0, Copyright (c) 1998-
2010 Zend Technologies
```

Look at the very first line that PHP displays: this tells you that you're running version 5.3.4.

If you want to get the very latest version of PHP, you can visit *www.php.net* and download the PHP source code. That's a little trickier than just using the preinstalled version on your Mac, though, so unless you're into commands like unzip and tar, you can stick with what's already on your computer.

By the way, this is a great time to remind you that if you're *not* using your Mac's Software Update frequently, you might want to do that now. It keeps your software current without all the hassle of downloading programs on your own.

PHP on the Mac (MAMP Installation)

Although it's nice that Macs come with PHP already installed, there might just be a better option—one worth doing a bit of downloading and installing for yourself. That better option is MAMP, which stands for Mac, Apache, MySQL, PHP. This is the Mac counterpart to WAMP, the easy Windows PHP installation (page 22) that you, as a Mac user, probably skipped.

MAMP doesn't improve on the PHP installation that came on your Macs; it does integrate MySQL—which you'll need before you know it—as well as the Apache web server and several helpful tools for working with PHP scripts and MySQL databases. You even get a simple control panel for starting up your local web server and MySQL database. Those additions are a nice perk, and coupled with how easy it is to install MAMP, you might just want to ditch the default PHP installation and get MAMP going.

First, using your favorite web browser, visit *www.mamp.info*. A site like the one shown in Figure 1-18.

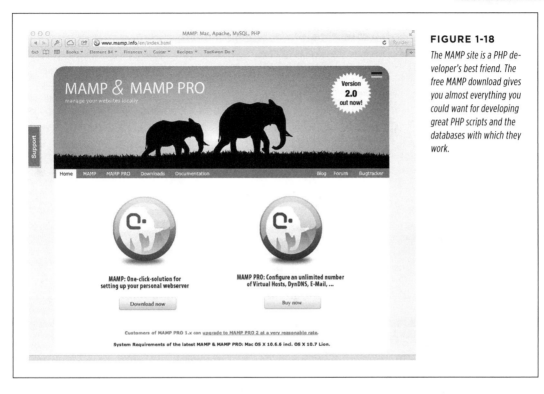

FIGURE 1-18

The MAMP site is a PHP developer's best friend. The free MAMP download gives you almost everything you could want for developing great PHP scripts and the databases with which they work.

Simply click the "Download now" button under MAMP and then grab a coffee and wait for the installer to download.

Now, launch the installer. Click Next a few times to select your hard drive and agree to the license. Keep going until the installer informs you that MAMP is ready to install, as shown in Figure 1-19.

NOTE Some versions of MAMP don't have a correctly signed security certificate. This results in a nasty message popping up when you try to launch the installer: "MAMP_2.1.1.pkg can't be opened because it is from an unidentified developer."

Fortunately, you can safely ignore this for MAMP. Just Control-click the installer, and then in the popup menu that appears, you can click "Open." This will in turn give you a dialog box, and you can click "Open" yet again. Finally, you'll have your program ready to run. Fortunately, you should only have to do this once.

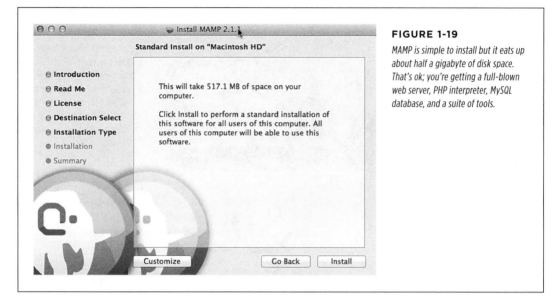

FIGURE 1-19

MAMP is simple to install but it eats up about half a gigabyte of disk space. That's ok; you're getting a full-blown web server, PHP interpreter, MySQL database, and a suite of tools.

Once the installation is complete, go to Applications→MAMP. You'll see a nifty control panel, a la Figure 1-20.

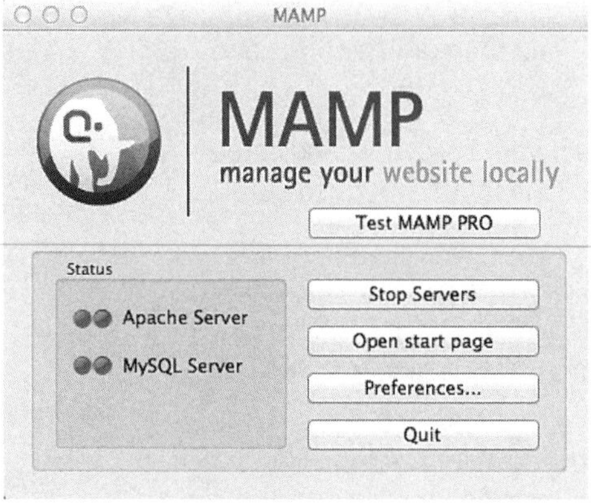

FIGURE 1-20

This control panel is MAMP's home base. You can start and stop software components and make all your configuration changes here. While you're getting your PHP feet wet, you may want to move the MAMP icon into your dock; you'll be using it a ton.

Your installation might try to automatically start both an Apache server and the database. Still, you can configure these easily by clicking the Preferences button. You should probably check the Ports tab and ensure that there aren't any issues with any other software on your computer. You can do this all within MAMP, as shown in Figure 1-21.

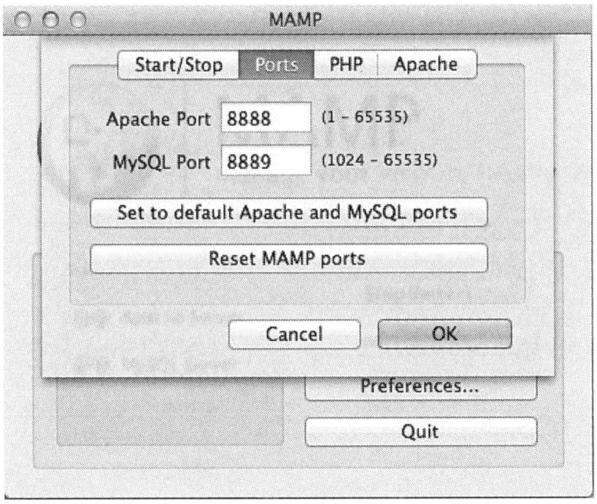

FIGURE 1-21

MAMP lets you change both the port that Apache (the web server) runs on, as well as the port that MySQL runs on. Be especially careful with the MySQL port. Most programs that use MySQL will need to be updated to the value you use here.

NOTE If all this talk of ports is starting to give you a headache, that's okay. It probably just means that your machine is set up without any software running on weird ports, and that makes things easy here: just accept the defaults. These are pretty standard ports, and will almost always work perfectly with a system.

You can also click the PHP Preferences option and see a few things that, honestly, probably don't matter much to you (see Figure 1-22). Just leave these alone. In fact, there's almost never a reason to mess with these selections. Mostly, it's good to know that yes, MAMP did indeed install PHP (along with a web server and MySQL) with just a few mouse clicks.

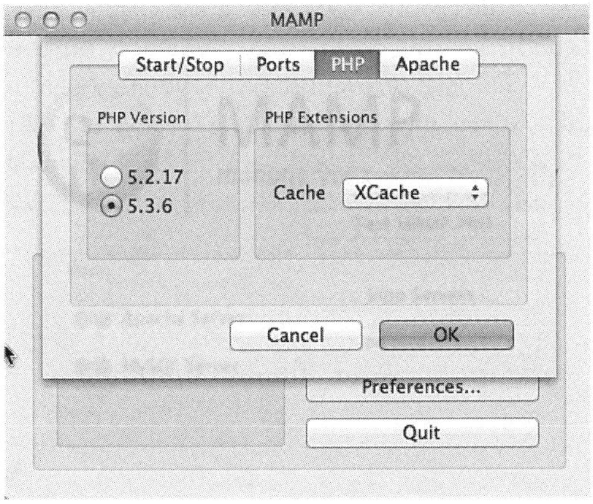

FIGURE 1-22

There are some reasons you might one day want to jump back from PHP 5.3 to 5.2, but that's far down the line. For now, just accept these options as they are and get ready to start scripting.

There's not much else to do now, so you can close Preferences and click the "Open start page" option to get a nice browser page like the one shown in Figure 1-23. Here's where you'll spend lots of your troubleshooting time as well as digging into databases once you've mastered the command line tools for MySQL that you'll learn about in Chapter 4.

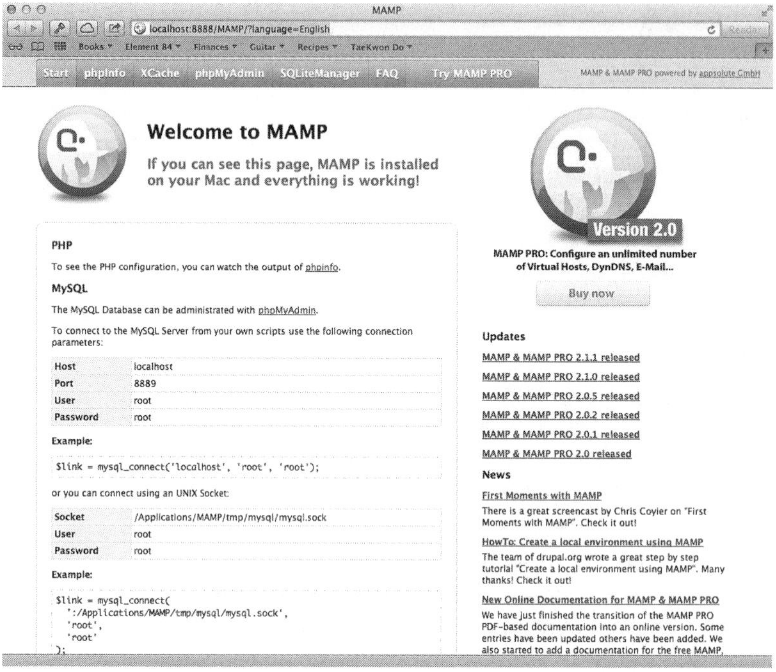

FIGURE 1-23

Here's where you'll do most of the work once you have your MAMP software running. Think of the MAMP control panel as the place you'll control the programs, and this start page as where you'll interact with those programs.

Before moving on, you can verify that this is all doing what it should. At the top of the MAMP start page, click the "phpInfo" tab. A screen appears, similar to that in Figure 1-24. What's significant here isn't all the information listed; you needn't concern yourself with that just yet. What *is* cool, though, is that you're looking at a PHP script that's been interpreted by a PHP interpreter (installed as part of MAMP). The interpreter then fed the output of that script to your new MAMP-installed web server, which in turn handed that response to your web browser. Proof that you're already running PHP.

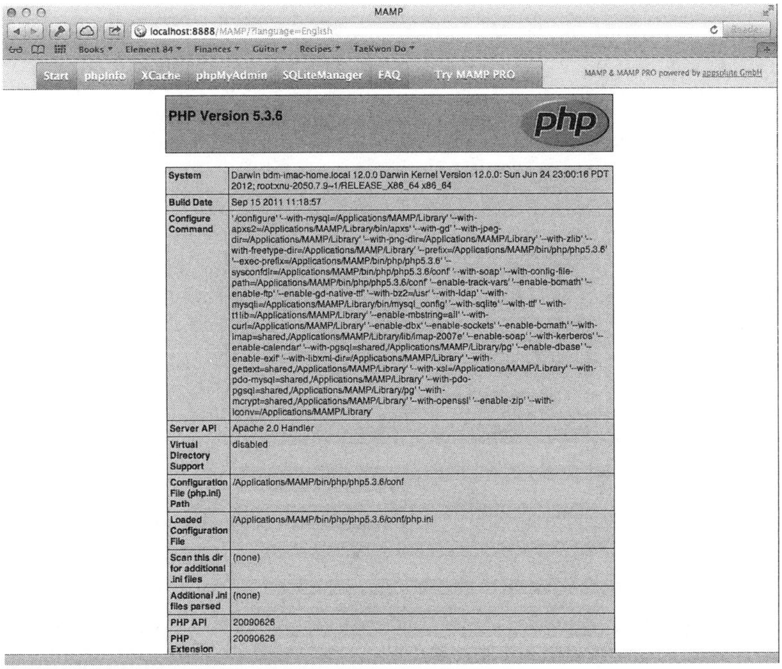

FIGURE 1-24

This page is actually the output of the phpinfo function in PHP. Here's the proof that you've got what you need to run PHP scripts on your local machine. In fact, you just ran one.

Get Out Your Text Editor

All the programs you're going to write in PHP are plain, old text files. Writing PHP isn't a lot different than writing HTML or CSS or JavaScript. You'll type different things, of course, but these are all just text files saved with a special extension. You use *.html* for HTML, *.css* for CSS, *.js* for JavaScript, and now you'll use *.php* for PHP files.

Because PHP is just text, you'll want a good text editor in which to work. If you're in Windows, you can use Notepad. As simple as that program is, it's perfect for coding in PHP. If you're on a Mac, TextEdit is a great choice. The good news is that each of these programs comes preinstalled on your computer, so you don't have to download or buy anything. The bad news is that none of these programs *know* you're writing PHP, so you don't get much help if you type something wrong or want to organize your files without resorting to Windows Explorer or the Finder. These programs are simple, but limited.

On the other hand, there are quite a few editors out there that are built specifically to handle PHP. For instance, for Windows, you can download NuSphere PhpED (*nusphere.com/products/phped.htm*), which is shown in Figure 1-25. You'll pay a bit for a program like NuSphere—usually between $50 and $100—but you'll get fancy color coding, help with special language features, and in a lot of cases, some nifty file organization features and the ability to upload your PHP directly to your web server.

FIGURE 1-25

NuSphere PhpED gives you a ton of features and supports JavaScript, CSS, and HTML, as well as PHP. It also has great documentation for most of the PHP functions and libraries.

If you're on a Mac, the two leading candidates for editors that do text plus lots of other cool things are BBEdit (*www.barebones.com/products/bbedit/index.html*) and TextMate (*www.macromates.com*). Both are Mac-only programs, and both offer similar features on the Mac as does PhpED for Windows: color-coding, file management, help documentation, and support for HTML, CSS, JavaScript, and a lot more. You can see BBEdit in action in Figure 1-26; you'll need to drop $100 to get your own copy, though.

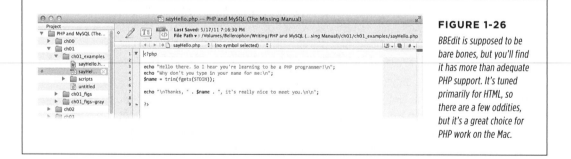

FIGURE 1-26

BBEdit is supposed to be bare bones, but you'll find it has more than adequate PHP support. It's tuned primarily for HTML, so there are a few oddities, but it's a great choice for PHP work on the Mac.

You can see what TextMate looks like in Figure 1-27. It's a little simpler than BBEdit, so if you've never used a programming editor, this might be easier to begin with. TextMate costs around $60, slightly less than BBEdit.

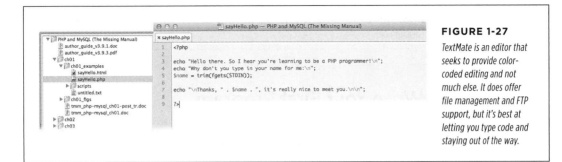

FIGURE 1-27

TextMate is an editor that seeks to provide color-coded editing and not much else. It does offer file management and FTP support, but it's best at letting you type code and staying out of the way.

UNDER THE HOOD

Text Editors: Mashing Up Programs

Although programs like PhpED, BBEdit, and TextMate are billed as text editors, they're actually lots of programs rolled into one. Imagine having a text editor, a file management tool like Windows Explorer or Finder, a telnet or terminal program, an FTP client, and some glue to hold them all together. That's more or less what these programs give you: a bunch of things all rolled into one single software package.

What's great about these "text editors plus" is that they offer you all sorts of features, and you don't need five or six icons in your Mac's Dock or shortcuts on your Windows desktop. You have access to almost everything you'll typically need to build web pages or program in PHP, right at your fingertips.

What's not so great, though, is that generalized tools aren't often as fully featured as specific tools. In other words, a program that tries to do everything usually does lots of things

decently, as opposed to lots of programs that only do one thing, but do that one thing really well.

Much of the time, you're making a choice between convenience and features. If you only use FTP to upload files to a server on occasion, you almost never work with your computer's command line, and you get a kick out of colored editors, the bundled text editors with lots of extra features might be a good fit.

Whether you use a more full-featured text editor or not, though, at some point you might need to ditch the editor and use an actual FTP or telnet program. As long as you're comfortable diving into those programs *without* the use of an editor from time to time, by all means, go forth in code in TextMate or PhpED without worry.

Once you're comfortable writing PHP code, you can spend some time playing with all these different enhanced editors. You can see what you like, discover whether an editor is perfect for you, or realize you're a Notepad or TextEdit programmer at heart. There's no one right option for PHP; all of these choices work just fine.

If you're just starting out, though, try to use a simple text editor—Notepad on Windows or TextEdit on the Mac. You'll learn a lot more about PHP this way, even if you don't get all the bells and whistles of one of the full-featured editors. Besides, once you understand PHP and have learned to work with it manually, you'll appreciate and be able to use the features of the other editors a lot more effectively.

NOTE Once you've become familiar with PHP, you can also check out Eclipse PHP (*www.eclipse.org*). The Eclipse IDE has long been a favorite for Java developers, and there are now enough plug-ins for PHP that it's a legitimate option for PHP programmers, too. However, there's a lot going on in Eclipse—tons of tools and gadgets—so you might want to wait a bit before you dive head first into it. Come back to it later, though; it's well worth checking out.

Write Your First Program

You've got PHP installed locally and you've got a text editor. Now all you need is an actual program. Start your text editor and type the following code, exactly as shown here:

```php
<?php

    echo "Hello there. So I hear you're learning to be a PHP programmer!\n";
    echo "Why don't you type in your name for me:\n";
    $name = trim(fgets(STDIN));

    echo "\nThanks, " . $name . ", it's really nice to meet you.\n\n";

?>
```

NOTE You can find a copy of this script on this book's Missing CD page at *www.missingmanuals.com/cds/phpmysqlmm2e*.

A lot of this probably looks weird, and that's OK. You'll soon understand every bit of this code. Right now, just get used to looking at PHP, which is quite different from HTML or JavaScript.

WARNING Some of the editors you might use, like TextEdit, will try to save the document as *rich text*. Rich text lets you use formatting, like bolding and underlining. You don't want that in your PHP code, so look for the option to use *plain text*, which doesn't provide formatting.

If you're using TextEdit, choose Format→Make Plain Text. (You won't see that option if you're already working in plain text.) If you're using Notepad, rich text isn't an option, so you've got nothing to worry about.

Once you're done, your editor should look similar to Figure 1-28.

```
○ ○ ○                      Untitled
<?php

echo "Hello there. So I hear you're learning to be a PHP programmer!\n";
echo "Why don't you type in your name for me:\n";
$name = trim(fgets(STDIN));

echo "\nThanks, " . $name . ", it's really nice to meet you.\n\n";

?>
```

FIGURE 1-28

PHP is just text, but it uses several weird characters. Start getting used to typing the dollar sign ($), angle brackets (< and >, just like in HTML), and the backslash (\). You'll be using those characters a lot.

NOTE You won't see the nice color-highlighted syntax until you save your file with a *.php* extension.

This program does just a few simple things:

- Identifies itself as PHP by using <?php.

- Prints out a welcome message by using the echo command.

- Asks the user for her name, again by using echo.

- Gets the user's name and stores it in something called $name.

- Says hello to the user by printing out a message that includes the information stored in $name.

- Finishes up with the ?> characters.

It's okay if not much on this list makes sense yet, especially the weird line beginning with $name =. There are also some strange characters like \n and STDIN that you'll learn about soon. But see if you can follow the plain-English words through the basic path: the opening <?php, the printing, the request for the user's name, another bit of printing, and the closing ?>.

Now, save this program. Name it *sayHello.php*, and ensure that you add that *.php* extension! Otherwise, you'll have a lot of problems down the line. Save the file some place handy, like on your desktop, your home directory, or a folder you're using to keep all your PHP programs in as you're learning.

WARNING Most programs in Windows and on the Mac append a default extension, like *.txt*. Make sure you replace this with *.php*. Windows especially tends to hide extensions, so verify that your full filename is *sayHello. php*, not something like *sayHello.php.txt*.

That's it; you've written your first PHP program!

Default to Plain Text

Most of the popular text editors let you change from rich text to plain text on a per-file basis, but they automatically start out in rich text mode. That can become a pain, so you might want to change the setup of your editor to always start out in plain-text mode.

For TextEdit on the Mac, open the Preferences menu. At the very top, under Format, select "Plain text" (as shown in Figure 1-29).

In Windows, if you use Notepad, you avoid this entire issue, so you've got nothing to worry about.

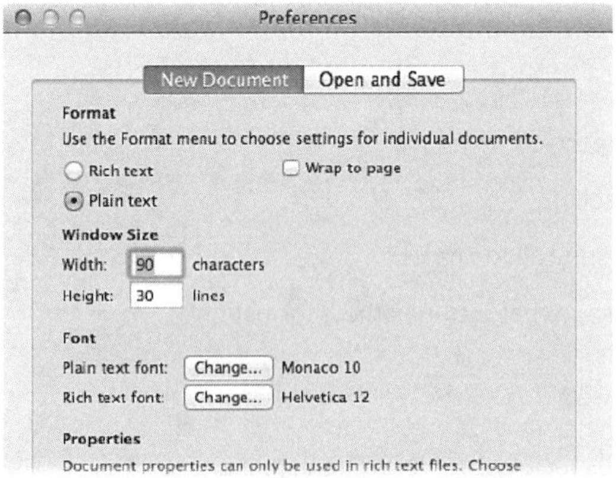

FIGURE 1-29

You can get to the TextEdit preferences via the Preferences menu, or by using the shortcut combination ⌘-period. In the Preferences box, you've got lots of options, but the text format and font used for plain text are the most important for now.

■ Run Your First Program

What good is it to get all this code typed in if you can't see if it works? This particular program isn't ready to run on the Web yet; first you need to add something to it in your command-line terminal program, so go ahead and fire that up. If you're on the Mac, you should open up Terminal. In Windows 7 or earlier, go to Windows Start→Run and then run command or cmd from the menu to get a command line. In Windows 8, at the start screen, press Windows key + R and then type cmd (as shown in Figure 1-30).

FIGURE 1-30

In Windows 7 (left) and earlier, you can get to the command line via the Start menu. Since Windows 8 doesn't have a Start menu, just go to the Start screen and press Windows key+R. That opens the Run box where you can type cmd.

Now, go to the directory in which you saved your program, *sayHello.php*. You can do a directory listing with `dir` (in Windows) or `ls` (on the Mac) to ensure that you're in the right directory. Once you're in the right directory, type this into your command line:

```
php sayHello.php
```

This instructs the php program to run and gives it your program, *sayHello.php*, as the script to run. In short order, you should see the welcome message you typed, and then the program asks you for your name. Type your name and press Enter. The program should then greet you, just as shown in Figure 1-31.

```
bdm-imac-home:ch01_examples bdm0509$ php sayHello.php
Hello there. So I hear you're learning to be a PHP programmer!
Why don't you type in your name for me:
Brett

Thanks, Brett, it's really nice to meet you.

bdm-imac-home:ch01_examples bdm0509$
```

FIGURE 1-31

Eventually, you'll run most of your PHP scripts through a web browser. For now, though, the command line lets you take control of the php command and give it a particular script to run so that you can see the output on the command line.

That's it! Your first program works, and you're ready to go deeper into PHP.

But Where's That Web Server?

Before you take that well-deserved break, there's one question left to answer. Remember way back to the discussion about a PHP interpreter interacting with a web server? All that business about PHP running locally or running remotely? Uploading files, web hosting providers; remember all that stuff? If not, Figure 1-32 should be a helpful refresher as to how PHP usually functions.

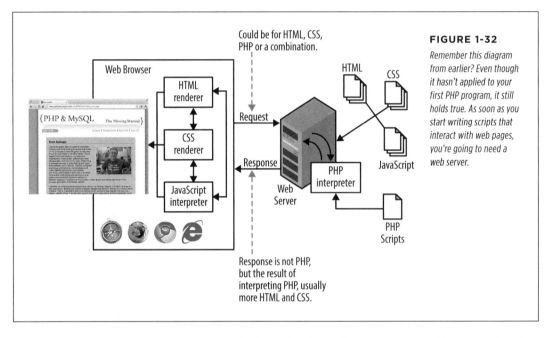

FIGURE 1-32

Remember this diagram from earlier? Even though it hasn't applied to your first PHP program, it still holds true. As soon as you start writing scripts that interact with web pages, you're going to need a web server.

So what gives? You installed PHP locally and ran your script without problem, but a web browser wasn't involved

The PHP Interpreter Is a Program You Can Run

The PHP interpreter that's shown in Figure 1-32 is just a program, like `dir` or `ls` or `which` or anything else you can type into a command-line or terminal window. And just like those other programs, you can run it on your scripts manually. In fact, that's just what you did. You ran the PHP interpreter (php) on your script, because you installed WampServer or, if you're on a Mac, because php is already installed.

But, this sort of script—where all it does is output some text—is not the typical PHP script. It's more of a "blow bubbles in the kiddie pool" script: helpful to get started, but just the tiniest taste of what's coming.

So, you don't need a web browser or a web server. You just needed the PHP inter-preter. Because of that, there's no sense uploading your script and trying to find the PHP interpreter on your hosting provider, which requires shell access, which in turn might require calling up tech support and spending 20 minutes on the phone giving out maiden names and birthdates...in other words, it's just not worth it.

But, the HTML Is Coming...

Keep those credentials handy, though, because in the next chapter, you *will* start uploading your scripts. You'll move beyond simply outputting text and begin to output HTML. You'll take input from an HTML form and churn back out styled, web-friendly responses. And, you'll move from using just a local PHP installation to using a remote one.

Buckle up, take that break, and head on over to Chapter 2.

PHP Meets HTML

With your first PHP script under your belt, you've made some real progress. But that PHP script might not have been what you expected. Most web developers don't fall asleep at night dreaming of seeing this in a terminal window:

```
Hello there. So I hear you're learning to be a PHP programmer!
Why don't you type in your name for me:
Brett

Thanks, Brett, it's really nice to meet you.
```

Even less impressive than its complexity (or lack thereof) is the script's format. It's just plain text. There's no formatting; in other words, no HTML.

In this chapter, you're going to inject HTML into your scripts. No command-line prompts and boring text. By the time you're through, your script will be speaking the language of the Web—HTML. In addition, you'll see how PHP does one of its core tasks: respond to an HTML form.

■ Script or HTML?

Before you can start doing fancy party tricks with PHP, you've got to get over a bit of a conceptual hurdle. So far in your web programming journey, you're probably used to thinking about the technologies you've learned in strict categories: HTML is markup, the structure of your page; CSS applies style to that structure; and JavaScript adds some interaction, with everything from alert boxes to validation, redirection, and widgets.

In the process, you probably also built some syntax categories. Your HTML is angle brackets, <title> and <head> and <ul>, and the like. CSS is curly braces and style keywords like p.warning and { } and border-style: dotted. The same is true with JavaScript: you've got alert and strings in quotes like "Please enter a valid phone number." And those categories are distinct. Your HTML is separate from your CSS, which is separate from your JavaScript, even though they all interact with one another.

But with PHP, you're going to have to abandon some of those categories. PHP happily—and sometimes confusingly—mixes these categories. You can write a PHP script that does programming tasks and then outputs HTML, CSS, and even JavaScript.

Determination by Extension

PHP scripts are identified by the extension *.php*. Accordingly, web servers that supports PHP see a file with a *.php* extension and hand that file off to the PHP interpreter for processing. The interpreter does its thing and hands the result of the interpreted script back to the web server, which in turn passes that response along to a user's web browser. Another look at this process, which is shown in Figure 2-1, might help.

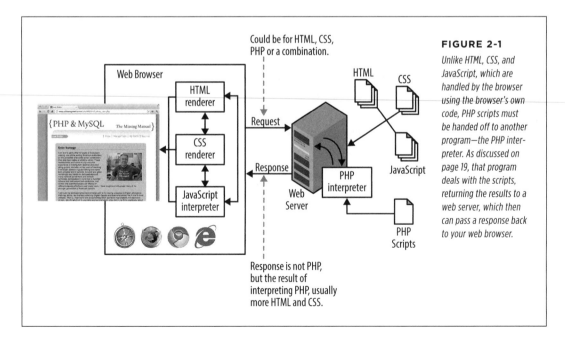

Could be for HTML, CSS, PHP or a combination.

Response is not PHP, but the result of interpreting PHP, usually more HTML and CSS.

FIGURE 2-1

Unlike HTML, CSS, and JavaScript, which are handled by the browser using the browser's own code, PHP scripts must be handed off to another program—the PHP interpreter. As discussed on page 19, that program deals with the scripts, returning the results to a web server, which then can pass a response back to your web browser.

But what's inside that script can be...well, all sorts of things. Remember, it's the output of a PHP script that is ultimately handed off to a browser, so that response *can't* be PHP. It must be some combination of HTML, CSS, and JavaScript—the things that a web browser knows how to handle.

In other words, a PHP script might be made up of PHP commands, but it also must be able to output more than just text, like *sayHello.php* from Chapter 1 does. It must be able to output HTML, CSS, and JavaScript. Fortunately, this isn't as difficult or tricky as it might sound.

HTML Is Treated as HTML

You might be thinking, "Ok, I get it. I can use that echo command from Chapter 1 to output HTML, right?" Or maybe if you've used jQuery, you're already a step beyond that: "Maybe there's some cool PHP toolkit that makes building up an HTML and CSS response easy." Although both of those thoughts are true, as you'll see in this section, they're actually not the simplest way to have a PHP script generate an HTML response.

For example, here's some HTML for a simple web form, sort of like the program you already built in Chapter 1.

```html
<html>
 <head>
  <link href="css/phpMM.css" rel="stylesheet" type="text/css" />
 </head>

 <body>
  <div id="header"><h1>PHP & MySQL: The Missing Manual</h1></div>
  <div id="example">Example 2-1</div>

  <div id="content">
    <h1>Welcome!</h1>
    <p>Hello there. So I hear you're learning to be a PHP programmer!</p>
    <p>Why don't you type in your name for me:</p>
    <form action="scripts/sayHelloWeb.php" method="POST">
      <p><i>Enter your name:</i> <input type="text" name="name" size="20" /></p>
      <p><input type="submit" value="Say Hello" /></p>
    </form>
  </div>

  <div id="footer"></div>
 </body>
</html>
```

Type this code into a text editor (for a refresher on text editors, see page 35) and save it as *sayHelloWeb.html*. For advice on where to save your files, see the box below.

Directory Assistance

If you open *sayHelloWeb.html* locally, you should also put the CSS and images referenced in the page alongside the file in the correct directory structure. So, if your HTML is in *phpMM/*, you should have *scripts/*, *css/*, and *images/* subdirectories inside *phpMM/*. Your HTML files go directly in *phpMM/*, *sayHelloWeb.php* goes in *scripts/*, and your CSS and images go in *css/* and *images/*, respectively.

If you download the book's examples, things are organized even a little more tightly. You have a core folder like *ch01/*, and

then subdirectories for each chapter's major headings: *01/*, *02/*, and so on. Then, in each of those directories, you see the HTML alongside *scripts/*, *css/*, and *images/*. You can use that layout, or just drop all the downloaded files as-is into your own location, and things should work just fine.

Or, you can put those files somewhere else and update the paths in the HTML and CSS to point to that location. Either way, you need to realize that if you just double-click this file on your desktop, you might not see the correct images and styles.

NOTE You can download this HTML, along with the rest of the book's sample files, from *www.missing manuals.com/cds/phpmysqlmm2e*. Along with the HTML, you also get the CSS and images used by the samples, which will give your programs a little extra visual pizzazz. Still, especially as you're just getting started, you'll learn a lot more if you'll type the PHP code for these programs yourself.

Nothing new here other than the form's target: *scripts/sayHelloWeb.php*. Don't worry about that for now, though; you'll deal with that shortly.

Open the page locally on your own computer. (Check out the box on page 22 for more on getting your local web server going.)

If you get things in the right place, you'll see something like Figure 2-2.

Your web browser sees all the HTML here and knows what to do: show a web page.

How do I access my local web server?

Even though you can count on your computer's web browser to know what to do with an HTML file, like *sayHelloWeb.html*, you'll want more than that before you go much further. If you've followed along from Chapter 1, you should have MAMP or WampServer installed. That means you've got a web server ready to go on your local machine.

In Windows, WampServer serves HTML by default out of *C:\wamp\www*. You can also click the small, green "W" icon

in the taskbar at the bottom right of your screen and select "www directory" to go directly to this location. Then, you can access your files in a web browser by visiting *http://localhost*.

In Mac OS X, the default directory for your web files is */Applications/MAMP/htdocs*. You can drop *sayHelloWeb.html* in that directory and access it through *http://localhost:8888/sayHelloWeb.html*. That also gives you a place to drop in the downloaded CSS and images you should have by now.

FIGURE 2-2

*If there's anything confusing
here, you might want to take
a look at HTML5: The Missing
Manual by Matthew MacDonald
(O'Reilly) to regain your
bearings. Hopefully, though,
this HTML is straightforward for
you, and the biggest challenge
is making sure that it's in your
working directory alongside
css/, images/, and so on, or
that your path in your HTML
matches your own directory
structure choices.*

PHP Is Not HTML (by Extension)

Just for the sake of experience, do something that might seem utterly bizarre to you: rename *sayHelloWeb.html* with a *.php* extension, to *sayHelloWeb.php*. If you then double-click this file, a number of things might happen—none of which you want. If you have a code editor like Dreamweaver, XCode, or Eclipse, those editors might launch and show you your file. Or, you might get an error because your computer doesn't know how to open the file.

Even worse, if you open the file in your web browser (using the browser's Open command, for example), the browser won't know what to do with it. It will probably ask you if you want to save the file (as demonstrated in Figure 2-3).

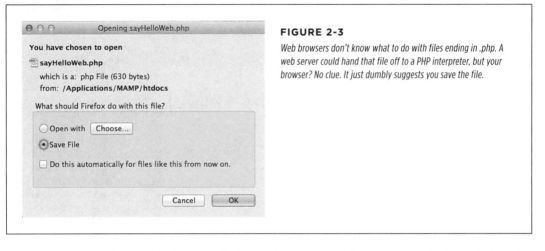

FIGURE 2-3

Web browsers don't know what to do with files ending in .php. A web server could hand that file off to a PHP interpreter, but your browser? No clue. It just dumbly suggests you save the file.

The *sayHelloWeb.php* file is definitely not HTML in terms of the file type. But the file contains HTML, so there must be some way to display that HTML. This time, instead of double-clicking the file or opening it with the browser's Open command, type the file's URL directly into the browser's address bar. (If you're not sure what this URL is, refer back to the box on page 48.)

This time, you should see something that might surprise you; check out Figure 2-4 for the details.

FIGURE 2-4

Your web browser couldn't open sayHelloWeb.php, and you know it's not an HTML file, based on the .php extension. But this sure looks like HTML. In fact, it looks exactly like the HTML file sayHelloWeb.html from Figure 2-2, as it well should: it contains the exact same HTML.

PHP Can Be HTML—by Response

As you learned in the previous section, the browser can't handle reading a PHP script, but when you access the page through a locally running web server, things just work. That's because the PHP interpreter is perfectly happy to take the HTML in the PHP script and push that HTML out as a response. The web server sends that HTML on to a browser, and this time—because the browser is getting HTML, not a file with a *.php* extension—it displays the HTML as a web page.

Now you've seen how a PHP script can return a full-blown HTML web page that any browser can display. Well, that's actually what you're going to be doing a lot in this book, starting in the next section: you'll do some programming in your scripts, and return HTML as a response.

But first, rename *sayHelloWeb.php* back to *sayHelloWeb.html*. Then, look back at the form line in the HTML file:

```
<form action="scripts/sayHelloWeb.php" method="POST">
```

This means that your form is going to submit its information to a program called *sayHelloWeb.php*, a new PHP program you're just about to write. (This time it will do more than just crank out HTML without any programming at all!) Once the form is submitted, *sayHelloWeb.php* takes over, the PHP interpreter runs the code, sends out the response from *sayHelloWeb.php*, and hopefully that response is something a user's web browser can understand and display.

■ PHP Talks Back

Now that you have an HTML page sending information to *sayHelloWeb.php*, you need to write some PHP. The PHP that you're about to write to run on the Web is not that much different than the program from Chapter 1 that you've already written. You have to get information a little differently because there's no command line that a user can use to enter information. But other than that, things stay pretty much the same.

Write Another PHP Script

Open a new text editor and type the PHP shown here; it should look sort of like an HTML-ized version of the *sayHello.php* program you've already written:

```
<html>
 <head>
  <link href="../css/phpMM.css" rel="stylesheet" type="text/css" />
 </head>

 <body>
  <div id="header"><h1>PHP & MySQL: The Missing Manual</h1></div>
  <div id="example">Example 2-1</div>
```

```
<div id="content">
  <h1>Hello, <?php echo $_REQUEST['name']; ?></h1>

  <p>Great to meet you. Welcome to the beginning of your
     PHP programming odyssey.</p>
</div>

<div id="footer"></div>
</body>
</html>
```

Save this program as *sayHelloWeb.php* within the *scripts/* subdirectory, and be sure that your file is in plain text and is using the right extension, *.php*.

NOTE You can download the example files for this section from this book's Missing CD page at *www.missingmanuals.com/cds/phpmysqlmm2e*.

Once you realize that a lot of this script is just HTML, you can probably already guess what most of this program does. Here's a section-by-section breakdown:

- The page starts out with a normal <html> element and head section.
- The body section begins and sets up the page heading and example number, just like the regular HTML page, *sayHelloWeb.html*.
- The page defines a heading with <h1> and prints "Hello,".
- The <?php tells the browser some PHP code is coming. Then, the $_REQUEST variable is accessed, and a property called name within that variable is printed by using echo.
- The end of the PHP code is indicated with ?>.
- The rest of the HTML is output, just as in *sayHelloWeb.html*.

WARNING To be extra clear, you should now have *sayHelloWeb.html*, an HTML page with a form, and *sayHelloWeb.php*, a PHP script that outputs HTML.

This program, like most PHP programs you'll write, accepts its input from a web page, either from one built in HTML like the pages you've created before, or from another PHP program. It's the job of that web page—*sayHelloWeb.html* in your case—to let the user enter information, and then send that information on to this program. The information from that HTML page is stored in $_REQUEST, which is a special variable in PHP.

Variables Vary

A *variable* in PHP (or any other programming language) is simply a piece of code that stores a value. Variables have names, and in PHP, those names can be almost anything you want. You can tell that something is a variable in PHP because its name begins with a $. So, $myHeight is a variable called "myHeight," and $_REQUEST is a variable called "_REQUEST."

> **NOTE** Technically, the name of a PHP variable does not include the $, but most PHP programmers consider that $ a part of the variable itself. Therefore, you'll hear PHP programmers say things like "dollar-sign my height" instead of just "myHeight" to refer to the variable $myHeight.

Variables are not just names, either. They also have a value. So the value of $myHeight might be the number 68 (for 68 inches) or the text "68 inches." In PHP, though, you're not stuck with that value forever. You can change the value of a variable, which is where the word "variables" comes from: a variable *varies*, or changes.

In *sayHelloWeb.php*, you're using the special PHP variable $_REQUEST to get the user's name, which she entered into the form you built in *sayHelloWeb.html*. PHP gives you the ability to get to anything a user entered into a form by using $_REQUEST and the name of the form entry field—in this case, "name." So, $_REQUEST['name'] returns the information a user put into a web form, specifically into an input field called "name." If the user also entered in her phone number, say into a form field called "phoneNumber," you could get that value in PHP with $_REQUEST['phoneNumber'].

> **NOTE** It's okay if you're still a little fuzzy on the details of how variables and $_REQUEST work. You'll learn a lot more about variables and, in particular, special variables in PHP like $_REQUEST in the next few chapters.

Once your PHP program grabs the value from the "name" form field, it prints out that value by using echo, something you've already used in your first PHP program (page 38). That value is dropped right into the HTML that's sent back to the browser—something you'll want to check out for yourself by running your new program.

Check Things Out Locally

Because you should have MAMP or WampServer installed, you can check the files you've created so far on your own computer, although you'll need to go through your local web server. Start a browser and visit *sayHelloWeb.html* on *http://localhost:8888* (in Mac OS X, using the default MAMP Apache port) or *localhost* (in Windows, using the default installation).

> **WARNING** *Do not* just double-click *sayHelloWeb.html*. As discussed in the box on page 48, even though your browser will open up the HTML file, it won't know what to do when that file submits to a PHP script.

Enter a name, click Say Hello, and you should get a response similar to that shown in Figure 2-5.

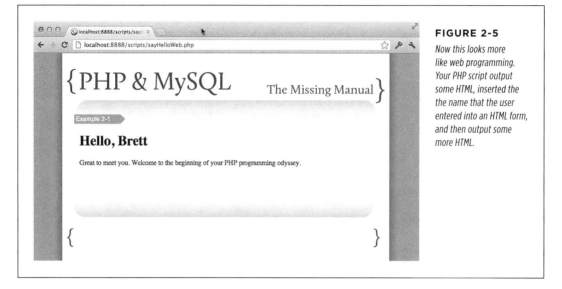

FIGURE 2-5

Now this looks more like web programming. Your PHP script output some HTML, inserted the the name that the user entered into an HTML form, and then output some more HTML.

So far, you've got an HTML page, a PHP script, and some CSS and images that are used by both. But, unless you plan on parading your user base through your office or den and letting them use your computer, things are pretty limited. This script only works on your local machine, and that's got to change.

Run PHP Scripts Remotely

It's time to get your programs out to the masses (or at least your buddy a few cubes down who doesn't believe you're a real programmer). That means you need a *hosting provider,* often called an *Internet Service Provider* (ISP) or web hosting company. All a hosting provider does is provide you with server space to house your web sites and applications; software to serve up your HTML and CSS and JavaScript—and now your PHP and MySQL; and some connection with the domain name service (DNS) so that people can access your site with a name like *coolPhpSites.com* instead of 98.234.1.23.

> **NOTE** You don't need to understand everything you just read to keep going. The basic idea is what's important: you need a place to put your files that makes them available on the Internet rather than just on your local computer.

Once you've got a hosting provider, it's just a matter of getting the right connection information, and getting your files online. Finding a hosting provider that fits what you're looking for is probably the hardest task; for some help on that tricky problem, check out the box below.

Once you've selected a provider, there are a couple of key bits of information that you'll need: the hostname to which you can FTP (page 8) and connect via SSH or telnet, and the directories into which your web files should go. If you're unfamiliar with connecting by using FTP or SSH, your hosting provider probably has some helpful tutorials on how to do all of this.

FREQUENTLY ASKED QUESTION

The Host with the Most

How do I choose a good hosting provider?

This is one of the toughest questions in the entire book. There are so many factors to consider, and everyone reading this has different priorities. Are you looking for an inexpensive solution or is stability and support at the top of your wish list? Will you use a gamut of technologies from PHP to Ruby on Rails to MySQL and PostgreSQL to WordPress to CoffeeScript—or is HTML, CSS, JavaScript, and PHP and MySQL enough? Do you want upgradeable server software and mailed-out logs and the ability to configure CPUs and online backups, or is a simple SSH/telnet session enough for you?

In the long run, only *you* know the answers to those questions. But, to work through this book, here's what you absolutely *will* need:

- PHP support (version 5 or higher)

- MySQL support (version 5 or higher, preferably 5.5 or higher)

- Some type of terminal access to your account, like telnet or SSH.

- Some type of FTP access to your account.

These are going to be the bare minimum. And if you can, you'd probably also like a few other things, too:

- The ability to drop a PHP script anywhere in your web directories and have them be treated as PHP (no configuration or special directories).

- phpMyAdmin setup to access your MySQL databases and tables.

- Email support (often better than phone support, because you have a record of communications!) that gets a response with 24 hours.

Now, that might seem like a lot, but you can find a ton of hosting providers that give you all this for a reasonable price. You could check out Bluehost (*www.bluehost.com*) or Kattare (*www.kattare.com*), or if you want to get a littler higher-end, try Engine Yard (*www. engineyard.com*) or Heroku (*www.heroku.com*).

Once have your hosting provider set up, it's time to upload some files.

Upload your HTML, CSS, and PHP

When you're building a web page, you have to upload your HTML, CSS, and any JavaScript you've written to your own web server. Then, you access those files with a browser, through a web address like *yellowtagmedia.com/phpMM/sayHello.html*. Typing that web address into your browser causes your server to supply your HTML to whatever web browser requested the page.

PHP works the same way. Once you've written your PHP programs, you upload them to your web server along with your HTML and CSS. Typically, you'll end up with files and directories like this:

- **Root or Home Directory (/).** This is your web root in which you put all of your HTML. This usually is the location referenced by a URL like *yellowtagmedia. com/,* without any specific file after the web server name.

- **CSS Directory (css/).** This is the directory in which all of your site's CSS is stored.

- **JavaScript Directory (js/).** Your JavaScript files go here. You'll often see this directory also called *scripts/,* but because PHP programs are also called scripts, it's a good idea to be more explicit in your naming.

- **PHP Directory (scripts/).** Here's where you'll put all of your PHP programs. Again, you could call this something more specific like *php/* or *phpScripts/,* but more often than not, websites use *scripts/* for this directory, so following that lead is a good habit to get into.

- **Examples Directory (ch01/, ch02/, and so forth).** As you're working through the examples, you're going to end up with a lot of PHP programs, and fast. To keep everything organized, you should have a separate directory for each chapter. For example, when you upload *sayHello.html* and *sayHelloWeb.php,* upload them into *ch02/sayHello.html* and *ch02/scripts/sayHelloWeb.php.*

NOTE   You don't have to organize things this way, but if you do, all the examples you download for this book will work without any changes. If you do change this directory structure, you'll need to change all the references in your HTML and PHP to CSS, JavaScript, and other PHP programs to reflect that change.

Now that you have your HTML and PHP ready, you need to upload those files to the appropriate directories on your web server. You should also download *phpMM.css* as well as the accompanying images from the book's website at *www.missingmanuals .com/cds/phpmysqlmm2e.*

Once you have everything in place, your web server directory structure should look something like Figure 2-6.

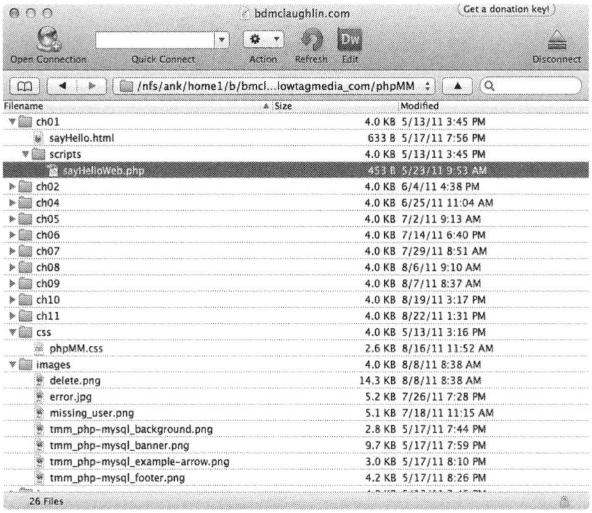

FIGURE 2-6

The HTML and PHP files you created are specific to this chapter, so they belong in ch02/. But phpMM.css is for all the book's examples you'll be building, so put it in css/ under the root of your web server.

Run Your Second Program

If you followed along in the previous section, you've got your HTML and CSS in their proper places, and your HTML form has your PHP program set as its action. You also should have *sayHelloWeb.php* in your *ch02/scripts/* directory. All that's left is to take your PHP for a spin. Start a web browser, go to your web server, and then add *ch02/sayHelloWeb.html* to your server name.

> **NOTE** You might need to add a prefix, like *phpMM/*, if you added a subdirectory under your web root. So, if your examples are in *[WEB ROOT]/phpMM/ch02/*, your URL would be *http://[your-host-name]/phpMM/ch02/sayHelloWeb.html*.

You should see the HTML you created in *sayHelloWeb.html*, just like in Figure 2-7.

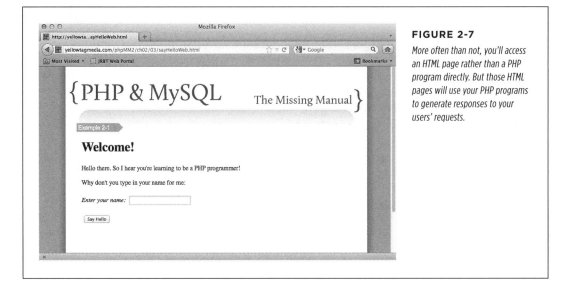

FIGURE 2-7

More often than not, you'll access an HTML page rather than a PHP program directly. But those HTML pages will use your PHP programs to generate responses to your users' requests.

Type your name and then click the Say Hello button. This cleverly labeled submit button sends your name as part of the form to the form's action, which is your *sayHelloWeb.php* program. That program then runs on your web server. You should get a response back, similar to Figure 2-8.

This is the same form and response you saw back in Figure 2-5. Whether it's on your own computer or a remote server, the web page looks the same.

FIGURE 2-8

The web browser doesn't actually run your program. Instead, it asks your server to run the program, and that server then gives the result of running sayHelloWeb.php back to the browser, which shows you a personalized welcome message.

Welcome to Programming!

It might seem like you've done a lot of work just to have a web browser tell you your name. In fact, you could probably write the same program in JavaScript if you wanted. But now that you've created a few PHP programs, you can see how easy it is to write this sort of code.

And before you know it, you'll be doing a lot more than telling users their names. You'll be talking to a database, doing advanced calculations, making decisions based on information the user gave you and what you have stored in a database, and more. But it all begins with a little HTML, a PHP program like the ones you've just written, and the directory structure you've put in place.

FREQUENTLY ASKED QUESTION

PHP and Your Provider

Where do all my files go?

As you've probably already realized, when it comes to running your scripts, the hardest part often isn't the PHP. Instead, it's figuring out where things go for your particular hosting provider.

Where do your web files go? A *public_html/* directory, or somewhere else altogether? Usually, you'll see either a *www/* or *public_html/* directory. Or, to be even safer, just call or email your hosting provider and ask them. They'll have an easy, definitive answer to this question.

Where do scripts go? In a special directory, or anywhere, as long as they have a *.php* extension? Most hosting providers let you drop PHP scripts anywhere you want, and the host's web server will serve anything with a *.php* extension via the PHP interpreter. But this is another question for which your hosting provider should supply a clear answer.

How can you organize things on your local computer so that it's easy to upload your HTML and images and scripts directly to your hosting provider? This one is up to you. You should spend some time coming up with your own ideas and preferences, and then just try your best to be consistent.

Fortunately, these are all issues that once you figure them out the first time, you usually don't have to figure them out again. So, take the time now to ensure that you can run your PHP on your hosting provider. Even though it's nice to have PHP running locally, it's online that PHP really shines, and the same will be true for MySQL soon.

Going forward, it will be assumed you're running things online, as well. So, although you can use a tool like Dreamweaver, NuSphere, or Eclipse to edit your scripts locally, all the examples and instructions expect that you're uploading and running things remotely, on a hosting provider.

PHP Syntax: Weird and Wonderful

You've got a couple of PHP programs running, and have a handle on how PHP can interact with an HTML form. Still, although you're a little more comfortable with how PHP as a whole interacts with web servers and web browsers, what's actually going on *in* those PHP scripts? It's time to dig a good deal deeper and start to *understand* what's going on in the code you're writing. In this chapter, you're going to get comfortable with a lot of the PHP syntax. That means learning what special words—usually called *keywords*—you type into your programs and what each one of those keywords instructs PHP to do.

Fortunately, this learning doesn't mean you can't still build interesting programs that run in a web browser. In fact, because almost everything that's done with PHP involves web pages, all of your scripts in this chapter will accept information from a web form and work with that information. So, you're not just learning PHP; you're learning to write web applications.

■ Get Information from a Web Form

In *sayHelloWeb.php*, you used the following line to get the value of a variable called "name" from the *sayHello.html* web form:

```
echo $_REQUEST['name'];
```

You might remember that $_REQUEST is a special PHP variable that lets you get information from a web request (page 53). You used it to get one particular piece of information—the user's name—but it can do a lot more.

> **NOTE** You can find the finished example code for this section on this book's Missing CD page at *www .missingmanuals.com/cds/phpmysqlmm2e*.

Accessing Request Parameters Directly

In fact, to see just how handy $_REQUEST really is, go ahead and start your text editor. Enter the code that follows, which lets your user enter in his name and several other important bits of contact information, like his Twitter handle, Facebook page URL, and email address.

```
<html>
 <head>
  <link href="../css/phpMM.css" rel="stylesheet" type="text/css" />
 </head>

 <body>
  <div id="header"><h1>PHP & MySQL: The Missing Manual</h1></div>
  <div id="example">Example -1</div>

  <div id="content">
    <h1>Join the Missing Manual (Digital) Social Club</h1>
    <p>Please enter your online connections below:</p>
    <form action="scripts/getFormInfo.php" method="POST">
      <fieldset>
      <label for="first_name">First Name:</label>
      <input type="text" name="first_name" size="20" /><br />
      <label for="last_name">Last Name:</label>
      <input type="text" name="last_name" size="20" /><br />
      <label for="email">E-Mail Address:</label>
      <input type="text" name="email" size="50" /><br />
      <label for="facebook_url">Facebook URL:</label>
      <input type="text" name="facebook_url" size="50" /><br />
      <label for="twitter_handle">Twitter Handle:</label>
      <input type="text" name="twitter_handle" size="20" /><br />
      </fieldset>
      <br />
```

```
        <fieldset class="center">
          <input type="submit" value="Join the Club" />
          <input type="reset" value="Clear and Restart" />
        </fieldset>
      </form>
    </div>

    <div id="footer"></div>
    </body>
  </html>
```

HTML Should Be Semantically Meaningful

You might have noticed some pretty big changes in this HTML from the simple form in Chapter 2. In that chapter, the form used <p> tags to break up the form labels and input boxes, and manually formatted the form labels with <i> tags. That got the job done, but it's not a good use of HTML.

Whenever you're writing HTML, you're actually structuring your page. So a form tag doesn't really do anything visually; it just lets a browser know, "Hey, here's a form." When you use tags like <i>, though, you're not describing structure; you're telling the browser how something should *look*. That's really not what HTML is for, though—it's a job for CSS.

In this form, however, all the formatting has been pulled out. Instead, all the labels are identified with the <label> element and a for attribute. That identifies the labels *as* labels—regardless of how those labels end up looking—and also connects each label with the specific input field to which it matches. There's also a <fieldset> element that surrounds the different blocks within the form: one for the labels and text fields, and a second for the form buttons. This also provides *semantic information*; in other words, it provides information that has meaning.

By making the HTML mean something, a browser (and other HTML authors) knows what things actually *are* in your form: labels are meant for...well...labeling things. Fields are grouped together with <fieldset>. And italic and boldface formatting are left to your CSS, as they should be.

What's really cool here is that now your CSS can do an even *better* job of styling your form. Because you've eliminated formatting in the HTML itself, you can style all your form labels the same way—perhaps by bolding them, right-aligning them, and adding a right margin of 5 pixels. The same is true of your sets of fields; you might put a border around related fields, which is exactly what's going on in the CSS applied to this form. In fact, to see how the CSS affects these HTML elements, check out Figure 3-1.

In truth, if you're new to making your pages semantically meaningful, it might take time to get used to using HTML just for structure and keeping all your style in CSS. But, stick with it; your pages will look better, and anyone who has to update your pages down the line will thank you.

Save this file as *socialEntryForm.html*. To ensure that your HTML is just the way you want, go ahead and upload it to your server, in the *ch03/* directory. Make sure you've got the book's CSS in the right place—under *css/* in your server's root—and then open a browser and head over to your HTML form. You should see something like Figure 3-1.

FIGURE 3-1

This web form is a typical entry page for a user to fill in. But, what happens when this form is submitted? You're about to find out (see page 65), and, in fact, take control of all this entered information.

In *sayHelloWeb.php*, you used $_REQUEST to extract submitted form information and asked specifically for the "name" value. With this new form, however, there's a lot more information contained in the form.

To get all that information, you need to create a new script called *getFormInfo.php*, and enter the following code:

```
<html>
 <head>
  <link href="../../css/phpMM.css" rel="stylesheet" type="text/css" />
 </head>

 <body>
  <div id="header"><h1>PHP & MySQL: The Missing Manual</h1></div>
  <div id="example">Example 3-1</div>

  <div id="content">
    <p>Here's a record of what information you submitted:</p>
    <p>
```

```
      First Name: <?php echo $_REQUEST['first_name']; ?><br />
      Last Name: <?php echo $_REQUEST['last_name']; ?><br />
      E-Mail Address: <?php echo $_REQUEST['email']; ?><br />
      Facebook URL: <?php echo $_REQUEST['facebook_url']; ?><br />
      Twitter Handle: <?php echo $_REQUEST['twitter_handle']; ?><br />
    </p>
  </div>

  <div id="footer"></div>
  </body>
</html>
```

> **NOTE** If you want to start taking a little more control of your scripts, you can name this program something other than *getFormInfo.php*. Just be sure that you also update *socialEntryForm.html* and change the form's action attribute value to match that custom script name.

By examining this code, you can already see what's going on here. In addition to grabbing the value of the "first_name" and "last_name" fields—similar to getting the value of the "name" field in *sayHelloWeb.php* (page 53)—the code uses $_REQUEST to pull in the values the user entered into the other form fields.

Go back to your *socialEntryForm.html* web form, enter your information, and then submit the form. You should see the result of *getFormInfo.php* running, and your browser should show you something similar to Figure 3-2.

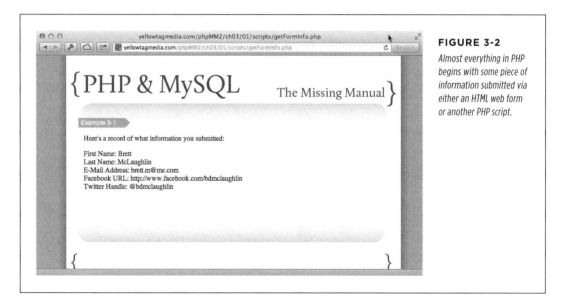

FIGURE 3-2

Almost everything in PHP begins with some piece of information submitted via either an HTML web form or another PHP script.

In fact, the following line is the way you'll use the $_REQUEST variable in most of your PHP programs:

```php
echo $_REQUEST['FORM_INPUT_FIELD_NAME'];
```

Create Your Own Variables

Of course, there might be times when you don't want to just display out the value of a field. Think back to your first program, *sayHello.php* (the version from page 48 that didn't run on the web). In that program, you created your own variable:

```php
$name = trim(fgets(STDIN));
```

PHP lets you create all the variables you want. Just give each one a descriptive name (as described in the box below) and put a dollar sign before that name, like this:

```php
$numberSix = 6;
$thisIsMyName = "Brett";
$carMake = "Honda";
```

> **WORD TO THE WISE**
>
> ### What's in a Name? A Whole Lot!
>
> PHP doesn't actually require you to use descriptive names. In fact, there are thousands of PHP programs on the Web with code that looks like this:
>
> ```php
> $x = $_REQUEST['username'];
> $y = $_REQUEST['password'];
> ```
>
> This code runs just as well as similar code that uses much more descriptive names:
>
> ```php
> $username = $_REQUEST['username'];
> $password = $_REQUEST['password'];
> ```
>
> So, what's the big deal? Many programmers will try to convince you that it's a lot of extra work to type in these longer descriptive names. That's true, too.
>
> Then again, how much work is it when you've got to track down the username variable in a piece of code you didn't write, or code that you did write, but many months ago? Suppose you've got a line much later in a script like this:
>
> ```php
> echo "Welcome back to the site, " . $y;
> ```
>
> Suddenly, it's not so clear what $x is and what $y is. Was $x the user name? Or was it $y? Be careful: Nobody wants his password printed out instead of his user name!
>
> Using descriptive names, even if they're longer and take a little extra time to type, will make your code easier to read, for you and anyone else who might need to look at it down the road.

Now that you know the basic code for creating a variable, go back to your new program, *getFormInfo.php*. Instead of just using echo to print out the submitted information, store each piece of information in a variable. By doing so, you can use that information however you want, and as many times as you want. Here's what your variables might look like:

```php
<?php

$first_name = $_REQUEST['first_name'];
$last_name = $_REQUEST['last_name'];
$email = $_REQUEST['email'];
```

```
$facebook_url = $_REQUEST['facebook_url'];
$twitter_handle = $_REQUEST['twitter_handle'];

?>

<html>
 <head>
  <link href="../../css/phpMM.css" rel="stylesheet" type="text/css" />
 </head>

 <body>
    <!-- Existing HTML code -->
 </body>
</html>
```

Notice that you can create blocks of PHP code—beginning with <?php and ending with ?>—anywhere you want. In this script, there's now a block of PHP before any HTML and then several small blocks of PHP within the big chunk of HTML. It's up to you when and where your PHP goes, as long as it gets the job done. You could have put this block of PHP between the page's opening html and head element or between the head and the body elements; that choice is up to you.

WARNING Sometimes, just because you *can* do something doesn't mean you should. It's usually best to do as much of your PHP work as you can before you output any HTML and then output as much of your HTML as you can in a single place. That keeps most of your code in one place and most of your HTML in another place.

Of course, you'll still have lots of times when you insert PHP into your HTML, as in *getFormInfo.php*, and that's okay. Those little bits of PHP fit into the HTML, and they certainly don't mix things up as much as 20 or 30 lines of PHP stuck in the middle of your HTML.

You can check out your form in a browser, but you shouldn't see anything different from what you already saw (take a look back to Figure 3-2). That's because your HTML—the part of the script that the browser displays to a user—hasn't changed at all.

But now there's a little bit of wasteful programming going on. You're getting the value of each form field through the $_REQUEST variable once, in the PHP block before all your HTML, and then you're getting all those variable values again in the HTML itself. Anytime you're doing something twice, you're wasting valuable web server resources.

Fortunately, it's easy to do away with this redundancy. That's because you have all the values you want, stored in your variables, $first_name, $last_name, and so on. So, in the HTML part of *getFormInfo.php*, you can just *echo out* those variables; you don't need to deal with $_REQUEST anymore. Here's how to update the "content" <div>:

```
<div id="content">
  <p>Here's a record of what information you submitted:</p>
  <p>
```

```
       First Name: <?php echo $first_name; ?><br />
       Last Name: <?php echo $last_name; ?><br />
       E-Mail Address: <?php echo $email; ?><br />
       Facebook URL: <?php echo $facebook_url; ?><br />
       Twitter Handle: <?php echo $twitter_handle; ?><br />
    </p>
  </div>
```

Take a moment to submit values into your *socialEntryForm.html* again to ensure that your updated script works. You should see the exact same result as before (compare your results to Figure 3-2 again). It might surprise you that you've done all this work just to get the same result, but that's actually a big part of good programming. To learn more about this approach to programming, see the box that follows. This version has all the submitted values in variables, though, and that's an improvement.

WORD TO THE WISE

Refactor as You Go

Whenever you rearrange code, especially to organize it better or to divide your code's behavior into separate chunks, you're *refactoring*. For example, when you created a PHP block at the beginning of *getFormInfo.php* to grab all the information from the submitted form and then just echoed out each variable within the HTML, you actually were refactoring your script.

When you're writing code, you want to refactor constantly. Anytime you can better organize your script—or, as you'll do later, better organize lots of scripts that all work together—you should do it. Even if you're not sure how your better organization might help your program, it's worth the effort. When you come back to your code a week from now, a month from now, or even a year from now, it's going to be a lot harder to remember what everything does. Even worse, it's going to be tough to remember *where* things are in your script. (Your scripts are going to get a lot longer soon, too.)

By refactoring as you go, you're ensuring that it's easy to see what a script does from a quick look. It also means that when you need to make changes, you can jump right to the spot within your script where those changes need to be made, get your work done, and go back to living the high life of a PHP programmer.

But be warned: refactoring isn't usually the most fun way to spend a Friday night. A lot of the time, the goal in refactoring is to *not* change how your code works, and especially to not change what it outputs in a browser. Because you're rearranging—and sometimes optimizing, which is just making things run as smoothly as possible—your goal is keep things looking just the same.

That's the case with your refactoring of *getFormInfo.php*. You added some PHP, created a bunch of variables, and then used those variables in your HTML. The result? Exactly the same as your original version. But now your code is a lot easier to understand, and you're actually going to get some nice benefits by having those variables available shortly.

But, why put values into a variable? Right now, it's a little silly: all you're doing is changing the place within your script where you grab information from the $_RE-QUEST variable. That's not doing you any real good. So, what can you do with these variables once you've placed information in them? PHP gives you a lot of options, particularly when you have variables that contain text.

■ Working with Text in PHP

PHP sees all text the same: a meaningless collection of characters. Those characters can be letters, numbers, spaces, punctuation marks, or just about anything else. In PHP, an English word like "caterpillar" is just as ordinary a piece of text as is something nonsensical like "!(gUHa8@m.@." To you, "caterpillar" looks like a word. That second group of letters, however, looks like something QBert might have said. To PHP, though, both of them are just text. In fact, because it's such an important part of the language, PHP and most programming languages have a special word to refer to text: a string. So, a piece of text can also be referred to as a *string*; thus instead of text searching or text matching, you'll often hear programmers talk about *string searching* or *string matching*.

NOTE If you have no idea what QBert is, take a moment to Google it. Then take another moment to weep for your lost youth.

Combine Text

The good thing about PHP seeing all text the same way is that you can do all sorts of interesting things with it, regardless of what that text is. So, going back to your script, *getFormInfo.php* you have five variables, all of which contain text:

```
$first_name = $_REQUEST['first_name'];
$last_name = $_REQUEST['last_name'];
$email = $_REQUEST['email'];
$facebook_url = $_REQUEST['facebook_url'];
$twitter_handle = $_REQUEST['twitter_handle'];
```

Two of these are related: $first_name and $last_name. It's pretty common to take in information this way—with the names separated—but it's just as *uncommon* to print them out separately. Imagine walking into your local Pier 1 Imports and being greeted by an old friend like this: "Hey there, First Name Brett, Last Name McLaughlin!" That's pretty awkward; and it's just as awkward on the Web.

NOTE You can find the finished example code for this section on this book's Missing CD page at *www. missingmanuals.com/cds/phpmysqlmm2e.*

There's no reason to settle for this separation, though. You can easily combine these two strings by using a technique called *concatenation*. That's a fancy word that just means "combine," and in the case of strings in particular, combining two pieces of text end-to-end. So, if you concatenate "my" and "girl," you get a new string, "mygirl."

In PHP, you concatenate with the period (.). For *getFormInfo.php*, therefore, find the two lines of HTML that print out the first and last name:

```
First Name: <?php echo $first_name; ?><br />
Last Name: <?php echo $last_name; ?><br />
```

Now, change these to a single line, and concatenate the first and last names:

```
Name: <?php echo $first_name . $last_name; ?><br />
```

Go back to *socialEntryForm.html*, enter some information, and then submit your form. You should see something like Figure 3-3: the first name Brett and last name McLaughlin are successfully concatenated. However, if you look closely, you'll see that the first name and last name are smashed together. What you need is a space between those two bits of text.

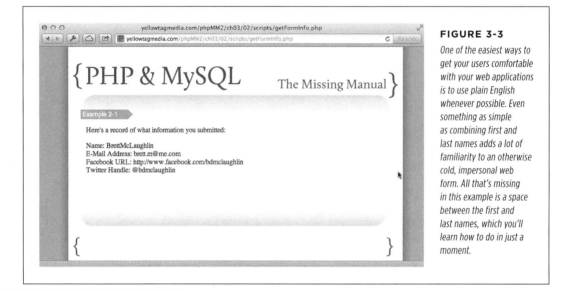

FIGURE 3-3

One of the easiest ways to get your users comfortable with your web applications is to use plain English whenever possible. Even something as simple as combining first and last names adds a lot of familiarity to an otherwise cold, impersonal web form. All that's missing in this example is a space between the first and last names, which you'll learn how to do in just a moment.

This is a situation for which PHP treating all text the same really helps. To add a space, all you have to do is put it in quotes, like this: " ". PHP doesn't see that text as any different from the text in your variables. You can just concatenate that string—the empty space—to $first_name, and then concatenate $last_name to the space, like this:

```
Name: <?php echo $first_name . " " . $last_name; ?><br />
```

Try your form out again, and you should see a proper space between the first and last names. Check out Figure 3-4, which should match what your page now looks like.

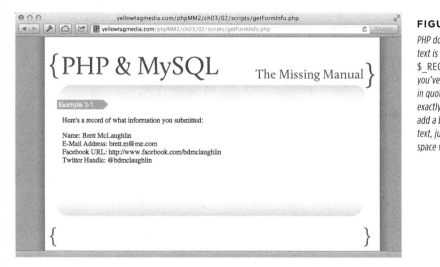

FIGURE 3-4

PHP doesn't care if text is in a variable like $_REQUEST, a variable you've created yourself, or in quotes. It treats all text exactly the same. So, to add a blank space to your text, just surround the space with quotes.

Searching Within Text

Of course, if all you could do with strings was smash them together, that would be pretty boring. Thankfully, PHP offers a lot more options. One of the most common things you'll do with PHP text is search it. For example, take the $facebook_url variable in *getFormInfo.php*. Suppose you want to turn that into a live, clickable link. First, add the HTML <a> tag, like so:

```
<p>
  Name: <?php echo $first_name . " " . $last_name; ?><br />
  E-Mail Address: <?php echo $email; ?><br />
  <a href="<?php echo $facebook_url; ?>">Your Facebook page</a><br />
  Twitter Handle: <?php echo $twitter_handle; ?><br />
</p>
```

Now, instead of just showing the text of the URL, your web page shows a link that people can click, as demonstrated in Figure 3-5.

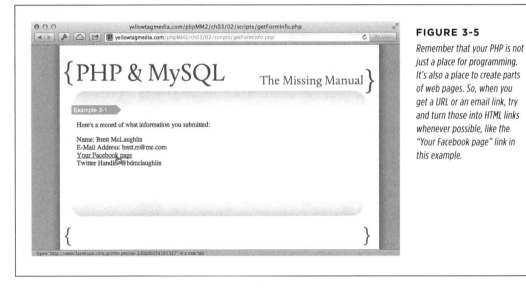

FIGURE 3-5

Remember that your PHP is not just a place for programming. It's also a place to create parts of web pages. So, when you get a URL or an email link, try and turn those into HTML links whenever possible, like the "Your Facebook page" link in this example.

But, what happens if someone forgets to put the *facebook.com* part of the URL in? Maybe he didn't read carefully, and he just threw in the part of the URL *after facebook.com*, like *ryan.geyer* or *profile.php?id=699186223*. In this case, the link you create won't be of any use.

What you need, then, is a way to see whether the text that was entered in your $facebook_url variable contains "facebook.com". If so, it's probably safe to turn the text into a URL link. If not, the link probably needs to have "http://www.facebook .com" added to the beginning of the variable's value. In other words, your PHP needs to search for the text "facebook.com".

The easiest way to do this in PHP is to look for the position of a piece of text inside a bigger piece of text to determine what the position of "facebook.com" is inside of $facebook_url, like this:

```php
$first_name = $_REQUEST['first_name'];
$last_name = $_REQUEST['last_name'];
$email = $_REQUEST['email'];
$facebook_url = $_REQUEST['facebook_url'];
$position = strpos($facebook_url, "facebook.com");
$twitter_handle = $_REQUEST['twitter_handle'];
```

The strpos() function, which just stands for "string position," returns a number that indicates where in the string the searched-for text exists. So, if $position was 5, that would mean that "facebook.com" appeared at position 5 within $facebook_url. (For more information on how these position numbers work, see the box on page 74.)

However, it's not enough to just determine a position. You need to do something with it. Better still, you need to figure out whether it indicates a position within $facebook_url—which would mean that $facebook_url contains "facebook.com"—or if $facebook_url doesn't have "facebook.com" within it at all. You can do this by seeing if $position is false, something PHP defines for you by using the keyword false. Otherwise, strpos() returns the position within $facebook_url at which the searched-for string appears.

NOTE The strpos() function, like most functions in PHP, can return two totally different things: a number indicating a position within the search string, or the value false.

```
$first_name = $_REQUEST['first_name'];
$last_name = $_REQUEST['last_name'];
$email = $_REQUEST['email'];
$facebook_url = $_REQUEST['facebook_url'];
$position = strpos($facebook_url, "facebook.com");
if ($position === false) {
  $facebook_url = "http://www.facebook.com/". $facebook_url;
}
$twitter_handle = $_REQUEST['twitter_handle'];
```

At first glance, it probably looks like there's a lot of new stuff going on here, but don't sweat it. You already understand almost all of this code.

1. **First, strpos() checks to see if $facebook_url has the text "facebook.com" within it.** The value returned from strpos() is stuffed into a new variable, $position.

2. **$position is compared to the special PHP value false by using an if statement.** You'll learn a lot more about if statements soon, but it does just what it looks like: if $position is false, then execute the code within the curly brackets, { and }.

3. **The code that's within { and } only runs if the statement above is true—in this case, if $position === false.** If that's true, then "http://www.facebook.com" is inserted before the string in $facebook_url, to make a real link to Facebook.

4. **There's also a hidden step in this if statement: if $position is not false, then nothing happens.** The line of code within { and } is completely skipped over.

Now that you've made these changes to your script, save it and go back to your web form, *socialEntryForm.html*. This time, enter a Facebook link without the "facebook.com" part of the URL; for example, profile.php?id=100000039185327. Then, submit your form and see what your result looks like.

At first glance, nothing might look different. The web page generated from your PHP probably still resembles Figure 3-5. But, look at the source of your page (see Figure 3-6) or click the link itself (see Figure 3-7). In both cases, you can see that *profile. php?id=100000039185327* was turned into an actual URL, *http://www.facebook .com/profile.php?id=100000039185327.*

UNDER THE HOOD

Programming Languages Like Zeroes

The more you program in languages like PHP, Java, C, or Perl, the more you'll see some unusual uses of the number 0. In almost all of these languages—and certainly in PHP—counting begins at 0, rather than 1. So, if you were counting the length of the text "That's weird," the first letter—the capital "T"—would be at position 0, not position 1.

This gets particularly tricky when you're searching for text within text, such as in *getFormInfo.php.* Suppose that someone typed "facebook.com/michael.greenfield" into the Facebook URL text box. Then, in your code, you did something like this to see if the form value was a real URL:

```
if (strpos($facebook_url, "facebook.com")
> 0) {
  $facebook_url = "http://www.facebook.
com/" .

                  $facebook_url;
}
```

On the surface, this statement looks good: if "facebook.com" doesn't appear in the first position or greater of $facebook_url,

add "http://www.facebook.com/" to the beginning of $face-book_url.

However, the result would not be good. You'd actually have a value like this in $facebook_url: "http://www.facebook .com/facebook.com/michael.greenfield." So, what happened?

Remember, PHP starts counting at 0, not 1. Therefore, position 0 is actually the first position in $facebook_url. And that position has an "f" in it. Position 1 has an "a," position 2 a "c," and so on. It turns out that the entire first part of $face-book_url is actually "facebook.com," the string for which your code is searching. As a result, strpos() returns a 0 to indicate that the searched-for string is in the first position of $facebook_url.

What this all means—besides the fact that programming languages count differently than humans—is that you need to be a zero-based thinker when you're writing code. So, if you're searching for something within a string, a position of 0 or greater means the string was found, rather than 1 or greater. Remember that, and you'll save yourself a ton of bug hunting.

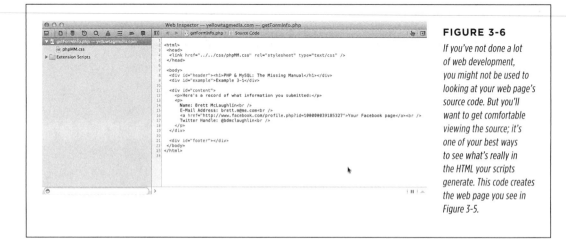

FIGURE 3-6

If you've not done a lot of web development, you might not be used to looking at your web page's source code. But you'll want to get comfortable viewing the source; it's one of your best ways to see what's really in the HTML your scripts generate. This code creates the web page you see in Figure 3-5.

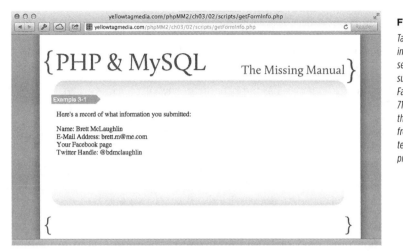

FIGURE 3-7

Taking a partial URL and making it into a clickable link might seem like a lot of work for such a minor feature, as in the Facebook link example (page 71). But users are forgetful, and the more you can protect them from making a mistake without telling them about their problems, the better it is.

Changing Text

You've combined two pieces of text, you've searched within text, so what's left? Well, changing text, of course. And it turns out that you've already got a lot of the information you need to do it.

Consider the Twitter handle people are entering into your web form. Most people put an @ before their Twitter handle, like so: @bdmclaughlin. But to see someone's Twitter profile on the twitter.com website, you actually don't want that @. So if the Twitter handle is @phpGuy, the Twitter URL to see that profile would be *http://www.twitter.com/phpGuy*.

Turning a Twitter handle into an active link requires a few steps. Here they are in plain English:

1. **Create a new variable, $twitter_url, and start by giving it a value of "http://www.twitter.com/".**

2. **Determine if the Twitter handle has an @ sign in it.**

3. **If there's no @ in $twitter_handle, add the handle to the beginning of $twitter_url.**

4. **If there *is* an @ in $twitter_handle, remove the @ from the handle and add the handle to the end of $twitter_url.**

5. **Display the Twitter handle as part of an <a> link element in your script's HTML output.**

You've done something similar to all of these steps except for step 4, so this shouldn't be a big problem for you.

First, create a new variable to hold the Twitter URL that you're building, and give it the first part of the Twitter URL:

```
$twitter_handle = $_REQUEST['twitter_handle'];
$twitter_url = "http://www.twitter.com/";
```

Then, you need to determine whether the Twitter handle—which you've got in the `$twitter_handle` variable—has the @ character anywhere in it. You can use `strpos()` again for this step:

```
$twitter_handle = $_REQUEST['twitter_handle'];
$twitter_url = "http://www.twitter.com/";
$position = strpos($twitter_handle, "@");
```

In this example, you need to do something whether there's an @ in `$twitter_handle` or not. So you'll have an `if`, but you'll also have an `else`:

```
$twitter_handle = $_REQUEST['twitter_handle'];
$twitter_url = "http://www.twitter.com/";
$position = strpos($twitter_handle, "@");
if ($position === false) {
  $twitter_url = $twitter_url . $twitter_handle;
} else {
  // Do something to remove the @ from the Twitter handle
}
```

If there's no @, this code simply adds the handle to the end of `$twitter_url`. If there is an @, you have more work to do to get rid of it and create the URL.

You've already seen that `strpos()` takes a string as a target in which to look, and then it takes another string, which is the item for which you're searching. PHP has a similar way to get just part of a string: the `substr()` function. `substr()` is short for for "substring," which, as its name implies, means a part of a string. You provide `substr()` with a string to search for and then a position at which to begin gathering the substring of the search text.

For example, `substr("Hello", 2)` would give you "llo". That's because the "H" is at position 0, the "e" is at position 1, and the first "l" is at position 2. Because you instructed `substr()` to start at position 2, you get the letters from that position to the end of the string, in this example, "llo".

WARNING Remember, most PHP functions like `substr()` and `strpos()` start counting at zero. If you're still unsure about how that works, check out the box on page 74.

In the case of the Twitter handle, you can use `substr()` in a similar way. But you want to cut off everything up to and *including* the @ sign, which you already know is at the position stored in the $position variable. So, you can use substr() and start your new string at the position after $position, or $position + 1.

```
$twitter_handle = $_REQUEST['twitter_handle'];
$twitter_url = "http://www.twitter.com/";
$position = strpos($twitter_handle, "@");
if ($position === false) {
  $twitter_url = $twitter_url . $twitter_handle;
} else {
  $twitter_url = $twitter_url . substr($twitter_handle, $position + 1);
}
```

NOTE You're starting to see a lot of new code quickly, but don't worry if something confuses you at first glance. Just take a moment and look at each piece of the new code, bit by bit. As you understand each individual piece, you'll find the overall picture quickly becomes clear.

All that's left to do at this point is to update the part of your script that outputs HTML:

```
<p>
  Name: <?php echo $first_name . " " . $last_name; ?><br />
  E-Mail Address: <?php echo $email; ?><br />
  <a href="<?php echo $facebook_url; ?>">Your Facebook page</a><br />
  <a href="<?php echo $twitter_url; ?>">Check out your Twitter feed</a><br
/>
</p>
```

Hop back to your entry page, fill it up with information, and then submit the form to your updated script. Try it with and without an @ character in your Twitter handle, and the results should be the same: an output page with links to your Facebook and Twitter page, with the @ correctly removed, as illustrated in Figure 3-8.

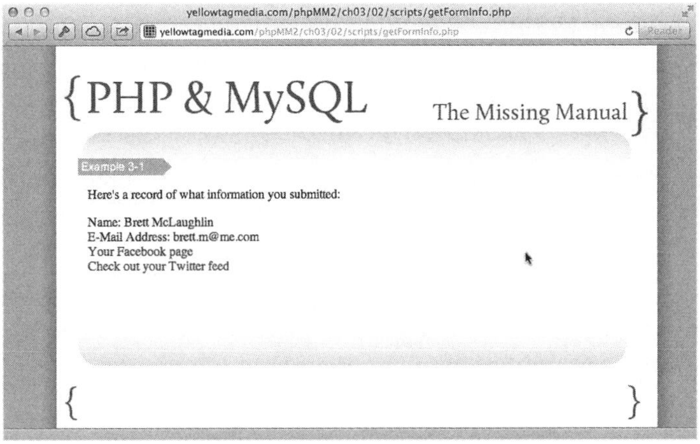

FIGURE 3-8

You might want to update your PHP script even further to add some additional style and formatting. You might want to change things to read from your user's perspective, such as "My name," and "Check out my Twitter page." Don't be afraid to experiment, particularly now that you're getting comfortable with your PHP script.

PHP's Angle on Brackets

What's with all the angle brackets?

When you're using PHP to show a lot of HTML and then dropping little bits of PHP into that HTML, things can get pretty confusing. Take a look at one of the lines that's in *getFormInfo.php*:

```
<a href="<?php echo $facebook_url; ?>">
  Your Facebook page
</a><br />
```

Some of this code looks strange, to say the least: there are two opening brackets before a single closing bracket, and then there's *another* closing bracket at the end of that first line. On top of that, you've got all the PHP within quotation marks.

Unfortunately, this is one of the downsides to inserting PHP into HTML. It's a necessary evil, and it's something you'll get used to, but it can still trip you up. Anytime you have PHP code, you *really* should surround it in <?php and ?>. (You don't have to, though; you can leave off ?> if you're ending your script with PHP, but that's generally considered a pretty lazy practice.) If you're using PHP to insert something into an element that's already in brackets, you'll get this strange double-bracketed code.

It's also pretty common to use PHP to generate a link, which in the case of an <a> element becomes the value of an attribute.

That means your entire PHP block will be surrounded by quotation marks. That's okay—as long as your PHP doesn't *also* have quotation marks. If you have a case for which you need quotation marks within your PHP, and that PHP is *already* within quotes, you can alternate single- and double-quote marks, like this:

```
<a href="<?php echo 'http://www.twitter.
            com/' .$twitter_handle; ?>">
  Your Twitter page
</a><br />
```

You can flip these around without a problem, too:

```
<a href='<?php echo "http://www.twitter.
            com/" .$twitter_handle; ?>'>
  Your Twitter page
</a><br />
```

Just be sure you don't open something with single quotes and then close it with double quotes, or vice versa. Mismatching quotes cause things to break, and nobody wants that.

There actually are some differences in how PHP handles double-quoted strings and single-quoted strings, but it's nothing you need to worry about right now.

Trim and Replace Text

Once you start trying to help your users by correcting possible errors in their form entry, the world of PHP strings becomes a big toolkit at your disposal. Take two other common problems in web forms, especially web forms in which users enter URLs:

- Users enter extra spaces around words, like " http://www.facebook.com/ryan.geyer " instead of "http://www.facebook.com/ryan.geyer" (note the spaces between the quotes and the text).

- Users mix up .com and .org URLs by putting in something like "http://www.facebook.org/profile.php?id=534643138" instead of "http://www.facebook.com/profile.php?id=534643138".

You'd be surprised how often people mix up .com and .org. In fact, lots of companies that own *domain-name.com* will also buy *domain-name.org* and redirect anyone that goes to *domain-name.org* to *domain-name.com* for that very reason.

You know how PHP strings work, and you've already used several PHP functions. You just need to learn two more functions to handle these common problems.

■ REMOVING EXTRA WHITESPACE BY USING TRIM()

PHP has a trim() function that eliminates any empty characters—what PHP calls *whitespace*—around a string. For example, trimming " I love my space bar. " gives you "I love my space bar." So, with just a couple of simple additions to your script, you can make sure that extra spaces around your users' entries is a thing of the past:

NOTE PHP also gives you rtrim( ), which trims just whitespace after a string (on its right side), and ltrim( ), which trims whitespace before a string (on its left side).

```php
$first_name = trim($_REQUEST['first_name']);
$last_name = trim($_REQUEST['last_name']);
$email = trim($_REQUEST['email']);
$facebook_url = trim($_REQUEST['facebook_url']);
$position = strpos($facebook_url, "facebook.com");
if ($position === false) {
  $facebook_url = "http://www.facebook.com/" . $facebook_url;
}

$twitter_handle = trim($_REQUEST['twitter_handle']);
$twitter_url = "http://www.twitter.com/";
$position = strpos($twitter_handle, "@");
if ($position === false) {
  $twitter_url = $twitter_url . $twitter_handle;
} else {
  $twitter_url = $twitter_url . substr($twitter_handle, $position + 1);
}
```

This change is simple to implement: every time you get a value from $_REQUEST, just wrap the value in trim(). You'll never have to worry about whitespace around your text again.

WARNING trim( ) (as well as rtrim( ) and ltrim( )) only remove whitespace on the *outside* of your text. Thus, trim( ) is great for dealing with something like " Way too much whitespace. " but won't help you at all with "Way too much whitespace."

■ REPLACING CHARACTERS IN TEXT BY USING STR_REPLACE()

It's also easy to replace text in a string. You use str_replace(), and give it three things:

1. **The text to search for, in quotes.** For example, "facebook.org".

2. **The replacement text.** If you want to replace every occurrence of facebook.org with facebook.com, your replacement text would be "facebook.com".

3. **The string in which to search; that is the value that the user typed into your web form.**

In PHP, you can put all this together on one line (see the box on page 81). You get something like this:

```
$facebook_url = str_replace("facebook.org", "facebook.com",
                            trim($_REQUEST['facebook_url']));
$position = strpos($facebook_url, "facebook.com");
if ($position === false) {
  $facebook_url = "http://www.facebook.com/" . $facebook_url;
}
```

Make these changes, and then visit your web form again. Enter some information that might have been a problem for a less-skilled PHP programmer, with lots of spaces and a bad facebook.org URL, as shown in Figure 3-9.

FIGURE 3-9

You'd be amazed at how often people fill out forms in a hurry. That usually means one of two things will happen: either all that problematic information will cause errors in a server-side script, or—if the programmer is a little more advanced—the script happily fixes those errors and keeps on chugging. It's good to be in the second category!

Submit this data. As you can see in Figure 3-10, *getFormInfo.php* doesn't miss a beat. It gets rid of all that extra space, and it even fixes the bad Facebook URL (see Figure 3-11).

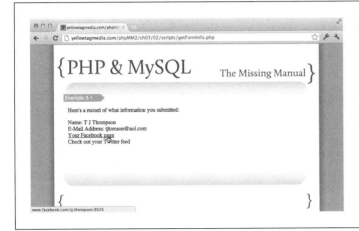

FIGURE 3-10

Using trim() *and* str_replace() *and
even* strpos() *is part of being a responsible
PHP programmer. In fact, you might eventually
build your own standard blocks of code through
which you run all your web form entries, just to
ensure that they're formatted exactly the way
you like.*

Chain Your Methods (Or Not!)

You might have noticed that PHP lets you do in a single step what might otherwise take several steps. For example, look at this line in your PHP script:

```
$facebook_url = str_replace("facebook.
org", "facebook.com", trim($_
REQUEST['facebook_url']));
```

This code actually combines several different things. You could rewrite this code like the following example, to make all those separate things a little clearer:

```
$facebook_url = $_REQUEST['facebook_url'];
$facebook_url = trim($facebook_url);
$facebook_url = str_replace("facebook.
org", "facebook.com", $facebook_url);
```

Both of these code examples carry out the same task, and from a performance and technical point of view, one isn't better than the other. That means it's up to you which version you prefer. So, how do you decide?

There are two basic schools of thought here. The first is common in programmer circles. It's the "brevity is the soul of wit" approach to programming. The concept is pretty simple: "Why do in multiple lines what you can get done in one line?"

Using this approach, anytime you can combine steps, you should. The code is a lot shorter, and you don't have a lot of those in-between steps. The result is called *method chaining*: you do one thing to a piece of text, for example, and then the result of that one thing is sent to another thing. In other words, each step is a link in a chain, and the entire line is the chain, complete and ready to use.

The other school of thought is a little less popular among programmers...unless those programmers have to teach what they're doing to someone else. This school of thought tries to make code really easy to understand. Of course, the more you can break down that chain of actions, the easier it is to quickly figure out what's going on. This takes a lot more code, but all that extra code is easier to understand, and (at least in theory) to fix if something goes wrong.

Realistically, you'll probably want to end up somewhere in the middle of these two approaches. For instance, your code in *getFormInfo.php* is nice and clear, even though a few things are chained together. But if you end up with lines that have 6, 7, or even 10 things attached to one another, it might be time to split things up (and lay off the triple ventis from Starbucks!).

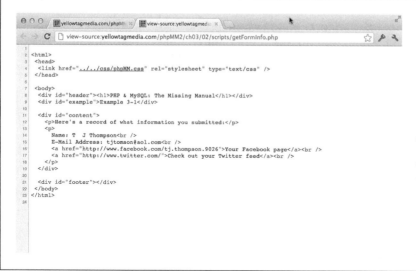

FIGURE 3-11

Once again, View Source is your friend. In most browsers, this option is under the View menu, the Page menu, or available by right-clicking the page. Be sure to view your page's source; it's what's really getting sent to the browser, no matter how things actually look on your screen.

TAKE IT FURTHER

PHP Offers a Slew of String Functions

Believe it or not, you've only just scratched the surface of what PHP has to offer in dealing with strings and text. Visit *php.net/ manual/en/ref.strings.php* to see a complete list of what you can do with text in PHP. But get your high-resolution monitor out; this is a long list that won't even fit on a single screen for most web browsers.

So, what do you do? Freak out about how much you *don't* yet know? Print out this web page and start memorizing a few functions every night? No, not at all. Just bookmark the page—and while you're at it, the PHP manual at *php.net/ manual*—and know that it's there when you need it. If you run across a string you need to manipulate, just pull up your bookmarked PHP manual and search through it until you find what you want.

The real surprise here is that *everyone* does it. Sure, there might be some Dustin Hoffman lookalike out there rattling off all the PHP numerical functions in a monotone voice, all Rain-Manned up in his gray suit. But that guy is the exception. Refer often to the online PHP manual—and books like this one—and when you forget something, just look it up.

Instead of worrying about memorizing the odds and ends of every function in the PHP language, work on understanding the *patterns* of PHP and how those patterns work. For instance, you now know that most string manipulation involves calling some function, passing it a few pieces of information, and assigning the result to a variable. *That's* what's important, and now, every time you do look up a string function in the PHP manual, you know exactly how to use that function correctly.

■ The $_REQUEST Variable Is an Array

It's probably no surprise to you that PHP is a lot more than a tool to work with text. You've been working with strings non-stop, but there are a lot more types of information you'll need to work with in your PHP scripts. As you might expect, there are all kinds of ways to work with numbers, and you'll work with them quite a bit before long.

But there's another important type of information you need to understand. In fact, you've already been working with this type as much as you've worked with text. This mystery type is an *array*, which is a sort of container that holds other values within it.

> **NOTE** You can find the finished example code for this section on this book's Missing CD page at *www .missingmanuals.com/cds/phpmysqlmm2e.*

Arrays Can Hold Multiple Values

An array is a *data structure*, which is an organization of data that can be referenced all at once. It's another one of those terms that will gain you respect at a local Google get together (but might get you some odd looks if you're having cocktails at a political fundraiser). But, arrays aren't hard to understand. Think of an array as a file cabinet of information, and you've got the idea.

As an example, if you have a variable called $file_cabinet that's an array, it can store other information within it. You might stuff URLs, and first names, and last names, and emails into that $file_cabinet. You can fill up the file cabinet by telling PHP where you want your information by using numbers surrounded by square brackets, right after the array variable name, like this:

```php
<?php

$file_cabinet[0] = "Derek";
$file_cabinet[1] = "Trucks";
$file_cabinet[2] = "derek@DerekTrucks.com";
$file_cabinet[3] = "http://www.facebook.com/DerekTrucks";
$file_cabinet[4] = "@derekandsusan";


?>
```

Think of these numbers as drawers in the file cabinet, or if you like things a little more compact, labels on file folders within the cabinet.

> **NOTE** Anytime you see a code example like this, you can type it, save it (using a name like *file_cabinet .php*), and run it with the php command. Go ahead and try it; you'll be changing things and making up your own programs in no time.

Then, you can get information out of $file_cabinet by using those same numbers within brackets:

```php
$first_name = $file_cabinet[0];
$last_name = $file_cabinet[1];
$email = $file_cabinet[2];
$facebook_url = $file_cabinet[3];
$twitter_handle = $file_cabinet[4];
```

WARNING It's probably old hat to you by now, but remember from the box on page 74 that most things in PHP start counting at 0. Arrays are no different. This means that the first item in $file_cabinet is $file_cabinet[0], not $file_cabinet[1].

From this point, you can do whatever you want with those values, including print them out. Here's a complete program that isn't very useful, but certainly puts an array through its paces. It fills an array, pulls information out of the array, and then does a little printing.

```php
<?php

$file_cabinet[0] = "Derek";
$file_cabinet[1] = "Trucks";
$file_cabinet[2] = "derek@DerekTrucks.com";
$file_cabinet[3] = "http://www.facebook.com/DerekTrucks";
$file_cabinet[4] = "@derekandsusan";

$first_name = $file_cabinet[0];
$last_name = $file_cabinet[1];
$email = $file_cabinet[2];
$facebook_url = $file_cabinet[3];
$twitter_handle = $file_cabinet[4];

echo $first_name . " " . $last_name;
echo "\nEmail: " . $email;
echo "\nFacebook URL: " . $facebook_url;
echo "\nTwitter Handle: " . $twitter_handle;

?>
```

This program does a fine job filing pieces of information away for use later—but there's a bit of a problem here. Are you really going to remember that you have a last name at position 2, and at position 4, you stored the Facebook URL? That's a disaster waiting to happen.

Fortunately, the wise folks that came up with PHP thought this through. PHP arrays are *associative*, which means simply that you can associate labels with each item in the array. Going back to the idea of each number being a folder in a file cabinet, you can use an actual label on the folder. Better yet, that label can be anything you want.

Following is that same simple program; this time it uses associative labels. You should make these changes to your own copy of this script if you're following along.

```php
<?php

$file_cabinet['first_name'] = "Derek";
$file_cabinet['last_name'] = "Trucks";
$file_cabinet['email'] = "derek@DerekTrucks.com";
$file_cabinet['facebook_url'] = "http://www.facebook.com/DerekTrucks";
$file_cabinet['twitter_handle'] = "@derekandsusan";

$first_name = $file_cabinet['first_name'];
$last_name = $file_cabinet['last_name'];
$email = $file_cabinet['email'];
$facebook_url = $file_cabinet['facebook_url'];
$twitter_handle = $file_cabinet['twitter_handle'];

echo $first_name . " " . $last_name;
echo "\nEmail: " . $email;
echo "\nFacebook URL: " . $facebook_url;
echo "\nTwitter Handle: " . $twitter_handle;
?>
```

By now, though, this $file_cabinet should be looking a bit familiar. You've seen something that looks awfully similar...read on for the full story.

PHP Gives You An Array of Request Information

Yes, you guessed it: $_REQUEST—that special variable PHP gave you to gather all the information from a web form—is an array! And when you've written code like $_REQUEST['first_name'], you've been grabbing a particular piece of information out of that array.

In fact, you've already seen that the most powerful way you use arrays is really behind the scenes. You (or a web browser) stick information into the array and then pull it back out and work with that information. The array just serves as a convenient way to hold things, like when a browser is sending a request to your PHP script.

You've seen that not only can you retrieve information in an array by a name— the label on a file folder—but also by number. This means that you can use $file_cabinet['first_name'], but you can also use $file_cabinet[0]. The same is true of $_REQUEST; it's just an array, therefore, using $_REQUEST[0] is perfectly fine with PHP.

What exactly is in $_REQUEST? Go ahead and create the following new program, and you can see for yourself.

```html
<html>
 <head>
  <link href="../../css/phpMM.css" rel="stylesheet" type="text/css" />
 </head>

 <body>
  <div id="header"><h1>PHP & MySQL: The Missing Manual</h1></div>
  <div id="example">Example 3-2</div>

  <div id="content">
    <p>Here's a record of everything in the $_REQUEST array:</p>
    <?php
      foreach($_REQUEST as $value) {
        echo "<p>" . $value . "</p>";
      }
    ?>
  </div>

  <div id="footer"></div>
 </body>
</html>
```

This is another one of those scripts that can look intimidating at first, but it's really not bad at all. In fact, the only thing you've not seen before is the line with the foreach construct. Take a closer look at this line, which begins a PHP loop:

```php
foreach($_REQUEST as $value) {
```

The foreach construct is a nifty PHP element that lets you quickly get at the values of an array (you'll learn a lot more later, on page 466). In this case, foreach takes an array ($_REQUEST) and then pulls each value out of that array, one at a time. Each time it pulls out a single value, it assigns that value to a new variable called $value; that's the as $value part of the foreach line. Inside the foreach loop, a $value variable is assigned a single value from within the array. This is repeated until there are no more values from left in the array.

Just as with the if statement you've used a few times, the curly braces ({ and }) tell PHP where the beginning and the end of this loop are:

```php
foreach($_REQUEST as $value) {
  echo "<p>" . $value . "</p>";
}
```

Everything between the { and } runs once for each time through the loop. This means that for every item in $_REQUEST, this line is going to run one time:

```
echo "<p>" . $value . "</p>";
```

This echo line prints out $value with some HTML formatting. Every time foreach loops around, $value picks up the next value from $_REQUEST, which makes this statement is a quick way to print out every value in $_REQUEST.

Now, suppose that $_REQUEST has values within it like "Derek", "Trucks", and "@ DerekAndSusan". When PHP runs your code, it does something like this:

```
echo "<p>" . "Derek" . "</p>";
echo "<p>" . "Trucks" . "</p>";
echo "<p>" . "@DerekAndSusan" . "</p>";
```

Save this script as *showRequestInfo.php*. You'll also need to change where your *socialEntryForm.php* web form submits its information to the following:

```
<form action="scripts/showRequestInfo.php" method="POST">
  <fieldset>
    <label for="first_name">First Name:</label>
    <input type="text" name="first_name" size="20" /><br />
    <label for="last_name">Last Name:</label>
    <input type="text" name="last_name" size="20" /><br />
    <label for="email">E-Mail Address:</label>
    <input type="text" name="email" size="50" /><br />
    <label for="facebook_url">Facebook URL:</label>
    <input type="text" name="facebook_url" size="50" /><br />
    <label for="twitter_handle">Twitter Handle:</label>
    <input type="text" name="twitter_handle" size="20" /><br />
  </fieldset>
  <br />
  <fieldset class="center">
    <input type="submit" value="Join the Club" />
    <input type="reset" value="Clear and Restart" />
  </fieldset>
</form>
```

NOTE   You may want to create a copy of *socialEntryForm.html*, and call it something else, like *socialEntryForm-2.html* or *enterInformation.html*. This will give you two versions: one that sends information to *showRequestInfo.php*, and one that sends information to *getFormInfo.php*.

Visit your new web form, fill it out, and then submit it. The web form you get back is the result of running your new *showRequestInfo.php* script. This form finally gives you an idea of what's being sent between your web browser and a web server, and you can see it all in Figure 3-12.

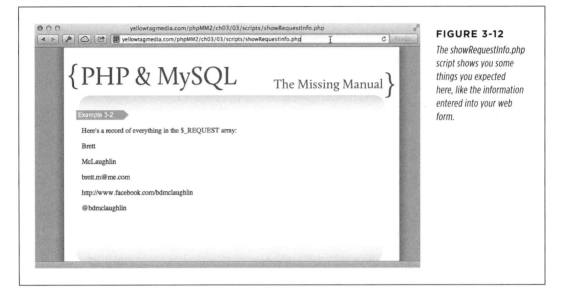

FIGURE 3-12

The showRequestInfo.php script shows you some things you expected here, like the information entered into your web form.

At this point, you have the raw information, but what does it all mean? The web page in Figure 3-12 is like seeing all the files on a computer, but having none of the names of those files. Or, if you like the file cabinet analogy, imagine having a cabinet of folders with all the labels torn off. It makes knowing what's going on a little trickier.

With the form data, you already know the labels: "first_name", and "last_name", "email", and so on. In an associative array such as what PHP uses, these are called the *keys*. You can get the value of a particular "folder" in an array with code like this:

```
$value = $file_cabinet[$key];
```

This line of code gets the value from the array that's attached to whatever label the $key variable holds. Thus, if $key were "first_name", the code would basically be the same as this:

```
$value = $file_cabinet['first_name'];
```

Therefore, in *showRequestInfo.php*, you just need to also get the keys from the $_REQUEST array, instead of just the values. Then, you can print out both the key *and* the value. And, wouldn't you know it, PHP makes that easy, again by using foreach:

```
<div id="content">
  <p>Here's a record of everything in the $_REQUEST array:</p>
  <?php
    foreach($_REQUEST as $key => $value) {
      echo "<p>For " . $key . ", the value is '" . $value . "'.</p>";
    }
  ?>
</div>
```

This time, you're instructing foreach to get both the key, as $key, and the value, as $value. That special => sign tells PHP you want the $key and then the $value attached to the key. In other words, you're grabbing a label and the folder that label is attached to, which is just what you want.

Fill out your form again and check out the results of your updated PHP script, as shown in Figure 3-13.

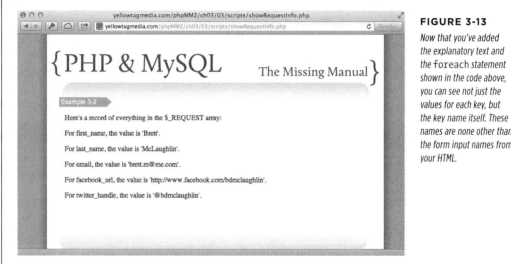

FIGURE 3-13

Now that you've added the explanatory text and the foreach statement shown in the code above, you can see not just the values for each key, but the key name itself. These names are none other than the form input names from your HTML.

■ What Do You Do with User Information?

At this point, you've got a lot of information stuffed into a lot of variables. In fact, your earlier web form, *socialEntryForm.html*, looks a lot like the signup forms you've probably filled out hundreds (or thousands) of times online. But there's a problem, isn't there? In fact, you might have already run across it as you worked through all the changes to your *getFormInfo.php* script: none of that information was ever saved! You had to enter in your name and social information, over and over and over.

Good PHP programmers are able to solve just about any technical problem you throw at them. They know all the PHP string functions, arrays, and a lot more, to boot. But *great* PHP programmers can solve a whole set of problems that those good PHP programmers never think about: user expectation problems. These are problems that really aren't technical—although you might need to be a good programmer to work around users.

Here's the million-dollar question: What does your user *expect* your pages and scripts to do? For instance, does your user expect to have to come back to your page and enter in the same information, each time? Absolutely not. You'd probably stop visiting a site like that yourself. What you have is a user expectation problem—and if you want users to hang around and use your site, you'd better solve this problem.

In fact, one of the best things you can do is actually *use* your own pages and programs. Get a cup of coffee, a notepad, and just sit down at your computer. Close all your text editors and programming tools, and think, "I'm a user!" Then, try out your web form, submit the form, enter weird information in it, and just see what happens. Take a few notes about things that bug you, but remember: you're just a user here.

WARNING You might be tempted to make all your notes in a text editor, or just start fixing things. Resist this urge! As soon as you start fixing things, or even getting immersed in your computer, you're not thinking like a user anymore, and you'll miss things.

You'll probably find all sorts of things you didn't even think about. So, now what? Well, you've got to start fixing those things. And first up is this pesky issue of having to enter the same information into your page, over and over.

MySQL and SQL:
Database and Language

Where is this supposed to go?

It's a question you ask every day. Where do these shoes go? Where does this new box of books go? Where do these receipts go? Because that's such a common question, it shouldn't surprise you too much that when you're building web applications, you need to ask the same thing:

Where does my information go?

For the kinds of web applications you've been building with web pages and PHP, the answer to this question is simple: in a database. But what do you get out of a database that makes it worth the effort of installing another tool and learning another language? And, why does everyone seem to agree that if you're writing PHP code, you need a database, too? Sit tight, because this chapter is about to reveal all.

■ What Is a Database?

A database is just a repository in which you can store information, add some layer of organization to the stored information, and grab that information when it's needed. In a literal sense, a file cabinet is a database. You can throw things into it, pull those things back out, and even use files and labels to keep your files organized.

Databases Are Persistent

You've already seen that PHP gives you arrays (page 83) that serve as a sort of programmer's file cabinet. An array might function as a database in a simplistic sense, but it won't serve your needs for long. For one thing, arrays and their contents in PHP are lost every time your program stops and starts again. That's not very helpful.

A good database provides long-term storage for your information. If your program stops running, or your entire web server has to be restarted, a database doesn't lose your information. Imagine if every time your web server had to be shut down for an upgrade, your database lost every user's first name, last name, and email address. Do you think your users would come back to your site if they repeatedly had to type everything in again? Not a chance.

Therefore, a good database needs to store information more permanently. In programmer jargon, this is called *persisting* your information. (At times, though, even permanent information can be lost; see the box that follows for advice on backing up your information in such cases.)

UNDER THE HOOD

Permanent Data Is Really Semi-Permanent

Even though databases store your information, and that storage lasts beyond your computer or even a database starting up and shutting down, your information is still not really permanent. Think about it: even if you write in ink instead of pencil, you can still throw away the piece of paper you wrote on. That's how databases work: they store information in a form that's harder to destroy, but that information still *can* be destroyed.

At some point, databases have to store information somewhere, usually on hard drives. If one of those hard drives crashes or becomes defective, your information is lost, no matter how good your database is. Additionally, threats to computers like overheating or natural disasters can wipe out your data by destroying the hard drives on which it exists.

That's why most databases offer some form of backup and replication. *Backup* is just creating a copy of your database so

that if something goes wrong, you can restore the database from the backup and recover all (or at least most) of the information that's been lost.

Replication is when an entire database is duplicated (the duplicated version might be running simultaneously). This means that in addition to having the main database and possibly a backup, you have an entirely different copy of the database running, as well. With replication, an entire database could fail, but all your applications keep running because they can switch to the replicated version.

Replication is expensive because you basically need another server with another copy of your database software running. Still, if you use an application extensively and it earns money as long as it's running, replication is a really important way to ensure that information isn't lost in a disaster.

If you think about it, you're constantly working with something like this on your computer: a system that stores your information over a long term. It's your hard drive and file system. The files on your computer are basically pieces of information; such as addresses, emails, your finances, or maybe what level you've made it to in Angry Birds. You can shut down your computer and start it back up, or even upgrade to a new computer, and all those files with all your information will still load up.

In other words, a file system is really a sort of database. In fact, lots of databases actually use files much like your computer does to persist information. So, why doesn't PHP just store information in files? It actually has an entire set of tools for working with files, including creating, writing, and reading files. Isn't that enough?

NOTE You learn about how to use PHP to work with files in Chapter 5.

Databases Are All about Structure

If you think about it, there's something pretty clunky about your computer's file system. Have you ever tried to remember the last time you sent an email to someone? Your email program might not know that person's email address. And, if you go to that person's card in your address book program, that address book program might not be connected to your email program.

Even if you actually find the email address, you might need to reference some documents related to the email message. Where are those documents? In another folder somewhere, probably in some highly-organized structure about which you've long forgotten.

That's why your computer gives you one or more ways to search for information. In Mac OS X, you can use Spotlight (see Figure 4-1) or a program like Quicksilver (*http:// quicksilver.en.softonic.com/mac*). If you have Windows, you can download Google's Desktop Search (*http://www.google.com/quicksearchbox*, see Figure 4-2). These programs find all occurrences of a certain word or topic across your entire system.

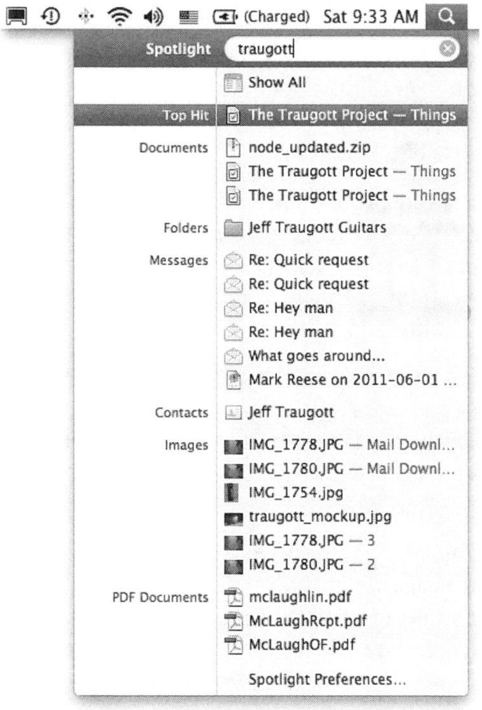

FIGURE 4-1

Spotlight in Mac OS X tries to relate files in different places by their name, the folder they're in, or their content. In other words, Spotlight tries to determine the relationships between different files and folders.

In fact, these search programs attempt to do what databases do by nature: locate and organize information. If you've ever tried to make these sort of connections on your computer—whether you're using Spotlight or Google Search or doing it by hand—you know it's a hassle and inconsistent, at best. What you need is a better way to connect two, three, or ten pieces of information together.

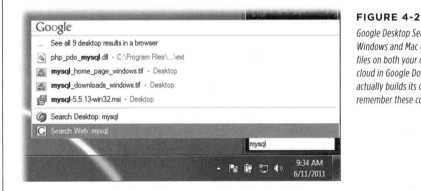

FIGURE 4-2

Google Desktop Search works in both Windows and Mac OS. It indexes and connects files on both your computer and in the cloud in Google Documents and Gmail. It actually builds its own database to make and remember these connections.

Good Databases Are Relational

There is one task for which a file system and your hard drive are lacking, but a database excels: creating *relationships* between different pieces of information. For example, you might have a person, and that person has several email addresses, phone numbers, and mailing addresses. This isn't anything new; your address book program already handles these sorts of relationships.

But a good database goes further. An email message is related to the email address of the sender, and that email is related back to the person's name and phone numbers and mailing address. A map with streets connects those streets to the streets used in a person's mailing address. The creator's name in a file description relates to that person, and their email, and their phone, and so on.

In a lot of ways, these relationships are really a giant web of connections. A good database both creates and manages all these relationships. In fact, relationships are so integral to MySQL, FileMaker, Oracle, and other big-time databases that they're called *relational databases*. (For a technical journey into how these databases operate, see the box on page 95.)

This means that in addition to instructing a database what information you want it to store for you and your programs, you also define how that information is *connected* to other pieces of information. Not only do you get to use this web of connections, but you specify to the database exactly how the web should be constructed. That's a lot of power, which is why you'll have to learn an entirely new language to work with these relational databases.

Objects and Relations in Databases, Oh My!

For decades, the relational database has been the de facto standard for high-end applications, whether those applications run on the Web or on an internal company network. These database programs—often called an RDBMS, which stands for *relational database management system*—are the best understood, and most data naturally fits into an RDBMS model. Not only that, but there are more stable and professional RDBMS's than any other type of database.

However, there are some competitors to the RDBMS model these days. Most of these are *object-oriented database management systems*, or OODBMS for short. Although the OODBMS has been around since the 1970s, it's really just in the past 10 years that these have gained popularity.

An RDBMS stores information in tables, rows, and columns. For example, you might have a table of users that has columns for their first name, last name, and email. This means that anything that's stored in the RDBMS involves some kind of mapping. This means that the information in your PHP script has to be mapped to particular tables and columns. You'd say, for example, the

information in $_REQUEST['first_name'] needs to be stored in the *Users* table, and then in the first_name column. This isn't a big deal, but it is an extra step in working with relational databases.

In an OODBMS, you'd create an *object* in your code. (You don't need to worry about the details of objects and how they work for now.) So, you might create a new User object, and assign it's first name the value in $_REQUEST['first_name']. Then, when you want to store that user's information, you just hand the OODBMS your entire User object. In other words, the database figures out how to deal with an object instead of you specifying where individual pieces of information go.

Of course, with an OODBMS, this means you have to have lots of objects in your code, so you're going to end up writing some code whether you're working with an RDBMS or an OODBMS. Still, the RDBMS is far, far more common in web applications than the OODBMS, which is why it's definitely the one you want to focus on learning.

◼ Installing MySQL

Before you can tackle the new language of databases, you've got to get a database installed on your computer. In this book, you'll be working with the MySQL database, which is one of the most common databases used in web applications. The reason for this is because it's easy to get, easy to install, and easy to use.

> **NOTE** Like most things in life, ease-of-use comes with some tradeoffs. There are some database programs that cost a lot of money and are really complicated to use, such as Oracle. But these programs typically offer features that programs like MySQL don't: higher-end tools for maintenance, and a whole slew of professional support options that go beyond what you can get with MySQL.
>
> Don't worry, though. Almost every single command, technique, and tool you'll learn for working with MySQL will work with *any* relational database, so even if you end up at a company or in a situation where Oracle (or an IBM product, or PostgreSQL, or something else entirely) is in use, you'll have no problems getting your PHP working with a database other than MySQL.

If you installed MAMP on your Mac or WampServer on your Windows-based PC (see Chapter 1, page 22), then you already have a local installation of MySQL. Pretty sweet, right? (And, if you didn't—you masochist, you!—check out Appendix B for detailed, step-by-step instructions on installing MySQL *without* MAMP or WampServer.)

Just as Chapter 1 deals with a local installation of PHP, this chapter starts out by focusing on a local installation of MySQL. Of course, just as your PHP work in Chapter 1 progressed into working with a remote installation of PHP in Chapter 2, the same applies here, so if you don't want to mess with WampServer or MAMP, you can jump on your hosting provider, fire up the mysql program, and get to typing. Of course, this assumes that your hosting provider lets you have shell access and lets you run the mysql console program—neither of which is a sure thing. If those become an issue, you can always resort to the already-installed MAMP/WampServer version on your local computer.

The mysql Console Program: Your New Best Friend

Regardless of how you install MySQL, your first step toward database mastery is to begin using the mysql console program. Although MySQL is a database, mysql is a program that lets you interact with that database from a command line. Every installation of MySQL comes with the mysql tool; you just have to know how to get at it.

But first you have to *start* the MySQL service. Otherwise, you'll get errors because the mysql program has nothing to which it can connect. For WampServer, on the right side of the taskbar, click the green "W" icon and choose Put Online or Start All Services and read on. For MAMP, start the program, select Start Servers, and then go to page 98.

> **WARNING** Many budding web developers have had their careers crashed against the rocks of their MySQL server not being started. You can bang your head against the MySQL console all day and get nowhere if you don't have MySQL started up on your computer.

Run the mysql Tool on WampServer

WampServer installs mysql along with the MySQL database. However, it doesn't set up your PATH to access that program, so you'll have to do a little digging around.

■ FIND THE MYSQL COMMAND-LINE PROGRAM

Once you've started up MySQL, change into the *wamp/* directory on the drive on which you installed WampServer. For example, if you put WampServer on the *c:* drive, go to a command prompt (Start→Run and then type command on Windows 7 and earlier; Windows key+R on Windows 8) and then type the following:

```
C:\Users\bdm0509> cd c:\wamp\bin\mysql\
```

Now, you'll have to do a little investigation, because things change based upon the version of MySQL your copy of WampServer installed. Do a directory listing:

```
C:\wamp\bin\mysql>dir
 Volume in drive C has no label.
 Volume Serial Number is 7C78-FE01

 Directory of C:\wamp\bin\mysql

08/01/2012  02:32 PM    <DIR>          .
08/01/2012  02:32 PM    <DIR>          ..
08/01/2012  02:32 PM    <DIR>          mysql5.5.24
               0 File(s)            0 bytes
               3 Dir(s)  52,739,547,136 bytes free
```

You should see just one directory, specific to the version of MySQL installed by
WampServer. Change into that directory. For MySQL 5.5.24, use the following:

```
C:\wamp\bin\mysql> cd mysql5.5.24
```

Now, you can go into yet another *bin* directory and finally run the `mysql` command:

```
C:\wamp\bin\mysql\mysql5.5.24> cd bin

C:\wamp\bin\mysql\mysql5.5.24\bin>mysql
ERROR 2003 (HY000): Can't connect to MySQL server on 'localhost' (10061)
```

■ GIVE `MYSQL` THE RIGHT USER AND PASSWORD

You have the right program, but the error message tells you that things aren't working yet. That's because you haven't told `mysql` what user to use for logging in. You
must specify the user with the -u option and then tell it to log in as "root". Here's
how it looks:

```
C:\wamp\bin\mysql\mysql5.5.24\bin>mysql -u root
Welcome to the MySQL monitor.  Commands end with ; or \g.
Your MySQL connection id is 2
Server version: 5.5.24-log MySQL Community Server (GPL)

Copyright (c) 2000, 2011, Oracle and/or its affiliates. All rights reserved.

Oracle is a registered trademark of Oracle Corporation and/or its
affiliates. Other names may be trademarks of their respective
owners.

Type 'help;' or '\h' for help. Type '\c' to clear the current input statement.

mysql>
```

And there you have it! Somewhat surprising, you don't need to provide a password
to WampServer. Of course, because this is all running on your own local installation,
security isn't the concern it will be when you start connecting to a MySQL database

on your web host out on the Internet. For now, you're ready to start interacting with your database.

Run the mysql Tool on MAMP

If you're on Mac OS X, MAMP came with a mysql tool, available through the Terminal. It's stored in */Applications/MAMP/Library/bin*, so you can run it like this:

```
$ /Applications/MAMP/Library/bin/mysql
```

■ SET UP MYSQL FOR YOUR USER PROFILE

You can make this easier with a few quick edits to your profile and setup:

1. **Create a directory called *bin* in your home directory:**

   ```
   mkdir ~/bin
   ```

2. **Go to that directory:**

   ```
   cd ~/bin
   ```

3. **Create a symbolic link to the mysql program in that directory:**

   ```
   ln -s /Applications/MAMP/Library/bin/mysql mysql
   ```

4. **Add your new *~/bin* directory to your path.** Edit your *~/.bash_profile*:

   ```
   vi ~/.bash_profile
   ```

5. **Find or add a line to update your PATH variable.** For example:

   ```
   export PATH=$PATH:~/bin
   ```

6. **Now save your *.bash_profile*, and restart Terminal.**

> **NOTE** If you're comfortable with the Mac OS X command line and see things here that don't apply to your system—such as bash needing to be replaced by a custom shell you've installed—then feel free to make those changes. You're probably a few steps ahead already, anyway, so if you know what to do, go on and make the changes for your system.

If you can power through this setup, all you have to do in the future is start a new Terminal and type the following:

```
$ mysql
```

If you don't want to go through that rigamarole, just type the full path to mysql every time:

```
$ /Applications/MAMP/Library/bin/mysql
```

■ GIVE MYSQL THE RIGHT USER AND PASSWORD

For MAMP installations, just as with WampServer installations, using the mysql tool log in to MySQL as the root user. You specify that by using the -u option and then the username root, like this:

```
$ mysql -u root
```

Running this command as is doesn't quite give you what you were hoping for. In fact, you'll probably see an error similar to this:

```
$ /Applications/MAMP/Library/bin/mysql -uroot
ERROR 1045 (28000): Access denied for user 'root'@'localhost' (using password:
NO)
```

That's because users have passwords, and you haven't supplied one. On top of that, for reasons too confusing to mention, the mysql program doesn't ask you for a password, unless you instruct it to. Add the -p option, and you'll be prompted for a password:

```
$ /Applications/MAMP/Library/bin/mysql -uroot -p
Enter password:
```

To find your root user password, go to the MAMP start page. That's the web page that fires up every time you start MAMP. If MAMP is already running, you can click "Open start page." You'll see something like Figure 4-3, and there, clear as can be, is your password.

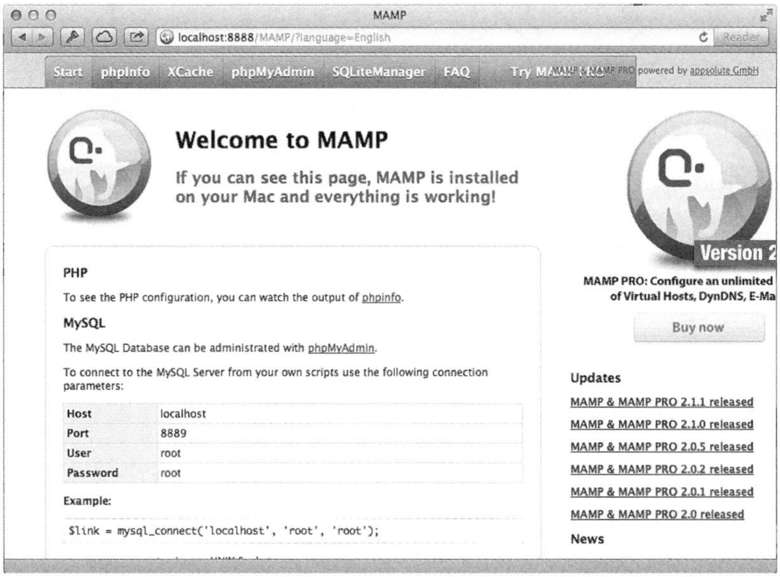

FIGURE 4-3

The MAMP start page is your first and best source for all things PHP, MySQL, and web server on your local installation of these programs. In this case, it displays the MySQL root password, which you'll need...a lot!

A root user password of "root" isn't particularly secure, but again, you're on your local computer, not the NASA user store. Now, you can give that password to the mysql prompt. You should see something like this in return:

```
$ /Applications/MAMP/Library/bin/mysql -uroot -p
Enter password:
Welcome to the MySQL monitor.  Commands end with ; or \g.
```

```
Your MySQL connection id is 6
Server version: 5.5.9 Source distribution

Copyright (c) 2000, 2010, Oracle and/or its affiliates. All rights reserved.

Oracle is a registered trademark of Oracle Corporation and/or its
affiliates. Other names may be trademarks of their respective
owners.

Type 'help;' or '\h' for help. Type '\c' to clear the current input statement.
Once you're logged in, you can type exit to quit:
mysql> exit
Bye
$
```

That's all there is to it! Now you're ready to start talking to MySQL.

Run Your First SQL Query

MySQL has installed a number of pre-created databases on your system. To see them, all you have to do is ask. Fire up the mysql command line tool again, and type this command:

```
show databases;
```

> **WARNING** Be sure you end your line with a semicolon, or you'll get unexpected results. All your MySQL commands must end with a semicolon, just like most of your PHP commands.

You should get a text response from MySQL that looks a bit like this:

```
mysql> show databases;
+--------------------+
| Database           |
+--------------------+
| information_schema |
| development        |
| eiat_testbed       |
| mysql              |
| nagios             |
| ops_dashboard      |
| performance_schema |
| test               |
+--------------------+
8 rows in set (0.25 sec)
```

You might not have as many databases that come back, or you might have different databases. That's OK.

The show command does just what you might expect: it shows you everything for a particular keyword; in this case, databases. To sum it up, show databases is just a way you can ask MySQL to show you all the databases installed on your machine.

On top of that, now you know something really important: MySQL really isn't so much a database, but a piece of software that can store and create databases. In this example, there are eight rows returned as a result of running the show databases command, which means there are eight databases on the system, not just one. Before you're done, you'll have created several databases, all running within MySQL.

For now, tell MySQL you want to work with the mysql database, which you have on your system even if you've only installed MySQL. You do that with the use command, like so:

```
use mysql;
```

Now, you're *in* the mysql database. This means that any commands you give to MySQL are run against just the mysql database.

At the beginning of this section, you asked MySQL to show you all the databases it has; now tell it to show you all the tables in the database you're currently using:

```
show tables;
```

You should get a nice long list, as illustrated here:

```
mysql> show tables;
+---------------------------+
| Tables_in_mysql           |
+---------------------------+
| columns_priv              |
| db                        |
| event                     |
| func                      |
| general_log               |
| help_category             |
| help_keyword              |
| help_relation             |
| help_topic                |
| host                      |
| ndb_binlog_index          |
| plugin                    |
| proc                      |
| procs_priv                |
| proxies_priv              |
| servers                   |
| slow_log                  |
| tables_priv               |
| time_zone                 |
| time_zone_leap_second     |
```

```
| time_zone_name               |
| time_zone_transition         |
| time_zone_transition_type    |
| user                         |
+------------------------------+
24 rows in set (0.00 sec)
```

A lot of these table names appear odd, but that's mostly because these are internal tables used by MySQL. As you create new tables and users and set up your database, all of that information is stored within another database: the mysql database.

To see some of this information, you must use the select command to access information from a specific table—for example, the *user* table. Type this command at your MySQL command prompt:

```
mysql> select * from user;
```

The asterisk (*) means "select everything." Then, from specifies to MySQL where to get the information: in this example, *user*, which is a table in your database.

Don't be surprised when you get a confusing stream of information back. In fact, it might look like something out of the Matrix; check out Figure 4-4 for an example.

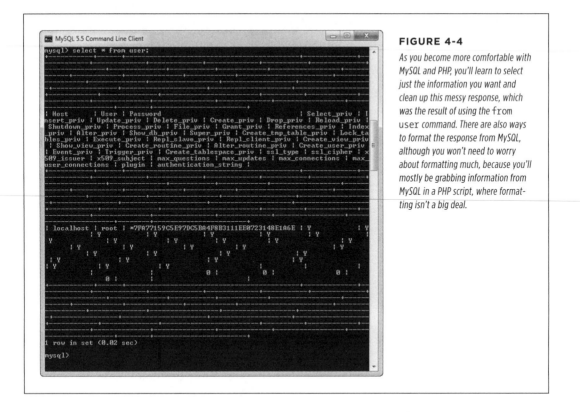

FIGURE 4-4

As you become more comfortable with MySQL and PHP, you'll learn to select just the information you want and clean up this messy response, which was the result of using the from user *command. There are also ways to format the response from MySQL, although you won't need to worry about formatting much, because you'll mostly be grabbing information from MySQL in a PHP script, where formatting isn't a big deal.*

The problem here isn't in anything you typed. It's just that you instructed MySQL to select *everything* from the *user* table, and in this case, everything is a *lot* of information. In fact, it's so much information that it won't all nicely fit into your command-line client, which is why you got all the strange looking lines in your response.

To tame this beast a bit, you can select just a little information from a table. You do this be replacing the * in the command with the specific column names you want, separated by commas:

```
mysql> select Host, User, Password from user;
```

You get back just the three columns for which you asked:

```
mysql> select Host, User, Password from user;
+-------------------------+-------+----------------------------------------
--+
| Host                    | User  | Password
|
+-------------------------+-------+----------------------------------------
--+
| localhost               | root  | *62425DC34224DAABF6995B46CDCC63D92B03D7E9
|
+-------------------------+-------+----------------------------------------
--+
1 row in set (0.00 sec)
```

This example shows that for your local computer (*localhost*), you have a single user named "root." The password is encrypted, so it isn't very helpful, but you can see that MySQL definitely has an entry for you. Because you only asked for three columns, this response is a lot more readable and actually makes a little sense.

So, what's a column? A column is a *single category of information* in your table. For example, in a table that stores users, you might have a `first_name` and a `last_name` column.

NOTE If you're starting to get a little dizzy or your nose is bleeding from the rush of new terms, don't worry. You'll be working with tables, columns, and these MySQL statements over and over and over again as you build your PHP programs. Just get what you can now, and you'll have all this new MySQL lingo under control in no time.

Now that you've dipped your feet into the MySQL pool, it's time to start to create your own tables and columns, and fill those tables and columns with your own information.

Going Local

My website is going to run on a server out there on the Internet. Why should I install MySQL on my own desktop?

You saw it already in the first few chapters on PHP, and now you're about to see it again: most of your programming is meant to be run on a web server. You might pay a monthly fee for hosting to a service like *kattare.com* for your own domain, you might own your own server that is connected to the Internet, or you might deploy your code to your company's servers, housed in a room that's kept too cold for normal human beings and requires a key card to even make it through the door. In all these cases, though, your code ends up somewhere other than your own desktop or laptop.

But, if that's the case, why go through the trouble of installing PHP and MySQL on your own computer? Truth be told, you could ask a lot of PHP developers and they'd admit that they don't even have PHP (let alone MySQL) on their own devices. Their programming lives are lived through telnet and ssh sessions, writing code on a distant server, somewhere out on the Web.

Although your code rarely will ultimately run from your own computer, there are some really good reasons to install your entire development setup on it. First, you're not always in a place where you can connect to the Internet. You might be on a plane, in the back of a taxi, or lost in West Texas with nothing but an old leather-covered compass and a MacBook Pro. In all these cases, if you've got PHP and MySQL on your laptop, you can code away, testing your code against a real database, and never miss a beat.

Second, it's common to write a lot of code, run it, find out you messed up something (or a lot of somethings), rewrite code, try again, and again, and again. The same is true when you start accessing a database. Although you could do this on the server on which your code will ultimately reside, that's a lot of time spent on a network connection, using that machine's resources, and potentially adding and deleting and adding data to a database. It's a lot simpler to work on your own computer, and then at certain milestones, upload all your working code to your server.

And finally, you learn a ton by installing these programs from scratch. You get a better handle not just on your own device, but how these programs work. If someone is getting a particular error, you might recognize that same error as something you got when a Windows service wasn't running, or the MySQL instance on a Mac OS X computer didn't have the right table permissions set up. Your installation is a way to learn more about the tools you use, and that's always a good thing.

You can run the examples in this book on your own computer and on your web server. Just make sure that if you're working on your own machine you can either get to its code with a web browser or you upload your code every time you're ready to make sure things are working correctly. That way, you can follow along with all the examples. Beyond that, it's up to you where you develop your code, test it, and run it.

■ SQL Is a Language for Talking to Databases

So far you've been using a program called MySQL, and you've been talking to that program using SQL, the *Structured Query Language*. And you've already written a couple of SQL queries:

```
mysql> select * from user;
...
mysql> select Host, User, Password from user;
...
```

Both of those commands are SQL queries, or expressed more accurately, SQL. The Structured in SQL comes from the idea that you're accessing a relational database, something with a lot of structure, and you're using a language that itself is very structured. You'll soon see that SQL is very easy to learn, mostly because it's very predictable. That's why you can look at a command like the following and probably figure out what it does:

```
mysql> select User, Password
          from users
        where first_name = 'Dirk'
          and country = 'Germany';
```

Even though you've never seen the where keyword, it's obvious what it does: this returns only the User and Password column from the *users* table, where the user's first_name field is "Dirk" and the country field is "Germany."

WARNING   The pronunciation of SQL is more hotly contested than most presidential elections. Some folks say "sequel" while others insist on "S-Q-L," saying each letter individually. Although you probably want to stick what with the folks around you are using, both are perfectly fine. (By the way, this book goes with the "sequel" pronunciation.)

You could buy a SQL book and start memorizing all the keywords, but it's a much better idea to simply begin building your own tables and learn as you go. To do that, though, you need to get connected to the database with which all your PHP programs will talk to.

Logging In to Your Web Server's Database

Now that you've got a basic lay of the land for how MySQL behaves, it's time to get things set up on the database your web server uses. You'll probably need to use a tool like telnet or ssh to log in to your web server.

NOTE   If you've never used telnet or ssh before, you should Google either program's name; you'll find a ton of resources. You might also want to call whoever hosts your domain and ask how you can best access your server. Many web providers now have a graphical version of SSH that you can use right from their control panel. Most good hosting providers also have detailed online instructions to help you get logged in and started, usually applicable to both Windows and Mac OS X.

Once you're logged in, you should be able to use the MySQL command-line client, mysql. Almost every hosting provider that supports PHP also supports MySQL, which means that just typing mysql is usually the way to get started.

Unfortunately, you're likely to get an error like the following, right out of the gate:

```
bmclaugh@akila:~$ mysql
ERROR 2002 (HY000): Can't connect to local MySQL server through socket '/tmp/
mysql.sock' (2)
```

This usually means that MySQL isn't installed on your server, or at least that it's not been configured correctly. But that's probably by intention: most hosting providers keep their MySQL installation either on a different machine, or they at least limit accessibility by using a different domain name, like *mysql.kattare.com*. That adds some protection, isolation, and security to the MySQL databases they host, all of which are good things.

> **NOTE** If running mysql doesn't work, you might also try mysql --host=localhost. Some MySQL installations are configured to only answer to *localhost* rather than what's called the *local socket*. That adds a bit of security to a MySQL installation, but isn't something you need to worry much about at this point. Just ensure that you can get mysql running, one way or another.

No matter where MySQL is installed, your task is simple. Run mysql and instruct it exactly where to connect. The --host= option lets you give mysql the hostname of your MySQL database server, and --user= lets you give it your own user name.

> **NOTE** You'll almost certainly have a user name other than "admin" or "root" for your domain provider's MySQL installation. You can ask what it is when you ask about telnet or ssh access. Or, if you want to try something out on your own, start with the user name and password you use for logging in to your web server itself. Be cautious, though: good database systems will have different user names and passwords than the web servers that talk to them.

Put all this together on the command line, and you' get something like this:

```
bmclaugh@akila:~$ mysql --host=dc2-mysql-02.kattare.com
                        --user=bmclaugh --password
Enter password:
```

That last option, --password, instructs MySQL to ask you for a password. You could put your password on the command itself, like --password=this_is_not_very_secure, but then that slightly nosy cube-mate would be able to log in to your MySQL server. And, if you're wondering what happened to the -u and -p options for mysql, you might want to check out the box that follows.

You Say Potato, I Say P

Back on page 98, you used the -u option for a username, and the -p option to instruct MySQL to prompt you for a password. And, as you might guess, there's a -h option you can use for specifying the host; it works like --host.

In fact, there's *no difference* between using -u brett and --user=brett. The same is true for --password and -p, and --host and -h. There's no subtle variation; each pair is identical.

Why two options?

Well, it's really about brevity and convenience. You've probably heard it before, and it remains true: programmers are lazy typists. Given the choice between typing six characters (--user) and two (-u), programmers will choose the smaller amount every time. So the -p and -u and -h options are sort of a programmer-friendly shorthand.

There's no right or wrong way to do it, which is a good thing. For clarity, this book uses the longer, easier-to-read versions most of the time. But now that you know the shortcuts, feel free to use them anytime you like.

Once you type your password, you should see the standard MySQL welcome screen, as demonstrated in Figure 4-5.

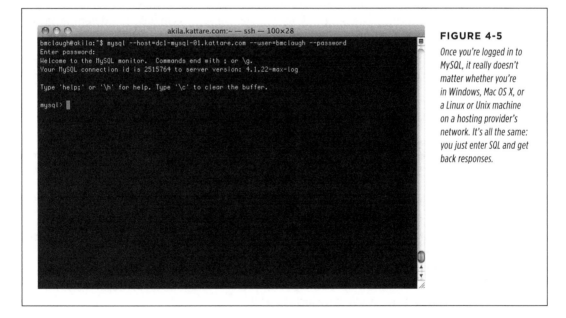

FIGURE 4-5

Once you're logged in to MySQL, it really doesn't matter whether you're in Windows, Mac OS X, or a Linux or Unix machine on a hosting provider's network. It's all the same: you just enter SQL and get back responses.

Now, you're ready to actually do something with this new SQL you've been learning.

Selecting a Database with USE

On most MySQL installations that hosting providers give you, you don't have nearly as much freedom as you do on your own installation. For example, on a remote server, suppose that you type the SQL show command you used on page 100:

```
myqsl> show databases;
```

If you ran this earlier on your own computer, you probably saw a lot of databases listed here. But now, on your hosting provider, you'll probably only see one:

```
myqsl> show databases;

+----------+
| Database |
+----------+
| bmclaugh |
+----------+
1 row in set (0.09 sec)
```

That's because your privileges on your hosting provider's server are limited, and as such, the company certainly isn't going to let you log in to the mysql system databases and see what users are in the system's *user* table. What you probably see is a single entry: a database named something similar to your login name. So, if you log in to your system with the user name "ljuber", you might see a database named ljuber or perhaps db-ljuber or something similar.

In fact, you're probably already set up within the database that's named after you. Go ahead and inform MySQL that's the database in which you want to work:

```
mysql> use bmclaugh;
Database changed
```

> **WARNING**   On some systems, you're automatically set up to use your user's database when you log in to MySQL. Still, the use command won't give you any problems if you point it to the current database, so it's always a good idea to begin your MySQL sessions with use [your-database-name].

While you're acclimating yourself to your new MySQL environment, you also want to get used to seeing and typing SQL commands in all capital letters. So if you get an email from your database buddy and she suggests that you use a WHERE clause or tells you that your SELECT query is goofy, she's not actually yelling at you. She's saying (or more accurately, writing) SQL commands in all uppercase letters, which is the way most database jockeys do it.

In fact, the commands you've seen thus far are more commonly written and typed like this:

```
mysql> SELECT * FROM user;
...
mysql> SELECT Host, User, Password FROM user;
...
```

```
mysql> SELECT User, Password
          FROM users
        WHERE first_name = 'Dirk'
          AND country = 'Germany';
```

This creates a nice clear distinction between the SQL keywords like SELECT, FROM, WHERE, and AND, and the column and table names. As you've guessed, though, MySQL accepts keywords in either uppercase or lowercase letters. They all work the same way.

NOTE In this book, an all-capitals word like SELECT means the same thing as select written in code font.

Again, though, you don't *have* to use capital letters in MySQL for keywords like SELECT and WHERE. Although it makes the code easier to decipher, lots of programmers get tired of all-caps and just go straight for the lowercase letters.

Using CREATE to Make Tables

When you could get to and USE the mysql database, you had some tables ready for you to SELECT from: the *users* table, for example. However, now you're on a database server from which you can't get to those tables. So, before you can get back to working on your SELECT skills, you need to create a table.

As you might have already guessed, you can do that with another handy-dandy SQL keyword: CREATE. The objective is to create a table, put data in it, get data out, and generally have all kinds of database fun.

Type this command into your MySQL command line:

```
CREATE TABLE users (
```

This time, don't add the usual semicolon at the end. When you press Enter, you'll see something a little weird:

```
mysql> CREATE TABLE users (
    ->
```

As you know, MySQL commands should end in a semicolon, so when you leave it off, you're telling MySQL, "Hey, I'm writing a command, but I'm not done yet." What this demonstrates is that, you don't have to jam a lot of SQL onto one line; you can split it up over several lines by pressing Enter. As long as you don't type that semicolon, MySQL won't try to do anything with your command. And that little arrow, ->, lets you know that MySQL is waiting for you to continue typing.

So be obliging! Keep typing the following lines, each of which sets up a different column of information in your table:

```
mysql> CREATE TABLE users (
    -> user_id int,
    -> first_name varchar(20),
    -> last_name varchar(30),
```

```
-> email varchar(50),
-> facebook_url varchar(100),
-> twitter_handle varchar(20)
-> );
```

Press Enter after this last semicolon, and you get a very unimpressive response:

```
mysql> CREATE TABLE users (
    -> user_id int,
    -> first_name varchar(20),
    -> last_name varchar(30),
    -> email varchar(50),
    -> facebook_url varchar(100),
    -> twitter_handle varchar(20)
    -> );
Query OK, 0 rows affected (0.18 sec)
```

This last line is MySQL's very modest way of saying, "I did what you asked." If you get an error message instead, see the following box for advice on handling typos.

FREQUENTLY ASKED QUESTION

How to Fix a SQL Typo

I got an error message because I mistyped something in one line of my command. Now what do I do?

Even for PHP and MySQL wizards, typos are a problem. In fact, because programmers tend to type way too fast, typos are a real source of frustration in MySQL.

In some cases, MySQL will simply display an error and let you try again:

```
mysql> use
ERROR:
USE must be followed by a database name
mysql>
```

No big deal. Other times, though, you'll make a mistake in the middle of a command, and even worse, press Enter:

```
mysql> SELECT *,
    -> FROM
```

```
    ->
    ->
```

There's an extraneous comma after the * in your SELECT line here. But MySQL is just giving you extra -> prompts every time you press Enter. What do you do?

The problem is that from the perspective of MySQL, you haven't ended the SQL command. So, it isn't processing your command—including your mistake—and isn't giving you a chance to start over.

When you get into a situation like this, your best bet is to enter a semicolon, and then press Enter. This ends your current command—however broken that command might be—and instructs MySQL to process that command. This will usually cause an error, but then you're back in control and can make fixes.

Without even thinking very hard, you probably know at least a bit about what's going on in your CREATE command:

1. **CREATE informs MySQL you want to create a new structure in the database.**

2. **TABLE specifies to MySQL what kind of structure.** In this case, you want a table.

3. **"users" is the name of the table you're creating.**

4. **The opening parenthesis (`(`) indicates to MySQL that you're about to describe the table to create, one line at a time.**

5. **Each line has a column name, such as** `user_id`, **and a type, such as** `int` **or** `varchar(20)`.

6. **When you're done describing the table, you use a closing parenthesis (`)`) to let MySQL know you're done describing the table, and then end the whole enchilada with a semicolon.**

You'll learn a ton more about all the different types of columns as you go, but for now, there are just two to worry about. The first is `int`, which is short for `integer`. An integer, as you recall from math class, is any whole number; 1, 890, and 239402 are ints, but 1.293 and 3.1456 are not.

> **NOTE** MySQL is just as happy to accept `integer` as `int`. In fact, 'it considers them identical.

The second type to which you need to pay some attention is a little less obvious: `varchar`. The `varchar` type stands for *variable character*, which means that it holds character data—strings—of variable lengths. Referring back to our example, a `varchar(20)` can hold a string as short as the length of 0 all the way up to a length of 20 characters. For advice on deciding on how big to make your columns, see the box below.

DESIGN TIME

The Size of Your Columns Really Does Matter

When most people are creating their tables, they spend a lot of time thinking about what they want to store in their database, and very little time thinking about things like how big the maximum length of a `varchar` field can get. So you'll see lots of tables that have 10 or 20 `varchar(100)` columns, even though those columns hold totally different pieces of information.

But it's better to stop and think about these things when you're designing your tables. Make your columns as long as they need to be—but not longer. Yes, it may seem "safe" to just come up with crazy, overly long lengths, but then you're not really doing a very good job of making your database really look like the information it's going to store.

If you're storing a first name, there's really no way the maximum length of that first name is as long as, for example, a Facebook URL. A really, really long first name might be 15

characters (and that would be *really* long!). But you can barely fit "www.facebook.com" into a 20-character column. So your columns should have different maximum lengths.

But this is about good design, not making your database hum. Your database only uses space for the information it holds; you don't get penalized by wasted disk space or bad performance if all your `varchar` fields are super-long. What you do get, though, is a database that looks sloppy, making *you* look like you didn't spend much time thinking about your information.

Take the time to do good design now, and it will pay off later. Make your `varchar` columns as long as they need to be, and maybe even a *little* bit longer, but always remember what information will go in those columns.

The upshot of all these new terms is you've directed MySQL to create a table comprising several new columns, one that's an int (user_id), and several that are varchars of various maximum lengths.

Did this command work? Well, look for yourself by using the SHOW command:

```
mysql> SHOW tables;
+-----------------------------------+
| Tables_in_bmclaugh                |
+-----------------------------------+
| users                             |
+-----------------------------------+
1 row in set (0.06 sec)
```

No doubt about it, you definitely created a table. But, what's actually in the table? For that, you need a new command: DESCRIBE. Try it out on your *users* table:

```
mysql> DESCRIBE users;
+----------------+--------------+------+-----+---------+-------+
| Field          | Type         | Null | Key | Default | Extra |
+----------------+--------------+------+-----+---------+-------+
| user_id        | int(11)      | YES  |     | NULL    |       |
| first_name     | varchar(20)  | YES  |     | NULL    |       |
| last_name      | varchar(30)  | YES  |     | NULL    |       |
| email          | varchar(50)  | YES  |     | NULL    |       |
| facebook_url   | varchar(100) | YES  |     | NULL    |       |
| twitter_handle | varchar(20)  | YES  |     | NULL    |       |
+----------------+--------------+------+-----+---------+-------+
6 rows in set (0.04 sec)
```

NOTE You can also use DESC (or desc) for DESCRIBE. Thus, DESC users; is a perfectly acceptable SQL command, too.

Now, you can see that MySQL did what you commanded it to: It created a table called *users* with all the columns you specified, using the types you gave it. There's a lot more information there, too, but you don't need to worry about that just yet.

Using DROP to Delete Tables

What goes up must come down, or so the saying goes. For everything MySQL and SQL let you do, there's a way to undo those things. You've created a table, but now you need to delete that table. However, DELETE isn't the command you want; instead, it's DROP.

Suppose that you decide you no longer like that *users* table, or you want to practice that fancy CREATE command again, you can ditch *users* with a simple line of SQL:

```
mysql> DROP TABLE users;
Query OK, 0 rows affected (0.10 sec)
```

Boom! It's gone. But, just to be sure, confirm it:.

```
mysql> SHOW tables;
+-----------------------------------+
| Tables_in_bmclaugh                |
+-----------------------------------+
0 rows in set (0.06 sec)
```

How simple is that? But wait…now you have no tables again, and nothing from which to SELECT. It's back to creating tables again. Type that CREATE SQL statement into your MySQL tool one more time and create the *users* table again.

> **NOTE**   On many systems, you can press the up arrow key and you'll see the last command you ran. Press the up arrow key a few times, and it will cycle back through your command history. This is a great way to quickly reuse a command you've already run.

INSERT a Few Rows

At this point, you've created and dropped, and created the *users* table. But it's still empty, and that's no good. What do you do? Easy: INSERT some data.

Try entering this command into your command-line tool:

```
mysql> INSERT INTO users
    -> VALUES (1, "Mike", "Greenfield", "mike@greenfieldguitars.com",
    -> "http://www.facebook.com/profile.php?id=699186223",
    -> "@greenfieldguitars");
Query OK, 1 row affected (0.00 sec)
```

What a mouthful! Still, you can probably just look at this SQL and figure out what's going on. You're inserting information into the *users* table and then you're giving it that information (VALUES), piece by piece.

You can actually trace each value and connect it to a column in your table. You might want to DESCRIBE your table again:

```
mysql> DESCRIBE users;
+----------------+--------------+------+-----+---------+-------+
| Field          | Type         | Null | Key | Default | Extra |
+----------------+--------------+------+-----+---------+-------+
| user_id        | int(11)      | YES  |     | NULL    |       |
| first_name     | varchar(20)  | YES  |     | NULL    |       |
| last_name      | varchar(30)  | YES  |     | NULL    |       |
| email          | varchar(50)  | YES  |     | NULL    |       |
| facebook_url   | varchar(100) | YES  |     | NULL    |       |
| twitter_handle | varchar(20)  | YES  |     | NULL    |       |
+----------------+--------------+------+-----+---------+-------+
6 rows in set (0.29 sec)
```

The first value, 1, is assigned to user_id; the second, "Mike", to first_name; and so on.

And really, that's all there is to it. You can insert as much into your table as you want, anytime you want. There are lots of ways to fancy up INSERT, and you'll learn about most of them as you start to work with INSERT in PHP.

Using SELECT for the Grand Finale

Finally, you're back to where you can use good-old SELECT. By now, that command should seem like ancient history, given that you've used DROP and CREATE and INSERT and a few others since that first SELECT * FROM users. But, now you've got your own *users* table, so try it out again:

```
mysql> SELECT * FROM users;
+---------+------------+------------+---------------------------+--
------------------------------------------------+------------------
-+
| user_Id | first_name | last_name  | email                     |
facebook_url                                    | twitter_handle
  |
+---------+------------+------------+---------------------------+--
------------------------------------------------+------------------
-+
|       1 | Mike       | Greenfield | mike@greenfieldguitars.com |
http://www.facebook.com/profile.php?id=699186223 | @greenfieldguitars
  |
+---------+------------+------------+---------------------------+--
------------------------------------------------+----------------
---+
1 row in set (0.00 sec)
```

No big surprises here; you got back the row you just inserted. However, just like earlier, the screen is a bit of a mess. Too many columns make the results hard to read.

To simplify things, grab just a few columns. For example, let's assume that you don't really need to see Mike's entire Facebook page URL right now. From the code on page 103, you know how to select specific columns of information:

```
mysql> SELECT first_name, last_name, twitter_handle FROM users;
+------------+------------+--------------------+
| first_name | last_name  | twitter_handle     |
+------------+------------+--------------------+
| Mike       | Greenfield | @greenfieldguitars |
+------------+------------+--------------------+
1 row in set (0.00 sec)
```

That's a lot more readable. And once you're writing PHP to talk to MySQL, this formatting won't be such a problem. PHP doesn't care about fitting everything into a nice line or two. It's happy to take a big messy set of results and handle them.

If you'd like, take some time to insert a few more rows of users and then play with SELECT. If you want to get really fancy, try using a WHERE clause, like this:

```
mysql> SELECT facebook_url
    ->   FROM users
    ->   WHERE first_name = 'Mike';
+---------------------------------------------------+
| facebook_url                                      |
+---------------------------------------------------+
| http://www.facebook.com/profile.php?id=699186223 |
+---------------------------------------------------+
1 row in set (0.00 sec)
```

As you can see, WHERE lets you choose a specific person or record of information. You'll see that again on page 152. Try creating tables with more columns, selecting different columns, choosing records with WHERE, and see how far you can get with all the SQL you've already picked up.

POWER USERS' CLINIC

SQL or MySQL? They're Not the Same

It's one thing to know what SQL stands for, and how to install MySQL. But it's something else altogether to know what the difference is between SQL and MySQL. In fact, ask around at your local water cooler. You'd be surprised how many novice programmers are not sure what the difference is between SQL the language and MySQL the database program.

SQL is in fact a language. It's something that exists separately from MySQL or any other database program, like PostgreSQL or Oracle. That means that SQL can change, or be updated, without your database automatically changing. In fact, the way it usually works is that SQL gets a new keyword or instruction, and then all the database programs release new versions to support that new keyword. Of course, SQL has been around for a long time, so this sort of thing doesn't happen very often anymore.

MySQL is a database program. It lets you work with and administrate databases, and you do that with SQL. In other words, MySQL is really just a tool that lets you use SQL. That makes the name—MySQL—either terribly helpful or terribly confusing. Either way, in this book, you'll be executing SQL commands against your MySQL database.

If you can keep the difference between SQL and MySQL in your mind, you're going to be ahead of the game. That's because when you work with your PHP, you'll be connecting to a MySQL database, but you'll be writing SQL commands and queries. Why does that matter? Because you can change to another database, and almost all of your SQL will work, as long as your new database accepts SQL. That's the beauty of separating SQL from the database that you use, in this case MySQL. You can change one—moving to PostgreSQL or Oracle—without having to rewrite all your code.

Now, notice that *almost* all of your SQL will keep working. Each database adds its own twists to how it implements the SQL standard. And most databases add some database-specific features to "add value." (You can read that as "to sell their product over another product.") So, you can run into some problems moving from one database to another. But, your understanding of SQL helps there, too, because you'll be able to diagnose any issues and quickly solve them.

The takeaway here is to learn SQL, use MySQL, and end up with code that works on just about any SQL database.

Dynamic Web Pages

Connecting PHP to MySQL

Now that you've seen a bit of the power of PHP and MySQL, it's time to bring these two juggernauts together. With many programming languages, any time you want to interact with a database, you have to download and install extra code or small plug-ins. PHP isn't like that, though; it comes ready to connect to MySQL from the moment you run the php command.

Even though you've only recently begun your journey to PHP mastery, you're ready to use a database from within your scripts. You'll just need to learn a few new commands and how to deal with the problems that can come up when you're working with a database. In fact, you're going to build a simple form with which you can enter SQL and run it against your MySQL database. Who needs the mysql command-line tool when you're a PHP programmer?

Then, to put a cherry on top of your towering sundae of PHP and MySQL goodness, you'll write another script. This one takes all the information from the forms you've already been building, adds that information into a database, and then adds one more form to with which your users can search for another user by name. All that in one chapter? Yes indeed.

■ Writing a Simple PHP Connection Script

No matter how simple or advanced your PHP scripts, if they communicate with a database, they'll begin with the same few steps:

1. **Connect to a MySQL installation.**

2. **USE the correct MySQL database.**

3. **Send SQL to the database.**

4. **Get the results back.**

5. **Do something with the results.**

Depending on the application you're writing, steps 3, 4, and 5 will change a bit based on what you're doing. A script that creates tables looks different than a script that searches through existing tables.

But, those first couple of steps—connecting to MySQL and using the right database—are always the same, no matter how fancy your script is. Just think, then: the code you're about to write is the same code that programmers making $150 or $200 an hour are writing somewhere. (They're just writing that code in expensive houses with robots serving them ice tea as they lounge by the pool.)

NOTE You can find the finished example code for this section on this book's Missing CD page at *www. missingmanuals.com/cds/phpmysqlmm2e*.

Connect to a MySQL Database

Because your form is going to take in SQL and run it against your MySQL database, first you've got to instruct your PHP script how to connect to a database. Essentially, you're directing PHP to do the same thing you did when you started up your MySQL command-line client (page 105). When you connected to your web server's database, you probably used a command like this:

```
bmclaugh@akila:~$ mysql --host=dc2-mysql-02.kattare.com
                        --user=bmclaugh --password
```

You'll need to give PHP the same pieces of information (database host, your user name, and a password) so that it can connect.

Fire up your text editor and create a new script. Call it *connect.php*. This script is going to be as simple as you'll ever see because all you need it to do is connect to your database, USE the right database, and then run a sample SQL query to ensure that things are working correctly.

In your script, type the following lines:

```
<?php
  mysql_connect("your.database.host",
                "your-username", "your-password")
```

```
    or die("<p>Error connecting to database: " .
        mysql_error() . "</p>");

  echo "<p>Connected to MySQL!</p>";
?>
```

> **NOTE** Be sure to change "your.database.host", "your-username", and "your-password" to the values for
> your own database.
>
> If you're running your database on the same computer as your PHP and web-serving files, your database host
> name is usually *localhost*. Remember, *localhost* is just a way to say "the local machine."

Yes, it's really that simple! And, like most of the other PHP scripts you've been writing, although there are some new commands, you probably already know almost exactly what's going on here.

First, there's a new command: mysql_connect. No surprises here; this just takes in a database host, a user name, and a password, and makes a connection. It's just as if you're running your mysql tool and connecting to a remote database.

That's pretty self-explanatory. But what about the die bit? Sounds a little gruesome (like *Lord of the Flies* gruesome, not *Twilight* teen-angst gruesome). In fact, it is a bit nasty: you use die when something might go wrong in your script. Think about die as saying, "If my code dies, then do something less nasty than throwing an error code on my user." In this case, die prints out an error message that won't scare off your users. (If you're not sure why that's so important, see the box on page 124.)

But before you can understand die, you need know a little bit about the inner workings of mysql_connect. When mysql_connect runs, it either creates or reuses an existing connection to your database. It then returns that connection to your PHP program and makes all the other PHP-to-MySQL commands you'll learn about soon available. But, if mysql_connect can't create that connection—for example, if your database isn't running or you have a bad host or user name—mysql_connect returns a very different value: false.

What's really happening in your script is something like this:

```
<?php
  // This isn't working code, but you get the idea
  if (i_can_connect_to_mysql_with("my.database.host",
                      "my-username", "my-password"))
    go_do_cool_database_stuff();
  else
    send_error_to_user_using_die
?>
```

That's a lot of typing, though, so PHP lets you shorten it to this:

```php
<?php

  mysql_connect("your.database.host",
                "your-username", "your-password")
    or die("<p>Error connecting to database: " .
           mysql_error() . "</p>");

  echo "<p>Connected to MySQL!</p>";
?>
```

Not only is this shorter, but it flips things around a bit. It's saying, "try to connect (using `mysql_connect`), and if the result isn't true (the or part of the code), implement `die`." Now, `die` prints out an error message, but it also "dies." In other words, it ends your script. So, if `mysql_connect` returns false, and `die` runs, your script will exit. Your users won't ever see the "Connected to MySQL!" line because the script will have stopped running. It's dead on the server room floor, in search of a working database connection.

Not only that, but `mysql_connect` sets up another function when it can't connect. It makes available the errors it ran into while trying to connect by using another command, `mysql_error`. Thus, you can call `mysql_error` as part of your `die` statement to show what really happened.

NOTE Technically, `mysql_connect`, `mysql_error`, and `die` are all examples of *functions*. A function is a block of code, usually with a name assigned to it, that you can call from your own code anytime you need to carry out the task that the block of is designed to do. It's a lot quicker and neater to call a function by name than rewrite the block of code that function represents, over and over again.

Don't worry about functions for now, though. Just use them like any old PHP command. Before long, not only will you understand functions better, but you'll be writing your own.

If `mysql_connect` does connect without any problems, it will return that connection. That means the `die` line is skipped, and the next thing PHP does is execute this line:

```php
  echo "<p>Connected to MySQL!</p>";
```

To see this script in action, create a simple HTML form and call it *connect.html*. You can use this HTML to get started:

```html
<html>
 <head>
  <link href="../css/phpMM.css" rel="stylesheet" type="text/css" />
 </head>
```

```
<body>
  <div id="header"><h1>PHP & MySQL: The Missing Manual</h1></div>
  <div id="example">Example 5-1</div>

  <div id="content">
    <h1>SQL Connection test</h1>
    <form action="scripts/connect.php" method="POST">
      <fieldset class="center">
        <input type="submit" value="Connect to MySQL" />
      </fieldset>
    </form>
  </div>

  <div id="footer"></div>
</body>
</html>
```

This form is about as simple as it gets: build the form, drop a single button into
place, and attach that button to your new *connect.php* script. Load up your form in
a browser (see Figure 5-1), and click "Connect to MySQL."

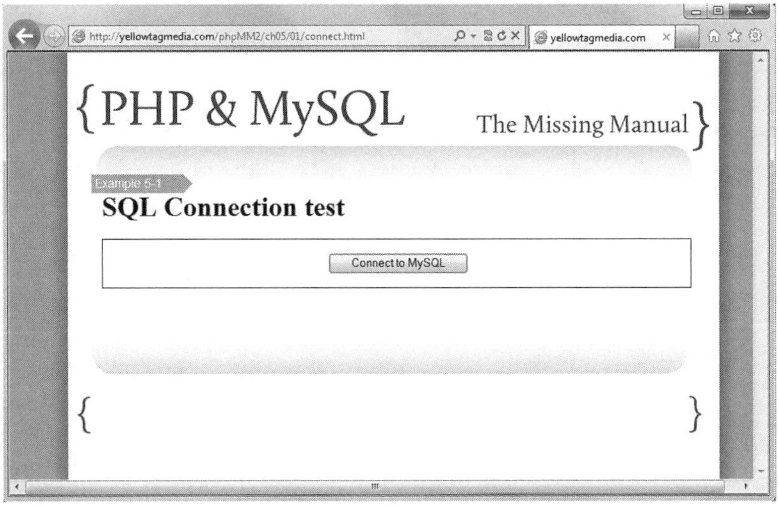

FIGURE 5-1

*Sure, you could have made
connect.html even simpler.
You could have ditched all
the structure and CSS referencing. But who wants
to connect to a database
without showing off a
little? Besides, customers
like a nice, clean site. You
don't have to spend hours
on CSS, but if you make
even your most basic
demos look professional,
your clients will love you
for it.*

Hopefully, you see one of the simplest, happiest messages of your burgeoning PHP
and MySQL programming career: you're connected! Check out Figure 5-2 to see
the triumphant, if simple, result.

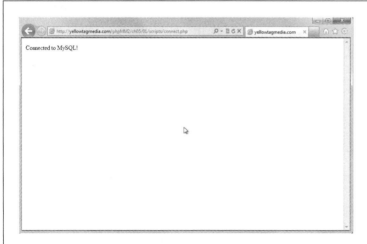

FIGURE 5-2

These three words mean that your PHP script now can do virtually anything you can imagine with your database. But there's something missing: how does MySQL know which database is yours? You still need to direct PHP toward which database to USE.

POWER USERS' CLINIC

Everybody Dies at Some Point

It's really, really, really easy to forget to add those die statements to your PHP scripts. PHP doesn't require them, so it's perfectly happy to take in something like this:

```
mysql_connect("database.host.com", "user-
name", "password");
```

That's the same code you've already written, except it leaves off the die part.

But, here's the thing: leave off that die, and when something goes wrong, your script is going to crash and provide something that's either a really useless error or something so cryptic that you can't even tell *what* it is. For example, drop off your die and enter in a wrong password, run your script, and you'll get something like this as an error:

```
Can't connect to local MySQL server
through socket '/tmp/mysql.sock' (2)
```

Believe it or not, this is actually a pretty good error message, as messages go when you don't use die statements. So, adding that one line of error handling can make a huge difference for a user when things go wrong.

In fact, as you begin to build much bigger, full-blown web applications, you might redirect your user to a nicely formatted error page, complete with contact information for an administrator and a CSS-styled error report. Of course, none of that is possible without die.

Now, at this point, some of you—already flush with PHP power—are already thinking about how few errors you're making. You're thinking that die is for rank amateurs who don't write flawless code. Unfortunately, when you're up at 2 a.m. trying to hit a deadline so that you can get paid, your brain starts to resemble a rank amateur. Everyone makes mistakes, and die (and other error handling techniques) is one of those lifesavers that helps you look prepared and professional when those inevitable mistakes do occur.

In fact, the slickest, highest-paid programmers in the world are error-handling gurus. At the same time, they're probably *not* using die. They're more likely to use a more robust error-handling system; something like the error handling in Chapter 8. For now, though, a healthy and liberal use of die will get you used to adding in a form of error handling. You can come back and improve upon it later.

Select the Database with PHP

There's something wonderful waiting around the programming corner now. Almost all of the mysql_ family of functions works the same: you give them some values, and they give back something useful. If something bad happens, you usually get back either false or a non-existent object (something most programmers call *null* or *nil*).

Now, you need to instruct MySQL which database your PHP script wants to use. There's a function for that: mysql_select_db.

> **NOTE** The family of mysql_ functions is quite extensive. You might want to bookmark this documentation page: *www.php.net/manual/en/ref.mysql.php*. If you ever get stuck, head over there and see if a function might do what you need.

You give mysql_select_db a database name, and it uses that database—or returns false. Update *connect.php* to use the right database:

```
<?php
  mysql_connect("your.database.host",
                "your-username", "your-password")
    or die("<p>Error connecting to database: " .
          mysql_error() . "</p>");

  echo "<p>Connected to MySQL!</p>";

  mysql_select_db("your-database-name")
    or die("<p>Error selecting the database your-database-name: " .
          mysql_error() . "</p>");

  echo "<p>Connected to MySQL, using database your-database-name.</p>";
?>
```

> **NOTE** If you're unsure of what database name to use, flip back to page 100 in Chapter 4. You can use SHOW DATABASES; in a MySQL terminal to see what databases you have available on your hosting provider. Failing that, you could also just call up your hosting provider, and they should be able to help you out with the name of the database you can use.

You should already see the pattern. The die command ensures that if bad things happen, an error displays, your users can actually read that error, and then the script exits. If things do go well, another happy message should print.

Try this new version out. Visit *connect.html* again and try to connect (and now USE) your database. You should see something similar to Figure 5-3.

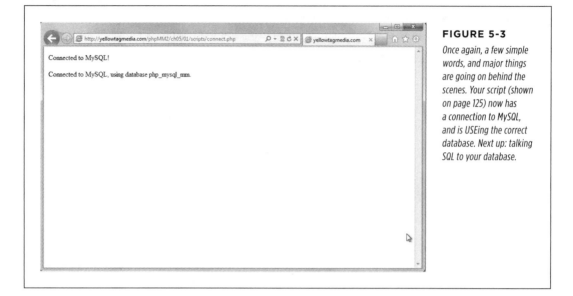

FIGURE 5-3

Once again, a few simple words, and major things are going on behind the scenes. Your script (shown on page 125) now has a connection to MySQL, and is USEing the correct database. Next up: talking SQL to your database.

Viewing Your Database's Tables by Using SHOW

Now that you have a connection, and you're tied in to the right database, you need to see which tables are available on your hosting provider. When you were working directly with the MySQL command-line tool, one of the first things you did was to see what tables existed and then start creating tables of your own (page 100). You can do that same thing now with a PHP script and a little bit of simple output.

But before diving into that, you can easily have your script reveal which tables are available in your database. Open *connect.php* again, and add in this line:

```php
<?php
  // All your existing database connection code

  $result = mysql_query("SHOW TABLES;");
?>
```

Here's another new PHP-to-MySQL function: `mysql_query`. You'll become very familiar and friendly with this one; it's the key to passing SQL in to your database. This function takes in SQL, and you've given it some really simple SQL:

```
SHOW TABLES;
```

This command does *exactly* the same thing as when you type the SQL SHOW TABLES command into your command-line tool.

■ HANDLING ERRORS BY DETERMINING IF YOUR RESULTS ARE NOT

But what about die? What about error handling? There's none of that yet, and by now, you know there should be. But there's something different about this line: whatever comes back from mysql_query is stuffed into a variable called $result.

It's really $result that you want to examine. The result should either have a list of tables, from SHOW TABLES, or report an error of some sort. If it's reporting an error, $result is false because the mysql_ functions return false when there's a problem.

You know how to check for a false value, though (page 73), so you can add the following code to handle problems:

```php
<?php
  // All your existing database connection code

  $result = mysql_query("SHOW TABLES;");

  if ($result === false) {
    die("<p>Error in listing tables: " . mysql_error() . "</p>");
  }
?>
```

This code works, but it's really not how most PHP programmers do things. The three equal signs (===) is an unusual thing to use in PHP, at least for checking to see whether a variable is false. What's a lot more common—and the way it's usually done in PHP—is to use the *bang* or *negation* operator, which is an exclamation mark (!). So, if you want to see whether a variable called $some-variable is false, you could say if (!$some-variable). By adding that exclamation mark, you're saying something like, "see if $some-variable is false."

Even better, think of ! as meaning *not*. So, what you really want to say in your code is, "If *not* $result, then die." That means you could rewrite your code to look like this:

```php
<?php
  // All your existing database connection code

  $result = mysql_query("SHOW TABLES;");

  if (!$result) {
    die("<p>Error in listing tables: " . mysql_error() . "</p>");
  }
?>
```

This example shows much better PHP, and now you have any problems covered.

NOTE It might seem weird to hear about "the way it's done in PHP." If code works, then it works, right? Well, yes...but have you ever heard someone who's just learning English speak? Often, the words are correct, but the order, usage, and idiom are all wrong. It sounds awkward, and you can have trouble figuring out what the person means.

Programming languages are the same. There's writing code that works, and there's writing code in a way that shows you really know the language. Sometimes, this is called being *eloquent*. It's worth learning not just how to write working PHP, but to write PHP that looks natural. (There are even books devoted to "speaking properly" in JavaScript and Ruby called *Eloquent JavaScript* by Marijn Haverbeke [No Starch Press] and *Eloquent Ruby* by Russ Olsen [Addison-Wesley].)

In fact, to ensure that your code deals with errors, change your SQL query to include a typo:

```php
<?php
  // All your existing database connection code

  $result = mysql_query("SHOWN TABLES;");

  if (!$result) {
    die("<p>Error in listing tables: " . mysql_error() . "</p>");
  }
?>
```

Load *connect.html* in a browser and run your connection test. Figure 5-4 is similar to what you should see: still a little cryptic, but clearly your code realized there was a problem and handled it with an error message rather than a massive meltdown.

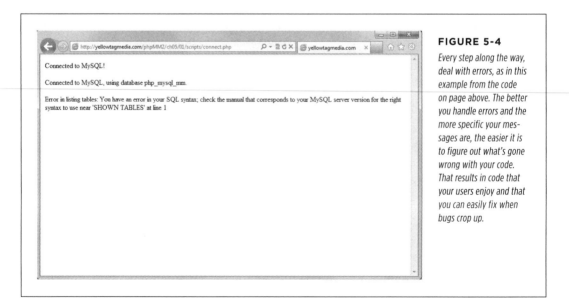

FIGURE 5-4

Every step along the way, deal with errors, as in this example from the code on page above. The better you handle errors and the more specific your messages are, the easier it is to figure out what's gone wrong with your code. That results in code that your users enjoy and that you can easily fix when bugs crop up.

■ PRINT OUT YOUR SQL RESULTS

So far, the PHP script you've created in this chapter handles errors, reports problems, and lets you deal with what's in $result when things don't go wrong. Unfortunately, that's where things get trickier. $result is actually not a PHP type that you've used, or even one that you'll need to learn how to work with directly. It's something called a *resource*, which is PHP-speak for a special variable that's related to something outside of PHP.

Think about it this way: In the case of mysql_query, you've asked for the SQL results from running the query SHOW TABLES. But, although PHP can talk to MySQL, it doesn't know how to interpret SQL. Therefore, it can't know that $result should hold a list of rows, each of which containing one value: a table name. All it knows is that something else—your MySQL database—is getting a query through the mysql_query function. Think about it for a moment. Depending on what query you pass mysql_query, $result might hold rows with multiple pieces of information, like a first name and Facebook URL, or just an indication of whether a CREATE TABLE statement worked or not.

In these cases, you usually end up with a PHP resource. That resource means something; it's just that PHP doesn't really know what that something is. So, your PHP needs help. What it needs is something that knows about MySQL and can figure out how to work with $result. That's exactly what you get with another MySQL function, mysql_fetch_row. You pass this function in a resource returned from mysql_query, and it lets you cycle through each row in the results returned from your SQL query.

Here's the basic pattern:

1. **Write your SQL query and store it in a string or a variable.**

2. **Pass your query into mysql_query and get back a PHP resource.**

3. **Pass that resource into mysql_fetch_row to get back rows of results, one at a time.**

4. **Cycle through those rows and pull out the information you need.**

5. **Buy a really nice musical instrument with all the cash you're making.**

> **NOTE** That last step is optional, but highly recommended.

You've got a resource in $result, now pass it in to mysql_fetch_row, like this:

```php
<?php
  // All your existing database connection code

  $result = mysql_query("SHOW TABLES;");

  if (!$result) {
    die("<p>Error in listing tables: " . mysql_error() . "</p>");
  }
```

```php
echo "<p>Tables in database:</p>";
echo "<ul>";
while ($row = mysql_fetch_row($result)) {
  // Do something with $row
}
echo "</ul>";

?>
```

WARNING If you changed your SQL to SHOWN TABLES to produce an error earlier, be sure to change it back to SHOW TABLES.

Even though PHP doesn't know what to do with the resource returned from mysql_query, mysql_fetch_row does. It takes in your $result resource and starts creating rows, one at a time, in an array.

And then there's that while loop, something else that's new, but not tough to grasp. A while loop continues to loop for as long as a specified test condition is true. In this case, it keeps looping while $row—which is the next row of results from your SQL query—is getting a value from mysql_fetch_row($result). When there are no more result rows, mysql_fetch_row doesn't return anything, so $row is empty, and the while loop says, "Ok, I'm done. I'll stop looping now."

Finally, you've got a nice unordered list (<ul>) ready to emerge from each row. There's just one thing left to add:

```php
<?php
  // All your existing database connection code

  $result = mysql_query("SHOW TABLES;");

  if (!$result) {
    die("<p>Error in listing tables: " . mysql_error() . "</p>");
  }

  echo "<p>Tables in database:</p>";
  echo "<ul>";
  while ($row = mysql_fetch_row($result)) {
    echo "<li>Table: {$row[0]}</li>";
  }
  echo "</ul>";

?>
```

Each time mysql_fetch_row returns $row, it's actually returning an array, something with which you've already worked (page 83). That array has all the different pieces of information from your SQL query. For SHOW TABLES, that's just one thing, at

$row[0]: the table name. Pretty soon, you'll write some more complex queries, and you might need to grab the value in $row[1], $row[2], or even $row[10].

In this case, you get back $row, you grab the table name by getting the first item in the array (index 0), and then you print that out by using echo. There's just one other wrinkle here: those curly braces inside the string that's passed to echo. What's up with those?

Well, you could rewrite this line like this:

```
while ($row = mysql_fetch_row($result)) {
  echo "<li>Table: " . $row[0] . "</li>";
}
```

Nothing wrong there, except for all the extra quotation marks and periods to stick strings together.

> **NOTE** Major bonus points if you nerded out and remembered that mashing strings together is called *concatenation*.

But PHP is pretty savvy, and the folks that wrote the language are programmers, too. They realized, like you do, that you constantly need to drop variables into the middle of strings. So, instead of constantly ending a string and adding a variable, you can just wrap a variable inside of { and }, and PHP will print the value of that variable instead of "$row[0]". It makes for a lot simpler code, and that's a good thing.

At this point, save *connect.php*, revisit *connect.html* in your browser, and see what tables are in your database. Figure 5-5 shows *connect.php* running against a database with a lot of tables. You might have only one or two, or none at all, and that's fine. Just so long as you get a list of the tables that you do have or an empty response. What you *don't* want here is an error.

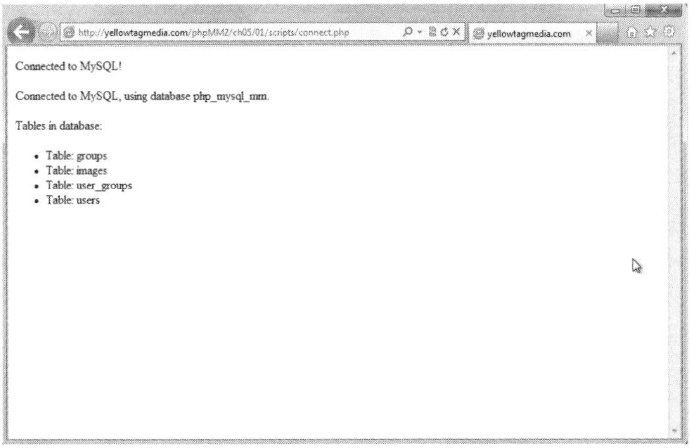

FIGURE 5-5

The SHOW TABLES command, as used in the connect.php script on page 130, is a bit clunky, and took quite a few lines to do something relatively simple. And, you might not even see any tables! Still, now you know how to run a SQL query. And for now, this kind of code is a really easy way to ensure that your PHP scripts are talking to your MySQL databases.

■ Cleaning Up Your Code with Multiple Files

Even if you don't realize it yet, there's something problematic about the *connect.php* script you created in the previous section. Look at the first few MySQL calls you make:

```php
<?php
mysql_connect("your.database.host",
              "your-username", "your-password")
    or die("<p>Error connecting to database: " .
          mysql_error() . "</p>");

echo "<p>Connected to MySQL!</p>";

mysql_select_db("your-database-name")
    or die("<p>Error selecting the database your-database-name: " .
          mysql_error() . "</p>");

echo "<p>Connected to MySQL, using database your-database-name.</p>";

// And so on...
?>
```

You're manually typing your database host, your user name, your password, and your database name into your script. Suppose that you have 10 scripts; you're typing that 10 times. The chances for misspelling something are pretty high.

Not only that, what happens when you change your password? Or if you upgrade to a better hosting plan to handle all the web traffic your apps are generating and need to change your database host? You've got to track down every place you used that information, in every PHP script. That's not only a nightmare, it also keeps you from writing new code and making more cash. Not good.

What you need is a way to store those pieces of information where you can keep them up to date, and where your code can refer to them correctly every time. Programmers call that *abstracting out* the information. *Abstraction* is a way of hiding the implementation—the way something works—from programs that use that something. You basically have a symbol, or a name, and that name refers to some bit of information with a lot more detail. And even if that detail changes, the name still points to the right information.

It's like saying "Bob" and meaning your friend, instead of calling him "that 29-year-old guy with the full head of hair." That way, every year you can call the same friend "Bob," without changing your (and his) description.

In PHP, abstraction uses variables, and you'll see how that works in the next section.

NOTE   You can find the finished example code for this section on this book's Missing CD page at *www
.missingmanuals.com/cds/phpmysqlmm2e*.

Replacing Hand-Typed Values with Variables

Instead of including your actual host name, user name, and password as in the code
on page 132, you want your code to look more like the following:

```php
<?php
  mysql_connect($database_host, $username, $password)
    or die("<p>Error connecting to database: " .
         mysql_error() . "</p>");

  echo "<p>Connected to MySQL!</p>";

  mysql_select_db($database_name)
    or die("<p>Error selecting the database your-database-name: " .
         mysql_error() . "</p>");

  echo "<p>Connected to MySQL, using database your-database-name.</p>";

  // And so on...
?>
```

You're really just writing something that looks a bit like a variable in place of hand-
typing the user name or database name. Now, you can define those variables above
your connection code:

```php
<?php
  $database_host = "your.database.host";
  $username = "your-username";
  $password = "your-password";
  $database_name = "your-database-name";

  // Database connection code
?>
```

But is this really that much better? You're still entering these hand-typed values into
your script. You haven't solved the problem; you've just moved it to a different part
of the script. What you need to do is to store your values in a separate file.

Abstracting Important Values into a Separate File

To avoid typing values such as your database name and user name into every
script—and keep them up to date—you need to put them some place where all your
PHP scripts, including *connect.php*, can access them. Open a new file, and call it
app_config.php. Now, drop your variables into this new file:

```php
<?php
// Database connection constants
$database_host = "your.database.host";
$username = "your-username";
$password = "your-password";
$database_name = "your-database-name";

?>
```

> **NOTE** Be sure to save *app_config.php* somewhere that makes sense for all your application's scripts to access it. In this book's examples, *app_config.php* is in the root of the site, under *scripts/*. So, if you're in the *ch05/02/ scripts/* directory, you'd access this file at *../../../scripts/app_config.php* or *[site_root]/scripts/app_config.php*. You can save the file wherever you want, as long as you get the path right in your PHP scripts that reference it.
>
> When you move to a production version of your application, you definitely want to place this file *outside* of the site root. That way, hackers can't simply type the path to your configuration script and gain access to all your passwords. Alternatively, you could add security to this directory; however, simply getting it out of the web serving directories altogether is usually easiest.

Now, you can have all your different PHP scripts use these shared variables. If you change a variable here, in *app_config.php*, that change affects all your PHP scripts that use these shared variables.

But how do you actually access these variables? Go back to *connect.php* and remove where you defined these variables manually. If you try to access *connect.php* through *connect.html* now, though, you'll get a nasty error, as demonstrated in Figure 5-6.

FIGURE 5-6

You defined your variables in app_config.php, but connect.php doesn't know that; that's why it can't connect to your database and you get the error shown here. You need to instruct your connection script to not run until it loads app_config.php. Then, things will behave because the variables connect.php uses will be set properly.

You can see the user name *yellowta* in screenshot in Figure 5-6. That user name will be different for you, and that's good! You'll see your own user name, rather than *yellowta*.

This error is thrown because *connect.php* now has no idea what $username or $password refer to. You need to instruct PHP that before it tries to do anything in *connect.php*, it needs to load *app_config.php*. In fact, this is a requirement for *connect.php*. That's (almost) exactly what you type in your script:

```php
<?php

  require '../../scripts/app_config.php';

  // Database connection code
?>
```

Now, PHP loads *../../scripts/app_config.php before* it runs your `mysql_connect` function. In fact, `require` says, "Hey PHP, if you can't load the file I'm telling you to load, throw a nasty error, because nothing else is going to work."

WARNING Ensure that the path and file name that you give to `require` matches where you actually put *app_config.php*, or you'll get to see the error that `require` produces, up close and personal.

Try to run your connection script again; you should see your table listing, exactly as in Figure 5-5, which means things are working again.

UNDER THE HOOD

Require or Include?

There's another command in PHP that's very similar to require: include. include does exactly what require does in that it says to PHP to load another file. The difference is that if that file can't be loaded, include just issues a warning, and lets PHP continue to run the later commands in your script. require completely shuts things down, but include allows your script to keep going.

But here's the thing. Are you *really* going to bother including a file if you don't need that file? In most cases, probably not. You're including that file because you need it; you really *require* that file to run. So, in almost every situation, you should use require to grab another file, not include. If something goes wrong, you want to know about it. You don't want the rest of your code running, because it's probably going to error out anyway.

Variables Vary, but Constants Stay Constant

There's just one more nagging little problem with your code: you're still using variables for your user name and password, along with the database host and database name. And what's a variable? Something that *varies* or *changes*. So, PHP will happily let you do this in *connect.php*:

```
mysql_connect($database_host, $username, $password)
  or die("<p>Error connecting to database: " . mysql_error() . "</p>");

// This is allowed, but some bad mojo
$password = "hijinks"
```

What happens when some other script—one which also requires *app_config.php*—tries to connect with mysql_connect? It's going to use $password, but now $password is no longer correct. It's set to "hijinks," and chaos ensues.

What you really want is for those values in *app_config.php* to be constant and never change. You can do this with the special define function. Open up *app_config.php* and change your code:

```
<?php
// Database connection constants
define("DATABASE_HOST", "your.database.host");
define("DATABASE_USERNAME", "your-username");
define("DATABASE_PASSWORD", "your-password");
define("DATABASE_NAME", "your-database-name");
?>
```

You define the name of a constant and the value for that constant, and PHP creates a new constant. Now, you can type DATABASE_HOST into your code, and PHP *really* sees your.database.host, which is the name of your database's host server. Perfect! In addition, because this is a constant, not a variable, your scripts can't change it anywhere along the line.

Note that the constants are also in all-uppercase letters. That's not required, but it's another one of those "speak like a PHP programmer" things, as described in the note on page 128. You want constants to look different than variables, and using all uppercase names is one way to do that. Constants also don't have the $ character before their names.

At this point, you need to make some quick changes to *connect.php* to use these new capitalized constant names:

```
<?php
  require '../../scripts/app_config.php';

mysql_connect(DATABASE_HOST, DATABASE_USERNAME, DATABASE_PASSWORD)
  or die("<p>Error connecting to database: " .
        mysql_error() . "</p>");

echo "<p>Connected to MySQL!</p>";

mysql_select_db(DATABASE_NAME)
  or die("<p>Error selecting the database " . DATABASE_NAME .
        mysql_error() . "</p>");
```

```
echo "<p>Connected to MySQL, using database " . DATABASE_NAME . "</p>";

    // SQL query-running goodness proceeds...
?>
```

WARNING You can't use the { and } inside your quotes to print out constants. It's only when you surround a variable (which starts with $) with { and } that PHP will print out the value of that variable. Instead, use the normal string concatenation approach by which you end your string and add the constants using the dot (.).

Go ahead and try out *connect.php* again. You should get a perfectly good list of table names. But this time, you have constants for your important information, safely tucked away in a file separated out of *connect.php*.

NOTE It's also a good idea to add some additional security to *app_config.php*, and any other scripts that contain special values like this. You can set the permissions on the file to be more restrictive or move the file to some place your PHP script can access, but your web users can't. Ask your web or server administrator for help if you're not sure how to do that.

DESIGN TIME

Start Small, Add Small, Finish Small

You might be wondering why you couldn't have just started with *app_config.php* and the completed, working version of *connect.php*. Or, at a minimum, you could have just dropped all the database connection code into *connect.php* at once and then handled the printing code all at once. Isn't that how real developers write code?

Well, yes and no. Lots of developers do write code like that. They type anywhere from 10 to 50 lines of code into their script and then try it out. Lots of things will break because developers type too fast and make mistakes. But then, they'll fix each problem, one by one by one. And for lots of developers, that's just fine.

But, that's not very efficient. On top of that, you're usually focused on the last step (like printing out the tables), and so you might not spend much time figuring out the best way to handle the in-between steps. You might not use { and } to simplify the statement that prints $row[0], or you might skip a die because you're thinking about HTML output, not handling the case in which the database password isn't right.

The reality is that the best developers work on really, really small chunks of code at a time. They test that code, and then they move on to something else. In fact—and this goes a bit beyond this book, but it's still important—a lot of really elite developers actually write tests *before* they write anything else. They write those tests, and the tests obviously fail, because they haven't written any code. Then they write just enough code to pass their test, and then they write another test.

Now, this rigmarole probably sounds insane. Write tests for code that doesn't exist? Here's what's really nuts: often, this approach results in more test code than actual application code! It's a lot of work, and it's all based on the idea that you should write just enough code to get one thing working at a time.

But, here's the big reveal, and why these elite developers are elite: this results in better code. Working small, from start to finish, means that you're focusing on one thing and doing that one thing really well. You aren't rushing to something else. And that means what you're working on is solid and works. This approach does take more time in the beginning, but results in rock-solid code that breaks far less often.

So take your time, and work small. Your code will be better, and your customers will love you because your code is still running while they're on the phone trying to get help with a broken app from "the other guys."

■ Building a Basic SQL Query Runner

Now that you can connect to SQL, you're ready to take on something more ambitious: building your own version of a MySQL command-line tool. Of course, you're a PHP developer and programmer now, so mentally scratch out "command-line" and replace it with "web-based."

It turns out that you already have most of the tools you need. You can easily build an HTML form with which you and your users can enter in a SQL query; you know how to connect to MySQL and select a database; and you can run a query. All that's left is to figure out how to interpret that PHP resource that mysql_query returns when it's not a list of table names.

> **NOTE** You can find the finished example code for this section on this book's Missing CD page at *www.missingmanuals.com/cds/phpmysqlmm2e*.

Creating an HTML Form with a Big Empty Box

Before getting to mysql_query and its results, though, start with what you know: an HTML form. Keep things simple for now by creating a form with a few basic buttons and a single text area into which you can type queries.

Start your text editor and create *queryRunner.html* with the following code:

```
<html>
 <head>
  <link href="../css/phpMM.css" rel="stylesheet" type="text/css" />
 </head>

 <body>
  <div id="header"><h1>PHP & MySQL: The Missing Manual</h1></div>
  <div id="example">Example 5-2</div>

  <div id="content">
    <h1>SQL Query Runner</h1>
    <p>Enter your SQL query in the box below:</p>
    <form action="scripts/run_query.php" method="POST">
      <fieldset>
        <textarea id="query_text" name="query"
                  cols="65" rows="8"></textarea>
      </fieldset>
      <br />
      <fieldset class="center">
        <input type="submit" value="Run Query" />
        <input type="reset" value="Clear and Restart" />
      </fieldset>
    </form>
```

```
     </div>

     <div id="footer"></div>
   </body>
</html>
```

Fire up your favorite browser and ensure that things look like Figure 5-7.

FIGURE 5-7
Whoever said you wouldn't spend plenty of time writing HTML and CSS when you became a full-fledged web programmer? Even with a basic SQL query runner, good structure and style make a huge difference in presentation and how easy your code is to update.

Connecting to Your Database (Again)

Now that you have your HTML form, exactly as with the *connect.html* page you created on page 122, you need to write a script that connects to MySQL and then USEs your database. This code should be pretty familiar by now; create a new script in your *scripts/* directory called *run_query.php* and go to work:

```php
<?php
require '../../scripts/app_config.php';

mysql_connect(DATABASE_HOST, DATABASE_USERNAME, DATABASE_PASSWORD)
  or die("<p>Error connecting to database: " .
        mysql_error() . "</p>");

echo "<p>Connected to MySQL!</p>";

mysql_select_db(DATABASE_NAME)
  or die("<p>Error selecting the database " . DATABASE_NAME .
```

```
      mysql_error() . "</p>");

  echo "<p>Connected to MySQL, using database " . DATABASE_NAME . "</p>";
?>
```

You've already written this code before (page 133), and in fact, you have to write it every single time you connect to MySQL. That sort of duplication isn't good for the same reason why you moved your database constants into *app_config.php*: you wanted to be able to keep code that's always the same in a single place rather than ten or a hundred.

You've seen how easy it is to `require` a file, and pull in some constant values. And you can do the same thing with your database connection code. Open a new file and call it *database_connection.php*. Save this new script right alongside *app_config.php* (in your entire site's *scripts/* directory, not alongside your chapter-specific examples) and enter the following code:

```
<?php
  require 'app_config.php';

  mysql_connect(DATABASE_HOST, DATABASE_USERNAME, DATABASE_PASSWORD)
    or die("<p>Error connecting to database: " .
        mysql_error() . "</p>");

  echo "<p>Connected to MySQL!</p>";

  mysql_select_db(DATABASE_NAME)
    or die("<p>Error selecting the database " .
        DATABASE_NAME . mysql_error() . "</p>");

  echo "<p>Connected to MySQL, using database " .
      DATABASE_NAME . ".</p>";
?>
```

> **NOTE** Ensure that your path to *app_config.php* matches where you stored that file. If you're saving *database_connection.php* in the same directory as *app_config.php*, you just need the file name, without any directory paths.

You now have all your database code tucked nicely away, so you can radically overhaul *run_query.php*. Instead of all the code at the top of this section, you just need the following:

```
<?php
  require '../../scripts/database_connection.php';
?>
```

How's that for short code? More important, notice that there's no longer a reason to require *app_config.php*. Your script requires *database_connection.php*, and it's *database_connection.php* that handles bringing in *app_config.php*. Things are much neater now.

To verify that this works, visit your *queryRunner.html* page and click the "Run Query" button. You should see something like Figure 5-8, all without anything but a single `require` in your main script.

FIGURE 5-8

In queryRunner.html, clicking "Run Query" produces this page. The script run_query.php requires database_connection.php (which connects to the server and selects the database), which in turn requires app_config. php (which contains your password and other constants you need to connect). It might seem strange to write a script that appears to do nothing more than require another script. Actually, the more comfortable you get coding, the more you'll favor this sort of reuse. You want to write just enough new code to get the job done. If you can reuse lines of existing code, you should do so.

Running Your User's SQL Query (Again)

You're finally ready to combine what you know about PHP and what you know about SQL. You've already captured anything the user puts into the big text area on your form through the $REQUEST variable (which, as explained on page 83 in Chapter 3, is an array), and you also can use mysql_query to run a query.

In *run_query.php*, here's how you put those two things together:

```php
<?php
require '../../scripts/database_connection.php';

$query_text = $_REQUEST['query'];
$result = mysql_query($query_text);
```

```
if (!$result) {
  die("<p>Error in executing the SQL query " . $query_text . ": " .
      mysql_error() . "</p>");
}

echo "<p>Results from your query:</p>";
echo "<ul>";
while ($row = mysql_fetch_row($result)) {
  echo "<li>{$row[0]}</li>";
}
echo "</ul>";
?>
```

In other words, grab the correct field from the input from your HTML form, pass it to mysql_query, and you're good to go. You can then pass in the returned PHP resource, $result, to an error-handling if statement, and finally to mysql_fetch_row to print out the results from the query.

This looks pretty good, so now you're ready to actually try things out.

FREQUENTLY ASKED QUESTION

When Not to Abstract Out

The mysql_query *function seems like something I'm going to be using a lot. Why not just abstract it out in the same manner as* mysql_select_db *and the defined constants?*

Good question! You've correctly noticed that just as you're constantly connecting to MySQL—with the same user name and password, repeatedly—and selecting a database—often the same database, repeatedly—you'll be calling mysql_query, over and over and over. At first glance, it seems to make sense to place that in another file and then require that file.

Well, the reason is actually in the code you wrote on page 141: what you pass to mysql_query is going to change almost every time you call it. Earlier, in *connect.php*, you passed the SHOW TABLES query to it; now you're passing it a query from the form field in *queryRunner.html*. So, even though you're calling mysql_query over and over, what you're giving that function is changing. It's not going to help you to pull out that function from your main scripts.

You could move mysql_query out of your main script, and pass to it the part of the statement that keeps changing: the SQL query. You'd need to create a custom function that takes in your query from your main script and hand that query to

mysql_query. Then, when mysql_query finished running, the custom function would need to pass back anything it returned to your main script.

That might sound like a mouthful, and a lot of work. It's actually pretty easy, though, and once you start writing your own functions—something you'll be doing in Chapter 8 quite a bit—you'll have no problem doing just this. But, what would you gain? You'd still have to pass in a query and get back a response. you wouldn't actually gain anything from building your own function; it would basically replace mysql_query, but you wouldn't get any extra functionality, and it wouldn't add any protection from changes or anything like that to your code.

However, before you go thinking that you shouldn't worry about this sort of thing, take a minute. Asking yourself, "Could I pull this code out into another general file? Should I make this a custom function?" is a very good thing! You want to think like that, even if you decide—as is the case here—that it's *not* a good thing. The more you roll around new ideas and ways to approach your code, the better a programmer you'll be. So, keep asking yourself these questions; just don't be afraid to answer your own questions with "No, that's not such a great idea...in *this* case."

Entering Your First Web-Based Query

In *run_query.php*, you're connecting to a database and you have a way to run a query, but you probably don't have much *in* your database yet, so start by creating a new table. Call the table *urls* (it's going to contain web addresses). Here's the SQL you'll need:

```
CREATE TABLE urls (id int, url varchar(100), description varchar(100));
```

Of course, because you have a nice big text area on *queryRunner.html*, you could also spread that out:

```
CREATE TABLE urls (
   id int,
   url varchar(100),
   description varchar(100)
);
```

Either way, you want a form that looks something like Figure 5-9.

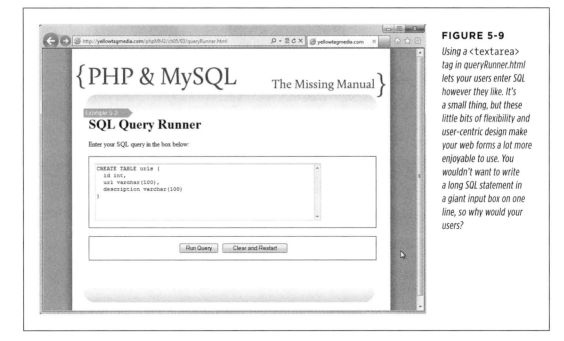

FIGURE 5-9

Using a <textarea> tag in queryRunner.html lets your users enter SQL however they like. It's a small thing, but these little bits of flexibility and user-centric design make your web forms a lot more enjoyable to use. You wouldn't want to write a long SQL statement in a giant input box on one line, so why would your users?

Go ahead and click Run Query. What did you get?

Not so good, right? You're probably staring at a surprising screen, sort of like the one shown in Figure 5-10.

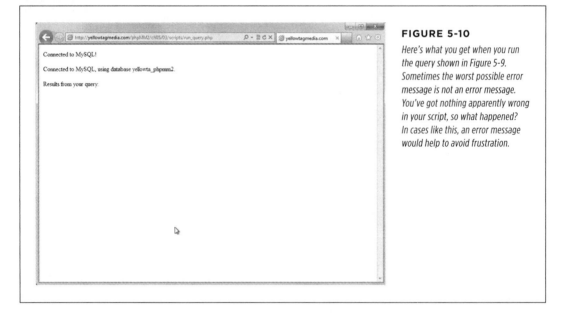

FIGURE 5-10

Here's what you get when you run the query shown in Figure 5-9. Sometimes the worst possible error message is not an error message. You've got nothing apparently wrong in your script, so what happened? In cases like this, an error message would help to avoid frustration.

If you want to really become confused, press the Back button on your browser and run your CREATE query again. You'll see a message like the one shown in Figure 5-11.

FIGURE 5-11

Huh? First, you got nothing (Figure 5-10). But now, you're being told that something did happen, and trying to make that (invisible) thing happen again has caused an error. Your script couldn't create the urls table, because you already created it the first time you ran the query.

First, nothing happened—no results at all (Figure 5-10). Now, MySQL is reporting that the *urls* table already exists (Figure 5-11). In fact, if you hop out to your command-line tool, you'd see that, yes, the table *does* exist in your database:

```
mysql> describe urls;
+-------------+--------------+------+-----+---------+-------+
| Field       | Type         | Null | Key | Default | Extra |
+-------------+--------------+------+-----+---------+-------+
| id          | int(11)      | YES  |     | NULL    |       |
| url         | varchar(100) | YES  |     | NULL    |       |
| description | varchar(100) | YES  |     | NULL    |       |
+-------------+--------------+------+-----+---------+-------+
3 rows in set (0.00 sec)
```

Look carefully at your code again:

```php
<?php
  require '../../scripts/database_connection.php';

  $query_text = $_REQUEST['query'];
  $result = mysql_query($query_text);

  if (!$result) {
    die("<p>Error in executing the SQL query " . $query_text . ": " .
      mysql_error() . "</p>");
  }

  echo "<p>Results from your query:</p>";
  echo "<ul>";
  while ($row = mysql_fetch_row($result)) {
    echo "<li>{$row[0]}</li>";
  }
  echo "</ul>";
?>
```

The if (!$result) code block is not running; clearly $result came back as something other than false. However, the while loop never ran, so you never saw any results.

Wait a second, though. Your query was a CREATE query. What rows would be returned from that sort of query? There wouldn't be any rows, because you weren't asking for rows. You were just asking MySQL to create a table; in fact, a place to *put* rows.

Handling Queries That Don't SELECT Information

The important point demonstrated in the previous section is that mysql_query is happy to take in a CREATE statement. It even did what you asked, which is why the second time you entered that query in Figure 5-11, MySQL returned an error, saying that the *urls* table was already created. When `mysql_query` receives a CREATE statement, it returns `false` if there was an error—which your script handles—but true if there's not an error. If there's not an error, *it will not return any rows.* You get a `true` value in `$result`, but nothing else. And that's where things went wrong.

In fact, that's what `mysql_query` does when it gets most of the SQL statements that don't select data, such as CREATE, INSERT, UPDATE, DELETE, DROP, and a few others. For each of these, you just get back `true` (if things worked) or `false` (if they didn't).

NOTE   A few of those SQL commands (for example, UPDATE and DELETE) might look new to you. Don't worry, though. First, they do just what it appears they do: UPDATE updates information in a table, and DELETE removes it. Second, when you need to use those functions, you'll get a lot more detail about exactly how to use each of them.

Fortunately, now that you know this is going on, it's not too hard to deal with the problem. You just need to see whether the SQL query string that the user supplied has one of these special words. If so, it must be handled differently. But, it just so happens you're plenty comfortable with searching through strings (page 73).

Take a moment to think this through; what you really want is something like this:

1. **Grab the user's query from the HTML form.**

2. **Pass the query into `mysql_query` and store the result in a variable.**

3. **See if the result is false, which is bad no matter what type of SQL was passed in.**

4. **If the result is not false, see if the query has one of the special keywords in it: CREATE, INSERT, UPDATE, DELETE, or DROP.** (There are others, but this covers the most common ones.)

5. **If the query has one of these special words, just see whether the result of running the query was true, and let the user know that things went well.**

6. **If the query does not have one of these words, try to print out the result rows as you've already been doing.**

You know how to do all of these things individually; all you need to do is put them together. Start out with a variable that indicates whether the user's SQL will return anything and set it to false:

```
$return_rows = false;
```

Now you can search the user's query by using `strpos`, looking for one of the SQL keywords that tells you, "No, rows will not be returned by this query."

```
$return_rows = false;
$location = strpos($query_text, "CREATE");
```

If nothing was found, check the next keyword...and the next...and so on:

```
$return_rows = false;
$location = strpos($query_text, "CREATE");
if ($location === false) {
  $location = strpos($query_text, "INSERT");
  if ($location === false) {
    $location = strpos($query_text, "UPDATE");
    if ($location === false) {
      $location = strpos($query_text, "DELETE");
      if ($location === false) {
        $location = strpos($query_text, "DROP");
        if ($location === false) {
          // If we got here, it's not a CREATE, INSERT, UPDATE,
          //   DELETE, or DROP query. It should return rows.
          $return_rows = true;
        }
      }
    }
  }
}
```

WARNING Be sure to use that *triple*-equal sign (===) in your if statements to check whether $location is false.

That code might look complicated, but it's clear when you walk through it, line by line. Basically, you have the same if statement, repeated over and over, with each of those statements containing another nested if statement:

```
$location = strpos($query_text, "SEARCH_STRING");
if ($location === false) {
  // Try again with another SEARCH_STRING
}
```

Finally, if all of the if statements fail, CREATE, INSERT, UPDATE, DELETE, or DROP are not in the query string:

```
// This is the innermost if statement
if ($location === false) {
  // If we got here, it's not a CREATE, INSERT, UPDATE,
  //   DELETE, or DROP query. It should return rows.
  $return_rows = true;
}
```

The challenge here is that you really want to search the user's query string not just for a single matching word, like CREATE or INSERT, but for several matching words. That's a little tricky, so you've got to do it with one call to strpos at a time.

NOTE Make sure that you understand this code, but don't get too attached to it. It's really ugly, and in the next chapter, you're going to add an extremely new tool to your PHP programming kit and rework this code to be a *lot* slimmer and sleeker.

At each step, if the search string is found, it means that the user has entered one of those special SQL keywords that does not return rows, so the variable $return_rows is set to false, which is different from its original value, true.

Finally, at the end of this curly-brace love fest, the if statements unwind back to the main program, and either $returns_rows has a value of true because none of the searches matched, or it's false because one of them did.

You're ready to use $returns_rows to print out a result:

```php
<?php
  // require and database connection code

  // run the query

  // handle errors in the result

  $return_rows = false;
  $location = strpos($query_text, "CREATE");
  if ($location === false) {
    $location = strpos($query_text, "INSERT");
    if ($location === false) {
      $location = strpos($query_text, "UPDATE");
      if ($location === false) {
        $location = strpos($query_text, "DELETE");
        if ($location === false) {
          $location = strpos($query_text, "DROP");
          if ($location === false) {
            // If we got here, it's not a CREATE, INSERT, UPDATE,
            //   DELETE, or DROP query. It should return rows.
            $return_rows = true;
          }
        }
      }
    }
  }

  if ($return_rows) {
    // We have rows to show from the query
    echo "<p>Results from your query:</p>";
    echo "<ul>";
    while ($row = mysql_fetch_row($result)) {
      echo "<li>{$row[0]}</li>";
```

```
    }
    echo "</ul>";
  } else {
    // No rows. Just report if the query ran or not
    if ($result) {
      echo "<p>Your query was processed successfully.</p>"
      echo "<p>{$query_text}</p>";
    }
  }
?>
```

> **NOTE** Remember that if ($return_rows) is the same as if ($return_rows === true). The same goes for if ($result).

Most of this is familiar. All of the code you've been using to print out rows stays the same. That code just moves inside the if ($return_rows) block, because it only applies if the user entered something like a SELECT that returns (potentially) lots of results.

Then, in the else branch of that if, your script reports whether things went OK. As an additional aid, this branch of the if statement prints out the original query so that the user can know what was executed.

Technically, you don't really need that if ($result). Because you tested earlier to see if $result is false, if your script gets to this last bit, you know that $result is true, so you can simplify things at the end a bit:

```
if ($return_rows) {
  // We have rows to show from the query
  echo "<p>Results from your query:</p>";
  echo "<ul>";
  while ($row = mysql_fetch_row($result)) {
    echo "<li>{$row[0]}</li>";
  }
  echo "</ul>";
} else {
  // No rows. Just report if the query ran or not
  echo "<p>Your query was processed successfully.</p>";
  echo "<p>{$query_text}</p>";
}
```

This script is getting to be long, but you now know what every single line is doing at this point. Go ahead and try it out.

You probably created the *urls* table earlier—even though your PHP script didn't let you know that. Try entering DROP TABLE urls; as your SQL query. Then, run your query, and this time, you should get a helpful message back, specific to your rowless query, as you can see in Figure 5-12.

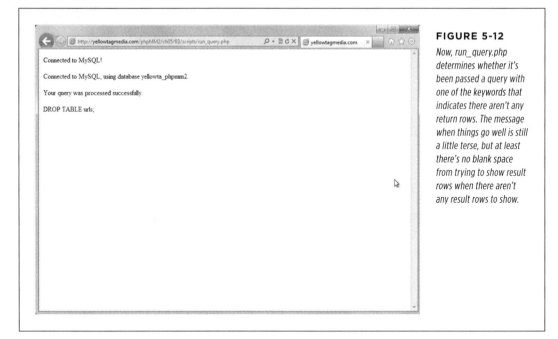

FIGURE 5-12

Now, run_query.php determines whether it's been passed a query with one of the keywords that indicates there aren't any return rows. The message when things go well is still a little terse, but at least there's no blank space from trying to show result rows when there aren't any result rows to show.

Dealing with Humans

Unfortunately, there's still a problem in one of those lines. Right now, if your user types the query DROP TABLE urls;, your set of if statements catches that DROP is part of the query, realizes it has no return rows, and does the right thing: reports that the query either ran without problems or that an error occurred.

But what about this query?

```
drop table urls;
```

Do you see a problem? Here's the if statement that should indicate a match:

```
$location = strpos($query_text, "DROP");
if ($location === false) {
  // this should return true, and so there are no return rows
}
```

But that line searches for "DROP", which will not match "drop" at all. strpos searches for strings, but it sees a lowercase letter, like "d," as a different letter than an uppercase "D." Thus, that search will find "DROP" but not "drop" or "dRoP."

And, as always, it's humans who are using your app, not robots. You can't simply assume that those humans will be good SQL citizens and always use capital letters. You could even put a little message on the form: *Please type your SQL in all capital letters.* But, humans will be humans, and they tend to ignore instructions like that.

In fact, you'll spend *at least* as much of your time dealing with the human factor in your code as writing code that handles the normal flow of operation. In fact, once you add real people to your line of thinking, you'll realize that "normal" isn't a useful term. Instead, your code simply has to deal with what's *possible*.

So, how do you fix the issue of lowercase and uppercase? It turns out to be fairly simple: you convert $query_string to all CAPITAL letters before starting to search through it:

```
$return_rows = false;
$query_text = strtoupper($query_text);
$location = strpos($query_text, "CREATE");
// All the nested if blocks.
```

Now, if a user enters "drop table urls" or "DROP table UrLS," the search string becomes "DROP TABLE URLS," and searching for "DROP" will return a match.

But there's another problem! Do you see what it is?

NOTE Yes, there really are this many wrinkles and problems with just a single simple program. That's why there are lots of programmers, but so few really great programmers: the difference is handling all these little details without throwing your iPhone through a nearby wall.

Avoid Changing User Input Whenever Possible

This one is a bit trickier, and it really is a potential problem, as opposed to something creates havoc right now. Here's the last bit of your code that's run if the user enters a rowless query like DROP or INSERT:

```
// No rows. Just report if the query ran or not
echo "<p>Your query was processed successfully.</p>"
echo "<p>{$query_text}</p>";
```

To see this in action, again, load *queryRunner.html* and then enter DROP TABLE urls; again. You'll get something like Figure 5-13.

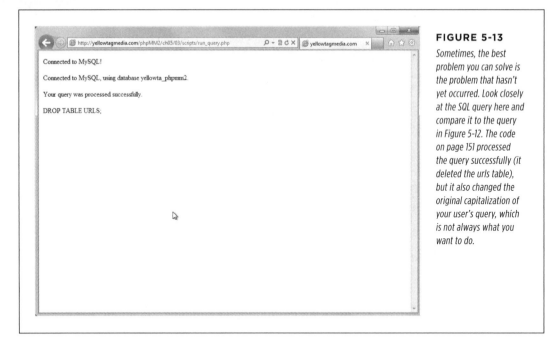

FIGURE 5-13

Sometimes, the best problem you can solve is the problem that hasn't yet occurred. Look closely at the SQL query here and compare it to the query in Figure 5-12. The code on page 151 processed the query successfully (it deleted the urls table), but it also changed the original capitalization of your user's query, which is not always what you want to do.

NOTE If you're following along, you might need to CREATE the *urls* table before you can DROP it. You can flip back to Figure 5-9 for that SQL if you don't recall it off the top of your head.

What's the big deal? Look closely, and then flip back to Figure 5-12. Do you see the problem? In the latter version, in Figure 5-13, everything is in uppercase. That makes sense, because to make searching easier, you added this line to your script:

```
$query_text = strtoupper($query_text);
```

Then, when you output $query_text at the end, the output is shown in all uppercase letters. Is this a big deal? Well, it doesn't seem to be, at least not here. However, it does reveal something: after that $query_text string is converted to uppercase, any time it's used, it's coming back with all uppercase letters.

Suppose that the original query was something like this:

```
SELECT *
  FROM users
 WHERE last_name = "MacLachlan";
```

Now, consider this same query, converted to all uppercase letters:

```
SELECT *
  FROM USERS
 WHERE LAST_NAME = "MACLACHLAN";
```

Believe it or not, these are *not* the same query. SELECT—and most of the other SQL queries—are going to treat a last name of "MacLachlan" as totally different than "MACLACHLAN". As a result, those two queries are not identical at all.

Right at this juncture, this doesn't create any trouble. Your script never reruns the query, and mysql_query runs with $query_text before its turned into its uppercase version. But, this is a problem waiting to happen.

In general, you want to try and avoid directly changing input from a user to steer clear of exactly this sort of problem: you might need to use that input again, and once you've changed it, you can't go back.

Luckily, this is a really easy fix: you just don't change the user's input. Instead, you use a new variable to store the uppercase version of the query:

```
$return_rows = false;
$uppercase_query_text = strtoupper($query_text);
$location = strpos($query_text, "CREATE");
```

Now, you should use this new variable in all your string comparisons:

```
$return_rows = false;
$uppercase_query_text = strtoupper($query_text);
$location = strpos($uppercase_query_text, "CREATE");
if ($location === false) {
  $location = strpos($uppercase_query_text, "INSERT");
  if ($location === false) {
    $location = strpos($uppercase_query_text, "UPDATE");
    if ($location === false) {
      $location = strpos($uppercase_query_text, "DELETE");
      if ($location === false) {
        $location = strpos($uppercase_query_text, "DROP");
        if ($location === false) {
          // If we got here, it's not a CREATE, INSERT, UPDATE,
          //   DELETE, or DROP query. It should return rows.
          $return_rows = true;
        }
      }
    }
  }
}
```

As small a change as that is, it protects you in case you ever need to use that query string again.

And just like that, you've got a tool that will execute any SQL query you throw at it. But there's work still to do. All that search code clutters up your script, and there's just no getting around it: your script is pretty hard to understand at first glance (and even at second glance). In the next chapter, you'll tackle all of this, transforming your handy little form to a really nice exercise of your PHP muscle.

POWER USERS' CLINIC

Get Specific with Position and Whitespace Trimming

You're definitely making *run_query.php* a lot better, but there are still problems. Suppose that someone wrote SQL like this:

```
SELECT *
  FROM registrar_activities
WHERE name = 'Update GPA'
   OR name = 'Drop a class'
```

This is a SELECT statement, so *run_query.php* should run the SQL and print out all the rows returned from this query. But there's a nasty little problem, isn't there?

Yup. Your code that searches for "update" and "drop" will report that this query has both words in it, and simply return "Your SQL was run without any problems." But that *is* a problem!

What can you do? Well, think about the structure of SQL. Those special keywords—CREATE, INSERT, and their friends—all are the *first* word in the query. Thus, you'd need to get the position of the match and check whether that position is position 0. You can do that by adding to your if conditions and using the logical or || operator in PHP:

```
if ($location === false || $location > 0)
{
```

The double-pipe (||) means "or" to PHP. So, this line says if there's no match at all ($location === false) or the match isn't starting at the first position (position 0), then look for the next keyword. Of course, you'd have to change all your if statements, which is even messier. Clearly, this is an improvement, although it's one that clutters up your code even further.

Wait; it gets worse! You're dealing with real humans, and humans do funny things. Suppose that someone enters this SQL into your form:

```
    CREATE TABLE urls (id int, url var-
char(100),
                          description var-
char(100));
```

Here, you have a new problem: this isn't a SELECT, but your search code won't find one of those special words at the beginning. The first character is just a space: " ".

You can solve this problem, too, by using another familiar function: trim. trim gets rid of whitespace, and if you do that before you search, you should be in good shape:

```
$uppercase_query_text =
trim(strtoupper($query_text))
```

That probably seems like a ton of work for a really simple form with one text area. But, when you're working with user input, this is exactly how you want to think: what would users do? What might they type to screw things up, and can I help keep them from seeing something weird or making a mistake? Think like that, and you're going to build better, more stable, more enjoyable web applications.

And, as something to look forward to, you're just about to learn some handy techniques to make all this messy code a lot simpler. So keep going, dealing with human-type input, and know that your code is only going to get cleaner and simpler.

Regular Expressions

In the example in the last chapter example—a web form that lets users run SQL against a MySQL database—you did one of the most common things programmers do. You wrote code that solves a problem, but it's ugly, messy, and a little hard to understand. Unfortunately, most programmers *leave* code in that state. That's something you want to avoid.

Bad code is like sloppy plumbing or a poorly constructed house frame. At some point, things are going to go bad, and someone is going to have to fix problems. And, if you've ever had an electrician tell you what he has to charge you because the guy who did the work initially did it wrong *before*, you know how expensive it is to fix someone else's mistakes.

But here's the thing: Even good code is going to fail at some point. Any time you have a system that involves humans, at some point, someone will do something unexpected, or maybe just something you never thought about dealing with when you wrote your code. And that's when *you're* the electrician, trying to fix things when the customer's unhappy—but in this scenario, there's nobody else to blame.

So, writing ugly code that works really isn't an option. At the moment, the code in *run_query.php* right now is very ugly. It's all those `if` statements that are trying to figure out whether the user entered a CREATE or an UPDATE or an INSERT, or maybe a SELECT...or who knows what else? What you really need is a way to search the incoming query for all those keywords *all at once*. And then there's converting text to uppercase, and dealing with whitespace, and making sure the SQL keyword you want is at the beginning of the query.

Unfortunately, there's no way to solve this problem elegantly by using `strpos` and the string manipulation you've done so far. Fortunately, though, you have another option: *regular expressions*. Regular expressions (also know in programmer-ese as *regexes*) are like a keg of gunpowder: extremely powerful, but perfectly capable of blowing up your program and creating hours of frustration. That's okay, though, because you're not running off to battle just yet.

Before you're done with *run_query.php*, you'll have learned how to use regular expressions, cut out all but one of those annoying `if` statements for searching through `$query_text`, and made your program easier to troubleshoot when problems occur down the line.

> **WARNING** It's pretty common knowledge that most people—and even most programmers—see regular expressions in particular as a complicated, difficult programming art. That's okay; you're more than ready to tackle them. Once you understand how they work, you'll wonder why anyone wouldn't want to use them all over the place.

◼ String Matching, Double-Time

So far, you've been using `strpos` to perform string searching, and you've been passing into that function your string and then some additional characters or a string for which to look. The problem is that using `strpos` in this way limits you to a single search string at a time; you can search for UPDATE and you can search for DROP, but not at the same time.

Here's where regular expressions come into the picture. A regular expression is just what it sounds like: a regular sequence of characters or numbers or some other pattern—an expression—for which you want to search. If you had a string like "abcdefghijklmnopqrstuvwxyz," you could search for the pattern, or regular expression, "abc". It would show up once, of course, which isn't very "regular."

However, suppose that you had an entire web page, and you wanted to search for links. You might use an expression like "<a" to find all the link elements. You might find none, or one, or ten; with a regular expression, you can search for practically anything you want. It does get a bit murky though, so the best place to start is at the beginning.

> **NOTE** You can find the finished example code for this section on this book's Missing CD page at *www.missingmanuals.com/cds/phpmysqlmm2e*.

A Simple String Searcher

Just about the simplest regular expression you can come up with is a single simple letter, like "a" or "m". Thus, the regular expression "a" will match any "a". Simple, right?

In PHP, if you want to search by using regular expressions, you use the `preg_match` function. Even though that sounds like something related to childbirth, it actually stands for "p-reg," as in "PHP regular (expressions)." However, no matter how you say it (and what thoughts it conjures up), it's used like this:

```php
<?php
$string_to_search = "Martin OMC-28LJ";
$regex = "/OM/";
$num_matches = preg_match($regex, $string_to_search);

if ($num_matches > 0) {
  echo "Found a match!";
} else {
  echo "No match. Sorry.";
}
?>
```

WARNING   Be sure that the first thing you give to `preg_match` is the regular expression, *not* the string in which you want to search. This might seem backward compared to how you've been working, but you'll soon be using the `preg_match` and related functions so often, putting the search string first will feel odd.

Save that program as *regex.php* and run it from the command line. You should get a result like this:

```
--(08:25 $)-> php regex.php
Found a match!
```

Admittedly, this isn't very exciting. Before you can walk, though, you gotta crawl. And part of crawling is understanding just how you write a regular expression.

First, regular expressions are just strings, so you wrap them in quotes. You'll typically use double quotes (") rather than single quotes (') because PHP doesn't do as much helpful processing on single-quoted strings as double-quoted ones. (For more advice on how to use quotes in PHP, see the box on page 158.)

Additionally, regular expressions begin and end with a forward slash. It's everything between those slashes that makes up the meat of the expression. For example, "/OM/" is a regular expression that searches for OM.

More specifically, "/OM/" searches for exactly OM; it won't match "om" or "Om" or "OhM". It has to be an uppercase O followed by an uppercase M. So far, this is just like the string matching you've already done.

Of course, `preg_match` has some wrinkles, too. First, as you've seen, it takes a regular expression as the first argument, and then the string in which to search as the second. Then, it returns the number of matches, rather than the position at which a match was found. Here's the first real wrinkle: `preg_match` will *never return anything other than 0 or 1*. It returns 0 if there are no matches, and 1 upon the first match, and then it simply stops searching.

If you want to find all the matches, you can use preg_match_all. Thus, preg_match("/Mr/", "Mr. Mranity") will return 1, but preg_match_all("/Mr/", "Mr. Mranity") will return 2.

UNDER THE HOOD

Which Quote Is the Best Quote?

Almost every programming language seemingly treats single-quoted strings ('My name is Bob') and double-quoted strings ("I am a carpenter.") the same way. However, also in almost every programming language, there's a lot more going on than you might realize, all based upon which quotation mark you use.

In general, there is *less* processing performed on single-quoted strings. But, what processing occurs in the first place? Take the statement I'm going to the bank. If you put that in a single-quoted string, you get 'I'm going to the bank.' But PHP is going to bark at you, because the single-quote in I'm looks like it's ending the simple string 'I', and all the rest—m going to the bank—must just be something else. Of course, that's not what you mean, so you do one of two things: you either switch to double quotes and move on, or you *escape* the single quote.

Escaping a character is when you instruct the programming language to *not treat this as part of the language; it's just part of my string.* Typically, you escape characters by typing a backslash (\) in front of the potentially problematic character. In the string I'm going to the bank., you'd write it in single quotes like this: 'I\'m going to the bank.' That backslash directs PHP to ignore both the backslash and the character that follows it.

Now, what if you want to actually write a backslash? Suppose you're writing a program for your great-great-great granddad, the one that still runs DOS on his PC/AT? You might want to say, 'Never, ever, ever type \'del C:*.*\' and hit

Return!' Well, you handled the single-quotes handily, but now PHP is trying to escape the character following that in-string backslash: *. That just confuses PHP. * isn't a special character, so what is going on? Well, in this case, you need to escape the backslash itself. To do that, you just put in the escape character—the backslash—and then the character to be escaped; in this case, another backslash. The result is 'Never, ever, ever type in \'del C:*.*\'

So, what does all this have to do with single and double-quotes? Well, other than the single quote (') and the backslash (\), PHP doesn't do any other processing to your single-quoted strings. But there are lots of other things you might need processing for: a new line (\n), a tab (\t), or that slick way of inserting variables right into a string with {$variable} or just using $variable.

With a single-quoted string, you get very little. With a double-quoted string, you get all the extra processing. As a result, most programmers tend to use double quotes. That way, they don't have to stop to think, "Now do I need extra processing on this string? Or can I use single quotes?"

One last note: in 99 percent of the applications you write, the type of quotes you use doesn't matter. The processing involved in handling those extra escape characters and variables isn't going to frustrate your customers or send server hard drives or RAM chips into a frenzy. You can happily use double-quoted strings all the time, and you'll probably never notice any issues at all.

NOTE There are also several additional things you can pass into—and get out of—preg_match and preg_match_all. You can find out about all of this online at *php.net/manual/en/function.preg-match.php*. For now, though, just get comfortable with regular expressions.

Search for One String...Or Another

So far, there's not a lot that preg_match seems to offer that you don't already have with strpos. But there's a lot more that you can do, and one of the coolest is search-ing for one string *or* another. To do this, you use a special character called the *pipe*. The pipe looks like a vertical line: |. It's usually above the backslash character, over on the right side of your keyboard.

Anytime you want to search for one string or another, you put those two strings together surrounded by parentheses, separated by the pipe, as shown here:

```
/(Mr|Dr)\. Smith/
```

First, though, notice the wrinkle: the backslash (\). This is escaping the period, be-cause that period usually means in a regular expression, "match any single character." But in this case, you want to match an actual period. So, \. will match a period, and nothing but a period.

> **NOTE** You can read more about back slashes and the escape character in the box on page 158.

/Mr\. Smith/ matches "Mr. Smith" but will skip right over "Dr. Smith." However, /(Mr|Dr)\. Smith/ matches either "Mr. Smith" or "Dr. Smith."

That means that this little code snippet would find a match in both cases:

```php
// This will match
echo "Matches: " . preg_match("/(Mr|Dr)\. Smith/", "Mr. Smith");

// So will this
echo "Matches: " . preg_match("/(Mr|Dr)\. Smith/", "Dr. Smith");
```

With this new wrinkle, you should be able to make some pretty massive changes to *run_query.php* from the last chapter. Open that file and take a look. As a reminder, here's the old version:

```php
<?php
  require '../../scripts/database_connection.php';

  $query_text = $_REQUEST['query'];
  $result = mysql_query($query_text);

  if (!$result) {
    die("<p>Error in executing the SQL query " . $query_text . ": " .
        mysql_error() . "</p>");
  }

  $return_rows = false;
  $uppercase_query_text = strtoupper($query_text);
  $location = strpos($uppercase_query_text, "CREATE");
  if ($location === false) {
```

```php
      $location = strpos($uppercase_query_text, "INSERT");
    if ($location === false) {
      $location = strpos($uppercase_query_text, "UPDATE");
      if ($location === false) {
        $location = strpos($uppercase_query_text, "DELETE");
        if ($location === false) {
          $location = strpos($uppercase_query_text, "DROP");
          if ($location === false) {
            // If we got here, it's not a CREATE, INSERT, UPDATE,
            //   DELETE, or DROP query. It should return rows.
            $return_rows = true;
          }
        }
      }
    }
  }

  if ($return_rows) {
    // We have rows to show from the query
    echo "<p>Results from your query:</p>";
    echo "<ul>";
    while ($row = mysql_fetch_row($result)) {
      echo "<li>{$row[0]}</li>";
    }
    echo "</ul>";
  } else {
    // No rows. Just report if the query ran or not
    echo "<p>Your query was processed successfully.</p>";
    echo "<p>{$query_text}</p>";
  }
?>
```

It's all that if stuff that really is messy. But with regular expressions, you can make some pretty spectacular changes:

```php
<?php
  // require and database connection code

  $return_rows = true;
  if (preg_match("/(CREATE|INSERT|UPDATE|DELETE|DROP)/",
                strtoupper($query_text))) {
    $return_rows = false;
  }

  if ($return_rows) {
    // display code
  }
?>
```

NOTE   You might want to save this version as another file, or in another directory, so you can always see what you started with. In the book's examples, you'll find the original version of *run_query.php* in the example *scripts/* directory as *run_query.orig.php*, and this new version in the example *scripts/* directory as simply *run_query.php*.

Take a close look here, especially at the fairly long condition for the if statement. Here's the breakdown of what's going on:

1. **You start by setting $return_rows to true, instead of false.**

    This is because your regular expression search is determining whether you have return rows. This is easier to read than the older version, in which you're constantly doing a comparison, and then if there's *not* a match, setting $return_rows to true.

2. **Then, the if condition: it begins with preg_match.**

    There's no need to use preg_match_all, because you only care if the search strings are found at all, not if they're found more than once.

3. **The regular expression is actually pretty simple: it's each keyword for a SQL statement that doesn't return any rows, all separated by that pipe symbol.** So, it's basically an expression for matching a string that contains CREATE *or* INSERT *or* UPDATE *or* DELETE *or* DROP.

4. **This expression is evaluated against the uppercase version of $query_text.**

    Not only do you not change the value of $query_text, but you don't even really need to save the uppercase version. If you need an uppercase version again later, you can call strtoupper again.

5. **You know that preg_match returns 0 if there's no match, and PHP sees 0 as false.** preg_match returns 1 if there's a match, which PHP sees as true. Therefore, you can drop the whole preg_match in as your if statement's condition and know that if there's a match, the if statement code will run; if there's not a match, it won't.

6. **Inside the if, $return_rows is set to false, because a match means this is a query that doesn't have return rows.**

Not only is this code easier to read and makes more sense to a human brain, but you cut 20 lines of code down to 4.

WARNING   It's not *always* good to have less lines of code. Sometimes you can sacrifice readability and clarity to save a few lines, and that's not helpful. But, if you can condense four or five conditions into one or two, that usually *is* a good thing.

Getting into Position

One of the problems with even this streamlined version of *run_query.php* is that it looks for a match anywhere within the input query. If you read the box about whitespace trimming on page 154, you know there are still problems. You need to trim your user's query string, which is pretty simple:

```
if (preg_match("/(CREATE|INSERT|UPDATE|DELETE|DROP)/",
                  trim(strtoupper($query_text)))) {
    $return_rows = false;
}
```

But there's another, trickier problem: you really only want to search for those special keywords at the beginning of the query string. That prevents a query like the following from being mistaken as an UPDATE or DROP query:

```
SELECT *
  FROM registrar_activities
 WHERE name = 'Update GPA'
    OR name = 'Drop a class'
```

This query, a SELECT, returns rows, but if it's interpreted as an UPDATE or DROP, your script will not show return rows.

It took some additional if conditions to get this to work before, but that was before you were taking over the world one regular expression at a time. With regular expressions, it's easy to tell PHP, "I want this expression, but only at the *beginning* of the search string."

To accomplish this feat of wizardry, just add the carat (^) to the beginning of your search string, which basically says, "at the beginning."

```
// Matches
echo "Matches: " . preg_match("/^(Mr|Dr). Smith/",
                               "Dr. Smith") . "\n";
// Does NOT match
echo "Matches: " . preg_match("/^(Mr|Dr). Smith/",
                               "  Dr. Smith") . "\n";
```

Looking back in the first case, /^(Mr|Dr). Smith/ matches "Dr. Smith" because the string begins with "Dr. Smith" ("Mr. Smith" would be okay, too). But the second string does not match, because the ^ rejects the leading spaces.

Taking this back to your query runner, you'd do something like this:

```
if (preg_match("/^(CREATE|INSERT|UPDATE|DELETE|DROP)/",
                trim(strtoupper($query_text)))) {
    $return_rows = false;
}
```

That one little carat character makes all the difference. You can do the same thing at the end of the search string by using the $ character, as demonstrated here:

```
// Does NOT match
echo "Matches: " . preg_match("/^(Mr|Dr). Smith$/",
                               "Dr. Smith  ") . "\n";
```

```
// Matches
echo "Matches: " . preg_match("/^(Mr|Dr). Smith$/",
                              "Dr. Smith") . "\n";
```

WARNING Ensure that your ^ and $ are inside the opening / and closing /. If you were to put, for example, /^(Mr|Dr). Smith/$, PHP would complain about that last $, alerting you that $ is an unknown modifier. This is an easy error to make, and it can be pretty frustrating to track down.

In the first case, there's no match because the regular expression, which uses $, doesn't allow for the trailing spaces in "Dr. Smith ". The second check does match, though, because there's no leading space (which matches the ^(Mr|Dr) part) and no trailing space (which matches the Smith$ part).

In fact, when you have a ^ at the beginning of your expression and a $ at the end, you're requiring an exact match not just within the search string but to the string itself. It's like you're saying that the search string should equal the regular expression. Of course if you were doing a real equivalency in PHP (with == or ===), you couldn't have those nifty or statements with |, or any of the other cool things regular expressions offer.

Ditch `trim` and `strtoupper`

As long as you're simplifying your code with some regular expression goodness, try taking things further. Right now, you're converting $query_text to all uppercase characters by using `strtoupper` and then searching for "CREATE", "INSERT", and the like within that uppercase version of the query.

But, regular expressions are happy to be case-insensitive, meaning that they don't care whether they match uppercase or lowercase versions of a word. Just add an "i" to the end of your expression, *after* the closing forward slash:

```
// Matches
echo "Matches: " . preg_match("/^(MR|DR). sMiTH$/i",
                              "Dr. Smith") . "\n";
```

This expression produces a match, irrespective of the case of the expression and the search string not matching. You can change your search in *run_query.php* to take advantage of that fact:

```
$return_rows = true;
if (preg_match("/^(CREATE|INSERT|UPDATE|DELETE|DROP)/i",
               trim($query_text))) {
  $return_rows = false;
}
```

No more `strtoupper`, and a new "i" at the end of the expression. With this change, the sort of query shown in Figure 6-1 will still happily be recognized as DROP, which returns no result rows.

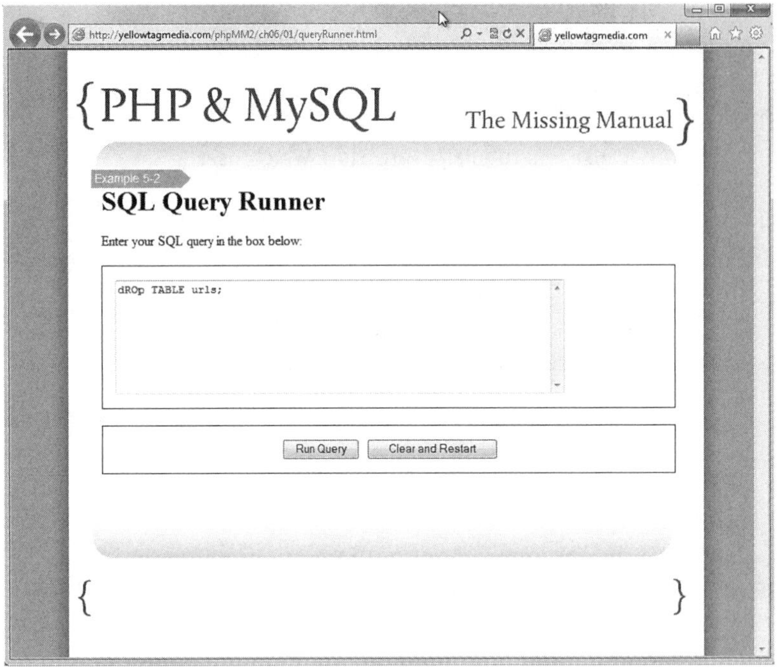

FIGURE 6-1

Even though you're not really adding functionality with these regular expressions, you're definitely improving your code. You're searching for what you want in the original $query_text, instead of changing $query_ text to work with your search. That's the way it should be: Always search an unchanged input string whenever possible.

What about trimming whitespace? Well, you really don't need to trim $query_string; instead, in your regular expression, you just want to ignore leading spaces. At least, that's the result you want. In PHP, you have to think of it this way:

1. **Begin by matching any number of spaces—including when there are no spaces.**

2. **Then, after some indeterminate number of spaces, look for (CREATE|INSERT |UPDATE|DELETE|DROP).**

This means that while you're ignoring those spaces in your particular situation—figuring out whether the query is a CREATE, or UPDATE, or whatever—you're really just doing another type of matching.

Now, you know how to match a space: you just include it in your regular expression. For example, /^ Mr. Smith/ requires an opening space. "Mr. Smith" would not match, but " Mr. Smith" would.

But, that requires a space. How can you say that more than one space is okay? That's when you need + (plus) character. The + character says, "The thing that came just before me can appear any number of times."

```
// Matches
echo "Matches: " . preg_match("/^ (MR|DR). sMiTH$/i",
                              " Dr. Smith") . "\n";
// Does NOT match
echo "Matches: " . preg_match("/^ (MR|DR). sMiTH$/i",
                              "    Dr. Smith") . "\n";
// Matches
echo "Matches: " . preg_match("/^ +(MR|DR). sMiTH$/i",
                              "    Dr. Smith") . "\n";
```

The first and second expressions look for exactly one space, and so the first entry matches, but the second—with multiple leading spaces—doesn't. However, the third expression accepts any number of spaces, so once again, it matches.

Wait, though, try this:

```
// Does NOT match
echo "Matches: " . preg_match("/^ +(MR|DR). sMiTH$/i",
                              "Dr. Smith") . "\n";
```

Uh oh! Apparently "any number of spaces" for + really means "any non-zero number of spaces." If you are okay with nothing *or* any number of characters, use *.

```
// Matches
echo "Matches: " . preg_match("/^ *(MR|DR). sMiTH$/i",
                              "Dr. Smith") . "\n";
```

Now you can look for spaces within your $query_text in *run_query.php* and avoid touching the input string at all, even temporarily:

```
$return_rows = true;
if (preg_match("/^ *(CREATE|INSERT|UPDATE|DELETE|DROP)/i",
               $query_text)) {
  $return_rows = false;
}
```

Back to Square One?

If I'm ignoring all the leading spaces, isn't that just the same as
`$location = strpos($query_text, "CREATE");`
and all its if-based brethren?

It might seem like all this regular expression work has brought you back to where you began: a search for CREATE or INSERT or UPDATE anywhere within $query_text, but you're worlds away from all those `if` statements. First, to restate the obvious, you have a script that you should be happy to show any of your programmer friends. You've used regular expressions, and used them well, so you don't have a shoebox of conditions to sort through.

Second, your code is more sensible. It starts with the presumption that you'll return rows. Then, based on a condition, it might change that presumption. This is natural human logic: start one way, if something else is going on, go another way. That's a lot better than the sort of backward-logic of your earlier version of *run_query.php*.

Most important, you're still not searching anywhere within $query_text for those SQL keywords. You're searching anywhere within the string beginning with *the first non-space character*. For example, the following query still comes across as a SELECT and isn't mistaken for a DROP:

```
SELECT *
  FROM registrar_activities
 WHERE name = 'Update GPA'
    OR name = 'Drop a class'
```

And you did it without a lot of messy and obscure hard-to-read code. (Well, it might be a little tricky for your friends still scared off by regular expressions. But, now you can teach them what's up, and that's a good thing, too.)

Searching for Sets of Characters

Now that you've taken care of leading spaces, you need to handle what your user types regardless of case and extra line breaks, like the example in Figure 6-2. Not only is there questionable use of the Shift key, there might also be leading spaces. But even if there isn't leading space, there's something else here: a return. Your clever, endearing users have done something you'd probably never think about: They pressed Enter a few times before typing in their SQL.

Your regular expression might not handle the query in Figure 6-2 as a DROP, despite you handling leading spaces and issues with capitalization. That's because Enter produces some special characters, usually either \n, or in some situations, \r\n, or, just to keep things interesting, occasionally just \r.

> **NOTE** These are all just varying flavors of new lines. \n is called the *line feed character*, and \r is called a *carriage return*. In general, Windows uses \r\n, Unix and Linux use \n, and Macs (in particular, older, pre-OS X Macs) use \r.

Fortunately, there aren't nearly as many cross-system problems with these characters as there were just a few years ago. You can pretty safely use \n to create a new line, but when you search, you need to account for all the variations.

FIGURE 6-2

This innocent-looking query has some lurking problems, at least with your regular expression as it currently stands. Can you see what they are? There might be leading spaces—you can't tell by looking at this screen image, or even if you were looking at an actual browser. There might also be leading line breaks, as with this case in which the SQL starts below the top of the text field.

So, what can you do? Well, it's easy to account for multiple characters like this: the regular expression \n* will match any number of new lines, and \r* will match any number of carriage returns. But what about \r\n? \r*\n* would match that, but what about spaces? You could do \r*\n* * and match Enter followed by spaces, but if you start to think about spaces and then Enters and then more spaces...and more Enters...(you get the idea).

Of course, the whole point of regular expressions is to get away from that sort of thing. To do so, you search for *any* of a set of characters. That's really what you want: accept any number (including zero) of any of a set of characters, a \r, a \n, or a space. You don't care how many appear, or in what order, either.

You could do something like (\r|\n|)*, which is using the | to represent "or" again, and then the * applies to the entire group. But when you're dealing with just single characters, you can skip the | and just put all the allowed characters into a set, which is indicated by square brackets ([and]), as demonstrated here:

```
$return_rows = true;
if (preg_match("/^[ \t\r\n]*(CREATE|INSERT|UPDATE|DELETE|DROP)/i",
               $query_text)) {
  $return_rows = false;
}
```

This code handles spaces, the two flavors of new lines, and tosses in \t for tab characters. No matter how many leading spaces, tabs, or new lines there are, your regular expression is happy to handle them. In fact, this sort of whitespace matching is so common that regular expressions can use \s as an abbreviation for [\t\r\n]. And, you can simplify things even further:

```
$return_rows = true;
if (preg_match("/^\s*(CREATE|INSERT|UPDATE|DELETE|DROP)/i",
                $query_text)) {
  $return_rows = false;
}
```

Try this out. Enter the SQL shown back in Figure 6-2 and submit your query. You'll probably get something similar to Figure 6-3, which means you're not done yet. The problem here isn't your regular expression. It's really that you're trying to pass into mysql_query some queries that haven't been screened much for problems—like all those extra \r\ns at the beginning.

FIGURE 6-3

Just as you're getting your regular expression and search code bulletproof, there's a new error to deal with. This error occurs before your search ever runs. But it definitely shows a problem: mysql_query *did not seem to like those leading* \r\n *sequences.*

In fact, there are *lots* of queries that will create problems for *run_query.php*, regardless of how clean your regular expression code is. Try entering this query:

```
SELECT *
  FROM urls
 WHERE description = 'home page'
```

That might seem simple enough, but it's still going to break your script. It doesn't matter whether you have anything in the *urls* table; you'll still get an error, as shown in Figure 6-4.

FIGURE 6-4

Don't be misled by this error. You do not have an error in your SQL; you have some overly-simplistic code in your script. No worries, though, with a good base of regular expressions under your belt, you're ready to tackle more robust PHP and MySQL integration.

Frankly, you could spend weeks writing all the code required to handle every possible SQL query, make sure the right things are accepted and the wrong ones aren't, and to handle all the various types of queries.

But that's not a good idea. Just taking in any old SQL query is, in fact, a *very* bad idea. What's a much better idea is to take a step back and think about what your users really need. It's probably not a blank form, and so in the next chapter, you'll give them what they need: a normal web form that just happens to talk to MySQL on the back end.

Regular Expressions: To Infinity and Beyond

It's not an over-exaggeration to say you've just barely scratched the surface of regular expressions. Although you have a strong grasp of the basics—from matching to ^ and $ and the various flavors of preg_match, from position and whitespace to + and * and sets—there are more than a few trees that have sacrificed themselves to produce all the paper out there with text on regular expressions.

But don't be freaked out or daunted, and don't think you have to stop working your PHP and MySQL skills until you've mastered regular expressions. First, mastery is elusive, and even the best regular expression programmers use Google to refresh their memories on how to get just the right sequence of characters within their slashes. Just be on the lookout for chances to use regular expressions. And, as you get better at PHP, you'll use them more often, and they'll slowly become as familiar to you as PHP, or HTML, or any of the other things you've been doing over and over.

Regular Expressions Aren't Just for PHP

As you're probably seeing, it does take some work to get very far with regular expressions. There are lots of weird characters both to find on your keyboard, and to work into your expressions. Without a doubt, it doesn't take long for a regular expression to start to look like something QBert might say: *SD)!!@8#.

But, the work rewards you in more ways than you might realize. For instance, JavaScript has complete support for regular expressions, too. Methods like `replace()` in JavaScript take in regular expressions, as do the `match()` methods on strings. So, everything you've learned in PHP translates over, perfectly.

You also get some nice benefits in HTML5. You can use regular expressions in an HTML5 form to provide patterns against which data is validated. Take heart; this work in PHP is helping you out in almost every aspect of web programming.

In fact, there's hardly a serious programming language that doesn't support regular expressions. If you decide to learn Ruby and Ruby on Rails, you'll be swimming in regular expressions, and they're also hugely helpful as you move into using testing frameworks like Cucumber or Capybara or TestUnit. If all that sounds intimidating, relax! You've got regular expressions down, even before you've learned what lots of these languages are.

The moral of this story? What you're learning about SQL applies to more than MySQL, and what you're learning about regular expressions applies to more than PHP. Your skills are growing; use them!

A Little Cleanup: Remove the echo Statements

Before moving on, there's just one last thing you need to take care of. Right now, your *database_connection.php* script should look like this:

```php
<?php
  require 'app_config.php';

  mysql_connect(DATABASE_HOST, DATABASE_USERNAME, DATABASE_PASSWORD)
    or die("<p>Error connecting to database: " .
         mysql_error() . "</p>");

  echo "<p>Connected to MySQL!</p>";

  mysql_select_db(DATABASE_NAME)
    or die("<p>Error selecting the database " .
         DATABASE_NAME . mysql_error() . "</p>");

  echo "<p>Connected to MySQL, using database " .
      DATABASE_NAME . ".</p>";
?>
```

There's nothing wrong here, and it's quite informative with those echo statements. But, in the next chapter and beyond, you're going to start responding in your PHP scripts by using HTML rather than plain old text. As you'll soon see, your PHP will *usually* send back HTML when its called and interpreted.

Now, when your scripts respond with HTML, and they require or include *database_connection.php*, you really don't want those echo statements. They'll show up before your script's HTML, and generally look like either debugging information or a programming error. So, go ahead and get rid of those. When you're done, *database_connection.php* should look like this:

```php
<?php
require 'app_config.php';

mysql_connect(DATABASE_HOST, DATABASE_USERNAME, DATABASE_PASSWORD)
  or die("<p>Error connecting to database: " .
        mysql_error() . "</p>");

mysql_select_db(DATABASE_NAME)
  or die("<p>Error selecting the database " .
        DATABASE_NAME . mysql_error() . "</p>");
?>
```

NOTE To keep things clear, the examples for this chapter use the older version of *database_connection.php*, which has all the echo statements. That way, if you're following along, your response will look like the figures in this chapter.

Beginning in Chapter 7, though, these changes will be in *database_connection.php*, both within the chapter and in the downloadable examples. You'll need to make these changes in your own version so that your output matches the book's going forward.

Generating Dynamic Web Pages

You've been building up quite a robust set of tools. You have PHP scripts to receive requests from your HTML forms. You have MySQL to store information from your users. You have regular expressions to massage information into just the formats you need, and some basic flow controls in PHP like if and for to let you build scripts that make decisions based on what information your users give you.

But, at the end of the day, your goal in learning PHP and MySQL was probably to make dynamic and interesting web applications. Unfortunately, you've not done much of that yet. You do have a few interesting forms, but even those are simple: take in some information; print it back out; accept a SQL query (and do that quite imperfectly). So, where are the web applications? Heck, where are the pages that are built dynamically using your user's information?

Thankfully, you have everything you need to start building these kinds of web pages. You can get information from your users, store it in a database, and even do some basic data manipulation. All you need to do now is put it all together and create the basic web pages that most users expect: a place to enter their information, a place to look at their information, and in most cases, a place to look at all the related user's information.

Revisiting a User's Information

In Chapter 3, on page 62, you built a form in which users can enter their basic social media profile: a Twitter handle, a Facebook URL, and some basic contact information. As shown in Figure 7-1, it's a perfectly good form: simple and easy to use.

FIGURE 7-1

You can design forms that interact and submit to PHP scripts the same way you create any other web page: you use HTML and CSS to create a clean, easy-to-understand page. Then, get users to visit your page, fill out fields, and click buttons. It's the behind-the-scenes work that brings PHP and MySQL into the picture.

There's really no reason to change this form. However, the script that accepts its information is pretty lame. It does nothing more than manipulate some text and then send that text back (see Figure 7-2). It doesn't even save the form's information for later use. That's where the work is: making the script *do something* with the user's information.

Getting from a simple form on the Web to a script that interacts with a database involves a surprising amount of work. You need to figure out, design, and create tables, interact with those tables, potentially deal with errors from your database, and so on.

> **NOTE** If you haven't done so already, copy the HTML web form (page 62) to the directory in which you're working. You can leave the file named as it is, but you might want to rename it as *create_user.html*. For reasons you'll see soon, this little change can really pay off as your site grows more complex.

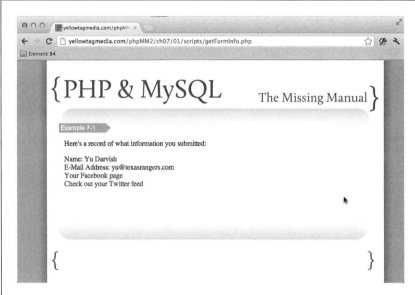

FIGURE 7-2

This HTML is generated by your old getFormInfo. php script (page 64). It's uninspiring, and you can do a lot better. Even more frustrating, this information is never stored anywhere. Once your user moves on, his information is lost.

■ Planning Your Database Tables

Building web applications is a lot like working a tricky maze: Sometimes the hardest part is figuring out where to start. Usually a web form needs a script to which it can submit data. That script needs a table into which it can insert and store information. But, where's the table? In a MySQL database, you need to create or set up tables for web access. Of course, the table itself needs structure. That's the way almost every form of every application goes: What starts out as a page that users see often ends up at a back-end structure that's invisible to everyone but you, the programmer.

It's always easiest to start with the information you want to store. You've actually already done some of this when you created your entry form (look back at Figure 7-1). Here's basically what you're collecting from your users right now:

- First name
- Last name

- Email address
- Facebook URL

- Twitter handle

Each of these items are individual components that when combined describe a single "entity"—a user. What you need, therefore, is a table to store users, and for each user, you need to store a first name, last name, e-mail address, a Facebook URL, and a Twitter handle.

All you need to do now is to translate this into a SQL CREATE statement:

```
CREATE TABLE users (
        user_id int,
        first_name varchar(20),
        last_name varchar(30),
        email varchar(50),
        facebook_url varchar(100),
        twitter_handle varchar(20)
);
```

WARNING You might not want to dive into your MySQL command-line tool or your web form and run this command just yet. There are some important additions still to be made before it's ready for prime time.

You might remember this SQL from Chapter 4, but that was ages ago, when you had but a fragile understanding of databases. Now, you know exactly what is going to be dropped into this table: information from the web form that you already have.

UP TO SPEED

One of These Things *Is* Like the Other

You'll quickly find that when you start talking with database people, there are a lot of interchangeable terms.

A table has rows, and each entry in that table is a row. But you'll also hear a row called an *entry* in the table as well as a *record*. These are really all the same thing, and even though it might be technically better to say a table has rows rather than entries or records, you can't guarantee that people will actually use those terms.

In the same vein, the *fields* in a table, like first_name or last_name, are also called *columns*. In those fields (or columns), you have *values*, or information, or for the technically stodgy, *data*. Lots of different terms, all with identical meaning.

Although you'll have to identify all these different terms, you can help matters a bit by not mixing and matching if you don't have to. Thus, a table that has rows usually has columns; a table with records usually has fields. Rows and columns go together; so do records and fields.

That said, even though you might want to try to be completely consistent—always using rows instead of records, and columns instead of fields—you'll invariably find yourself using all these same terms yourself.

Perhaps the best thing to remember here is that like any other bit of language, context is king. It's more important that you know what's an int and what's not than to be sure you say row instead of record. And, you need to not get mixed up on a complete entry (see; there's another term for record or row) and the individual *parts* of that entry. Just remember that a single entry, record, or row in the users table has multiple fields, columns, or pieces of information. Get that right, and you can solve the rest by listening carefully and asking the occasional question to clarify.

Good Database Tables Have ID Columns

Take a look at the first column created for this table: the user_id field. What exactly is that? Well, think about the most common thing you'll do with databases. Is it creating new entries in the table? Probably not. Honestly, if you think about how often you create a user ID or profile on the Web versus the number of times you log in to a site, you log in many, many more times.

In other words, you're creating information once for every ten, or twenty, or maybe one hundred times that you're *accessing* that information. That's a case where you're looking up information; you're searching for a user (usually yourself).

Of course, that then begs the question: How do you search for something? You can look things up by a last name and then find matching entries. Or, you can search by an email address or Twitter handle, which are supposed to be unique for each user. In fact, you've probably often had to create a user name that is unique (typically at great pain; who really takes all those normal user names and leaves you stuck with *m97f-ss0*, anyhow?).

Databases are no different in that they need something for which to look. Moreover, databases work best when they can identify every individual row in a table by a unique piece of information. Putting it more accurately still, databases function better with numbers than with text. The absolute preferred type of unique identifier—or ID—for a row in a table is a unique number.

That, then, is what user_id is about. It's a numerical value for each row that uniquely, identifies that row. It identifies each user as separate from all others, so your database can locate it, every time.

Auto Increment Is Your Friend

There's a bit of a problem lurking in the SQL bushes here, though. If the point of the user_id field is to provide a unique identifier for each user, whose job is it to keep up with that unique ID? How do all the scripts (and there will be more than one or two before you're done with any large web application) ensure that no two users are entered into the *users* table with the same user_id? Do you need yet another table just to keep up with the current count of users?

This isn't a trivial problem, because if you lose the ability to uniquely identify a user, things can go south from there quickly. On the other hand, nobody wants to spend hours writing number generators for every table or every web application.

The solution is not in your code, but in your database. Most databases, MySQL included, give you the ability to use an attribute called AUTO_INCREMENT. You specify this on a field in a table, and every time you add a row to that table, the field automatically creates a new number, incremented from the last row that was added to the table. For example, if one script adds a new user and MySQL sets the user_id to 1029, and another script later adds a new user, MySQL increments the previous number and assigns 1030 as the ID of the new user.

You can add this to your table CREATE statement like this:

```
CREATE TABLE users (
        user_id int AUTO_INCREMENT,
        first_name varchar(20),
        last_name varchar(30),
        email varchar(50),
```

```
        facebook_url varchar(100),
        twitter_handle varchar(20)
);
```

Much better. Now, you don't have to worry about IDs. In fact, you don't have to do anything special to let MySQL know to fill in the user_id column. Every time you add a new row, just trust that MySQL will also add a new value to user_id.

■ IDS AND PRIMARY KEYS ARE GOOD BEDFELLOWS

In addition to setting user_id to increment automatically, you've actually done something else subtly in MySQL: you've basically defined user_id as the *primary key* in the users table. The primary key is a database term for that special, unique value assigned to a particular row in a table.

> **NOTE** In some rather special cases, you might create a primary key out of multiple columns instead of just one. That's somewhat unusual, though, and it's not covered in this book.

Primary keys are important because databases typically create an *index* using a table's primary key. An index is a database-level mechanism by which a database can find rows based on that index quickly. With the user_id column indexed, you can find a row with a user_id of 2048 much faster than looking for a row with that same user_id, but on a table where user_id is *not* indexed.

Basically, an indexed field is like having a highly organized set of values. An unindexed field can still be searched, but in that case your database has to go through each value, one by one, until it finds the exact value for which you're searching. It's the difference between looking for a book in a well-organized library and looking for one in your great-great-grandfather's deserted attic.

When you instruct MySQL to automatically increment user_id, you identify that field as special. In fact, MySQL won't let you set more than one field to AUTO_INCREMENT, because it assumes that you put that on a field to use as a primary key.

There's just a little hitch, though: you have to instruct MySQL that you want user_id to be the primary key, by including the following:

```
CREATE TABLE users (
        user_id int AUTO_INCREMENT PRIMARY KEY,
        first_name varchar(20),
        last_name varchar(30),
        email varchar(50),
        facebook_url varchar(100),
        twitter_handle varchar(20)
);
```

This makes explicit what is implicit with AUTO_INCREMENT: user_id uniquely identifies each user entry in your table. In fact, if you don't do this, MySQL gives you an error. As an example, suppose that you have the following SQL, without the PRIMARY KEY keyword:

```
CREATE TABLE users (
    user_id int AUTO_INCREMENT,
    first_name varchar(20),
    last_name varchar(30),
    email varchar(50),
    facebook_url varchar(100),
    twitter_handle varchar(20)
);
```

If you were to run this query, MySQL would give you a bit of a weird error in the phpMyAdmin console, as illustrated in; Figure 7-3.

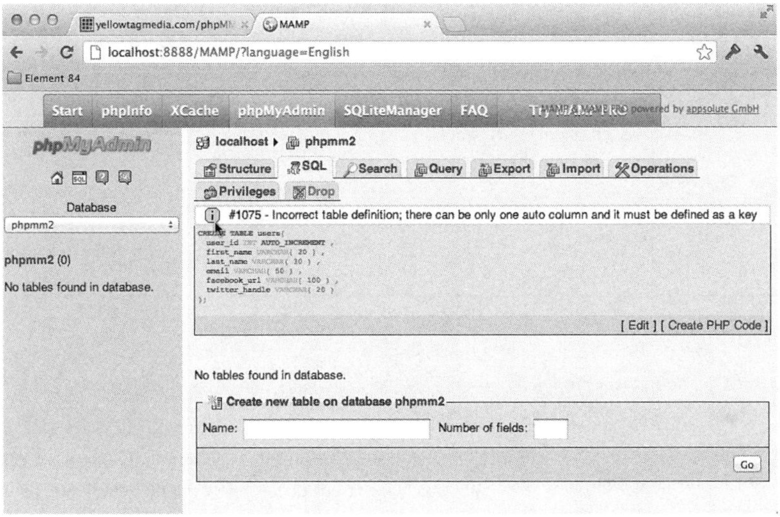

FIGURE 7-3

phpMyAdmin is a great tool for running queries. It clearly indicates where you're going wrong, as with this example, in which you left out the primary key in your CREATE statement. You can avoid spending lots of time in a text-based tool, you can browse your tables visually, and best of all, most web hosting companies that provide MySQL and database services offer phpMyAdmin. That means if you learn it on one host, you'll still (most likely) be able to use the same tool on another host.

This error—the infamous #1075 if you've been around MySQL for long—informs you that since you have an AUTO_INCREMENT column that you need to mark as PRIMARY KEY. It would be nice if MySQL would take care of that for you, but alas, it's up to you, so be sure to include PRIMARY KEY. At this point, you're *almost* ready to create this table for real.

Adding Constraints to Your Database

Remember that the purpose of a field like user_id is to facilitate easy searching. Adding AUTO_INCREMENT (and setting the field as a primary key) helps in that, but there's something subtle that also happens behind the scenes when you create an AUTO_INCREMENT column. You are also saying, "No matter what, this column will have a value." That's because MySQL is filling in that value.

More than likely, there are additional fields that you almost always want to be filled in. For example, there's really never a good time to let a user not put in her first or last name. And you should probably require an email address, too. Twitter handles and Facebook URLs are not always going to be attached to a user, so those can be left off, but the rest is mandatory.

Of course, could just decide to have your PHP scripts and web pages deal with requiring this information. But is that really safe? What if someone else forgets to add validation on a web page? What if *you* forget, writing code on a coffee-high one day, typing away at 2 a.m.? It's never a good idea to *not* validate when you *can* validate.

Again, MySQL has what you need. You can require a value on a field by instructing MySQL that field can't be *null* (which is programmer-talk for "not a value"):

```
CREATE TABLE users (
    user_id int NOT NULL AUTO_INCREMENT PRIMARY KEY,
    first_name varchar(20) NOT NULL,
    last_name varchar(30) NOT NULL,
    email varchar(50) NOT NULL,
    facebook_url varchar(100),
    twitter_handle varchar(20)
);
```

DESIGN TIME

To Null or Not to Null

Although the *users* table makes figuring out which columns should be NOT NULL fairly easy, that's not always (or often) the case. In fact, even with *users*, there's ambiguity: are you sure you want to require an email address? It is possible that someone might not have one (it still happens, although why email-less folks would be surfing the Internet might be quite a mystery), or you might have users concerned with you spamming them, and they don't want to enter an email. Are you *sure* that you want to require that as part of a user's information?

It might surprise you, but making a column NOT NULL is one of the most important decisions you make with regard to an individual table. This is particularly true if you decide *not* to make a column NOT NULL. Every record added might have a null value there, and if you decide down the line, "Oops, I really did need that value," you're stuck for all the old entries that don't have it. You can't ever un-ring that bell.

However, don't get too trigger-happy with NOT NULL, thinking that it's just safer to use it frequently and grab more data rather than less. Users can become upset if they're forced to fill out 28 fields just to use your site. Even mega-sites like Facebook and Twitter require only minimal information: usually

a name, email, user name, and password. Everything else can be added later.

In general, the rule of thumb is to require only what you absolutely need; but to absolutely require that information. That's a tongue-twister, but a useful one. Think carefully, make a decision, and then realize that you'll always upset someone. Your goal is to please most of your users, most of the time; if you can pull that off while still getting the information from them that you need, you're well on your way to Web stardom and Internet fame.

And one last subtle bit of advice: you're working at the table level with NOT NULL, not the application level. In other words, you're essentially saying, "This column can't be null *if (and only if) there's an entry in this table.*" You might decide that users don't have to enter an address (so it's not required they have an entry in a mythical addresses table), but *if* they enter an address, it should also be required that they enter the street, city, and country. Thinking along these lines—what data is essential for this particular table, rather than your entire app—will help you lock down your database with good, useful data, and still not go crazy with NOT NULL.

NOTE Even though MySQL handles auto incrementing and inserting values into user_id, it's still a good idea to make it NOT NULL. That makes it clear that the value in that column is required, regardless of how MySQL or any other code actually fills that value. For more detail, see the box on page 180.

Like AUTO_INCREMENT, this change is quick, easy, and goes a long way toward protecting the integrity of your information (or, to be more accurate, your user's information).

You should have a useful SQL statement, so go ahead and create your *users* table. Log in to MySQL by using your command-line tool, the web form you built earlier, or another web tool like phpMyAdmin, and create the table. You're about to need it.

WARNING You might need to DROP a previous version of the table. You can simply use DROP TABLE users; if you get an error trying to create the table. That should clear out any existing version of the table that might exist. Also, remember to ensure that you're in the right database when you run your CREATE statement!

If you're using a tool like phpMyAdmin, you can now view your created table. It should look something like Figure 7-4.

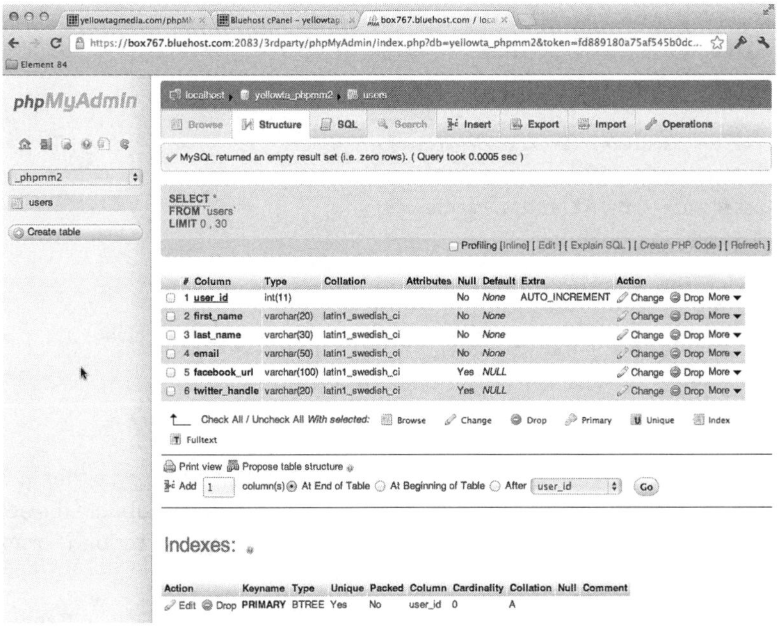

FIGURE 7-4

Ask your web hosting provider if it provides access to phpMyAdmin. Its GUI is a lot friendlier than the mysql *console tool, and it lets you view tables, like the users table you should by now have created.*

■ Saving a User's Information

You've had a table before, and now you've got a version of the *users* table that's a little sturdier, with AUTO_INCREMENT and validation of values in a few key fields. Plus, your web form grabs just the information you need to stuff into that table. All that's left is tying these things together via PHP, and you actually have almost everything you need for that, too.

You can start with a new script or use your old version of *getFormInfo.php* as a starting point. Either way, your first task is to capture the user's entered information and do a little text manipulation to get the values just the way you want them:

```php
<?php

$first_name = trim($_REQUEST['first_name']);
$last_name = trim($_REQUEST['last_name']);
$email = trim($_REQUEST['email']);
$facebook_url = str_replace("facebook.org", "facebook.com", trim($_
REQUEST['facebook_url']));
$position = strpos($facebook_url, "facebook.com");
if ($position === false) {
  $facebook_url = "http://www.facebook.com/" . $facebook_url;
}

$twitter_handle = trim($_REQUEST['twitter_handle']);
$twitter_url = "http://www.twitter.com/";
$position = strpos($twitter_handle, "@");
if ($position === false) {
  $twitter_url = $twitter_url . $twitter_handle;
} else {
  $twitter_url = $twitter_url . substr($twitter_handle, $position + 1);
}

?>
```

Call this script *create_user.php* and save it in your *scripts/* directory, either in your site root or under your *ch07/* examples directory. You should also update the action the form for *create_user.html* form to submit this newly named script. (For more information on naming, see the box on page 183.)

This is the kind of code you've written before, and because you haven't changed your form, it still works perfectly well. Now, you just need to update it so it stores this information in your new *users* table.

> **NOTE** For some extra credit, see if you can convert *create_user.php* to use regular expressions instead of the strpos function to update these variables. If you think you've whipped things into great shape, tweet a link to your code to *@missingmanuals* and see what cool swag you might win.

Name Follows Function

When you have a few web pages here and there, names are really not that big of a deal. Whether you name a page *get-FormInfo.html* or *create_user.html* is almost irrelevant; you can see all your files in a single directory listing or window of your FTP client.

But, even with medium-sized web apps, you'll have a lot more files than that. In fact, if you start to do the testing that you absolutely should be doing, you can easily have hundreds of files. At that point, your names really need to be meaningful.

But there's more to meaning than just description. Many of your forms and scripts are going to map and work directly with a single table in your database, and do one particular thing

with regard to that table, such as creating a user via the *users* table. In these cases, you make it really easy on yourself and others who'll work on your code by naming your files after that functionality. This means that even though your form might get a user's social information, it ultimately creates a user; thus, *create_user.php* is a descriptive, simple, clear name.

On top of all that, you'll soon be learning about the three basic actions you can take on information: create it, update it, and delete it. Mapping your HTML pages and scripts to those basic actions (*create_user*, *update_user*, and so on) really helps you see what you have and what you don't.

Building Your SQL Query

Your goal with the *create_user.php* script for it to collect contact information from visitors to your site and store that information in the *users* table. First, you can use your existing database connection script to make connecting easy:

```php
<?php

require '../../scripts/database_connection.php';

// Get the user's information from the request into variables

?>
```

> **WARNING**   You might have some echo statements left in *database_connection.php* from an earlier version of the examples. If you do, go ahead and remove those now so that they won't disrupt the seamless experience you'll be giving your users.

With a database connection ready for use, you need to turn all that information into the INSERT statement so that you can drop the information into your database.

Rather than just diving into your code, though, start with a sample statement. For example, pick a set of random values (maybe your own), and build up the SQL you want.

```
INSERT INTO users (first_name,
                   last_name,
                   email,
                   facebook_url,
                   twitter_handle)
           VALUES ("Brett",
                   "McLaughlin",
                   "brett.m@me.com",
                   "http://www.facebook.com/bdmclaughlin",
                   "@bdmclaughlin");
```

> **NOTE** You can even use your MySQL tools (page 179) to test this SQL out until it works and is formatted just as you need it.

This statement now becomes sort of a template in the respect that you want to use this statement, but you need to replace your sample values with your user's request information. Given that you already have those values, this actually isn't too hard:

```
$insert_sql = "INSERT INTO users (first_name, last_name, " .
                     "email, facebook_url, twitter_handle) " .
              "VALUES ('{$first_name}', '{$last_name}', '{$email}', " .
                     "'{$facebook_url}', '{$twitter_handle}');";
```

> **WARNING** There is some real danger in your code at this point. The data you're sending in your INSERT statement is not being escaped. (For a refresher on what escape characters are and how to use them see the box on page 158.) This means that some nasty things could get into your database. You'll clean that up in a few chapters using mysql_real_escape_string, but for now, it's not the greatest and most secure code.
>
> Getting into mysql_real_escape_string at this point is just going to cloud things up. So, use this code, but don't go putting it into your million-user ordering system just yet. Just keep working through the chapters, and you'll lock this code down a lot better really soon.

The one gotcha here is that you must ensure that each value you're sending to the database—which will eventually go into a text field in the *users* table—must be surrounded by quotes. Using single quotes lets you use double quotes around the entire query. It also lets you use curly braces ({ and }) to drop your variables right into the query string.

Inserting a User

In the previous section, you created a new string that includes the SQL query. Now, you can pass the $insert_sql query to mysql_query and run it against your database. This is the easiest (and often the most fun) line of SQL-invoking PHP to write:

```php
<?php

// Handle user request

$insert_sql = "INSERT INTO users (first_name, last_name, email, " .
                        "facebook_url, twitter_handle) " .
              "VALUES ('{$first_name}', '{$last_name}', '{$email}', " .
                      "'{$facebook_url}', '{$twitter_handle}');";

// Insert the user into the database
mysql_query($insert_sql);

?>
```

Unfortunately, this code doesn't do anything in the event of an error—and there are a lot of things that can go wrong. What if the database reports an error? What if you forgot to add the *users* table first? What if you have a *users* table, but without a facebook_url column, or it has a misnamed or misspelled column?

There's really a lot of work to do when it comes to error reporting, but for now, take a really simple (and probably way too simple) approach. Add a die statement, like the one you saw in Chapter 5, on page 125:

```php
<?php

// Handle user request

$insert_sql = "INSERT INTO users (first_name, last_name, email, facebook_url, twitter_handle) " .
              "VALUES ('{$first_name}', '{$last_name}', '{$email}', " .
                      "'{$facebook_url}', '{$twitter_handle}');";

// Insert the user into the database
mysql_query($insert_sql)
  or die(mysql_error());

?>
```

> **WARNING** Don't forget to remove the semicolon at the end of the mysql_query line when you add your die statement.

This solution is far from perfect, but it works, and it gives you some kind of report in case of error.

At this point, you can actually try out your page, albeit a little clumsily. Go ahead and visit your web page and fill out some sample values, as in Figure 7-5.

FIGURE 7-5

By now, you're probably getting tired of entering users. That's good—your create_user.html form is finally almost to the point where once you enter a user, that user is saved in the database. In fact, that happens here; now you just need a way to show that something happened, and deal with errors when they occur.

Submit your page to run the new code. It constructs a SQL statement using your values, connects to the database, and inserts the data by using `mysql_query`. Hopefully, your `die` statement *won't* run.

Assuming that you don't get an error, you'll get almost nothing back. That's rather disappointing, but something did happen—especially if you *didn't* get an error message.

NOTE If you still have the HTML section of *getFormInfo.php* copied into *create_user.php*, you might get back some output from your form submission.

The interest here is in what happened in your database. So, fire up a SQL tool and enter this query:

```
SELECT user_id, first_name, last_name
  FROM users;
```

Hopefully you get back something like this:

```
+---------+------------+-----------+
| user_id | first_name | last_name |
+---------+------------+-----------+
|       1 | Yu         | Darvish   |
+---------+------------+-----------+
1 row in set (0.00 sec)
```

If you want to use phpMyAdmin (page 55), you can browse to your *users* table and check out any data that might be inside of it, as shown in Figure 7-6.

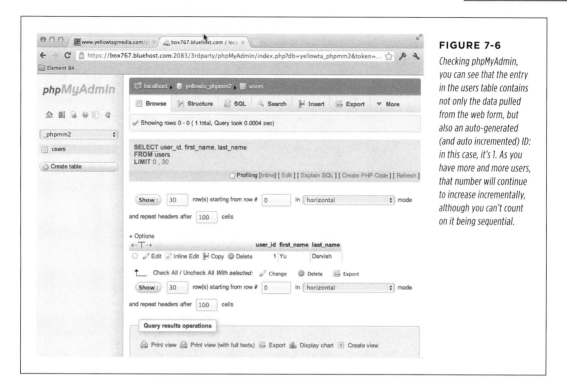

FIGURE 7-6

Checking phpMyAdmin, you can see that the entry in the users table contains not only the data pulled from the web form, but also an auto-generated (and auto incremented) ID: in this case, it's 1. As you have more and more users, that number will continue to increase incrementally, although you can't count on it being sequential.

A First Pass at Confirmation

So far, you've got your *create_user.html* page and a user (or many of them if you get cranking on your web form and enter more users) in your database, but your user—the person using your web application—sees nothing but a blank screen. That's not very helpful.

As a starting point, you can go back to the code from your older script, *get FormInfo.php*:

```php
<?php

// Get the user's information from the request array

// Connect to the database and insert the user

?>

<html>
 <head>
  <link href="../../css/phpMM.css" rel="stylesheet" type="text/css" />
```

```
  </head>
  <body>
   <div id="header"><h1>PHP & MySQL: The Missing Manual</h1></div>
   <div id="example">Example 6-1</div>
   <div id="content">
     <p>Here's a record of what information you submitted:</p>
     <p>
       Name: <?php echo $first_name . " " . $last_name; ?><br />
       E-Mail Address: <?php echo $email; ?><br />
       <a href="<?php echo $facebook_url; ?>">Your Facebook page</a>
       <br />
       <a href="<?php echo $twitter_url; ?>">Check out your Twitter feed</a>
       <br />
     </p>
   </div>

   <div id="footer"></div>
  </body>
 </html>
```

This is better than nothing, but there are some things you need to fix right off the bat. First, you're not printing out the user's Twitter handle; you're printing out the URL to his handle. Although that's probably more usable for clicking, it doesn't actually represent what was entered into the database. That leaves you with a tough choice:

- You can print out what was entered into the database, which is the value in $twitter_handle. That's what was actually inserted, but it doesn't have as much value in a web page, and it really is letting your users know what's in your database. But, is that what your users care about? Your database structure?

- You can print out the actual URL, which is better for clicking, but doesn't directly connect to what's in the database. It's a modification of the database value, which is OK, but might not be appropriate right on the heels of a form that is explicitly focused upon adding a user to the database.

All this may seem like a lot of fuss just for a Twitter handle. But the same issue comes up whether you show the first and last names or combine them together as this code does now:

```
Name: <?php echo $first_name . " " . $last_name; ?><br />
```

There's a deeper, bigger issue here: what exactly do you show your users with regard to data entered in the database? Do you show them the literal values as they're stored in the database, or do you show them values that are a little more massaged, a little more human-readable?

Users are Users, Not Programmers

The answer to that question is fairly simple: you *always* want to show your users things that make sense to them. Very rarely will someone care about the columns in your database, or what value is a primary key, or whether you store their Twitter handle with the @ sign, or without it. Therefore, you should *always* focus on what your users want to see, not what's literally and technically in your database. (Yes, that's two always-es in one paragraph.)

But, there's something else going on here: what is the *source* of the information you're showing? Implied in this idea of showing a user what makes sense to him is the idea that you, the wise programmer, take information from the database, work with it to get it into the right format, and then show that massaged information to the user.

In this first pass at a confirmation, are you showing what's in the database? Not at all; you're just sending back out what the user gave you. What if something did happen when that information was inserted into your database table? You'd never know it. By showing the user his own information, you could be masking what really was dropped into the database.

So, what do you do? You want to show users something that makes sense to them (there's that double-always again), but you also want to show those values based on the database, rather than just repeating a form, because that doesn't show any problems in the database.

Hopefully, you do both! How, though? Well, suppose you had a way to pull the user's information from the database, perhaps by using a SQL SELECT, and then based upon that information—information from the database, problems or not—construct something the user can see and read and that makes sense.

Here's one solution: After inserting the user, reload that same information, a bit like this:

```php
<?php

// Get the user's information from the request array

// Connect to the database and insert the user

$get_user_query = "SELECT * FROM USERS WHERE ..."
mysql_query($get_user_query)
  or die(mysql_error());

// Load this information and ready it for display in the HTML output

?>

<!-- HTML output -->
```

That query gets you the user from the database and it still lets you modify those values as needed for good, human-readable display. You'd have to figure out how to find the particular user who was just inserted, but that's something you'll soon be able to handle.

The issue is that you're doing a bunch of text manipulation on the request information, and then you need to do some of that again with the response from the database. Think about your application as a whole: Is there anywhere else you might want to display a user? Yes, absolutely. Every good application has a place where you can check out your own profile. If that's the case, you'd need to take the code in the back part of *create_user.php* and then copy it into a *show_user.php* script later. That's not good; remember, you really, *really* don't want the same code in more than one place. That's why you have the *database_connection.php* script that you can use over and over.

What you need is another script, one that shows user information. Then, you can simply throw users from *create_user.php*, which creates users, to this new script, and let it figure out what to do in terms of a response. So, leave *create_user.php* somewhat incomplete for now; you can come back and fix it later.

◼ Show Me the User

You need a page that shows a user's information in a way that makes sense to the user. This means that this page is going to pull information from the *users* table, but it's not a form; there's no need (at least, not yet) to do anything but display information. Most of the work here isn't code; it's getting a good user profile page built. You'll want to start with HTML.

Luckily, most web servers are configured to take a request for a file ending in *.php* and create HTML output, which is handed to a user's browser. As a result, you can create HTML, drop it into a file ending in *.php*, and when you start adding actual PHP, you're ready to go. Your web server will send the HTML in that file to a requesting web browser, and your user's (or you) see HTML output.

Creating a Mockup of a User Profile Page

Figure 7-7 shows a solid-looking profile page. It shows the basics of each user's contact information as well as a short bio and a picture of the user.

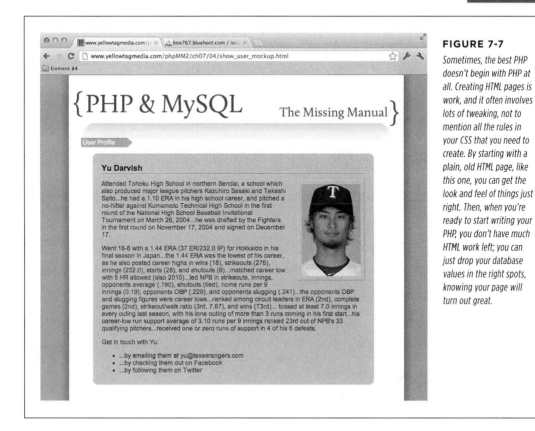

FIGURE 7-7

Sometimes, the best PHP doesn't begin with PHP at all. Creating HTML pages is work, and it often involves lots of tweaking, not to mention all the rules in your CSS that you need to create. By starting with a plain, old HTML page, like this one, you can get the look and feel of things just right. Then, when you're ready to start writing your PHP, you don't have much HTML work left; you can just drop your database values in the right spots, knowing your page will turn out great.

Here's the HTML for the page in Figure 7-7. Because of CSS, it stays pretty simple.

```html
<html>
 <head>
  <link href="../css/phpMM.css" rel="stylesheet" type="text/css" />
 </head>

 <body>
  <div id="header"><h1>PHP & MySQL: The Missing Manual</h1></div>
  <div id="example">User Profile</div>

  <div id="content">
    <div class="user_profile">
      <h1>Yu Darvish</h1>
      <p>
        <img src="../images/darvish.jpg" class="user_pic" />
```

Attended Tohoku High School in northern Sendai, a school
which also produced major league pitchers Kazuhiro Sasaki and Takashi
Saito...he had a 1.10 ERA in his high school career, and pitched a
no-hitter against Kumamoto Technical High School in the first round
of the National High School Baseball Invitational Tournament on
March 26, 2004...he was drafted by the Fighters in the first round
on November 17, 2004 and signed on December 17.</p>
        <p>Went 18-6 with a 1.44 ERA (37 ER/232.0 IP) for Hokkaido
in his final season in Japan...the 1.44 ERA was the lowest of his
career, as he also posted career highs in wins (18), strikeouts (276),
innings (232.0), starts (28), and shutouts (6)...matched career
low with 5 HR allowed (also 2010)...led NPB in strikeouts, innings,
opponents average (.190), shutouts (tied), home runs per 9
innings (0.19), opponents OBP (.229), and opponents
slugging (.241)...the opponents OBP and slugging figures were
career lows...ranked among circuit leaders in ERA (2nd), complete
games (2nd), strikeout/walk ratio (3rd, 7.67), and wins (T3rd)...
tossed at least 7.0 innings in every outing last season, with his
lone outing of more than 3 runs coming in his first start...his
career-low run support average of 3.10 runs per 9 innings ranked
23rd out of NPB's 33 qualifying pitchers...received one or zero
runs of support in 4 of his 6 defeats.</p>
        <p class="contact_info">Get in touch with Yu:</p>
        <ul>
        <li>...by emailing them at <a href="yu@texasrangers.com">yu@texasrang-
ers.com</a></li>
        <li>...by <a href="http://www.facebook.com/pages/Yu-
Darvish/55933782070">checking them out on Facebook</a></li>
        <li>...by <a href="http://www.twitter.com/YuDarTranslated">following
them on Twitter</a></li>
        </ul>
      </div>
    </div>

    <div id="footer"></div>
  </body>
</html>

> **NOTE** The bio and picture here are new, and not things that you would already have in your *users* table. They're just examples of what you might see on a user's profile page. Just a name and a few links for email and Twitter for this example was rather sparse.
>
> Don't worry, though. You'll be adding a profile picture and bio to your database soon, and then this page really will be something your app can display.

Even though this example is straightforward, what you need is really even simpler. Imagine (or type) this page without the placeholder text, but instead with variables in the place of the dummy text. For example, wherever the user's first name goes, envision $first_name, and then $last_name, $email, and so on. The result is clean:

> **WARNING** The HTML that follows is helpful to think through, but *it's not valid HTML or PHP*. Therefore, don't try to view this in a browser. Still, this example lets you see that almost everything on the page really just represents information in the database, all in a user-friendly format.

```html
<html>
 <head>
  <link href="../css/phpMM.css" rel="stylesheet" type="text/css" />
 </head>

 <body>
  <div id="header"><h1>PHP & MySQL: The Missing Manual</h1></div>
  <div id="example">User Profile</div>

  <div id="content">
    <div class="user_profile">
      <h1>$first_name $last_name</h1>
      <p><img src="$user_image" class="user_pic" />
        $bio</p>
      <p class="contact_info">Get in touch with $first_name:</p>
      <ul>
        <li>...by emailing them at
          <a href="$email">$email</a></li>
        <li>...by
          <a href="$facebook_url">checking them out on Facebook</a></li>
        <li>...by <a href="$twitter_url">following them on Twitter</a></li>
      </ul>
    </div>
  </div>

  <div id="footer"></div>
 </body>
</html>
```

But, wait a second...your *users* table doesn't have a bio ($bio), or a picture ($user_image)! In fact, that's exactly why it's a good idea to focus on your HTML first, rather than diving right into PHP. When you begin designing your page, you think about what you need.

Imagine this page with nothing more than a name and some contact links. What a bore for your users, as well as you. With this simple mockup, you've figured out several important things:

1. **You're missing some key information in your *users* table.** You'd like to have a bio, which is just a long chunk of text, and a way to load an image of the user.

2. **Once you update your table, you need to update your *create_user.html* and *create_user.php* form and code to let users enter that information, and then save the new information to your database.**

3. **Finally—and this is great news—with those changes, you can build a pretty nice-looking user profile page.**

The question now is, what do you do first? Well, the database is usually the center-piece of things, so you have to update your *users* table.

Changing a Table's Structure by Using ALTER

There are two pieces of information missing from *users*: a bio and an image. For now, leave the image thing alone. That takes a little bit of work, and you can always drop a placeholder in and come back to that. The bio, however, is easy.

First, you need to change your table's structure by adding a new column. That's not hard at all; the SQL ALTER command lets you do just that:

```
ALTER TABLE users
        ADD bio varchar(1000);
```

WARNING Be sure you type ALTER and not ALTAR; the first is a SQL command, and the second is where you sacrifice things, if you're so inclined. Either way, ALTAR will definitely not get your table in the shape you want.

This statement is as simple as it looks. You provide SQL with the name of the table to ALTER, and then specify how you want to alter it. In this case, you want to add a column, so you use ADD to give it the new column name and a type.

Of course, there are implications here:

• **Is it okay for a user to leave a biography blank, or should the bio column be NOT NULL?** It's probably okay if it's left blank, so NOT NULL really isn't required.

• **How in the world does information get into this column for new users?** For that, you need to update your *create_user* HTML web form as well as the script that does the database work. That's up next.

• **Can you alter a table any time you want?** Yes! That's the beauty of databases. They're pretty flexible.

Slugging in a Column

What happens to the old rows in a table when a new column is added?

Although it's easy to add a column to a database by using ALTER, and it's simple to update your forms to let your users get information into those columns (and show the results, if you've got a *show_user* script), there's something left that can be a pain: dealing with old data that suddenly has a new column.

Consider the *users* table. Imagine that it didn't have just one or two recent entries, but thousands of users from the past five years. As a result of your alteration, every one of those users has a glaring empty spot: the bio. Most databases happily leave the column blank, meaning you'll get NULL every time you try and pull something out of the new `bio` column.

In this case, adding the bio column isn't a big deal. In fact, you could probably call user bios a "new feature," throw together a press release, and tout the oversight as a brand new version, improved and usable by a whole new generation of bio-loving potential users. Existing users can log in and add a bio; this is exciting stuff!

What's not exciting is when you're adding a column that's required. Remember when your favorite site realized that using an email address as a user name wasn't always a great idea? They probably altered their tables, adding a user name

column, but had to make it NOT NULL. After all, the whole point of a user name is that each user has one.

In that case, you really do have a legitimate problem: you now have tons of rows that are missing required data. What do you do? Well, you can simply lock those users out, and the next time they try to access your site, build a mechanism that forces them to select a user name. That's typical, and even expected in these security-conscious days of the Web. But, what if that's not tenable? You're letting all those rows be in an invalid state until a user logs in.

If that's a problem—and it often is—you might need to insert some sort of placeholder data into your table, like "NEEDS_USERNAME", and then query the user to check whether that's her user name value when she does come back to your site. It's not the most elegant solution, but it keeps your data valid. Ultimately, the big issue with using ALTER is that you potentially end up with data in an invalid state for some amount of time, or you have to insert placeholder data to keep things running, although you know that data can't ultimately stay put. Neither solution is perfect, so you have to choose the lesser of these two evils. (Or, come up with something else altogether, and let us know by tweeting us at *@missingmanuals*. We'd love to hear what you come up with.)

NOTE   You'll deal with the user image later in this chapter. There's a lot to be said about image handling, and where to store images, so for now you can plan on having an image—and leave a spot for it in your web page and script—and just know that you'll add that later.

Building Your Script: First Pass

With the bio column in *users*, and an HTML mockup complete, you're ready to get down to the business of PHP. Create a new script and call it *show_user.php*. This goes along nicely with *create_user.php*, and you can probably already imagine you'll later add scripts like *delete_user.php* and *update_user.php* to complete the package.

At the outset, you don't need any PHP in this script at all. Instead, just drop in your HTML. Then, as you did earlier, you can replace all the instances where there will be information from the database with PHP variable names. What you end up with is shown in the code that follows.

```
<html>
 <head>
  <link href="../../css/phpMM.css" rel="stylesheet" type="text/css" />
 </head>

 <body>
  <div id="header"><h1>PHP & MySQL: The Missing Manual</h1></div>
  <div id="example">User Profile</div>

  <div id="content">
    <div class="user_profile">
      <h1>$first_name $last_name</h1>
      <p><img src="$user_image" class="user_pic" />
        $bio</p>
      <p class="contact_info">Get in touch with $first_name:</p>
      <ul>
        <li>...by emailing them at
          <a href="$email">$email</a></li>
        <li>...by
          <a href="$facebook_url">checking them out on Facebook</a></li>
        <li>...by <a href="$twitter_url">following them on Twitter</a></li>
      </ul>
    </div>
  </div>
  <div id="footer"></div>
 </body>
</html>
```

NOTE Remember, save this with a *.php* extension in your *scripts/* directory. That might be *ch07/scripts/* if you're using the book's structure, or just your website's *scripts/* directory if you're putting all your PHP from all the chapters in a single place.

Some things here are a bit odd:

- Where's the PHP? There's no <?php or ?> yet, and certainly no code.

- Those variables are PHP, not HTML. An HTML page won't know what to do with them.

- Where does the database interaction occur? There's no SQL, no SELECT from the database, or anything like that.

- How does the script know which user to load?

These are all the right questions to be asking. If you came up with a few of these, you're really getting your head around the big issues in PHP and web programming.

First, as to where the <?php and ?> tags are: they're coming later, but that's really incidental. You can give a file the *.php* extension and still put nothing but HTML within that file. Type the URL to your script into your browser and see what happens; Figure 7-8 is about right.

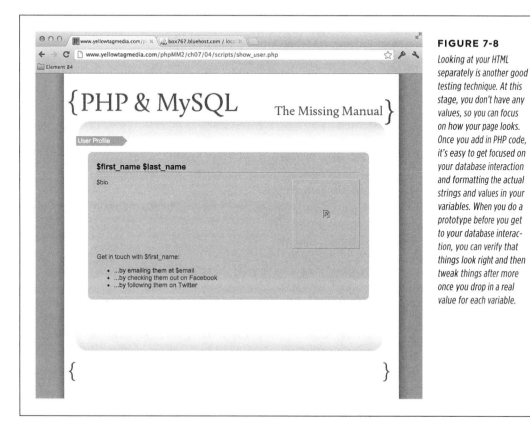

FIGURE 7-8

Looking at your HTML separately is another good testing technique. At this stage, you don't have any values, so you can focus on how your page looks. Once you add in PHP code, it's easy to get focused on your database interaction and formatting the actual strings and values in your variables. When you do a prototype before you get to your database interaction, you can verify that things look right and then tweak things after more once you drop in a real value for each variable.

WARNING If you get a page without any styling when you view your HTML, you might need to update the link element in your page's head section. Because you moved this page into your *scripts/* directory, the CSS is in a different relative location than when this was just an HTML page under your web root, or your *ch07/* examples.

There's nothing but HTML in *show_user.php*, so your web server supplies that HTML to a user's web browser. The result is a nice-looking web page. Of course, there's still a handful of issues to deal with, like those variable names that are coming across as plain, old text.

That's easy, though. Simply surround each variable with <?php and ?>, which signals to the browser, "Hey, treat this little bit as PHP." Then, you'll have to add an echo because you want to output the value of the variable:

```html
<html>
 <head>
  <link href="../../css/phpMM.css" rel="stylesheet" type="text/css" />
 </head>

 <body>
  <div id="header"><h1>PHP & MySQL: The Missing Manual</h1></div>
  <div id="example">User Profile</div>
  <div id="content">
    <div class="user_profile">
      <h1><?php echo "{$first_name} {$last_name}"; ?></h1>
      <p><img src="<?php echo $user_image; ?>" class="user_pic" />
        <?php echo $bio; ?></p>
      <p class="contact_info">Get in touch with <?php echo $first_name; ?>:</
p>
      <ul>
        <li>...by emailing them at
          <a href="<?php echo $email; ?>"><?php echo $email; ?></a></li>
        <li>...by
          <a href="<?php echo $facebook_url; ?>">checking them out
            on Facebook</a></li>
        <li>...by <a href="<?php echo $twitter_url; ?>">following them
            on Twitter</a></li>
      </ul>
    </div>
  </div>
  <div id="footer"></div>
 </body>
</html>
```

There's still an obvious issue here: These variables have no values. You haven't defined them, and if you try to access this page now, you're going to get some strange results (see Figure 7-9). But you're slowly moving toward a useful script, and that's a good thing.

The biggest problem here is that you don't know if this code works. For example, are there typos? Are there problems in the minimal PHP you have? It's a pain to move on to your database code when you're not sure that they'll work properly, even if you have the right values from the database.

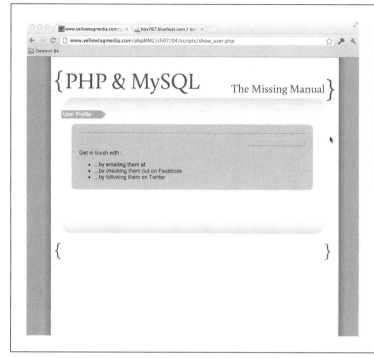

FIGURE 7-9

The state of show_user.php as shown on page 198 is one of those situations in which it's a little hard to tell what's going on. Look closely, though: Every time your PHP ran, it echoed out the value of a variable that didn't exist. The PHP is a little loose here, and simply throws out nothing. In other words, PHP does echo a nothing string, which is just whitespace. Once you put values in those variables, things will look much better.

One easy way to test before getting much further is to create a small section of PHP before the HTML. In that section, assign to each variable the sort of value you'd get from the database:

```php
<?php
$first_name = "Yu";
$last_name = "Darvish";
$user_image = "/not/yet/implemented.jpg";
$email = "yu@texasrangers.com";
$bio = "Attended Tohoku High School in northern Sendai, a school
which also produced major league pitchers Kazuhiro Sasaki and Takashi
Saito...he had a 1.10 ERA in his high school career, and pitched a
no-hitter against Kumamoto Technical High School in the first round
of the National High School Baseball Invitational Tournament on
March 26, 2004...he was drafted by the Fighters in the first round
on November 17, 2004 and signed on December 17.</p>
    <p>Went 18-6 with a 1.44 ERA (37 ER/232.0 IP) for Hokkaido
in his final season in Japan...the 1.44 ERA was the lowest of his
career, as he also posted career highs in wins (18), strikeouts (276),
innings (232.0), starts (28), and shutouts (6)...matched career
```

```
low with 5 HR allowed (also 2010)...led NPB in strikeouts, innings,
opponents average (.190), shutouts (tied), home runs per 9
innings (0.19), opponents OBP (.229), and opponents
slugging (.241)...the opponents OBP and slugging figures were
career lows...ranked among circuit leaders in ERA (2nd), complete
games (2nd), strikeout/walk ratio (3rd, 7.67), and wins (T3rd)...
tossed at least 7.0 innings in every outing last season, with his
lone outing of more than 3 runs coming in his first start...his
career-low run support average of 3.10 runs per 9 innings ranked
23rd out of NPB's 33 qualifying pitchers...received one or zero
runs of support in 4 of his 6 defeats.  ";
$facebook_url = "http://www.facebook.com/pages/Yu-Darvish/55933782070";
$twitter_url = "http://www.twitter.com/YuDarTranslated";
?>

<html>
  <!-- All your HTML and inline PHP -->
</html>
```

Now, you can view your page in a browser and get some useful results, like you see in Figure 7-10. This way, you can verify that your code is actually working; all that's left is to fill those variables with real values, and then figure out which user to look up in the first place.

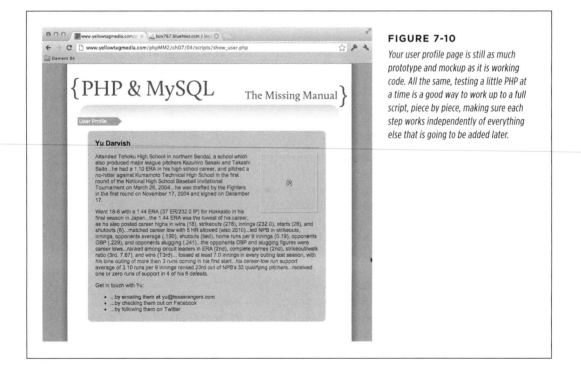

FIGURE 7-10

Your user profile page is still as much prototype and mockup as it is working code. All the same, testing a little PHP at a time is a good way to work up to a full script, piece by piece, making sure each step works independently of everything else that is going to be added later.

Using SELECT to Retrieve a User from Your Database

You've got your variables, and you've got your HTML. Now, you need to get your user. But, you know just what to do because you've already used SELECT a few times:

```
SELECT *
  FROM users;
```

In fact, you can run that command now on your database. What you get back are all the rows you have:

```
+---------+------------+-----------+----------------+--------------
----------------------------------------------+----------------+------+
| user_id | first_name | last_name | email          | facebook_url
| twitter_handle | bio  |
+---------+------------+-----------+----------------+--------------
----------------------------------------------+----------------+------+
|       1 | Yu         | Darvish   | yu@texasrangers.com | http://www.face-
book.com/pages/Yu-Darvish/55933782070 | @ YuDarTranslated
  | NULL |
+---------+------------+-----------+----------------+-------------------
----------------------------------------+----------------+------+
1 row in set (0.03 sec)
```

> **NOTE** This output is intentionally left as a bit of a mess because it's probably just what you see in your console window, too. The output of your SELECT is all the rows in the table, which won't fit in a normal command-line prompt, let alone the limited width of a book page.

In this case, there's just a single user. Once you retrieve this user, you can pull out the values for first_name and last_name, email, and so on and stuff them in $first_name, $last_name, and the rest of your variables.

There's still one big question lurking about: how do you know *which* user to get? Obviously, in the table output here, there's only one user. But, what about when your new app is a hit and you have hundreds, or thousands, or even hundreds of thousands of users? You need to be able to select just one of those users for *show_user.php* to display.

Think about the ways that users will end up at *show_user.php*. Here are a few:

- They are sent to this page after they've created a new user with *create_user .html* and *create_user.php*.

- They log in to your application and click a link such as My Profile or Update My Information.

- They select a particular user from a list of users, maybe all the users in the system, or all their friends, or all the users they're watching or following.

These situations all have one thing in common: Nobody ever goes to *show_user.php* directly by typing in a URL. In each case, someone selects a user, or creates a user, or logs in as a user, and then some link takes her to *show_user.php*.

The point is that in every reasonable situation, your code sends the user to *show_user .php*; therefore, so your code is really in control. If, for example, you need to send some information to *show_user.php*, that's possible. What might your code want to send to *show_user.php*? You want to send the unique ID of the user that *show_user .php* should load from the database and display.

Take a moment to revisit those same scenarios again:

- The *create_user.php* script creates a user, and the ID of that new user is handed off, along with your application user, to *show_user.php*.

- Clicking My Profile or Update My Information passes along the current logged-in user's ID to *show_user.php*.

- Selecting a user from a list—regardless of what's in that list—results in a link to *show_user.php* being followed, and the selected user's ID being passed to *show_user.php* at the same time.

In each case, your *show_user.php* script can use the ID that it received to look up the user and then display that user.

The beauty of this solution is not just that it's possible, because you have control over all the ways your users might get to *show_user.php*, but it's also perfect because you can pass in the ID of the user to show as part of the request, and you've already pulled information out of the request before, by using $_REQUEST.

Add the code highlighted in bold to *show_user.php*:

```php
<?php

$user_id = $_REQUEST['user_id'];

// Code to assign values to the page variables
?>

<html>
  <!-- All your HTML and inline PHP -->
</html>
```

Nothing new here; the only thing that's different from what you've done before is that you're pulling a request parameter with a new name: user_id.

Now, you can add a WHERE clause to your SELECT:

```sql
SELECT *
  FROM users
 WHERE user_id = $user_id;
```

So far, you've seen a few WHERE clauses (like the one on page 115), and they do just what you might expect. The WHERE clause narrows a set of results by applying an additional condition or restriction to the item you're looking for. In this case, you're saying, "Give me everything (*) from the *users* table, but only for the records (rows) that have a user_id of the value in $user_id."

Thus, if your sample user has a user_id of 1, and $user_id is 1, you'll get that sample user. If you don't have any rows that have a user_id of 1, you'll get nothing back from the SELECT. Here's what's really cool: you made user_id a primary key (with PRIMARY KEY), which means that you'll never have more than one result returned. This means that you don't have to see how many values are returned, or do anything special to handle one row or multiple rows. You'll either get nothing back because there was no match, or you'll get just a single row back.

When you put all this together, you can make some really important additions to *show_user.php*:

```php
<?php

require '../../scripts/database_connection.php';

// Get the user ID of the user to show
$user_id = $_REQUEST['user_id'];

// Build the SELECT statement
$select_query = "SELECT * FROM users WHERE user_id = " . $user_id;

// Run the query
$result = mysql_query($select_query);

// Assign values to variables

?>

<html>
  <!-- All your HTML and inline PHP -->
</html>
```

This script now connects to your database, builds the SELECT statement from the user_id request parameter that was passed to it, and then runs the query. All that's left is the one entirely new piece to this script: running through the actual result from a query, and pulling information from that result.

Pulling Values from a SQL Query Result

The $result variable is a resource, a special type of variable that holds a reference to more information, as explained in Chapter 5, on page 127. You can pass that resource to other PHP functions, and use it to get more information.

In the case of a SELECT query, what you really want is all the actual rows that the query returned, and then for each row, you want the different values. That's exactly what you can use a resource for, so you're all set to finish off *show_user.php* and start accepting requests.

You begin by ensuring that $result has a value. That's equivalent to ensuring that $result is not false, which is returned when there's a problem with your SQL:

```
// Run the query
$result = mysql_query($select_query);

if ($result) {
  // Get the query result rows using $result
} else {
  die("Error locating user with ID {$user_id}");
}
```

This if statement also (marginally) handles errors. If $result is false, something went wrong, which presumably means the user for whom you were searching by using $user_id doesn't exist, or there was a problem finding that user. So far, it doesn't format the error nicely, providing you with little information about what actually happened that caused the problem. For the time being that's OK; you'll beef up your error handling soon, so this if is a decent short-term solution.

Now, you need a new PHP function: mysql_fetch_array. This function takes a resource from a previously run SQL query. That's exactly what you have in $result:

```
if ($result) {
  $row = mysql_fetch_array($result);

  // Break up the row into its different fields and assign to variables
} else {
  die("Error locating user with ID {$user_id}");
}
```

Here's where things get a little odd. Take note of how the preceding script stores the result from mysql_fetch_array in $row. This implies that mysql_fetch_array returns a single row from your SQL query—and that's correct.

But, the function's name suggests something else: It leads you to believe that an *array* is returned—mysql_fetch_array, not mysql_fetch_row. So, is it a row or is it an array? Well, it's both. The mysql_fetch_array function does return an array, but it returns an array for a single *row* of the query associated with the result you pass into it.

This means that for mysql_fetch_array($result), you're going to get back a single row of results, but that the *way* that row is returned is in the form of an array.

> **NOTE** If you're already wondering, you can certainly get *every* row of results returned from a query, not
> just the first result row. You just keep calling `mysql_fetch_array`, over and over, and it keeps returning the
> next row from the results. Eventually, `mysql_fetch_array` will return `false`, which means there are no
> more results.
>
> Don't worry if this seems a little sketchy. Before long, you'll use `mysql_fetch_array` like this yourself, and it
> will all make perfect sense. For now, be aware that every time you call this function, you'll get one row of results
> (or `false` if there are no rows left to return), and that row is an array of values.

Because you know how to work with arrays, getting back an array in $row is good
news. In fact, $row is just like another array you know, the $_REQUEST array. And just
like $_REQUEST, you have not only a list of values, but values that are keyed based
on a name.

When a request came in with a parameter named "first_name," you pulled the value
for that parameter with $_REQUEST['first_name']. The same principle applies to
$row. You can give it the name of a column returned in your SQL query, and you'll
get the value for that column, in the specific row you're examining.

Once you have $row, you can just grab all the columns you want, and then stuff
them into some variables:

```
// Run the query
$result = mysql_query($select_query);
if ($result) {
  $row = mysql_fetch_array($result);
  $first_name    = $row['first_name'];
  $last_name     = $row['last_name'];
  $bio        = $row['bio'];
  $email         = $row['email'];
  $facebook_url  = $row['facebook_url'];
  $twitter_handle = $row['twitter_handle'];

  // Turn $twitter_handle into a URL
  $twitter_url = "http://www.twitter.com/" .
               substr($twitter_handle, $position + 1);

  // To be added later
  $user_image = "/not/yet/implemented.jpg";
} else {
  die("Error locating user with ID {$user_id}");
}
```

At this point, you have a fully functional script! In fact, other than figuring out how to use the $result resource with mysql_fetch_array, all of this should be no problem for you.

Passing a User ID into *show_user.php*

At this point, you need to get a user ID into your script so that it can use that ID to look up a user, get her information, and display it. But, before you spend a bunch of time on other scripts, it's a good idea to ensure that *show_user.php* works.

Fortunately, there's a very easy way to test your script. The $_REQUEST array has all the information passed into your script through its request, including extra information passed through the request URL itself. Remember, this isn't the ordinary way you'd either pass information into *show_user.php* or even access *show_user.php* in the first place. Instead, scripts like *create_user.php,* or maybe a My Profile button, would direct your users to this script.

But for now, you're just testing. So, go directly to the page by using a URL like *yellowtagmedia.com/phpMM/ch07/scripts/show_user.php.* As long as you're there, you can feed that script request data with request parameters on the URL itself. You can simply add these to the URL, after a ? (question mark) character. (For more information on using a */scripts* directory, see the box on page 208.)

The format is basically as follows:

`[scheme]://[domain-name]/[location-of-file]?[request-paramaters]`

For example, you might use *mysite.com/scripts/show_user.php?first_name=Mario.* Now, you could grab $_REQUEST['first_name'], and you'd get back "Lance." You can stack these up, too; just separate the parameters with an & (ampersand) character. You could go further and do *mysite.com/scripts/show_user.php?first_name=Mario&last_name=Beauregard.*

To do so, add the user ID of the user you created much earlier (or one of the users, if you inserted more than one) and try out *show_user.php*, with a URL like *yellowtagmedia.com/phpMM/ch07/scripts/show_user.php?user_id=1.* You'll get something back similar to Figure 7-11, which is a validation of all the work you've been putting into SQL and *show_user.php.*

FIGURE 7-11

There's always room for error when a form or web page sends information to another page or a script. Anytime you can test just a single script in isolation, you're going a long way toward removing potential errors and hard-to-find bugs that only pop up when two web pages talk to one another, as compared to when each is operating in isolation.

WARNING Request parameters are case-sensitive, as is PHP. Therefore, asking for $_REQUEST['user_id'] won't match a request parameter named USER_ID or user_Id. Be careful to ensure that your uppercase and lowercase letters all match up.

At this point, you've done just about everything you can to ensure that *show_user .php* is going to behave. It's missing some information, like the user's pic and bio, but you can deal with the picture later, and you can take care of the bio by updating *create_user.php.* Other than that, it's time to leave *show_user.php* alone and revisit the script that actually gets users to *show_user.php* in the first place.

NOTE There is probably one more thing you could do: manually INSERT a user with a bio into your users table and then try out *show_user.php* again. You might want to do that now and verify that *show_user.php* is just as you want it. You'll test that same bit of functionality in a little while once you update *create_user.php,* but there's no such thing as too much testing.

Is a *scripts/* Directory a Good Idea?

Storing all your scripts in a directory (or, technically, a subdirectory) called *scripts/* is a practice that largely dates back to older programming languages like Perl and CGI (*Common Gateway Interface*, a way of calling external programs like server-side scripts). In those days, programmers maintained a really firm separation between client-side programs, or views, and server-side programs. Thus, a script never really did anything that resulted directly in a web page being displayed; they were just programs called by other processes.

But PHP really blurs the line between what's a script, and what's a viewable page. The *show_user.php* script is actually a lot more HTML than it is PHP, and it's going to be common for a user to actually go to *show_user.php* directly. In other words, PHP is more than just a way to write scripts to which your forms submit behind the scenes. There will be lots of times when users click a link to a PHP page rather than an HTML page, or even type in a URL for the PHP script in his browser.

In fact, there are some popular pieces of software that essentially handle *all* HTML within PHP. WordPress (*www.wordpress.org*) is a hugely popular blogging and content management system that's built on PHP. In that system, your site's home page is actually *index.php*, not *index.html*.

At that point, a *scripts/* directory doesn't make sense. Your users don't care whether they're getting a page from an HTML file or a PHP script, as long as it looks and acts the way they expect. And adding a *scripts/* directory actually increases what your users have to know about your system rather than making things more transparent.

Therefore, beginning in Chapter 8, this change will kick into gear. It's good that you've been thinking about the difference between what you've been doing as a web page creator with HTML, CSS, and JavaScript, and your new PHP skills. But, now that you've moved beyond just submitting forms to PHP, it's time to blur the lines even further and let your PHP scripts live alongside your HTML.

■ Revisiting (and Redirecting) the Create User Script

The changes you made in the previous section are great, but there's more to do. For example, you have a new bio column, but no place to enter that information when users sign up. You need *create_user.php* to deal with that information when it comes in from your signup form. And then there's getting a user from the signup form to *show_user.php*—and passing along the newly created user's ID, as well. It seems like a lot, but with what you know, this change will be a breeze.

Updating Your User Signup Form

The first change—the bio—is one of the easiest. Open your *create_user.html* page and add a new form field so that your users can enter a biography. Leave plenty of space: Have you seen how much information people write about themselves on Facebook these days? Here's the updated version of *create_user.html*:

```html
<html>
 <head>
  <link href="../css/phpMM.css" rel="stylesheet" type="text/css" />
 </head>

 <body>
  <div id="header"><h1>PHP & MySQL: The Missing Manual</h1></div>
  <div id="example">User Signup</div>

  <div id="content">
    <h1>Join the Missing Manual (Digital) Social Club</h1>
    <p>Please enter your online connections below:</p>
    <form action="scripts/create_user.php" method="POST">
      <fieldset>
        <label for="first_name">First Name:</label>
        <input type="text" name="first_name" size="20" /><br />
        <label for="last_name">Last Name:</label>
        <input type="text" name="last_name" size="20" /><br />
        <label for="email">E-Mail Address:</label>
        <input type="text" name="email" size="50" /><br />
        <label for="facebook_url">Facebook URL:</label>
        <input type="text" name="facebook_url" size="50" /><br />
        <label for="twitter_handle">Twitter Handle:</label>
        <input type="text" name="twitter_handle" size="20" /><br />
        <label for="bio">Bio:</label>
        <textarea name="bio" cols="40" rows="10"></textarea>
      </fieldset>
      <br />
      <fieldset class="center">
        <input type="submit" value="Join the Club" />
        <input type="reset" value="Clear and Restart" />
      </fieldset>
    </form>
  </div>

  <div id="footer"></div>
 </body>
</html>
```

While you're at it, you might as well let your users pick an image for their profile.
You won't write any code in *create_user.php* to handle this, but it's coming soon,
and you'll save a trip back to *create_user.html* when you're ready to add images.

```html
<html>
 <!-- head section -->
```

```
<body>
  <div id="header"><h1>PHP & MySQL: The Missing Manual</h1></div>
  <div id="example">User Signup</div>

  <div id="content">
    <h1>Join the Missing Manual (Digital) Social Club</h1>
    <p>Please enter your online connections below:</p>
    <form action="scripts/create_user.php" method="POST"
          enctype="multipart/form-data">
      <fieldset>
        <label for="first_name">First Name:</label>
        <input type="text" name="first_name" size="20" /><br />
        <label for="last_name">Last Name:</label>
        <input type="text" name="last_name" size="20" /><br />
        <label for="email">E-Mail Address:</label>
        <input type="text" name="email" size="50" /><br />
        <label for="facebook_url">Facebook URL:</label>
        <input type="text" name="facebook_url" size="50" /><br />
        <label for="twitter_handle">Twitter Handle:</label>
        <input type="text" name="twitter_handle" size="20" /><br />
        <label for="user_pic">Upload a picture:</label>
        <input type="file" name="user_pic" size="30" />
        <label for="bio">Bio:</label>
        <textarea name="bio" cols="40" rows="10"></textarea>
      </fieldset>
      <!-- Buttons for submission and resetting the form -->

</body>
</html>
```

You need to change the form tag a bit, because now you're actually uploading a file to a server from your user's machine. To do this, add the new enctype attribute with the value "multipart/form-data". That alerts any scripts receiving this form's input to expect more than just the values in the input fields, like the name of the file. A form like this also submits the data associated with those fields; in this case, that's the actual file that the user selects to upload.

Then, you add a new input of type "file" which lets the user browse his hard drive, select a file, and upload that file. By the way, this code is almost boilerplate. Every time you give your users the opportunity to upload a file, this is the set of changes you'll need to make.

> **NOTE** If you want to start thinking ahead, the million-dollar question is, "Where do you store this image?" You have to set up to let the user upload the image; that's required for your scripts and code to work with it. However, do you save the image on your server's file system and reference it by using a field in your *users* table? Or, do you actually store it in your database? You'll develop your own answer to this question in just a few chapters.

Save your changes here and then open your form in a browser. You should see your updated form, similar to Figure 7-12.

FIGURE 7-12

Except for the new Choose File button, your form doesn't look much different when you add a new file input element or change your form to submit multipart data. Behind the scenes, though, your form is sending not just the name that ends up in each form field, but anything that's connected to that name—like the file that your user selects when he clicks that button.

If you fill in some values now, without changes to *create_user.php*, you'll create a new user without a bio.

Updating Your User Creation Script

The next change to *create_user.php* grabs the new bio request variable and adds it to your INSERT statement:

```php
<?php

require '../../scripts/database_connection.php';

$first_name = trim($_REQUEST['first_name']);
$last_name = trim($_REQUEST['last_name']);
$email = trim($_REQUEST['email']);
$bio = trim($_REQUEST['bio']);
// And other request variables follow...
```

```php
$insert_sql = "INSERT INTO users (first_name, last_name, email, bio," .
                            "facebook_url, twitter_handle) " .
                 "VALUES ('{$first_name}', '{$last_name}', '{$email}', '{$bio}' " .
 .
                      "'{$facebook_url}', '{$twitter_handle}');";

// Insert the user into the database
mysql_query($insert_sql);
?>
```

Submit your new form. Notice that there's a new column—bio—with values happily dropped into your database.

> **WARNING** Be sure you've run the ALTER TABLE statement that adds the bio column to your *users* table (page 194) before trying this out.

In fact, you can try this out by filling out *create_user.html* and clicking Submit. Then, try this SELECT statement:

```sql
SELECT first_name, last_name, bio
  FROM users;
```

Your result should speak for itself:

```
| first_name | last_name | bio
| Yu         | Darvish   |NULL |
| David      | Ramirez   |By breaking through heartache,
David Ramirez has gone on a search for understanding. The
Austin resident and frequent traveler to clubs, theaters
and listening rooms all over the country, has come to a
phase in his creative life where the tears have dried and
moving on looks like the best option.
```

You can also see that old users—in this case, the Yu Darvish entry—shows NULL for the bio, because that user was created before a bio column existed.

Next, you need to redirect your user over to the *show_user.php* script and then get the ID of the user you just created into that script, as well.

The first of these is easy:

```php
<?php

// Everything else you've already done

// Insert the user into the database
mysql_query($insert_sql);
```

```
// Redirect the user to the page that displays user information
header("Location: show_user.php");
exit();
?>
```

The header function sends a raw hypertext transfer protocol (HTTP) header to your user's browser. (HTTP is the language of web traffic. It's the same *http://* you put at the beginning of most of your URLs in your browser's address bar.) This function directly manipulates the location of your user's page.

In this case, you're changing the location from the current one to a new one: the *show_user.php* script. There are a couple things that are critical to get this working correctly, though:

1. **The header must be called *before* any other output in your script.** You can't echo out anything. Nor can you print out an <html> tag or anything else. The header is first, or problems arise.

2. **The location reference must be a URL, either relative or absolute.** This means that you could put *http://www.google.com* as the location, or *../../scripts/database_connection.php*, or in this case, a script in the same directory as this one, *show_user.php*.

These are simple rules but they're also really important ones. Get them right, or expect header to fail miserably.

All that's left now is getting that pesky user ID. To do that, you need something that's one step removed from your current PHP knowledge: an incredibly handy PHP function called mysql_insert_id. This isn't the sort of function you'll easily find unless you're looking for, say, a function to get the ID of the last row INSERTed into a database table with an AUTO_INCREMENT column.

Yes, that's the exact definition of mysql_insert_id! It's built exactly to do what you want to do: get an ID without any additional SELECTs or work.

NOTE To be fair, mysql_insert_id was always there, and it's a certain way of coding that makes it so useful. But, because you're coding that way—using tried-and-true PHP best practices—you get to use a function like mysql_insert_id just as it was intended, which makes your life a lot easier.

Even though you can pass a resource into mysql_insert_id, it will automatically use the last opened resource, which is perfect. Just add this after your INSERT is called via mysql_query, and it will automatically reference the resource returned from that call.

What does it return for a value? Just the ID of the user you want. You can actually tag that onto the URL, just as when you were typing in your URL manually:

```
<?php

// Everything else you've already done
```

```
// Insert the user into the database
mysql_query($insert_sql);

// Redirect the user to the page that displays user information
header("Location: show_user.php?user_id=" . mysql_insert_id());
?>
```

That's it. Add this to *create_user.php*, and you're ready to try things out.

> **NOTE** You might be tempted to try something like this:
>
> ("Location: show_user.php?user_id={mysql_insert_id()}");
>
> Unfortunately, it won't work. PHP is happy to insert variable values for variable names in curly braces, such as this:
>
> ("Location: show_user.php?user_id={$user_id}");
>
> However, it won't do the same for function calls.

Go ahead and visit your user creation form, fill out some data, and then submit it. You should be rewarded not by the output of *create_user.php*, but by *show_user .php*, loading the user that was just created. Figure 7-13 shows why this should be a fist-pumping moment.

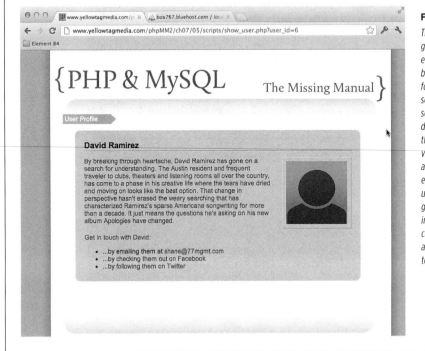

FIGURE 7-13

Think about all that's going on here. Your user enters data and clicks, but behind the scenes, that form is submitted to your script on the server. That script inserts data into a database. Then, it directs the user's browser to go visit another script, which asks the database for everything about a particular user. Finally, your user gets to see all this, mere instants later. This is a far cry from just HTML, CSS, and JavaScript. Welcome to web programming!

> **NOTE** Here's something to look forward to. It's really not great that you're dropping the user's ID right into the browser bar (see Figure 7-13). Any mildly inventive hacker would see that and start trying different IDs to see what they get. Never fear, though; before long, you'll not only remove that user ID from the URL, but also use sessions to enhance security, along with requiring passwords for seeing this sort of data.

Rounding Things Out by Using Regular Expressions (Again)

Your profile page (Figure 7-13) is *almost* perfect. But, that output looks awful with all that text run together. The user probably pressed Enter a few times to separate the bio into neat-looking paragraphs, but those paragraphs don't show up in HTML. What you really need is a quick and easy way to replace those Enter key presses with <p></p> tags.

You need a way to find certain specific characters and replace them with other characters. You know that each occurrence of Enter is represented by \r or \n or some combination of the two (Chapter 6, page 166), which means that you can use regular expressions to find them and then replace them.

Using preg_match, update show_user.php to change occurrences of Enter into HTML <p> tags:

```php
<?php

// Database connection code

// SELECT the correct user

if ($result) {
  $row = mysql_fetch_array($result);
  $first_name     = $row['first_name'];
  $last_name      = $row['last_name'];
  $bio            = preg_replace("/[\r\n]+/", "</p><p>", $row['bio']);
  $email          = $row['email'];
  $facebook_url   = $row['facebook_url'];
  $twitter_handle = $row['twitter_handle'];

  // Build the Twitter URL
}
?>

// HTML output
```

> **NOTE** Be sure you use [\r\n]+, and not [\r\n]*. The * would match *no* occurrence, and you'd end up with </p><p> between every character in the user's bio. Not so good! The + ensures that \r or \n (or both) appear *at least* once before replacing them with </p><p>.

Clearly, you can see why regular expressions are so powerful. You didn't need lots of looping and searching, and you don't have to figure out whether the user entered \r or \n or \r\n based on her platform. You just plug in the right regular expression, and you're off to the races.

All of this put together should give you a version of *show_user.php* like the following:

```php
<?php

require '../../scripts/app_config.php';
require '../../scripts/database_connection.php';

// Get the user ID of the user to show
$user_id = $_REQUEST['user_id'];

// Build the SELECT statement
$select_query = "SELECT * FROM users WHERE user_id = " . $user_id;

// Run the query
$result = mysql_query($select_query);

if ($result) {
  $row = mysql_fetch_array($result);
  $first_name     = $row['first_name'];
  $last_name      = $row['last_name'];
  $bio            = preg_replace("/[\r\n]+/", "</p><p>", $row['bio']);
  $email          = $row['email'];
  $facebook_url   = $row['facebook_url'];
  $twitter_handle = $row['twitter_handle'];

  // Turn $twitter_handle into a URL
  $twitter_url = "http://www.twitter.com/" .
                 substr($twitter_handle, $position + 1);

  // To be added later
  $user_image = "../../images/missing_user.png";
} else {
  die("Error locating user with ID {$user_id}");
}
?>

<html>
 <head>
  <link href="../../css/phpMM.css" rel="stylesheet" type="text/css" />
 </head>

 <body>
```

```
<div id="header"><h1>PHP & MySQL: The Missing Manual</h1></div>
<div id="example">User Profile</div>

<div id="content">
  <div class="user_profile">
    <h1><?php echo "{$first_name} {$last_name}"; ?></h1>
    <p><img src="<?php echo $user_image; ?>" class="user_pic" />
      <?php echo $bio; ?></p>
    <p class="contact_info">Get in touch with <?php echo $first_name; ?>:</
p>
    <ul>
      <li>...by emailing them at
        <a href="<?php echo $email; ?>"><?php echo $email; ?></a></li>
      <li>...by
        <a href="<?php echo $facebook_url; ?>">checking them out
          on Facebook</a></li>
      <li>...by <a href="<?php echo $twitter_url; ?>">following them
          on Twitter</a></li>
    </ul>
  </div>
</div>
<div id="footer"></div>
</body>
</html>
```

When you take this for a test spin, you'll finally see not just your user's information,
but a nicely formatted biography, as presented in Figure 7-14.

FIGURE 7-14

*Ensuring that your user's paragraph breaks are
maintained is another classic case of thinking
about your user. Is it functionally correct to pull
the user's bio from the database and show it?
Sure. Is it functionally correct to not insert weird
HTML into his bio when you store it? Again, sure.
But when you actually display that value to the
user, he doesn't care what's in your database. He
only cares that it looks good.*

The Match Name

Do my field names, variable names, and table column names have to match?

You may have noticed that there's a continuous line from the name of a field in your HTML in *create_user.html* to your *create_user.php* script, into other scripts like *show_user.php*, and then into your database table itself. `first_name` is consistent in your HTML, PHP, and MySQL (and therefore your SQL, too). That's not required; you can call a field `firstName` and call a variable `user_firstName` and call a column `first_name`, and as long as you keep things straight, all your code will work just fine. So no, your names don't all have to match.

But being consistent in your naming makes your life easier. You never have to think, "I know what I called that variable in my PHP, but what was the database column name again?"

Here's the flipside, though: There are some standard conventions for naming variables in different programming languages and database structures. The Java language favors less underscores, and more capitalization. Thus, `firstName` would be preferred over `first_name`; the same is true in C++, although PHP and languages like Ruby prefer underscores over capitalization. SQL definitely favors underscores.

What this boils down to is a sort of conditional rule of thumb: *if* you can be consistent without messing up the conventions of the language within which you're programing, do it! Your code is easier to read, from the outermost HTML page to the innermost database table. Because PHP is one of the languages that likes underscores, use them, and keep things simple and consistent across your different pieces of your application.

From Web Pages to Web Applications

When Things Go Wrong (and They Will)

You have a growing set of functional scripts. You have some web pages that interact with them, CSS to style both your HTML static pages and the HTML that your scripts dish out, and you could (and should) go in and add some client-side JavaScript validation. Things are looking pretty good.

But there's a monster lurking in the deep. Even though you've occasionally added a die or a conditional to ensure that your queries return a result row, your code really assumes the perfect user: one who always types exactly what you expect, never enters a phone number in the email field or spaces in the Facebook URL field; someone who never needs to go back—and in fact never clicks her browser's Back button at an inopportune time—and never enters her information into the same form twice by furiously clicking "Add my information" instead of waiting on her lousy Internet connection.

Of course, if you start thinking about your friends and family, you probably don't know a lot of those types of users. And that's a problem...a *big* problem. The reality of web software—and in fact any type of software—is that people will always find ways to break your best-intended pages, forms, and scripts. They'll supply you bad information, leave out required fields, and make a general mess of anything and everything.

NOTE Again, client-side JavaScript is worth a strong mention here. You can reduce a lot of this sort of problem by validating your user's information *before* it's sent to your scripts. For a lot more on how to do that, check out *JavaScript: The Missing Manual* by David Sawyer McFarland (O'Reilly).

Suppose you've typed something wrong in your database connection script. Will your users see a helpful error message? Or even an email to which they can report the problem? No, they'll get the rather disappointing screen shown in Figure 8-1.

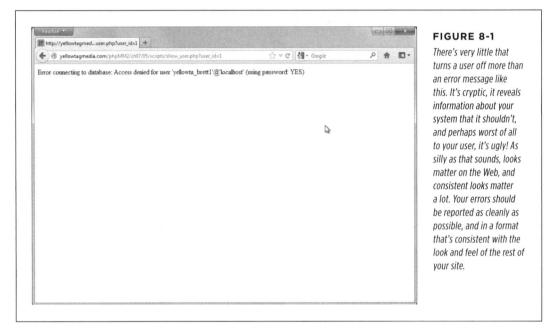

FIGURE 8-1

There's very little that turns a user off more than an error message like this. It's cryptic, it reveals information about your system that it shouldn't, and perhaps worst of all to your user, it's ugly! As silly as that sounds, looks matter on the Web, and consistent looks matter a lot. Your errors should be reported as cleanly as possible, and in a format that's consistent with the look and feel of the rest of your site.

A cryptic error message might be fine when it's only you using your system, testing things out, making sure your code is right. But this is a poor excuse for handling errors in any kind of system that's going to make it out there in the wilds of the Internet.

It gets even worse; try to visit the *show_user.php* URL again and supply a user ID that you know doesn't exist. Figure 8-2 shows that, instead of generating an error, the invalid user ID is being swallowed up by your script. You get an "empty" user profile, but otherwise it looks like nothing's wrong.

There's a lot of work to do here. First things first, though: What exactly should an error page have on it?

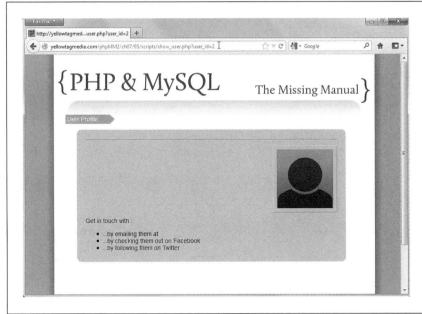

FIGURE 8-2

The problem with this web form is that it looks like there's no problem when in fact there's actually a big problem—someone entered an invalid user ID. The show_user.php script loads up its HTML, regardless of whether a SQL error occurred. Because PHP is happy to simply echo out empty strings for variables without values, this page looks almost normal... except for all the missing information.

Planning Your Error Pages

When you were creating the page that shows user profiles (page 196), you began with HTML. You created a mock-up of a simple page and then added PHP as you needed it. There's no reason to abandon that approach here, because you're basically trying to do the same thing. You want a nice-looking page for displaying errors, so before you start digging into PHP, get the page looking just right.

> **NOTE** You can find the finished example code for this section on this book's Missing CD page at *www.missingmanuals.com/cds/phpmysqlmm2e*.

Create a new HTML page and call it *show_error.html*. You can begin with the same structure you've been using for all your other pages:

```
<html>
 <head>
  <link href="../css/phpMM.css" rel="stylesheet" type="text/css" />
 </head>
```

```
<body>
  <div id="header"><h1>PHP & MySQL: The Missing Manual</h1></div>
  <div id="example">Error Page</div>

  <div id="content">
    <h1>Error Page</h1>
    <p>Error</p>
  </div>

  <div id="footer"></div>
</body>

</html>
```

At this point, you have an empty shell (see Figure 8-3), and it's time to get to work.

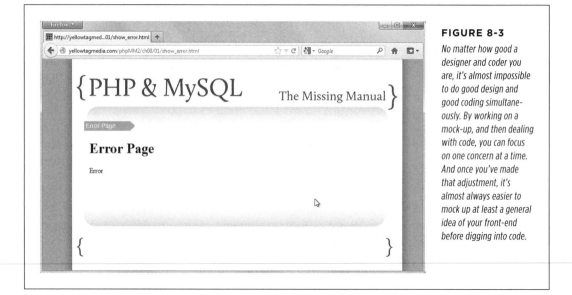

FIGURE 8-3

No matter how good a designer and coder you are, it's almost impossible to do good design and good coding simultaneously. By working on a mock-up, and then dealing with code, you can focus on one concern at a time. And once you've made that adjustment, it's almost always easier to mock up at least a general idea of your front-end before digging into code.

What Should Users See?

Here's your first question: what goes on this page that helps your users? To answer that, you really need to think about two things:

1. **What information does your user need when an error has occurred?**

2. **In what tone does that information need to be communicated?**

▨ TELL YOUR USERS THAT A PROBLEM HAS OCCURRED

The should be pretty obvious. Something has gone wrong; your user needs an explanation. But even in that, there's nuance. Should you print out an error that looks like the one here (which is the sort of thing MySQL might kick back to one of your scripts)?

```
#1054 - Unknown column 'firstname' in 'field list'
```

Certainly not. Unless the user is a MySQL or PHP programmer, this isn't helpful at all. Ideally, you want to translate that into normal human language, like the following:

```
We're sorry, we couldn't locate the user's first name.
```

That's much more readable, although it still doesn't give the user much to go on. "Why couldn't they fine me?" he might ask. "Is my record missing? Is my first name in the system? Uh oh, has my record been deleted? What's going on?!?"

NOTE Does that seem overly dramatic? Watch users who aren't particularly comfortable with computers and the Internet use a web application, especially if that application contains any of their personal information. It doesn't take much to create a lot of worry.

Maybe that error needs to be just as readable, but a lot less specific:

```
We're sorry! There's been an error processing your request.
```

Now, that's something most people can understand. Things can go wrong, and something has. The details aren't really relevant for your users; your job is simply to communicate a problem.

▨ BRING DOWN THE PANIC LEVEL IN THE PROCESS

By now, you've figured out that, in terms of information, your user really just needs to know that a problem has occurred. Details are probably irrelevant and could even potentially create more worry rather than less. But what about that second item:

In what tone does that information need to be communicated? This sounds pretty touchy-feely, and in fact, it is. You're dealing with human users, and that means human emotions. People become annoyed when the web application they're using throws up errors, and although you can reduce the stress and frustration, you can't get rid of it altogether.

Regardless of what you say when problems occur, you need to think about *how* you say it. A stern, bland error message isn't as comforting as a casual, conversational one. Sometimes you can even add in a little humor. Take a look at Figure 8-4 for one way to turn a problem into a conversation point. You can almost bet that a user who lands on this page—error or not—is going to come back to the site.

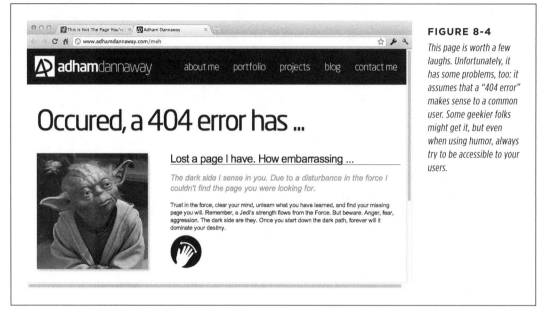

FIGURE 8-4

This page is worth a few laughs. Unfortunately, it has some problems, too: it assumes that a "404 error" makes sense to a common user. Some geekier folks might get it, but even when using humor, always try to be accessible to your users.

Going full on with humor might be a little strong for your example site, but at least ensure that you use conversational language. Just getting away from the stern-sounding, "Error 1282: An exception has occurred" goes a long way.

For example, make a few conversational improvements to your error page mockup, as in the following example, and notice how quickly this becomes a little more palatable when the inevitable error occurs:

```html
<html>
 <head>
  <link href="../css/phpMM.css" rel="stylesheet" type="text/css" />
 </head>

 <body>
  <div id="header"><h1>PHP & MySQL: The Missing Manual</h1></div>
  <div id="example">Uh oh... sorry!</div>

  <div id="content">
    <h1>We're really sorry...</h1>
    <p><img src="../images/error.jpg" class="error" />...but something's
gone wrong. Don't worry, though, we've been notified that there's a
problem, and we take these things seriously. In fact, if you want to
contact us to find out more about what's happened, or you have any
concerns, just <a href="mailto:info@yellowtagmedia.com">email us</a>
```

```
and we'll be happy to get right back to you.</p>
    <p>In the meantime, if you want to go back to the page that caused
the problem, you can do that <a href="javascript:history.go(-1);">by
clicking here.</a> If the same problem occurs, though, you may
want to come back a bit later. We bet we'll have things figured
out by then. Thanks again... we'll see you soon. And again, we're
really sorry for the inconvenience.</p>

  </div>

  <div id="footer"></div>

  </body>

</html>
```

This text doesn't say much more than "Yes, we know a problem has occurred, and we're working on it." Everything else is about presentation: conversational words, an image to break up the cold page (which at the end of the day still *does* say, "Hey, sorry, something's broken"), a contact link for email, and another link to revisit the offending page. (If you do invite users to contact you with problems, be sure to follow through. See the box on page 228.)

The error page in Figure 8-5 is a heck of a lot less annoying than that in Figure 8-3, and it took no more work to produce.

FIGURE 8-5

Simple things like error pages and testing are often what separate casual and mid-level programmers from high-end consultants and senior-level developers. Small things like this helpful error page keep systems running and users happy, which ultimately keeps the lights on and the bills paid.

Over-Promise at Your Own Risk

Nowhere other than error pages is it easier to over-promise and under-deliver. If you tell a user that you're looking into his problem, you'd better be looking into it. If you're going to supply a contact email address, ensure that it's real (yes, lots of times error pages have old, outdated addresses) and that the email actually gets to someone who will take care of the problem.

If your user thinks you're dealing with her issue, and she comes back in a few hours only to get the same error, all the clever images and language in the world won't keep her invested in your site. On top of that, she'll be annoyed not just that something went wrong, but that you lied (well, at least in her eyes) about working on her issue.

If you're just getting started or have limited resources, you might do well to simply state that you get notified when errors occur, and you usually fix problems within, say, 24 or 36 hours, or within some time period to which you can really commit. You might also give him an email address to use if things are urgent—but only if you watch your email! Another option is to preformat the email with something in the subject line to look for, like "URGENT" or "ERROR." You could even set a rule up on your email client to highlight such messages.

Whatever you do, make sure that your responsiveness matches what your error page promises, or you're going to have a lot more than a programming problem from which you'll need to recover.

One more bit of advice as you begin working in large companies: never let the marketing team write the error page text without supervision. The job of marketing people is to sell and promote, and if error pages are the easiest place to over-promise, marketing is the easiest place to over-sell capability. Get someone who is good with words to help you in crafting your error page, but ultimately, you're probably the person fixing problems; be certain that you can back up what ends up on your error pages.

Know When to Say When

You are now a capable PHP programmer, and you might have some other clever ideas as to what could go on this error page. You could grab the user's information from the database and personalize the page. You could set up a table that contains error codes, and associated with each error code, a helpful error message that's easy to read. Then when an error occurs, you could look up the error code and print out the corresponding error message from the database.

It's true that all this (and anything else you might come up with) would make for a pretty slick error page. But these are ideas that require fairly complex programming in and of themselves. There's a database to connect to and queries to execute. And every time you write a query, or connect to a database, you introduce the possibility of another error. Where do your users go when your error pages have errors?

As a rule of thumb, you want your error pages free from as much programming as possible; they shouldn't interact with databases, and they shouldn't be fancy. To put it simply; if your error page can cause an error, you're in trouble.

■ Finding a Middle Ground for Error Pages with PHP

On one hand, you want pages that are dead simple: some text, an image or two, and static content. Nothing can go wrong, which means your users get some level of reassurance and comfort. On the other hand, the error page in Figure 8-5 is awfully generic. It just doesn't *say* very much. It would be nice to see something about what actually went wrong, maybe like the following:

```html
<html>
 <head>
  <link href="../css/phpMM.css" rel="stylesheet" type="text/css" />
 </head>

 <body>
  <div id="header"><h1>PHP & MySQL: The Missing Manual</h1></div>
  <div id="example">Uh oh... sorry!</div>

  <div id="content">
    <h1>We're really sorry...</h1>
    <p><img src="../images/error.jpg" class="error" />...but something's
gone wrong. <span class="error_message">the username you entered couldn't
be found in our database.</span></p>
    <p>Don't worry, though, we've been notified that there's a
problem, and we take these things seriously. In fact, if you want to
contact us to find out more about what's happened, or you have any
concerns, just <a href="mailto:info@yellowtagmedia.com">email us</a>
and we'll be happy to get right back to you.</p>
    <p>In the meantime, if you want to go back to the page that caused
the problem, you can do that <a href="javascript:history.go(-1);">by
clicking here.</a> If the same problem occurs, though, you may
want to come back a bit later. We bet we'll have things figured
out by then. Thanks again... we'll see you soon. And again, we're
really sorry for the inconvenience.</p>

  </div>

  <div id="footer"></div>

 </body>

</html>
```

NOTE You can find the finished example code for this section on this book's Missing CD page at *www.missingmanuals.com/cds/phpmysqlmm2e.*

The result, Figure 8-6 seems to be a good compromise between a truly generic error page and one that is so tricked-out with user-specific information that it becomes prone to error itself.

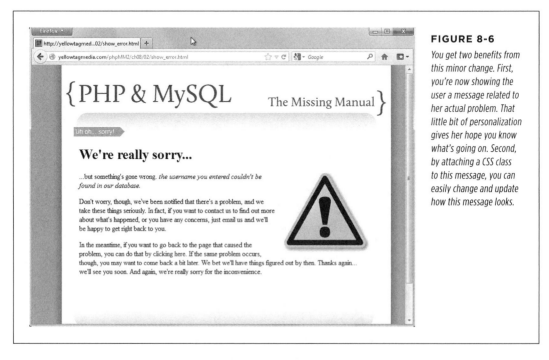

FIGURE 8-6
You get two benefits from this minor change. First, you're now showing the user a message related to her actual problem. That little bit of personalization gives her hope you know what's going on. Second, by attaching a CSS class to this message, you can easily change and update how this message looks.

In the next section, you'll put this personalized error message in place and still keep the programming minimal.

Creating a PHP Error Page

Almost everything on your template is straight HTML. The only thing that's dynamic—that would change from request to request—is the error message, so your task is relatively simple from a programming standpoint. Begin by putting in a variable for the error message; you'll come back and assign a value to that variable a little later.

```
<html>
 <head>
  <link href="../css/phpMM.css" rel="stylesheet" type="text/css" />
 </head>

 <body>
  <div id="header"><h1>PHP & MySQL: The Missing Manual</h1></div>
```

```
<div id="example">Uh oh... sorry!</div>

<div id="content">
  <h1>We're really sorry...</h1>
  <p><img src="../images/error.jpg" class="error" />
    <?php echo $error_message; ?>
    <span></p>
  <p>Don't worry, though, we've been notified that there's a
problem, and we take these things seriously. In fact, if you want to
contact us to find out more about what's happened, or you have any
concerns, just <a href="mailto:info@yellowtagmedia.com">email us</a>
and we'll be happy to get right back to you.</p>
    <p>In the meantime, if you want to go back to the page that caused
the problem, you can do that <a href="javascript:history.go(-1);">by
clicking here.</a> If the same problem occurs, though, you may
want to come back a bit later. We bet we'll have things figured
out by then. Thanks again... we'll see you soon. And again, we're
really sorry for the inconvenience.</p>

</div>

<div id="footer"></div>

</body>

</html>
```

Save this file as *show_error.php*. But, before you do, keep in mind that this error page is for all your scripts and HTML pages. So, don't save it in a *chapter08/* directory; put it in a *scripts/* directory in your site's root to ensure that it's easily accessible.

NOTE If you want to follow along exactly with the book's structure, save this file in *phpMM2/scripts/* (where *phpMM/* is the root directory in the examples you can download from online) or *phpMM2/ch08/scripts/*, depending on your directory structure.

Next, you need to get the error message. The least error-prone way to do that is by using request parameters and the $_REQUEST array.

```
<?php
  $error_message = $_REQUEST['error_message'];
?>

<html>
  <!-- Existing HTML and PHP -->
</html>
```

What's so good about this approach? First, it's about as basic as your PHP programming can be. You're not using a calculation, per se, you're just pulling a value out of an array, instead. Better still, it's not your own custom array, but one that PHP provides for you, and even fills for you, using information supplied in the request to *show_error.php*.

There's That *scripts/* Directory Again

I thought scripts/ *directories were an outdated practice. Why is* show_error.php *still in a* scripts/ *directory?*

In Chapter 7—specifically in the box on page 208—you learned about the benefits of moving your scripts from nested *scripts/* directories into the main parts of your site. This means that you probably started placing web forms like *create_user.html* directly alongside *create_user.php* and *show_user.php*. That's because your HTML pages and your PHP pages are starting to be a lot more alike than they are different.

However, *show_error.php* isn't just another HTML page. It's something special—something used across your application. In fact, it's just like *database_connection.php*, which you should *also* keep in your main *scripts/* directory. These scripts are really utilities, not pages that should live alongside other HTML pages.

The best practice is to move to organizing your files by function. Thus, you might have a directory called *users/* that contains all

your user-related files: *show_user.php, create_user.php,* and *create_user.html.* You might have other similar directories, like *groups/* and *social/* and the like.

When you begin to organize by function, your organization system becomes meaningful. It tells you what things do, rather than what they are (HTML, CSS, PHP, or whatever). Your PHP scripts live alongside your HTML pages because they *work* together. In fact, down the line, you might even break things up further, separating code that's for creating and displaying a web page from code that interacts with your database. That will come later, but for now, keep thinking *function over format.* It's more important to group user-related files together than to have all your PHP scripts together.

So, store your utility scripts in *scripts/* for now. And yes, you could look at renaming *scripts/* to something like *utilities/,* if you like. Organize wisely now; when you have 20, 50, or 100 files, you'll be grateful for the structure.

Testing Your Solution

With your request parameter now in place, it's time to test it out in a browser. Visit your script's URL and add a request parameter. For example, you might use something like this in your URL:

```
http://www.yellowtagmedia.com/phpMM2/ch08/scripts/show_error.php
?error_message=There%27s%20been%20a%20problem%20connecting%20to
%20the%20database.
```

NOTE That URL should all be on one line in your browser bar. Additionally, many browsers will convert spaces to the web-safe equivalent, that strange %20. That's a way of telling a browser "insert a space."

You should see something like Figure 8-7, which is a nice-looking error page that didn't take lot of work to produce.

This simplicity—using request parameters that are just plain text, passed from one page or script to another—is the beauty of *show_error.php*. There's very little that can go wrong. That's what you want in an error page: elegance and simplicity.

FIGURE 8-7

One of the nicest things about any script that uses request parameters and $_REQUEST is that you can easily test these scripts with a little command-line magic. Just name your parameters on the command line, separate the first one from your script with ?, and then separate multiple request parameters from one another with &.

You do need to make one fix, though: that backslash showing up before a single apostrophe ("There\'s" in the first sentence) is no good. You can get rid of that with a little regular expression magic. Replace all occurrences of a backslash with...well, with nothing:

```
$error_message = preg_replace("/\\\\/", '',
                    $_REQUEST['error_message']);
```

PHP has an oddity in that you need to actually use four back slashes to match a single backslash. So, \\\\ matches \, oddly enough. That's because you're sort of "fighting" the PHP escape mechanism—which uses a backslash (For a refresher see the box on page 158).

Expect the Unexpected

Things are looking good. But once again, you're assuming that things go just the way you want. In fact, that's exactly the sort of thinking that leads people to ignore error pages. If you need to deal with problems to the point that you're *creating* an error page, you'd better believe that problems can also occur when you're actually *on* the error page.

Thankfully, you've cut down on most of that by keeping your error page simple (read: less error prone). But what if there's no `error_message` request parameter? In that case, you get something like Figure 8-8.

FIGURE 8-8

The kind of error page you've created in the previous section is still a bit incomplete. There's no information about what went wrong, and not even an acknowledgement that there's been an error; look at Figure 8-6 for a comparison. Thankfully, that's easy enough to fix.

You're back to instilling your visitors with possible confusion, and that's no good. There's an easy solution, though: just deal with the situation when there's no request parameter:

```php
<?php
  if (isset($_REQUEST['error_message'])) {
    $error_message = preg_replace("/\\\\/", '',
                          $_REQUEST['error_message']);
  } else {
    $error_message = "Something went wrong, and that's " .
                  "how you ended up here.";
  }
?>

<html>
  <!-- Existing HTML and PHP -->
</html>
```

You haven't seen `isset` before, but here's how it works: if the `error_message` `$_REQUEST` parameter is set—which just means that it has a value—things are fine.

Go ahead and set the $error_message variable. If there's not a request parameter for error_message, set the $error_message variable to a conversational, albeit generic, message. isset returns true if a variable has been assigned something and is not null.

Go to your error page again, without anything on the URL, and you'll get a nice-looking page once again. Check out Figure 8-9 for what you should expect.

FIGURE 8-9

You could probably tweak the style on this page a bit. Although the italics worked well for the explicit error message in Figure 8-6, it's not quite effective here. If you want to get a little more fancy, you could set the CSS class on the span within which the error message prints, based on whether you have a generic error message, like the one shown here, or a specific one.

Welcome to Security and Phishing

And now, welcome to a big, fat, ugly problem. The way your page is set up at this juncture, anyone with a bit of programming prowess could supply his own error message to your web page, simply by adding it to any URL that points to your application: *?error_message=your custom error message.* That's one way to employ a technique of Internet vandalism called *phishing*.

■ PHISHING AND SUBTLE REDIRECTION

Phishing is a technique by which someone receives what *appears* to be a trusted URL that in fact sends that user to an untrusted website. Suppose you get an email with a link to a site that looks like this:

http://yellowtagmedia.com/phpMM2/ch08/scripts/show_error.php?error_message=%3Ca%20href=%22http://www.amctv.com/shows/breaking-bad%22%3EClick%20Here%20To%20Report%20Your%20Error%3C/a%3E

It has lots of gibberish at the end, but you recognize the important part, the host name: *yellowtagmedia.com*. Throughout this book, you've been seeing *yellowtagmedia.com* as a domain name. (It's the author's domain, so this is a perfectly fine site to visit.) So, you go ahead and click the link, and you see something like Figure 8-10.

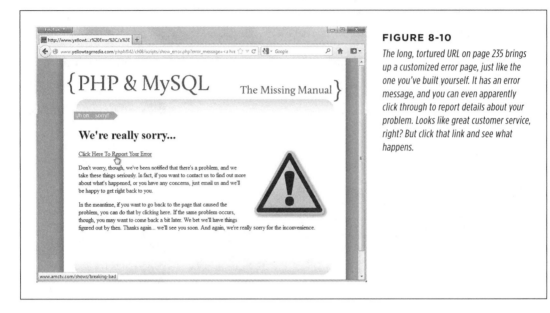

FIGURE 8-10

The long, tortured URL on page 235 brings up a customized error page, just like the one you've built yourself. It has an error message, and you can even apparently click through to report details about your problem. Looks like great customer service, right? But click that link and see what happens.

It's an error page, just like the one you've been creating. And, look, it has a link on it. Might as well trust the link, too. It appears on a trusted page. You click the link...and you end up on a completely different site—probably one you didn't expect (see Figure 8-11).

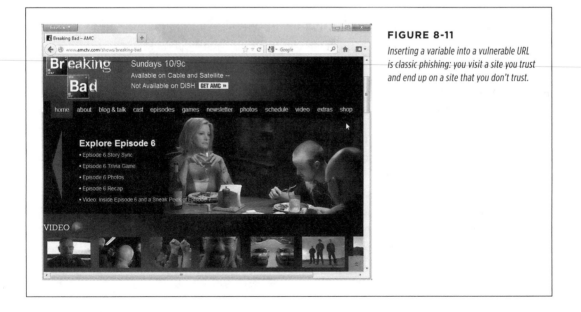

FIGURE 8-11

Inserting a variable into a vulnerable URL is classic phishing: you visit a site you trust and end up on a site that you don't trust.

Now, the AMC page for *Breaking Bad* is hardly anything to lose sleep over…and let's face it, *Breaking Bad* really is a great show. Suppose, though, that same link took you to a site that asks for your credit card or that is full of illicit material that could get you fired when you accidentally land on that site at work, or even just a simple site that asks you to "reconfirm" your user name and password: these are potential disasters.

A clever and not-so-well-meaning coder could easily use the same CSS that's used on *yellowtagmedia.com* to ensure that site looks just like the initial error page, and most users would never know the difference.

■ THE DANGERS OF REQUEST PARAMETERS

The problem is that anyone can actually type a request parameter in a URL. Look back at the URL that started all of this:

http://yellowtagmedia.com/phpMM2/ch08/scripts/show_error.php?error_ message=%3Ca%20href=%22http://www.amctv.com/shows/breaking-bad%22%3EClick%20Here%20To%20Report%20Your%20Error%3C/a%3E

It's the `error_message` parameter that creates all the trouble, because it accepts just about anything as a value. When you take away all the escaping, the URL really amounts to this:

http://yellowtagmedia.com/phpMM/ch07/show_error.php?error_message=<a href="http://www.amctv.com/shows/breaking-bad">Click Here To Report Your Error</a>

Suddenly, a link to a non-trusted site is dropped right into your trusted page. That's a big problem, and it can create massive headaches for your users.

Unfortunately, fixing this is going to take a lot of PHP wizardry that you don't have quite yet. Fortunately, it's coming…in about six chapters. For now, use this method of passing an error along via request parameters, but know that it's not quite ready for primetime. You'll need to use something called *sessions*, which is detailed in Chapter 14, to avoid ever becoming part of a phishing scam.

NOTE   Just so you know, this is a pretty subtle problem. It took a clever tech reviewer pointing it out to ever make it into print. But this is the price of coding on the big bad Internet: you always need to be aware of what a malicious, bored teenager can do to your site if you're not careful. Thankfully, though, you're learning everything you need to combat and prevent those attacks. Just hang tight until Chapter 14 on error handling, and then you can make some small changes that completely shut down any phishing attempts.

■ Add Debugging to Your Application

You've got some error pages that are very helpful to your readers. But what about you? Certainly, you're going to need to use your system, too. Although you want to have error pages that don't scare off your users, there are times when *you* need to figure out what's going on, not just in your code, but also on your front end. But, the error pages you've put in place are designed to *shield* users from seeing what's going on at the script level. What you need is to figure out a way to show the real errors that occurred—in a way that only you can see.

> **NOTE** You can find the finished example code for this section on this book's Missing CD page at *www. missingmanuals.com/cds/phpmysqlmm2e*.

Who's Using This App, Anyway?

Remember that this chapter started out by talking about the kinds of errors that your users see. The idea was to avoid unappealing, cryptic-looking errors like this:

```
#1054 - Unknown column 'firstname' in 'field list'
```

Sounds good...except when you're developing the application. In fact, if you're writing code, that's *exactly* the type of error you want to see. It's specific, helpful, and unlike your users, you aren't intimated (certainly not any more) by some techy details.

Put another way, you need a method to distinguish between debugging—when you're writing and fixing code—and production. You could have a way to set your application's mode. You could run in debug mode and see all the errors your script puts out, or you could run in production mode, in which error reporting isn't turned on. Then, you could simply run in debug mode until it's time to go live.

> **NOTE** You might even take this further: You could copy your code to a server, switch it to run in production mode, and then still run another copy in debug mode that you are working on and improving.

This arrangement is easy to set up; with *app_config.php*, you already have a nice central place to configure this sort of thing:

```php
<?php

// Set up debug mode
define("DEBUG_MODE", true);

// Database connection constants

?>
```

This gives you the ability to make a single change to DEBUG_MODE, and you get (or don't get) error reporting across your application. Now that you have a way to set your mode, it's time to make this new mode work.

Now You See Me, Now You Don't

Unfortunately, you've done a lot of work, but you still haven't solved one core problem: You need a way to display more information about an error to you and your programmer buddies without terrifying your users. Fortunately, you've laid some groundwork; the *app_config.php* file you created has a DEBUG_MODE, and that's the key ingredient.

What you need is a way to print out additional error information if you're in debug mode. To do this, you need to define a new function—call it debug_print—that only prints information if you're in debugging mode. Add the following code to *app_config.php*:

```php
<?php

// Set up debug mode
define("DEBUG_MODE", true);

// Database connection constants

function debug_print($message) {
  if (DEBUG_MODE) {
    echo $message;
  }
}
?>
```

With this function in *app_config.php*, it's available anywhere in your own code. All it does is selectively print a message; if debugging is enabled, it prints, and if it's not, $message never sees the light of day.

NOTE   You've just created your first custom function! Nice work. Although there's much more to learn about custom functions, notice how easy it is to create your own customized behavior for the rest of your application to use.

Next, you can add some additional information to your *show_error.php* page:

```php
<?php
  require 'app_config.php';

  if (isset($_REQUEST['error_message'])) {
    $error_message = preg_replace("/\\\\/", '',
                                  $_REQUEST['error_message']);
  } else {
    $error_message = "something went wrong, and that's how you ended up
here.";
  }

  if (isset($_REQUEST['system_error_message'])) {
    $system_error_message = preg_replace("/\\\\/", '',
                              $_REQUEST['system_error_message']);
```

```
    } else {
        $system_error_message = "No system-level error message was reported.";
    }
?>
```

NOTE   There are other ways to obtain this same result, but this one will avoid setting off any errors if you
have error_reporting turned on.

Then, down in your HTML, selectively print out this additional information:

```
<html>
 <head>
  <link href="../css/phpMM.css" rel="stylesheet" type="text/css" />
 </head>

 <body>
  <div id="header"><h1>PHP & MySQL: The Missing Manual</h1></div>
  <div id="example">Uh oh... sorry!</div>

  <div id="content">
    <h1>We're really sorry...</h1>
    <p><img src="../images/error.jpg" class="error" />
      <?php echo $error_message; ?>
      <span></p>
    <p>Don't worry, though, we've been notified that there's a
problem, and we take these things seriously. In fact, if you want to
contact us to find out more about what's happened, or you have any
concerns, just <a href="mailto:info@yellowtagmedia.com">email us</a>
and we'll be happy to get right back to you.</p>
    <p>In the meantime, if you want to go back to the page that caused
the problem, you can do that <a href="javascript:history.go(-1);">by
clicking here.</a> If the same problem occurs, though, you may
want to come back a bit later. We bet we'll have things figured
out by then. Thanks again... we'll see you soon. And again, we're
really sorry for the inconvenience.</p>
    <?php
      debug_print("<hr />");
      debug_print("<p>The following system-level message was received:
<b>{$system_error_message}</b></p>");
    ?>
  </div>

  <div id="footer"></div>
 </body>
</html>
```

Finally, you can put all this together: You have an error page, you have a means of printing information only if debugging is enabled, and you have *app_config.php* to tie everything together.

Before you're ready to conquer and selectively debug the world, though, there's something else to take care of. It's not quite error handling, but just plain, good coding.

Moving from `require` to `require_once`

If you look carefully at *database_connection.php,* you'll see this line at the top:

```
require 'app_config.php';
```

This means that any script such as the one that follows here, in turn requires *app_config.php*, as well.

```
require '../../scripts/database_connection.php';
```

So, if you wanted to get the setup from *app_config.php* in a script that already requires *database_connection.php*, you technically don't need to explicitly require *app_config.php*.

But—and this a big but—you've now hidden what's called a *dependency* in your code. Even though you're not requiring *app_config.php* explicitly, you're writing code assuming that *app_config.php* has been loaded. Suppose that you change a script to not use a database; the natural next step would be to remove the require for *database_connection.php*. Because your script no longer uses a database, requiring *database_connection.php* wouldn't make sense. With that removal, however, you also lose *app_config.php,* which causes a hidden problem that wouldn't show up until you realized none of your helpful constants and error messages are defined.

For this reason alone, it's a good idea to always be explicit in your requirements. To be sure, there's an obvious concern here: *app_config.php* will end up being required *twice* in database-driven scripts. You'll require *app_config.php* as well as *database_connection.php*, which in turn requires *app_config.php* again.

To get around this, you can use `require_once` instead of `require` in all your utility scripts. Therefore, in your main script—in whatever script your main code exists—use the normal require:

```
// main script you're writing code
require '../scripts/app_config.php';
```

Then, in any utility scripts that also need *app_config.php*, you would use require_once:

```
// database_connection.php and any other utility scripts
require_once '../scripts/app_config.php';
```

The require_once line checks whether the specified script has already been included (through include or require). It only includes the script if hasn't already been loaded. This ensures that *app_config.php* is only loaded once.

But, there's yet another problem: sometimes you have one script—like *create_user. php*—call another script—like *show_user.php*. In this case, you have two scripts that probably both use require, which will result in errors about constants being redefined. Is this a problem? Should you rethink and refactor *app_config.php*? Should you abstract out those constants into another file or move them into *database_connection.php*?

Honestly, you can just get around all of this by using require_once in *all* of your scripts. This rule of thumb is a good way to ensure that *app_config.php* is never loaded more than once. It also has another side effect: you're no longer trying to figure out which version of require to use. Just use require_once, unless you have a specific need to require something multiple times. That's something that rarely happens, so going with require_once as your standard is a good idea.

> **NOTE** In fact, you could have just started by using require_once right from the beginning. But, then you'd have no real idea *why* you're using that over require. By running through this process of actually seeing how some of your scripts call some of your other scripts multiple times (like the example on page 171), you can now explain to your coworkers why they too should almost always use require_once in their PHP scripts.

■ Redirecting On Error

You now have a complex mechanism in place to deal with error messages as they crop up, and you even have a way of printing out errors for your programming edification (with debug_print). Now, it's time to see how to use the error information.

Take a look at one of your simplest page/script combinations: *connect.html* and *connect.php*, from Chapter 5.

> **NOTE** For this exercise, copy these scripts into a new directory so that you can make changes to them. You should then change *connect.html* to submit to *connect.php*, without using a *scripts/* directory, and ensure that *connect.php* resides directly alongside *connect.html*. You should also be sure to require_once *app_config .php*, and ensure that your path to *app_config.php* reflects the new location of *connect.php*.

> Also, you can find the finished example code for this section on this book's Missing CD page at *www.missing manuals.com/cds/phpmysqlmm2e*.

Update *connect.php* to *show_user.php*

Right now, *connect.php* just uses die to report problems in connecting to your database:

```php
<?php

require_once '../scripts/app_config.php';
```

```
mysql_connect(DATABASE_HOST, DATABASE_USERNAME, DATABASE_PASSWORD)
  or die("<p>Error connecting to database: " .
        mysql_error() . "</p>");


// And so on...
?>
```

Right now, if `mysql_connect` fails, the entire script just goes down in a ball of flames. Not so great. One way you could fix the problem would be to do something like this:

```
if (!mysql_connect(DATABASE_HOST,
                DATABASE_USERNAME, DATABASE_PASSWORD)) {
  $user_error_message = "there was a problem connecting to the " .
                        "database that holds the information we need " .
                        "to get you connected.";
  $system_error_message = mysql_error();
  header("Location: ../scripts/show_error.php?" .
        "error_message={$user_error_message}&" .
        "system_error_message={$system_error_message}");
  exit();
}
```

NOTE   This is one of those sections of code that involves long lines that are ill-suited for print. You certainly don't need to break up these lines into multiple lines, although you can if you like. The downloadable code uses a single line for defining $user_error_message as well as for passing a URL to header.

This example uses your new error page in conjunction with PHP's redirect. In addition, it supplies both a friendly and system-level error, so it should work pretty well. For the sake of testing, type in a bad database host, like this one:

```
if (!mysql_connect(DATABASE_HOST, DATABASE_USERNAME, "foo")) {
  // handle error
}
```

Next, go to *connect.html* in your browser, submit the form to *connect.php*, and you should be rewarded with your error page, as in Figure 8-12. In terms of seeing errors, you have your users—and yourself—covered.

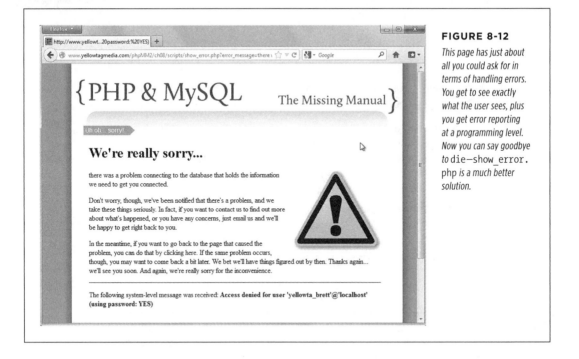

FIGURE 8-12

This page has just about all you could ask for in terms of handling errors. You get to see exactly what the user sees, plus you get error reporting at a programming level. Now you can say goodbye to die—show_error. php *is a much better solution.*

> **NOTE** Ensure that you have DEBUG_MODE set to true in *app_config.php* before you try this out (page 238) so that you'll see both the user-friendly and developer-friendly errors.

Now, set DEBUG_MODE to false in *app_config.php*:

```
// Set up debug mode

define("DEBUG_MODE", false);
```

Try going to *connect.html* and *connect.php* again; this time, you should only see the user-facing error (check out Figure 8-13).

FIGURE 8-13

What a difference some error-handling work makes. Remember back in the old days when a database error resulted in a blank page with a cryptic error message? This is a pretty massive upgrade. By now, you know that errors are going to happen, but now they happen in style, and that counts for quite a bit with the typical user.

Simplifying and Abstracting Your Code

Are you done yet? Well, almost. The error printing is great, but take another look at the code in your main script, *connect.php*:

```php
if (!mysql_connect(DATABASE_HOST,
                   DATABASE_USERNAME, DATABASE_PASSWORD)) {
  $user_error_message = "there was a problem connecting to the " .
                        "database that holds the information we need " .
                        "to get you connected.";
  $system_error_message = mysql_error();
  header("Location: ../scripts/show_error.php?" .
         "error_message={$user_error_message}&" .
         "system_error_message={$system_error_message}");
  exit();
}
```

That's a lot of code to handle the problem. In fact, you have a good bit more code dealing with the error than you do dealing with things that go right. That's not always a bad thing, but in this case, it's just not necessary. Do you remember how this code originally looked?

```
mysql_connect(DATABASE_HOST, DATABASE_USERNAME, DATABASE_PASSWORD)
   or die("<p>Error connecting to database: " . mysql_error() . "</p>");
```

This code has a line that does what you want. It also has a line if there are problems. Now multiply that by all the different places your code can fail; that's a lot of error handling code.

So, can you get your error handling to be that elegant? It's worth at try. Look closely at the code again and notice how regardless of what the error is, parts of the code will always be the same:

```
if (!mysql_connect(DATABASE_HOST,
                   DATABASE_USERNAME, DATABASE_PASSWORD)) {
  $user_error_message = "there was a problem connecting to the " .
                        "database that holds the information we need " .
                        "to get you connected.";
  $system_error_message = mysql_error();
  header("Location: ../scripts/show_error.php?" .
         "error_message={$user_error_message}&" .
         "system_error_message={$system_error_message}");
  exit();
}
```

The only things that ever change here are the actual error messages. The rest—the variable names, the header call, and the building of the URL—are always the same. This seems like it would be a good time create another function, a lot like debug_print, to handle the messages.

Add this function to *app_config.php*, further expanding your utility script:

```
<?php

// Set up debug mode
define("DEBUG_MODE", true);

// Database connection constants

function debug_print($message) {
  if (DEBUG_MODE) {
    echo $message;
  }
}

function handle_error($user_error_message, $system_error_message) {
  header("Location: show_error.php?" .
         "error_message={$user_error_message}&" .
         "system_error_message={$system_error_message}");
  exit();
}
?>
```

This bit of code is really just a variation on what you did with debug_print (page 239). You've taken something that's essentially the same code, over and over, and put it into a nice, handy, easy-to-reference custom function. The only change is the addition of exit. This line ensures that regardless of how the calling script is structured, once the header redirects the browser to your error page, nothing else happens. The error page displays, and PHP stops whatever else it might have planned to do.

Now, you can simplify *connect.php* by quite a bit:

```
if (!mysql_connect(DATABASE_HOST, DATABASE_USERNAME, "foo")) {
  handle_error("There was a problem connecting to the database " .
            "that holds the information we need to get you connected.",
            mysql_error());
}
```

This code is a *lot* neater, especially when you realize that it can fit into a single line in a terminal or editor. But, you can take this yet further:

```
mysql_connect(DATABASE_HOST, DATABASE_USERNAME, "foo")
  or handle_error("There was a problem connecting to the database " .
            "that holds the information we need to get you connected.",
            mysql_error());
```

Here, you've dropped the if statement and returned to the simple elegance of the or die you used to have, but with a much nicer function: your own handle_error.

redirect **Is Path-Insensitive**

There's just one problem with the current incarnation of *connect_php*, and it looks like Figure 8-14. You might see just this when you try out *connect.php* for yourself. You see a page indicating that something has gone wrong, but it's sure not the *show_error.php* page you were expecting.

This error is well known in PHP. Most web servers are set to treat any URL request that ends in *.php* as a PHP request. That's good, because it means that you don't have to stash all your PHP scripts in one directory. But it's bad, because the web server doesn't see whether the URL that ends in .php matches an actual file. It just hands the URL over to the PHP program. But if that URL isn't a pointer to a real file, PHP says, "I don't have anything to run." Or, more accurately, it says "no input file specified."

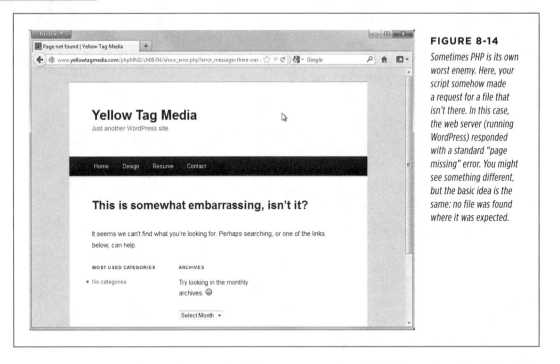

FIGURE 8-14

Sometimes PHP is its own worst enemy. Here, your script somehow made a request for a file that isn't there. In this case, the web server (running WordPress) responded with a standard "page missing" error. You might see something different, but the basic idea is the same: no file was found where it was expected.

Yet the question remains: *Why* are you getting this? It has to do with this little bit of code in *app_config.php*:

```php
function handle_error($user_error_message, $system_error_message) {
  header("Location: show_error.php?" .
         "error_message={$user_error_message}&" .
         "system_error_message={$system_error_message}");
}
```

In this code, the path to *show_error.php* is relative to *app_config.php*. Because *app_config.php* is in the same directory as *show_error.php*, there's nothing before the file name.

But this code is executed from your *connect.php* script, in (at least in the examples in this book) *ch07/*. Therefore, the path from *that* location to *show_error.php* is *../scripts/show_error.php*. Even though the handle_error function is defined in *app_config.php*, it's run from the *connect.php* script's context. The result? You're looking for *show_error.php* in the wrong place.

But, if you change the path in *app_config.php* to work with *connect.php*, and you later have a different script in a different location, you're going to get this same issue all over again. This begs the question: How is handle_error very useful anymore?

What you need, once again, is a way to indicate a common property—the root of your site—and then relate the path of *show_error.php* to that with an absolute path rather than using a relative path. (And if you need a refresher on the difference between the two, see the box below.)

Relative and Absolute Paths

A *relative path* is a path that references a file relative to the location of the current file. This usually means that the path begins with either the file itself, like *show_error.php*, or it moves back a directory using the .. indicator. So, relative paths look like *show_error.php* or *../scripts/show_error.php*. In both cases, your starting point is the current file indicating the path.

An *absolute path* is one that is not related to the current file; instead, it's related to the root of your site. You can always spot absolute paths because they start with a /, meaning that they begin looking for the file at the root, or "base," of your website. Thus, an absolute path would be something like */scripts/show_error.php*.

You can define your site root in *app_config.php* with a new constant:

```php
// Site root
define("SITE_ROOT", "/phpMM2/");
```

Now, you can use that constant in handle_error. Here's the final version of *app_config.php*, with all of the new constants, the completed handle_error function, and debug_print function:

```php
<?php

// Set up debug mode
define("DEBUG_MODE", false);

// Site root
define("SITE_ROOT", "/phpMM/");

// Database connection constants
define("DATABASE_HOST", "database.host.com");
define("DATABASE_USERNAME", "username");
define("DATABASE_PASSWORD", "super.secret.password");
define("DATABASE_NAME", "database-name");

function debug_print($message) {
  if (DEBUG_MODE) {
    echo $message;
  }
}
```

```
function handle_error($user_error_message, $system_error_message) {
  header("Location: " . SITE_ROOT . "scripts/show_error.php?" .
        "error_message={$user_error_message}&" .
        "system_error_message={$system_error_message}");
}

?>
```

> **NOTE** You can't use the curly braces trick to insert constants into a string; instead, you need to concatenate SITE_ROOT to your URL string in the call to header by using the dot (.) operator.

Now, you should finally be able to see *show_error.php* via an error in *connect.php*, in all its glory. Check out Figure 8-15 for the result of all this work.

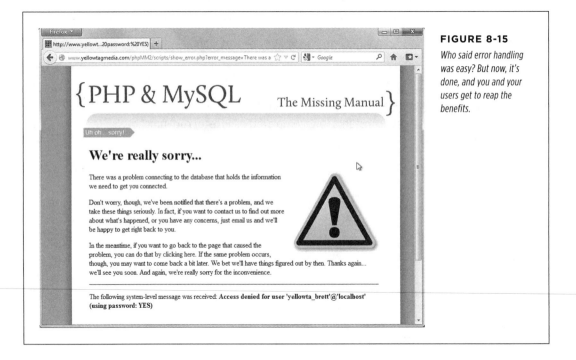

FIGURE 8-15

Who said error handling was easy? But now, it's done, and you and your users get to reap the benefits.

To finish up, take a blazing trip through all of your scripts and replace every bit of die and other error handling with calls to handle_error. Don't forget to update *database_connection.php* to use handle_error, too:

```php
<?php
  require 'app_config.php';

  mysql_connect(DATABASE_HOST, DATABASE_USERNAME, DATABASE_PASSWORD)
    or handle_error("There was a problem connecting to the database " .
            "that holds the information we need to get you connected.",
            mysql_error());

  mysql_select_db(DATABASE_NAME)
    or handle_error("There's a configuration problem with our database.",
                mysql_error());
?>
```

FREQUENTLY ASKED QUESTION

To Err Is PHP

A 20-plus–page chapter on error handling? Seriously?

It seems hard to believe, doesn't it? You've not added any real new functionality to your web app. Of course, you've learned a bit more about constants, you've defined two custom functions, you've added a utility class, and you've even managed to get a handle on require and require_once.

Still, error handling is usually something that books stick in the last chapter, figuring people won't mind if it's near the end where it can be ignored. Why spend all this time on something that (hopefully) your users never see? Well, mostly because an application that doesn't handle errors simply isn't complete.

And, like it or not, when you're just starting out programming, or programming in a new language, you're going to make more mistakes.

Tests and error handling are absolutely the best two ways to catch mistakes early and then provide the simplest path toward fixing those mistakes. Now that you have robust error handling, you'll be surprised how often a big problem is turned into a small problem because you spotted an error right away and could track it down without wading through all your code, hopelessly wondering what really went wrong.

Handling Images and Complexity

You've come to a watershed moment in your programming career, however brief you feel that career has been. Up until this point in the book, you've been using a lot of PHP constructs—from if statements to some basic functions to constants and even error handling. You've also become familiar with the basic MySQL interactions you'll need in most PHP scripts. With what you already know, you're ready to take on most of the basic programming problems you'll run across in a typical web application—as long as you're thinking on a single-page level.

In other words, if you have a form that gathers information, you can handle that. You can grab information from a table, and you can put information into a table. You can respond to errors, redirect users, and even distinguish between a good user experience and a bad one.

In spite of all that, you know that web applications are greater than the sum of their single-page interactions. Ten different pages that interact with ten different tables is a much simpler situation than a complete web application that has ten pages, particularly when those ten tables connect and interact with one another, and even relate information in one table to information in another. Add to that image handling (something you started to dig into in order to finish your user form), some interaction with Facebook and Twitter, and allowing users to actually log in, and things get a lot trickier.

And that's what's next: the jump from thinking about single forms and single scripts to thinking about entire systems. You're ready to begin interacting with the file system—the place where your scripts, files, and images live. You're ready to start thinking not just about a single table like *users* but working with multiple tables. And, custom functions? You've already built two—debug_print and handle_error—so you've got a foundation upon which to build.

NOTE   At this point, the changes to your code are coming fast and furious. In fact, you might be a little unsure as to whether you have everything right. If that's the case, you can always hop online and visit *www .missingmanuals.com/cds/phpmysqlmm2e* to get the chapter-by-chapter examples and make sure you're caught up and ready to keep programming.

Along the way, though, the decisions become trickier. Complexity brings with it not just the question, "What do I do next?" but also, "Of the two or three ways I *could* solve this problem, which one is the *best* way?" So, get ready: you're diving into deeper programming waters, which tend to comprise as much critical thinking and philosophy as they do new PHP and MySQL language features.

■ Images Are Just Files

The big glaring omission in your work with users is that pesky profile image that you worked with in Chapter 7 on page 208. You probably remember that the user's profile is pretty incomplete right now. The difference between your mock-up from that chapter (shown in Figure 9-1) and where your actual code is (shown in Figure 9-2) is easy to spot: it's all in that image.

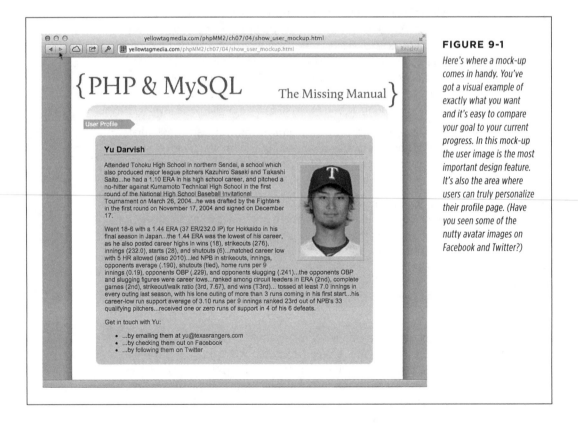

FIGURE 9-1

Here's where a mock-up comes in handy. You've got a visual example of exactly what you want and it's easy to compare your goal to your current progress. In this mock-up the user image is the most important design feature. It's also the area where users can truly personalize their profile page. (Have you seen some of the nutty avatar images on Facebook and Twitter?)

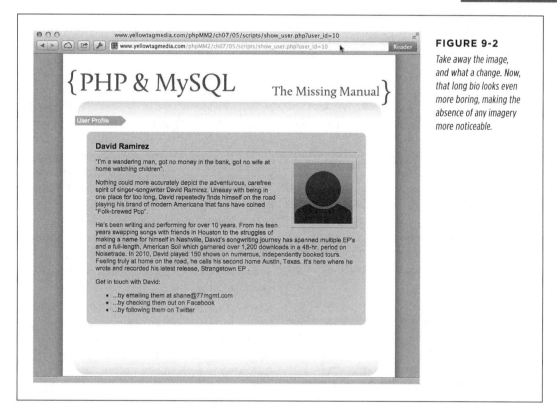

FIGURE 9-2

Take away the image, and what a change. Now, that long bio looks even more boring, making the absence of any imagery more noticeable.

To place a user image on the page, turn to the good old HTML <img> tag:

```
<img src="images/darvish.jpg" class="user_pic" />
```

The value of the src attribute is a reference to a file, although you don't have any image files yet. You have the user's name and information in your *users* table, but there's no image on your web server to which you can point. You need both a file and then a reference to that file.

It's a new PHP challenge: how do you get something other than text information from a user, and then what do you do with that information once you have it? (For more information on how files appear to PHP, see the box on page 256.)

Files, File Systems, and Client Versus Server

This might be the first time you've needed to get a clear understanding of the difference between what's on your user's computer and what's on the web server. You know what a file is: it's just a collection of bits and bytes that your computer knows how to handle. Your scripts, HTML, CSS, and JavaScript are ultimately just text: characters strung together and interpreted by a web browser or the PHP program. In the case of PHP, your web server (and specifically, the PHP interpreter interacting with your web server) interprets that PHP, turns it into HTML, CSS, and JavaScript for your browser, and then lets the browser take over. For the browser, it takes HTML, CSS, and JavaScript—whether in a static file or returned by a web server that's processed a PHP script—and renders those to your user's screen.

Images, on the other hand, are binary data. The same bits and bytes that make up your text files are used to indicate location and color of pixels. You need a different type of interpreter to read a binary file. Fortunately, web browsers are perfectly capable of taking an image file—be it a JPEG (.jpg), GIF (.gif), or PNG (.png)—and displaying it. Still, the process of getting a binary file is a bit different.

When users type the URL of your web application into their browser, they're running your program, which resides on a web server, somewhere, and is available via the Internet. They're running that program by using their web browser, which is a program that resides on *their* computer. There's a big difference between what's on their computer, and what's on your web server. Your web server can't reach into their computer and grab images, for example. The users—if they want to see one of their images in your program—have to upload that image to your web server. Your web server stores that image and can display it to whomever needs to see it.

Of course, most users don't know how to upload a file by using a program like FTP. It's up to you to get their file from their computer onto your file system. A *file system* is just a fancy word for the collection of files on your web server. It can also refer to the files on a user's computer.

Put another way, the user's computer is a *client*—a computer that's accessing your program. Your program runs on the *server*. This relationship is called a *client-server* interaction. Your job is to get an image file from the client to the server. Then, your server can give your PHP scripts access to that image file to be used in your programs (and, most important, in the user profile page).

HTML Forms Can Set the Stage

In this situation, your HTML is critically important to your PHP program. You need to ensure that the HTML form with which your user is working is set up correctly. Not only does that form need to give the user a place to select an image, but it needs to set up the process by which that image is uploaded correctly.

Copy your *create_user.html* page from your Chapter 8 examples into the directory in which you're working now. Here's where you left things; several steps are in place for uploading an image:

```
<html>
 <head>
  <link href="../css/phpMM.css" rel="stylesheet" type="text/css" />
 </head>
```

```
<body>
  <div id="header"><h1>PHP & MySQL: The Missing Manual</h1></div>
  <div id="example">User Signup</div>

  <div id="content">
    <h1>Join the Missing Manual (Digital) Social Club</h1>
    <p>Please enter your online connections below:</p>
    <form action="create_user.php" method="POST"
          enctype="multipart/form-data">
      <fieldset>
        <label for="first_name">First Name:</label>
        <input type="text" name="first_name" size="20" /><br />
        <label for="last_name">Last Name:</label>
        <input type="text" name="last_name" size="20" /><br />
        <label for="email">E-Mail Address:</label>
        <input type="text" name="email" size="50" /><br />
        <label for="facebook_url">Facebook URL:</label>
        <input type="text" name="facebook_url" size="50" /><br />
        <label for="twitter_handle">Twitter Handle:</label>
        <input type="text" name="twitter_handle" size="20" /><br />
        <label for="user_pic">Upload a picture:</label>
        <input type="file" name="user_pic" size="30" />
        <label for="bio">Bio:</label>
        <textarea name="bio" cols="40" rows="10"></textarea>
      </fieldset>

      <br />

      <fieldset class="center">

        <input type="submit" value="Join the Club" />
        <input type="reset" value="Clear and Restart" />
      </fieldset>

    </form>

  </div>


  <div id="footer"></div>

</body>

</html>
```

NOTE You also should change the action of the form to reflect that you're no longer using a *scripts/* directory. This HTML is in the *ch09/* example directory in this chapter's downloadable examples (*www.missingmanuals.com/ cds/phpmysqlmm2e*).

The key parts here are the enctype attribute on the <form> tag, and input type="file" for the user_pic. This code configures the form to upload not just text but also a binary image file.

Figure 9-3 shows that the user can already select an image now. But, there's something else this HTML needs: a size limit on the image. At one time or another, you've probably received that email from a friend that has a 22 MB picture of a cat blown up to 100 times its normal size, right? You want to avoid that in your forms. No 22 MB cat images; a single MB or two is plenty for any reasonable profile picture.

NOTE MB stands for *megabyte*, which is one million bytes. That's what the *mega* prefix represents: 1,000,000 of something. To get an idea of sizes, a Microsoft Word document of 20 or 30 pages is only about 1 MB. So, a 20 MB image is a *large* image.

In general, the only reason you'd want image files that big is for high-end photography sites or image-sharing sites like Flickr (*www.flickr.com*) for which detail is important. You don't need anything like that for a simple profile picture.

You can limit the size of an uploaded file by adding a hidden input element, and give it the name "MAX_FILE_SIZE." For the value, set it to the maximum size of the uploaded image you'll allow, in bytes. If you want to allow a 1 MB image, that's 1,000,000 bytes. Here's the HTML to permit a 2 MB image:

```
<input type="hidden" name="MAX_FILE_SIZE" value="2000000" />
<label for="user_pic">Upload a picture:</label>
<input type="file" name="user_pic" size="30" />
```

WARNING Ensure that you put this input *before* the "file" type input. You should also avoid any comments in the value attribute. Count those zeroes carefully, or you'll be back to shockingly large cats again. And no, for those concerned, no felines were harmed in the making of this book. Shrunk down to manageable sizes? Perhaps.

The form doesn't look any different with this input element, but now you're ready to let users upload an image, and do something with it (see Figure 9-3).

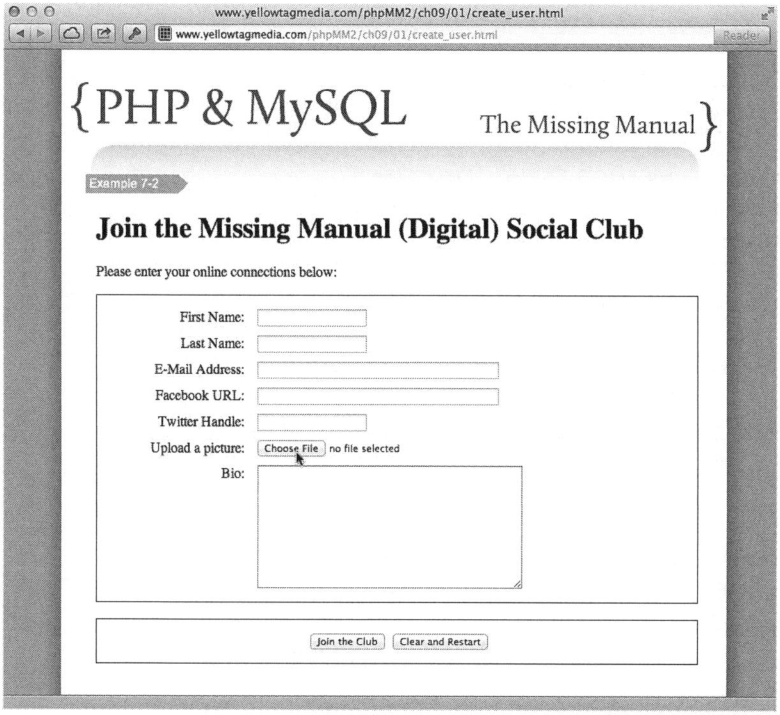

FIGURE 9-3

With much of your HTML in place, many of the changes you're starting to make are not noticeable when you look at the web page. Nothing looks different about this form, but with the addition of the code on page 258, it imposes limits on what your users can do—limits that you've set.

Try this out: select an image and then click Join the Club. Even though there's no PHP script waiting to receive this information, you'll see your browser slowly uploading something. Take a look at Figure 9-4 to see how Google's Chrome responds: a bit-by-bit indication of how the upload is progressing.

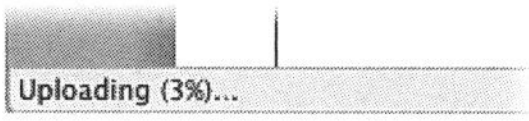

FIGURE 9-4

Sometimes, it's difficult to appreciate how much the web browser does for you. Just by using the input file type, you get a progress indicator, network connections, and an image upload, all for free. Now you've got time to write great PHP.

Uploading a User's Image to Your Server

It's time to grab that image and do something with it. Start by copying your old version of *create_user.php* into your current directory. Your script should look like this:

```php
<?php

require_once '../scripts/app_config.php';
require_once '../scripts/database_connection.php';

$first_name = trim($_REQUEST['first_name']);
$last_name = trim($_REQUEST['last_name']);
$email = trim($_REQUEST['email']);
$bio = trim($_REQUEST['bio']);
$facebook_url = str_replace("facebook.org", "facebook.com",
                           trim($_REQUEST['facebook_url']));
$position = strpos($facebook_url, "facebook.com");
if ($position === false) {
  $facebook_url = "http://www.facebook.com/" . $facebook_url;
}

$twitter_handle = trim($_REQUEST['twitter_handle']);
$twitter_url = "http://www.twitter.com/";
$position = strpos($twitter_handle, "@");
if ($position === false) {
  $twitter_url = $twitter_url . $twitter_handle;
} else {
  $twitter_url = $twitter_url . substr($twitter_handle, $position + 1);
}

$insert_sql = "INSERT INTO users (first_name, last_name, email, bio," .
                                 "facebook_url, twitter_handle) " .
              "VALUES ('{$first_name}', '{$last_name}', '{$email}', '{$bio}',
" .
                      "'{$facebook_url}', '{$twitter_handle}');";

// Insert the user into the database
mysql_query($insert_sql)
  or die(mysql_error());

// Redirect the user to the page that displays user information
header("Location: show_user.php?user_id=" . mysql_insert_id());
exit();
?>
```

NOTE You need to make a few changes to get your script to this point. Update the path to *app_config* *.php* and *database_connection.php* if you need to, and ensure that you're using `require_once` instead of `require`.

■ SET UP SOME HELPER VARIABLES

First, you need to add some basic information that you'll use for getting at the file, and for storing it. Add these variables to the top of your page:

```php
<?php

require_once '../scripts/app_config.php';
require_once '../scripts/database_connection.php';

$upload_dir = HOST_WWW_ROOT . "uploads/profile_pics/";
$image_fieldname = "user_pic";

$first_name = trim($_REQUEST['first_name']);
// Other variables

// Get request information

// Insert into MySQL
?>
```

One new element is HOST_WWW_ROOT. It looks a bit like the SITE_ROOT you defined in *app_config.php* in Chapter 8, on page 249:

```php
// Site root
define("SITE_ROOT", "/phpMM2/");
```

HOST_WWW_ROOT hasn't been defined yet. Right now, you have a SITE_ROOT, which is the web-specific path to your site's root, so if your website is hosted without any directory prefix, your SITE_ROOT is probably just /. If you're running within a *phpMM2/* directory, for example, your site root might be */phpMM/.* The takeaway here is that the SITE_ROOT is defined in terms of what a web server and a browser connected to that server see.

But what the browser sees isn't the complete (or absolute) path to that file on your host's server. A hosting server has tons of directories and subdirectories. Your directory, for example, might be */home/username,* and then within there, you might have a *www/* or *public_html/* directory. It's in that directory that your web files reside.

What this means is that your SITE_ROOT maps to a different path—one in terms of what your host's file server looks like—that represents the absolute path of a file. Here, you're calling this new constant HOST_WWW_ROOT. Add that path to *app_config.php*:

```php
<?php

// Set up debug mode
define("DEBUG_MODE", true);

// Site root
define("SITE_ROOT", "/phpMM2/");

// Location of web files on host
define("HOST_WWW_ROOT", "/home/bdmclaughlin/public_html/phpMM2/");

// Database connection constants

// Custom functions
?>
```

Of course, your HOST_WWW_ROOT will look different than the one in this example. If you're unsure how to get this path, see the box on page 263. You're using this root—and not SITE_ROOT—because the process of uploading and moving around files is going to involve your host's file server, not the browser. The uploaded user file is going to be stored on the host's file system, so you must deal with paths with respect to your host's file system. The browser will eventually show the file, at which point SITE_ROOT will come back into play. However, the upload process has nothing to do with what the browser sees. You need to look at things from the file system's perspective, which is just the sort of base path that HOST_WWW_ROOT provides.

Create that directory on your web server by using a terminal shell, command-line tool, or your FTP client. If your HOST_WWW_ROOT is /home/bdmclaughlin/public_html/phpMM2/, you need to create /home/bdmclaughlin/public_html/phpMM2/uploads/profile_pics.

Just as users can type the wrong information into your text fields, they can mess things up when uploading an image. Time for some error handling. The next variable—$php_errors—adds an array of potential errors:

```php
$upload_dir = HOST_WWW_ROOT . "uploads/";
$image_fieldname = "user_pic";

// Potential PHP upload errors
$php_errors = array(1 => 'Maximum file size in php.ini exceeded',
                    2 => 'Maximum file size in HTML form exceeded',
                    3 => 'Only part of the file was uploaded',
                    4 => 'No file was selected to upload.');
```

You've used arrays before, but there's something new about this one. You're creating a new array by using the array keyword and then defining the values that go in that array.

UNDER THE HOOD

What's my Host WWW Root?

It's not always easy to figure out the root of your website on your hosting provider's server, especially if you're not familiar with lots of Unix commands. The easiest approach here would be to telnet or SSH in to your hosting provider. (That's opening a command-line or terminal shell on your hosting provider's system.)

If you can do that—and lots of times, all you have to do is ask your hosting provider for access—you can determine your site's absolute path from the perspective of the file system by using the pwd command:

```
bdmclaughlin@yellowtagmedia.com [~]# pwd
/home/bdmclaughlin
```

Now, before you turn this into HOST_WWW_ROOT, realize that you might not actually be in your web root. Much of the time, when you telnet or SSH in to a web host, you're in your account's home directory. It's within that account that you'll find the web directory. In the following example, the *public_html/* directory is the one you want:

```
bdmclaughlin@yellowtagmedia.com [~]# ls
-d */

access-logs/

BackupNow/

etc/

mail/

perl5/
```

```
public_ftp/

public_html/

tmp/

www/
```

You can either tack that on to what you saw from the pwd command or change into that directory and run pwd again:

```
bdmclaughlin@yellowtagmedia.com [~]# cd
public_html/
bdmclaughlin@yellowtagmedia.com [~/pub-
lic_html]# pwd
/home/bdmclaughlin/public_html
```

Then, you can take the result of that pwd command and drop it right in as your HOST_WWW_ROOT:

```
// Location of web files on host
define("HOST_WWW_ROOT",
        "/home/bdmclaughlin/public_html/
phpMM2/");
```

In this case, the site files are within a subdirectory of the web root, called *phpMM2/*, so you append that to the result of running pwd.

Failing all of this, you could just call your hosting provider and explain that you need the actual path on its file system for your web files. That might seem easier, but if you can get into your system via SSH or telnet, you might find it fun to find it yourself.

Because an array is basically a list of values, you could do something like this just as easily:

```
// Potential PHP upload errors
$php_errors = array('Maximum file size in php.ini exceeded',
                    'Maximum file size in HTML form exceeded',
                    'Only part of the file was uploaded',
                    'No file was selected to upload.');
```

In this array, each value is automatically numbered, starting at O. Thus, $php_errors[0] has the value "Maximum file size in php.ini exceeded", for instance.

> **NOTE** Remember from the box in Chapter 3, on page 74, PHP, like most every programming language, starts counting at 0, rather than 1.

So, what are those numbers and funny arrows (=>)? They're there because PHP arrays are *associative arrays*. That's why you can say, for example, $_REQUEST['user_pic']. The $_REQUEST array doesn't just have values, it also has an *association* between those values (the information in an HTML form, usually) and the name of the fields in which those values appeared.

You can think of the mapping between the field name user_pic and the value of that field—something like *profile_pic.jpg*, for example—as being defined like this:

```
$_REQUEST = array('user_pic' => 'profile_pic.jpg');
```

> **NOTE** PHP is actually doing things in a much trickier way—that's how it lets you define any form field you want, of any type you want, with any name you want, and PHP handles it. Still, it all boils down to the creation of an associative array, with field names associated with, or *mapped to*, field values.

Going back to your array of PHP errors:

```
// Potential PHP upload errors
$php_errors = array(1 => 'Maximum file size in php.ini exceeded',
                    2 => 'Maximum file size in HTML form exceeded',
                    3 => 'Only part of the file was uploaded',
                    4 => 'No file was selected to upload.');
```

In this case, you're taking numbering into your own hands, rather than letting PHP define its own numbers. As such, $php_errors[1] is now "'Maximum file size in php.ini exceeded'," rather than letting PHP's zero-based numbering assign that string's value to $php_errors[0].

Tampering with PHP's numbering is generally a bad idea because you're changing behavior that all PHP programmers expect. In this case, though, it's for a worthy cause.

That's because PHP does more than give you a $_REQUEST array. When there are files involved, it gives you a $_FILES array. That array, just like $_REQUEST, is keyed to your field. Thus, $_FILES[$image_fieldname] is associated with the image uploaded (hopefully) from your form. (Remember, you defined $image_fieldname nearer the top of *create_user.php*.)

Furthermore, $_FILES[$image_fieldname] is itself an array, with information about the uploaded file, and any errors that might have occurred in the process. One of those pieces of information is $_FILES[$image_fieldname]['error']. This field returns a number: 0 for "Everything went OK," and non-zero for problems. Those non-zero numbers are none other than:

```
1 => 'Maximum file size in php.ini exceeded'
2 => 'Maximum file size in HTML form exceeded'
3 => 'Only part of the file was uploaded'
4 => 'No file was selected to upload.'
```

You can see why renumbering the $php_errors array makes sense: you've got a map of error codes that $_FILES[$image_fieldname]['error'] might return, and the human-readable errors that go with them.

At this juncture, you've got all the information you need; time to start using it.

■ DID THE FILE UPLOAD WITH ANY ERRORS?

Next, you need to check that $_FILES[$image_fieldname]['error'] piece of the $_FILES array and see whether any errors occurred. If the value is non-zero, something went wrong, and you need to handle the problem. Luckily, you have a handy-dandy function for just that: handle_error.

```php
<?php
// Require utility scripts

// Set up variables

// Get everything from the form aside from the image... down to...
if ($position === false) {
  $twitter_url = $twitter_url . $twitter_handle;
} else {
  $twitter_url = $twitter_url . substr($twitter_handle, $position + 1);
}

// Make sure we didn't have an error uploading the image
($_FILES[$image_fieldname]['error'] == 0)
  or handle_error("the server couldn't upload the image you selected.",
                  $php_errors[$_FILES[$image_fieldname]['error']]);

$insert_sql = "INSERT INTO users (first_name, last_name, email, bio," .
                                 "facebook_url, twitter_handle) " .
              "VALUES ('{$first_name}', '{$last_name}', '{$email}', '{$bio}',
" .
                      "'{$facebook_url}', '{$twitter_handle}');";

// Insert the user into the database
mysql_query($insert_sql)
  or die(mysql_error());

// Redirect the user to the page that displays user information
header("Location: show_user.php?user_id=" . mysql_insert_id());
exit();
?>
```

If the error field (`$_FILES[$image_fieldname]['error']`) is zero, things are great; just keep going. If it's non-zero, you want to show your user an error, using the error code to look up the exact problem in your $php_errors associative array—and display that, too, if debugging is on (page 238).

> **NOTE** Now would be a good time to check *app_config.php*, and verify that you have DEBUG_MODE set to true.

There's also a new wrinkle in here that you might have just skipped right over: This line is basically an `if` statement without the `if`. PHP will evaluate the following line:

```
($_FILES[$image_fieldname]['error'] == 0)
```

If that line is `true`, it will continue. If the line isn't true, it runs the `or` part of the code on the next line; in this case, that's `handle_error`.

Essentially, the preceding example does the same thing as the following code:

```
if ($_FILES[$image_fieldname]['error'] != 0) {
  handle_error("the server couldn't upload the image you selected.",
               $php_errors[$_FILES[$image_fieldname]['error']]);
}
```

> **WARNING** Watch your square brackets ([and]) and parentheses carefully here; it's easy to get them mixed up and cause a hard-to-find error.

But the code without the `if` is shorter and cleaner. Every bit helps. This is a nice trick to add to your growing PHP toolkit.

You can check your code out in action at this point. Visit *create_user.html* and find an image file that's bigger than 2 MB. Photos that come straight from your camera are likely to be large. (If you're on a Mac, you can export a full-size photo from iPhoto.) Select that image and then try and submit your form. You should see something like Figure 9-5. This page is the result of your code finding an error code, and that error code being matched up to an error in $php_errors—in this case, your image was larger than your HTML file allowed.

> **NOTE** You might have noticed that even though the image was rejected, your browser still uploads the image—regardless of how big the image is, or what your maximum file size is. That's because it's only *after* the image is uploaded that the size comparison is made. That's sort of a bummer, but it's a browser thing, and not something you can fix with PHP.

FIGURE 9-5

Here's one of those beautiful situations where the hard work you did earlier pays off. Rather than wading through your code or even writing custom PHP, you can quickly hand off an error to your handle_error *function and get a nice response. Now multiply that by the hundreds (thousands?) of times you'll use* handle_ error, *and you'll start to see the value of learning that utility function early in your PHP life (Chapter 8, page 246).*

POWER USERS' CLINIC

Breathing and Sleeping Matter

Any good programmer will tell you stories of at least a few all-night hacking sessions. And odds are, those stories will be tinged rosy, full of victories and excitement. But the truth of the matter is that fatigue slows the brain down, and no programmer is as effective on two hours of sleep as he is on six.

Why is this relevant? Because a tired brain isn't as useful as a rested one. And, because if you've been swimming in the pool of PHP programming for eight chapters before this one, by now you're well into the deep end. Chances are that you're having to read at least a few things twice, and some of this

new code introduces not just one or two new things, but three, or four, or five.

There's nothing at all wrong with this, but if you're getting worn out, nobody wins by you plowing ahead. Take a few hours off, ride your bike, jog a mile, or just set PHP aside for the night. You'll be stunned at how much clearer things seem after a bit of rest from programming. Don't think that rest and taking a few moments to breathe out of sight of the keyboard are a sign of weakness; in fact, it's just the opposite.

■ IS THIS REALLY AN UPLOADED FILE?

At this point, despite whether you have a real file, what your program needs to work with is a file *name*. That name is controlled entirely by what your users put into their file input box. This means that if a user is tricky, malicious, and thoroughly dishonest, he might try to put in a file name that does upload a file on the host provider's system, but also just so happens to match one of the special files on web servers that control things like, say, the user passwords (that file is usually */etc/passwd*). You need a way to stop that from happening. (More PHP books and tutorials than you can imagine leave this step out, but it's critical.)

You might think you're about to use regular expressions and check for all kinds of fancy file name characters, but there's an easier way. PHP gives you a function called is_uploaded_file whose purpose it is to ensure that for a given name, that name references a file uploaded with HTTP (the language of web browsers and HTML forms). In other words, if the supplied name targets a file on your web server, this function will return false, and you know that something's fishy.

Here's what you want to do:

```
// Make sure we didn't have an error uploading the image
($_FILES[$image_fieldname]['error'] == 0)
  or handle_error("the server couldn't upload the image you selected.",
                  $php_errors[$_FILES[$image_fieldname]['error']]);

// Is this file the result of a valid upload?
is_uploaded_file($_FILES[$image_fieldname]['tmp_name'])
  or handle_error("you were trying to do something naughty. Shame on you!",
                  "Uploaded request: file named " .
                  "'{$_FILES[$image_fieldname]['tmp_name']}'");


// Interact with MySQL
```

This code uses another property of $_FILES[$image_fieldname]: the temporary name of the file. This gives you the name of the file as it currently stands and lets you make sure it's an uploaded file.

But, there's a problem here: is_uploaded_file fires off an error if the file isn't uploaded. That sounds good, except that you've done a lot of work to handle errors your own way. You don't want is_uploaded_file to generate an error; you just want its return value, even if there's a problem.

You can instruct PHP to run a function but suppress errors by inserting the @ character directly before the function, and that's exactly what you need here:

```
// Is this file the result of a valid upload?
@is_uploaded_file($_FILES[$image_fieldname]['tmp_name'])
  or handle_error("you were trying to do something naughty. Shame on you!",
                  "Uploaded request: file named " .
                  "'{$_FILES[$image_fieldname]['tmp_name']}'");
```

If there's a problem when the function runs, handle_error takes over, rather than your script throwing out some unintelligible error of its own. You've avoided a nasty security hole. One more hacker thwarted. (For more on that @ character, see the box on page 269.)

Suppress Errors at Your Own Peril

There's perhaps no more intriguing operator in PHP than @. With one keystroke, all the problems that might come about from a user entering invalid data, or a SQL query having an incorrect column, or even just a poorly formed URL can be banished. Your code can continue without having to check for every possible mistake your users, you, and your code might make...and that's a lot of potential mistakes.

But @ is an atomic bomb waiting to turn your code into a smoldering slag heap. Use it frequently, and you'll quickly find that your code is riddled with potential problems. You'll never be sure if your problem is something your user did, something you did, or a legitimate bug you need to fix.

Regardless of what's causing the error, if you snuck around it with @, you have a legitimate bug. Make a rule for yourself:

when you use @ (as in the very next line), pair it with an or and explicit error handling. You'll be much better off for the discipline.

But—there's always a but, isn't there?—high-volume, production websites often use @ because they simply *can't* crash or stop working. In those cases, you should usually go with some sort of hybrid solution. On the one hand, use @, but then pair it with or that is triggered by a flag, like your debugging mode flag (page 238). Thus, in "normal" mode, things run without spewing tons of errors (or perhaps by only logging those errors). Then, by flipping on debugging mode, you can see what's really going on and track down problems and fix them.

IS THE UPLOADED FILE REALLY AN IMAGE?

You have a file uploaded, and you know it's not some fake file that has a name that points at a protected file on your server's file system. It's finally time to move on and show the image, right? Well, unfortunately, not quite. You have a file, but is it an image? There's nothing preventing a user from accidentally uploading a Word document, or a malicious user uploading some JavaScript or an executable file.

Remember, you can't assume that your users are going to do the right thing. Thankfully, PHP offers the getimagesize function, which checks the size of a given image file. And, best of all, this function kicks out an error if what it's evaluating is a non-image file. Add the following function to your script:

```
// Make sure we didn't have an error uploading the image
($_FILES[$image_fieldname]['error'] == 0)
  or handle_error("the server couldn't upload the image you selected.",
              $php_errors[$_FILES[$image_fieldname]['error']]);

// Is this file the result of a valid upload?
@is_uploaded_file($_FILES[$image_fieldname]['tmp_name'])
  or handle_error("you were trying to do something naughty. Shame on you!",
          "Uploaded request: file named " .
          "'{$_FILES[$image_fieldname]['tmp_name']}'");
```

```
// Is this actually an image?
@getimagesize($_FILES[$image_fieldname]['tmp_name'])
  or handle_error("you selected a file for your picture " .
                  "that isn't an image.",
                  "{$_FILES[$image_fieldname]['tmp_name']} " .
                  "isn't a valid image file.");

// Interact with MySQL
```

■ MOVE THE FILE TO A PERMANENT LOCATION

You're almost to the big finish. You have a valid HTTP upload that's an image. All that's left is to move this image from the temporary location that browsers use for uploaded files to someplace permanent. Here's where your image_fieldname variable from page 261 comes into use; remember this?

```
<?php

require_once '../scripts/app_config.php';
require_once '../scripts/database_connection.php';

$upload_dir = HOST_WWW_ROOT . "uploads/profile_pics/";
$image_fieldname = "user_pic";

// and so on…
```

> **NOTE** Create the *uploads/profile_pics/* directory if you haven't done so already.

At this point, it's important to understand what's happened to your user's uploaded file. When the server uploads this file, it uses a preconfigured location. It's also likely to use a name that isn't identical to what the user's file was originally called. Sometimes the name is completely changed; other times something is prepended (added before it) or appended to it.

Additionally, the file isn't in a place you want to leave it. It'll often be stuck into some sort of temporary storage, and that storage is probably cleared out every so often. You need to not only assign the file a name, but you also need to move it somewhere more permanent—for that, you can use $upload_dir.

There are lots of different approaches to naming a file. You could come up with something related to the user who uploaded the file, but often, it's just easiest to give the file a unique numeric name. And the easiest way to do this is to create the name based on the current time—a near surefire way to end up with a unique file name.

> **NOTE** Take a look at the image names on a site like Flickr or Facebook. Unless users have renamed their images, the names are often just a string of letters and numbers—often indicating a time.

Once you create a unique name, you can finally move the file from its current location to a permanent one.

First, figure out a name for the soon-to-be permanent image:

```
// Is this actually an image?
@getimagesize($_FILES[$image_fieldname]['tmp_name'])
  or handle_error("you selected a file for your picture " .
                 "that isn't an image.",
                 "{$_FILES[$image_fieldname]['tmp_name']} " .
                 "isn't a valid image file.");

// Name the file uniquely
$now = time();
while (file_exists($upload_filename = $upload_dir . $now .
                                     '-' .
                            $_FILES[$image_fieldname]['name'])) {
    $now++;
}
```

Here's the step-by-step breakdown:

1. **Create a new variable called $now and assign it the current time by using PHP's time function.**

2. **Start a loop by using while.** This instructs PHP that while a certain condition is true, keep doing the loop. As soon as that condition *isn't* true, stop looping.

3. **As part of the while condition, assign a value to $upload_filename: the $upload_dir plus the current time, a dash (-), and then finally the name of the original file.** This is a combination of a part that will be unique (the time) and the original name of the user's file (which is in $_FILES[$image_fieldname] ['name']).

4. **Complete the while condition by passing that calculated filename to** file_exists. If that file exists, the while loop runs. If not, you have a unique file name, so the loop will not run (or, run anymore, if it's already been looping).

5. **Within the loop, you need to change the filename.** Because the while loop is only going to run if you have a filename that's already in use, just add to $now and try again.

Here's the beauty of PHP: you can do all of that in just a few lines of code, and when this code completes, you'll have a unique file name for the user's file.

Now, move the file from its old temporary location to the permanent one:

```
// Is this actually an image?
@getimagesize($_FILES[$image_fieldname]['tmp_name'])
  or handle_error("you selected a file for your picture " .
                 "that isn't an image.",
```

```
                          "{$_FILES[$image_fieldname]['tmp_name']} " .
                          "isn't a valid image file.");

// Name the file uniquely
$now = time();
while (file_exists($upload_filename = $upload_dir . $now .
                                        '-' .
                                        $_FILES[$image_fieldname]['name'])) {
    $now++;
}

// Finally, move the file to its permanent location
@move_uploaded_file($_FILES[$image_fieldname]['tmp_name'], $upload_filename)
  or handle_error("we had a problem saving your image to " .
                    "its permanent location.",
                    "permissions or related error moving " .
                    "file to {$upload_filename}");

// Interact with MySQL
```

It's been a lot of work, but you should finally have your file in a permanent location—and you know that the file is a valid image. Your code should look something like this:

```php
<?php

require_once '../scripts/app_config.php';
require_once '../scripts/database_connection.php';

$upload_dir = HOST_WWW_ROOT . "uploads/profile_pics/";
$image_fieldname = "user_pic";

// Potential PHP upload errors
$php_errors = array(1 => 'Maximum file size in php.ini exceeded',
                    2 => 'Maximum file size in HTML form exceeded',
                    3 => 'Only part of the file was uploaded',
                    4 => 'No file was selected to upload.');

$first_name = trim($_REQUEST['first_name']);
$last_name = trim($_REQUEST['last_name']);
$email = trim($_REQUEST['email']);
$bio = trim($_REQUEST['bio']);
$facebook_url = str_replace("facebook.org", "facebook.com",
                            trim($_REQUEST['facebook_url']));
$position = strpos($facebook_url, "facebook.com");
if ($position === false) {
  $facebook_url = "http://www.facebook.com/" . $facebook_url;
}
```

```php
$twitter_handle = trim($_REQUEST['twitter_handle']);
$twitter_url = "http://www.twitter.com/";
$position = strpos($twitter_handle, "@");
if ($position === false) {
  $twitter_url = $twitter_url . $twitter_handle;
} else {
  $twitter_url = $twitter_url . substr($twitter_handle, $position + 1);
}

// Make sure we didn't have an error uploading the image
($_FILES[$image_fieldname]['error'] == 0)
  or handle_error("the server couldn't upload the image you selected.",
                  $php_errors[$_FILES[$image_fieldname]['error']]);

// Is this file the result of a valid upload?
@is_uploaded_file($_FILES[$image_fieldname]['tmp_name'])
  or handle_error("you were trying to do something naughty. Shame on you!",
                  "Uploaded request: file named " .
                  "'{$_FILES[$image_fieldname]['tmp_name']}'");

// Is this actually an image?
@getimagesize($_FILES[$image_fieldname]['tmp_name'])
  or handle_error("you selected a file for your picture " .
                  "that isn't an image.",
                  "{$_FILES[$image_fieldname]['tmp_name']} " .
                  "isn't a valid image file.");

// Name the file uniquely
$now = time();
while (file_exists($upload_filename = $upload_dir . $now .
                                      '-' .
                                      $_FILES[$image_fieldname]['name'])) {
    $now++;
}

// Finally, move the file to its permanent location
@move_uploaded_file($_FILES[$image_fieldname]['tmp_name'], $upload_filename)
  or handle_error("we had a problem saving your image to " .
                  "its permanent location.",
                  "permissions or related error moving " .
                  "file to {$upload_filename}");

$insert_sql = "INSERT INTO users (first_name, last_name, email, bio," .
                                 "facebook_url, twitter_handle) " .
              "VALUES ('{$first_name}', '{$last_name}', '{$email}', '{$bio}', " .
                      "'{$facebook_url}', '{$twitter_handle}');";
```

```
// Insert the user into the database
mysql_query($insert_sql)
  or die(mysql_error());

// Redirect the user to the page that displays user information
header("Location: show_user.php?user_id=" . mysql_insert_id());
exit();
?>
```

But, don't trust flawless coding. Try things out for yourself. Visit *create_user.php*, select an image from your hard drive (one that's within your size limit), and then upload it. Next, navigate to the *uploads/profile_pics/* directory in your web browser. If you have permissions set to view directories on your server, you'll see something like Figure 9-6.

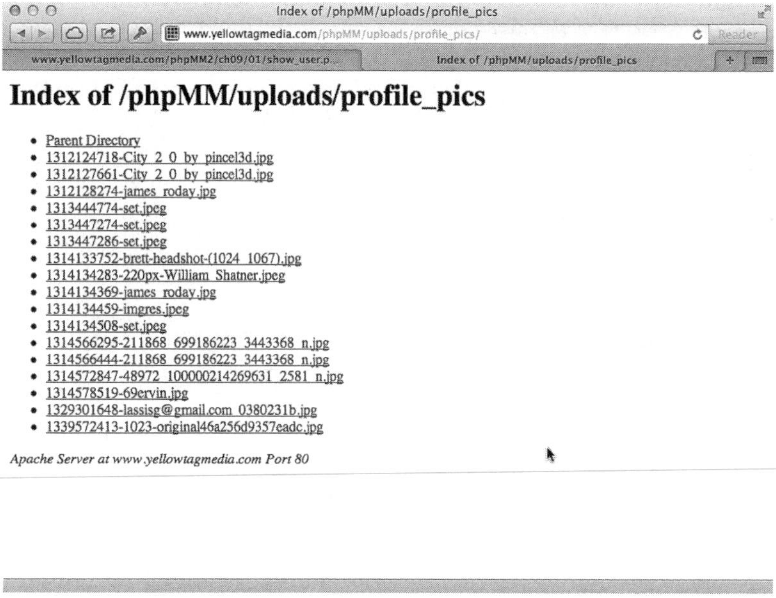

FIGURE 9-6

If you don't see a listing like this, or you get a message indicating that directory listings are denied, you can contact your web server provider or hosting company and ask it to turn on directory listings through the Internet. It's handy to be able to type a URL and look at a directory listing in your browser, but it's not the safest setup. It means that anyone with a web browser can navigate your site's directory structure. So although it's great for debugging, it's not something you want to leave on forever.

Now (finally!), you can click one of those file names, and you should get a glorious image uploaded from your computer to your web server, as demonstrated in Figure 9-7.

FIGURE 9-7

The image has landed! It's taken some work, but think about the best web applications out there: they all let users upload custom images. This is core functionality these days, and now you can do it, too. Nice work.

Storing the Image Location in the Database

It's taken some time, but you're finally ready to save this image—or at least its location—in your database table. You already have a query built:

```
$insert_sql = "INSERT INTO users (first_name, last_name, email, " .
                    "bio, facebook_url, twitter_handle) " .
            "VALUES ('{$first_name}', '{$last_name}', '{$email}', " .
                " '{$bio}', " . '{$facebook_url}', " .
                "'{$twitter_handle}');";

// Insert the user into the database
mysql_query($insert_sql);
```

■ CREATE A NEW DATABASE COLUMN

All you need to do, then, is add a column in which you can store the image location. This is a matter of using the ALTER command (Chapter 7, page 194), something with which you're already comfortable:

```
ALTER TABLE users
        ADD user_pic_path varchar(200);
```

Run this statement to test it, and then DESCRIBE your users table (Chapter 4, page 113) just to make sure the change was applied:

```
mysql> describe users;
+----------------+----------------+------+-----+---------+----------------+
| Field          | Type           | Null | Key | Default | Extra          |
+----------------+----------------+------+-----+---------+----------------+
| user_id        | int(11)        | NO   | PRI | NULL    | auto_increment |
| first_name     | varchar(20)    | NO   |     | NULL    |                |
| last_name      | varchar(30)    | NO   |     | NULL    |                |
| email          | varchar(50)    | NO   |     | NULL    |                |
| facebook_url   | varchar(100)   | YES  |     | NULL    |                |
| twitter_handle | varchar(20)    | YES  |     | NULL    |                |
| bio            | varchar(1000)  | YES  |     | NULL    |                |
| user_pic_path  | varchar(200)   | YES  |     | NULL    |                |
+----------------+----------------+------+-----+---------+----------------+
8 rows in set (0.00 sec)
```

This user_pic_path field is just a text column. This is because all you're storing is the path to the image rather than the image itself.

NOTE If you're starting to become curious about what it would look like to store the actual image in your database rather than just the path, sit tight. In the next section, that's exactly what you'll do.

■ INSERT THE IMAGE PATH INTO YOUR TABLE

The update to the INSERT query isn't difficult at all, now:

```php
$insert_sql = "INSERT INTO users (first_name, last_name, email, bio," .
                        "facebook_url, twitter_handle," .
                        "user_pic_path) " .
             "VALUES ('{$first_name}', '{$last_name}', '{$email}', '{$bio}', " .
                    "'{$facebook_url}', '{$twitter_handle}', " .
                    "'{$upload_filename}');";

// Insert the user into the database
mysql_query($insert_sql);
```

Things are definitely starting to flow quickly. With all your existing work already in place, adding a new column is simple. But, before you dive back into your HTML, there's one more thing that remains to be done.

■ CHECK YOUR WORK

Before you go any further, verify that things work. If you were just a PHP programmer, you'd have to try this code out and then either write a new script to select data from the *users* table, or jump right back into *show_user.php*. But why go to all that trouble? You know SQL and how to interact with MySQL.

First, create a new user, and use a name you haven't used before. Then, jump back into your SQL command-line tool and check the results of your work for yourself. Just SELECT the user you just inserted, focusing on the picture path:

```
SELECT user_pic_path
  FROM users
 WHERE last_name = 'Geyer';
```

You should see something like this:

```
mysql> select user_pic_path from users where last_name = 'Geyer';
+------------------------------------+
| user_pic_path                      |
+------------------------------------+
| /home/bdmclaughlin/public_html/phpMM2/uploads/profile_pics/1346084332-
370584_8323673_927214073_n.jpg |
+------------------------------------+
1 row in set (0.00 sec)
```

As you can see, the image is on your server, and now you've got the path to that image stored in your database. *Now*, you're ready to show your users their glorious images.

If you've had any issues, you might want to check out the completed version of *create_user.php* that follows. There have been a ton of additions, so check that everything is right where it belongs:

```php
<?php

require_once '../scripts/app_config.php';
require_once '../scripts/database_connection.php';

$upload_dir = HOST_WWW_ROOT . "uploads/profile_pics/";
$image_fieldname = "user_pic";

// Potential PHP upload errors
$php_errors = array(1 => 'Maximum file size in php.ini exceeded',
                    2 => 'Maximum file size in HTML form exceeded',
                    3 => 'Only part of the file was uploaded',
                    4 => 'No file was selected to upload.');

$first_name = trim($_REQUEST['first_name']);
$last_name = trim($_REQUEST['last_name']);
$email = trim($_REQUEST['email']);
$bio = trim($_REQUEST['bio']);
$facebook_url = str_replace("facebook.org", "facebook.com",
                            trim($_REQUEST['facebook_url']));
$position = strpos($facebook_url, "facebook.com");
if ($position === false) {
  $facebook_url = "http://www.facebook.com/" . $facebook_url;
```

```
}

$twitter_handle = trim($_REQUEST['twitter_handle']);
$twitter_url = "http://www.twitter.com/";
$position = strpos($twitter_handle, "@");
if ($position === false) {
  $twitter_url = $twitter_url . $twitter_handle;
} else {
  $twitter_url = $twitter_url . substr($twitter_handle, $position + 1);
}

// Make sure we didn't have an error uploading the image
($_FILES[$image_fieldname]['error'] == 0)
  or handle_error("the server couldn't upload the image you selected.",
                  $php_errors[$_FILES[$image_fieldname]['error']]);

// Is this file the result of a valid upload?
@is_uploaded_file($_FILES[$image_fieldname]['tmp_name'])
  or handle_error("you were trying to do something naughty. Shame on you!",
                  "Uploaded request: file named " .
                  "'{$_FILES[$image_fieldname]['tmp_name']}'");

// Is this actually an image?
@getimagesize($_FILES[$image_fieldname]['tmp_name'])
  or handle_error("you selected a file for your picture " .
                  "that isn't an image.",
                  "{$_FILES[$image_fieldname]['tmp_name']} " .
                  "isn't a valid image file.");

// Name the file uniquely
$now = time();
while (file_exists($upload_filename = $upload_dir . $now .
                                     '-' .
                                     $_FILES[$image_fieldname]['name'])) {
    $now++;
}

// Finally, move the file to its permanent location
@move_uploaded_file($_FILES[$image_fieldname]['tmp_name'], $upload_filename)
  or handle_error("we had a problem saving your image to " .
                  "its permanent location.",
                  "permissions or related error moving " .
                  "file to {$upload_filename}");

$insert_sql = "INSERT INTO users (first_name, last_name, email, bio," .
                                 "facebook_url, twitter_handle," .
```

```
                    "user_pic_path) " .
        "VALUES ('{$first_name}', '{$last_name}', '{$email}', '{$bio}', " .
                "'{$facebook_url}', '{$twitter_handle}', " .
                "'{$upload_filename}');";

// Insert the user into the database
mysql_query($insert_sql)
  or die(mysql_error());


// Redirect the user to the page that displays user information
header("Location: show_user.php?user_id=" . mysql_insert_id());
exit();
?>
```

NOTE   You can find this chapter's finished example code on this book's Missing CD page at *www.missingmanuals.com/cds/phpmysqlmm2e.*

■ Images Are for Viewing

Finally! It's time to show your users the fruits of all your hard work. They'll probably never realize how long you slaved to get one single image showing up—and protecting all their other information in the process.

Ensure that you have a copy of *show_user.php* alongside *create_user.html* and *create_user.php*. You need to update *show_user.php* to select the user's picture path from the *users* table and then display that picture.

NOTE   As with all scripts that you're updating, be sure to change `require` to `require_once`, include a reference to *app_config.php*, and update your paths such that you're not using chapter-specific *scripts/* directories. In any scripts that have HTML—like *show_user.php*—you should also check paths for things like the CSS files and external JavaScript references.

SELECTing the Image and Displaying It

This step turns out to be easy. First, you already have a SELECT that grabs everything for a particular user:

```
// Build the SELECT statement
$select_query = "SELECT * FROM users WHERE user_id = " . $user_id;
```

Next, you can just add a line that grabs the image path in the code that you already have pulling information out of the result of running this SQL INSERT:

```
if ($result) {
  $row = mysql_fetch_array($result);
  $first_name      = $row['first_name'];
  $last_name       = $row['last_name'];
  $bio             = preg_replace("/[\r\n]+/", "</p><p>", $row['bio']);
  $email           = $row['email'];
  $facebook_url    = $row['facebook_url'];
  $twitter_handle  = $row['twitter_handle'];
  $user_image      = $row['user_pic_path'];

  // Turn $twitter_handle into a URL
  $twitter_url = "http://www.twitter.com/" .
                 substr($twitter_handle, $position + 1);

} else {
  handle_error("There was a problem finding your " .
               "information in our system.",
               "Error locating user with ID {$user_id}");
}
```

> **NOTE** Take this opportunity to move from using die in the else block of your if statement to the much cooler handle_error function (page 247).

Be sure to remove this old code entirely:

```
// To be added later
$user_image = "../../images/missing_user.png";
```

Finally, you already have a place in this script's HTML that references the $user_image variable:

```
<div id="content">
  <div class="user_profile">
    <h1><?php echo "{$first_name} {$last_name}"; ?></h1>
    <p><img src="<?php echo $user_image; ?>" class="user_pic" />
    <!-- and so on... -->
```

Time to try things out again. Go to your *show_user.php* page with an existing user's ID in the URL bar of your browser, or create a new user with a picture and let *create_user.php* redirect you. You should see something similar to Figure 9-8.

To figure out why you can't see the image you uploaded, view the source for this page, and see what path was used for the image. You'll probably see something like Figure 9-9.

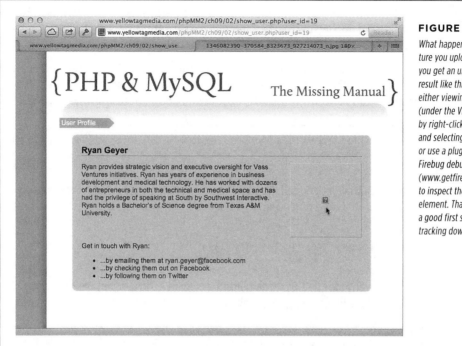

FIGURE 9-8

What happened to the picture you uploaded? When you get an unexpected result like this, start out by either viewing the source (under the View menu, or by right-clicking the page and selecting View Source) or use a plug-in like the Firebug debugger tool (www.getfirebug.com) to inspect the offending element. That's always a good first step toward tracking down a problem.

FIGURE 9-9

According to this HTML source code, the <img> element has the correct absolute path to the image. But, is that what a path in HTML pages should look like? How does the absolute path on a file system relate to the path on a web server?

You checked earlier to ensure that this is a valid image (page 269). This time, check to see if the path to the image is causing the problem.

Converting File System Paths to URLs

Currently, you have a path on your web server's file system (page 277) but what you need is a path that a web server recognizes. Remember the difference between SITE_ROOT—which is a path from a web server's perspective—and HOST_WWW_ROOT—which is from the perspective of a server's file system. That's exactly the issue here: your script provides a path on the file system to the web server.

Every web server has something called a *document root*. That's the directory into which you place files so that a web server and a browser can see them. That's also the directory you've already identified in *app_config.php* with HOST_WWW_ROOT (page 263).

> **NOTE** Old school programmers and HTML geeks will remember that *public_html/* used to be the almost universal standard for a document root. You'll still often see that, along with the newer *www/*.

To establish what your document root is, close *show_user.php* and create a new script called *test.php*. Type a single command between the opening and closing PHP syntax:

```php
<?php
echo "DOCUMENT ROOT: {$_SERVER['DOCUMENT_ROOT']}";
?>
```

$_SERVER is another one of those helpful associative arrays that PHP provides. The DOCUMENT_ROOT key reveals your web server's document root.

> **NOTE** Visit *www.php.net/manual/en/reserved.variables.server.php* to see all the various things you can discover by using $_SERVER.

Using a browser, go to this script. You'll get something like Figure 9-10: that's your document root. In this example, the root is */home1/b/bmclaugh/yellowtagmedia_com*. Therefore, the web path / is mapping to the file system path */home1/b/bmclaugh/yellowtagmedia_com*.

DOCUMENT ROOT: /home1/b/bmclaugh/yellowtagmedia_com

FIGURE 9-10

When you run your test.php script above, you should see the path on your hosting provider's file system. That's where your web files are located.

Now, you have the sort of hook you need: a mapping that relates a file system path to an actual web path. It's a pretty easy mapping, too. For any file path, you want to strip away everything from the beginning of the path up to and including *yellowtagmedia_com* (or whatever the end of your document root is).

To put that into action, start by adding a sample image path that you're currently storing in your database to your *test.php* script:

```php
<?php
echo "DOCUMENT ROOT: {$_SERVER['DOCUMENT_ROOT']}";
$image_sample_path =
  "/home1/b/bmclaugh/yellowtagmedia_com/phpMM2/" .
  "uploads/profile_pics/1346084332-370584_8323673_927214073_n.jpg";
?>
```

Next, use str_replace, a handy function you know quite well by now. You simply want to replace the file path equivalent of the document root with...well, nothing. You want to remove it:

```php
<?php
echo "DOCUMENT ROOT: {$_SERVER['DOCUMENT_ROOT']}";
$image_sample_path =
  "/home1/b/bmclaugh/yellowtagmedia_com/phpMM2/" .
  "uploads/profile_pics/1312128274-james_roday.jpg";
$web_image_path = str_replace($_SERVER['DOCUMENT_ROOT'],
                      '', $image_sample_path);
?>
```

Finally, echo the result back out:

```php
<?php
echo "DOCUMENT ROOT: {$_SERVER['DOCUMENT_ROOT']}";
$image_sample_path =
  "/home1/b/bmclaugh/yellowtagmedia_com/phpMMs/" .
  "uploads/profile_pics/1312128274-james_roday.jpg";
$web_image_path = str_replace($_SERVER['DOCUMENT_ROOT'],
                      '', $image_sample_path);

echo "<br /><br />CONVERTED PATH: {$web_image_path}";
?>
```

Go to your *test.php* again. Hopefully it will look like Figure 9-11.

NOTE As the name suggests, this script is for nothing other than testing purposes. For more on test scripts in PHP, see the box on page 285.

DOCUMENT ROOT: /home1/b/bmclaugh/yellowtagmedia_com

CONVERTED PATH: /phpMM/uploads/profile_pics/1312128274-james_roday.jpg

FIGURE 9-11

Adding the code on page 283 does exactly the conversion you want. It changes the image's path from the file system path that you need when working with the image directly, to the web path that your user's browser needs. In real life, though, don't display your file system path where everybody can see it (like, say, publishing it in a book?).

Take this path and drop it directly into your browser, following the slash after your domain name, and then press Enter. If all is well, you'll see that image you've been after for so long. Figure 9-12 shows the magic in action.

FIGURE 9-12

Finally! Just as it took a lot of work to get robust error handling in place, image uploading is a common but ultimately tricky exercise. Just think how much has to go on to get one image into the right place and easily viewable by your thousands (millions?) of users.

At this stage, you can turn the code in *test.php* into yet another helpful utility function. Open up your old friend *app_config.php* and create a generic version of the code from *test.php*:

```
function get_web_path($file_system_path) {

  return str_replace($_SERVER['DOCUMENT_ROOT'], '', $file_system_path);

}
```

Pretty streamlined, isn't it? Here's what this short bit of code does:

1. **Defines a new function by using** function **that you can call from any script that requires or includes *app_config.php*.**

2. **Names the function** get_web_path.

3. **Defines a single piece of information that the function gets from whatever script calls it: $file_system_path.** This will be the complete path on the web server's file system to the file that needs to be converted into a web-accessible path.

4. **Takes $file_system_path and replaces the document root in the path with nothing (' ').**

5. **Returns the result of running** str_replace **by using** return.

The only thing new here is return. return is a part of the PHP language, and it does just what you'd expect: it returns something to the program or script that called this function. So, if you passed in /usr/bbentley/web/images/profile.jpg, and your document root was */usr/bbentley/web*, the string /images/profile.jpg would be returned from a call to get_web_path.

POWER USERS' CLINIC

Prototype with Simple Scripts

Some languages and frameworks—Ruby on Rails, in particular—offer a means to run commands within the context of your programming or web environment. This is sort of like a command-line-plus, where you get all the benefits of a running web server, logging, your scripts loaded, and even a few additional bells and whistles.

Unfortunately, PHP isn't one of those languages. When it comes to testing out a bit of new functionality, your choices are typically to either just start coding in one of your existing scripts or to create a simple script like *test.php* and work with it until you get your functionality figured out.

Although using a simple command-line script can seem like a bit of a drag compared to a nice CSS-styled web environment, it's often the better choice. You can test things and get your code just right without having to worry about HTML or interactions across scripts. Then, once you have your code the way you want it, it's an easy drop-in to your full-blown web scripting environment.

WARNING There is one gotcha to this function: it assumes that you're sending it an absolute path, not a relative path. Thus, *../../../web/images/profile.jpg* won't match your document root in any form or fashion. Fortunately, your code that actually generates the path to an image uses absolute paths. This means that at least for your particular needs, this function works just fine.

Displaying Your User's Image: Take Two

It's time to turn back to *show_user.php*. This time, though, you're armed with a utility function. Use that function to convert the absolute path stored in your database into a web-safe path for viewing:

```php
if ($result) {
  $row = mysql_fetch_array($result);
  $first_name    = $row['first_name'];
  $last_name     = $row['last_name'];
  $bio           = preg_replace("/[\r\n]+/", "</p><p>", $row['bio']);
  $email         = $row['email'];
  $facebook_url  = $row['facebook_url'];
  $twitter_handle = $row['twitter_handle'];
  $user_image    = get_web_path($row['user_pic_path']);

  // Turn $twitter_handle into a URL
  $twitter_url = "http://www.twitter.com/" .
                 substr($twitter_handle, $position + 1);

} else {
  handle_error("there was a problem finding your " .
               "information in our system.",
               "Error locating user with ID {$user_id}");
}
```

It doesn't get much easier than that. Fire up your browser and try either creating a user again (with *create_user.php*) or visiting *show_user.php* and supplying a user_id parameter as part of the URL string. You should see *show_user.php* the way it's always been intended: resplendent with imagery, as shown in Figure 9-13.

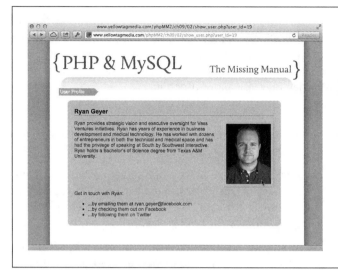

FIGURE 9-13

This chapter has been a bit of a never-ending story, hasn't it? Still, there's simply no doubt that you've got the most secure, well-built image-handling script around. (Well, okay, those guys from Facebook and Google+ might have a few additional tricks, but you're close.) Enjoy profile pictures for a moment, and then get ready for the next stage in your evolution.

FREQUENTLY ASKED QUESTION

Don't Store Paths in Your Database

Why not store a web path in the database?

Every single time you load an image from the database, you'll have to call `get_web_path` on that image path—at least if you want to show the image on the Web. Given that you're writing web applications, isn't that sort of the point? It might seem as though you could just cut that conversion step out and simply store the image in the database as a web path from the beginning.

There are a couple of reasons that's not a great idea, though. First, an absolute path is just that: it's absolute. Your web server software can change; your home directory can change; you can switch from PHP to Ruby to Perl and back to PHP; but short of you actually moving an image, its absolute path remains unchanged. Most importantly, you can change the entire document root of your site, and an absolute path will still work.

Why is that so significant? Because you might need to change the document root of your site at some point. If you stored a

web path in the database—a path related to your document root—and then your document root changed, all of your image paths would be invalid. You'd have to change every single one of them from being relative to your old document root to relative to your new document root. What a mess.

On top of that, a web path is a relative path, even if it begins with a /. That's because it's relative to your document root. An absolute path is fixed in relation to a specific computer, regardless of that computer's software. And as a general rule, you want to store things in a database that are as absolute and fixed as possible. Given the choice between a piece of information in an absolute form and one in a relative form, always go for the absolute form. It's usually easy to change from one form to the other, so store the more "reliable" one. You won't regret it.

■ And Now for Something Completely Different

Everything works now. Your users can upload images. You can get those images securely into a permanent location of your choice. You have a way to store the location in a database and to convert that location into a URL that works with your website and your personal document root. And then, to top it all off, you can show your users their images when they visit *show_user.php*.

So, what's next?

Suppose that you're using multiple web servers that share a single database. Are you really going to store the same image on each of those web servers?

Or suppose you're using a temporary computer for a web server, or think you might change to a higher-end hosting solution as your business expands. Do you want to have to copy not just your site—which might only be 10 or 20 MB zipped up—but all of your user's images, each one perhaps 1 or 2 MB in size?

These are just a few reasons why the solution you have in place might not be the best one for your particular web application. And there is another option, equally complex, but just as useful: you can store images not on the file system, but directly in your database.

This is one of the most common things you'll encounter in programming: you've got a solution that works, but there might be a better solution around the corner. In this case, there's a different solution, and it's in the next chapter. So turn the page, and see why you might just want your entire image stored in the database rather than just the path to that image.

Binary Objects and Image Loading

At this point, you have images on a file system, and the paths to those images stored in a database. In your PHP scripts, you convert that file system path to a web path, and then display the image. This works, and it works pretty well. In fact, you could run with that solution and likely never have any issues...but, then again, you might have a huge issue that crops up next week.

The downside of this approach is that you don't have a self-contained solution. Images are on the file system, paths are in the database, and then you need some PHP to convert from the location of the image on your server to a path that users' browsers can interpret correctly. To put it all together, you've created a real connection—sometimes called a *tight coupling*—between your file system, your PHP, and your database.

Taking all this into consideration, how do you make things more self-contained? You'd have to take these pieces of information and put them all in one place. Obviously, you're committed to a database, so that becomes the logical place to consolidate your information. Instead of *some* of your information going into your database, it *all* goes into your database.

In this approach, you take a user's uploaded image and put it in your database rather than just storing a reference to your image. Unfortunately, to do that, there's a lot more work to be done: you need not just a new column in your *users* table, but an entirely new table; you need a new data type; and you need more than just the SELECT and INSERT queries you've been using so far. If you need this type of solution, this chapter will show you how to do it.

Storing Different Objects in Different Tables

Up until now, you've been working with one table: *users*. That's because you've been working with a single entity: a representation of one of your users. Everything in that table—the first and last name, the email address, and the Facebook URL and Twitter handle—are parts of that user. Put another way, everything in the *users* table *describes* a user.

But, when you store an entire image within the database, you're no longer dealing with something that describes a user. In fact, although an image is *related* to a user—it's the image that a user wants to display when his profile is viewed—it's an object in its own right. Just like a user, it's a unique entity that might have other information describing it. And also like a user, an image should go into its own table.

> **NOTE** You can find the finished example code for this section on this book's Missing CD page at *www*
> *.missingmanuals.com/cds/phpmysqlmm2e.*

You're going to create a new table called *images* that's going to store not only a user's image, but several key details about that image:

- **An image ID**   This will uniquely identify the image, similar to a user_id in the *users* table. It will also let you associate an image to the *users* table a bit later.

- **The image name**   Even though you're storing the image's data, you still need a name by which you can refer to that image.

- **The image's MIME type**   This information is important for instructing a web server whether it needs to display a JPG, GIF, PNG, or something else entirely.

- **The file size**   This is more information that you supply to the browser for displaying the image.

- **The image data itself**   The raw bits and bytes that are turned into pixels and colors.

Translate this into SQL and you get a new CREATE statement:

```
CREATE TABLE images (
    image_id    int          AUTO_INCREMENT PRIMARY KEY,
    filename    varchar(200) NOT NULL,
    mime_type   varchar(50)  NOT NULL,
    file_size   int          NOT NULL,
    image_data  mediumblob   NOT NULL
);
```

You've seen all of this before, with the exception of a new column type: mediumblob. As you might expect, this implies there are a few other blob types, which are:

- **tinyblob**   This type stores objects up to 256 bytes.

- **blob**   You can store objects up to 65 KB (kilobytes) in a blob column.

- **mediumblob**   This has a capacity for up to 16 MB of data.

- **longblob**   This is the big one. You can store 4 GB of data in a longblob column.

The term *blob* stands for *binary large object*. It's a column designed for the very type of information that makes up an image; in other words, information that's neither a number nor a string, but is instead binary data. (For more detail on which type of blob to use and when, see the box that follows.)

DESIGN TIME

Planning for Growth and Describing Your Data

In the PHP world, there's a fair bit of disagreement about which blob type you should use for a given column. Some argue that you should always use longblob, whereas others argue that you should know exactly what size file you're dealing with, and use the blob that covers that size, and nothing more.

With those who argue for always using longblob, the thinking is that you're planning ahead. Because your database uses space as your actual data needs—and not the column's maximum size—a longblob holding a 2 MB image takes up just as much space, or more accurately, no more space than a mediumblob holding a 2 MB image. Then, why not use longblob all the time, and never have to change your column type as your storage needs change?

On the other hand, if you're allowing only images that are 2 MB or smaller, mediumblob best describes your data. You're doing more than just choosing an arbitrary type; you're providing information about what goes in the column.

For example, it's not a good idea to make everything a varchar(255) if you are only storing a first name because there's no first name that long (see the box on page 111). You lose a chance to say something about your data with that approach. The same is true for using a longblob *if* (and this is an important if) you've clearly decided that you're only accepting images up to a size that would fit in a mediumblob.

Go ahead and create this table. Ensure that it's in the same database as *users*. You should now be able to see both of these tables in your database:

```
mysql> USE phpmm2;
Database changed
mysql> SHOW tables;
+-----------------------------------+
| Tables_in_phpmm2                  |
+-----------------------------------+
| images                            |
| users                             |
+-----------------------------------+
2 rows in set (0.00 sec)
```

■ Inserting a Raw Image into a Table

It's time to revisit *create_user.php*. You're going to use a lot of your existing code, but there are also some changes to make. All of the checks you've put in place to ensure that your user uploaded a valid image, that no errors were generated by the server or PHP, and that the file is an image via getimagesize are just fine.

> **NOTE** Make a backup of *create_user.php* before you start making changes. Consider copying it to *create_user .php.bak* or something similar so that if you want to go back to storing just an image's path, you can.

Where things change is in the section of code that you used to move the temporary image into a final location (page 286). In this approach, the final location is the *images* table, so you must replace that code.

> **NOTE** You can find the finished example code for this section on this book's Missing CD page at *www .missingmanuals.com/cds/phpmysqlmm2e*.

Here's the *create_user.php* script with the path code removed.

```php
<?php

require_once '../scripts/app_config.php';
require_once '../scripts/database_connection.php';

// The errors array and variables related to images stay the same
$upload_dir = HOST_WWW_ROOT . "uploads/profile_pics/";
$image_fieldname = "user_pic";

// Potential PHP upload errors
$php_errors = array(1 => 'Maximum file size in php.ini exceeded',
                    2 => 'Maximum file size in HTML form exceeded',
                    3 => 'Only part of the file was uploaded',
                    4 => 'No file was selected to upload.');

$first_name = trim($_REQUEST['first_name']);
$last_name = trim($_REQUEST['last_name']);
$email = trim($_REQUEST['email']);
$bio = trim($_REQUEST['bio']);
$facebook_url = str_replace("facebook.org", "facebook.com", trim($_
REQUEST['facebook_url']));
$position = strpos($facebook_url, "facebook.com");
if ($position === false) {
  $facebook_url = "http://www.facebook.com/" . $facebook_url;
}
```

```php
$twitter_handle = trim($_REQUEST['twitter_handle']);
$twitter_url = "http://www.twitter.com/";
$position = strpos($twitter_handle, "@");
if ($position === false) {
  $twitter_url = $twitter_url . $twitter_handle;
} else {
  $twitter_url = $twitter_url .
                 substr($twitter_handle, $position + 1);
}

// Make sure we didn't have an error uploading the image
($_FILES[$image_fieldname]['error'] == 0)
  or handle_error("the server couldn't upload the image you selected.",
                  $php_errors[$_FILES[$image_fieldname]['error']]);

// Is this file the result of a valid upload?
@is_uploaded_file($_FILES[$image_fieldname]['tmp_name'])
  or handle_error("you were trying to do something naughty. " .
                  "Shame on you!",
                  "Uploaded request: file named " .
                  "'{$_FILES[$image_fieldname]['tmp_name']}'");

// Is this actually an image?
@getimagesize($_FILES[$image_fieldname]['tmp_name'])
  or handle_error("you selected a file for your picture that " .
                  "isn't an image.",
                  "{$_FILES[$image_fieldname]['tmp_name']} " .
                  "isn't a valid image file.");

// Name the file uniquely
$now = time();
while (file_exists($upload_filename = $upload_dir . $now .
                                     '-' .
                   $_FILES[$image_fieldname]['name'])) {
    $now++;
}

// Remove the code that used move_uploaded_file to move the temporary image

// Remove the column name and value for user pics.
$insert_sql = "INSERT INTO users (first_name, last_name, email, bio," .
                                 "facebook_url, twitter_handle)" .
            "VALUES ('{$first_name}', '{$last_name}', '{$email}', '{$bio}', " .
                    "'{$facebook_url}', '{$twitter_handle}');";
```

```
// Insert the user into the database
mysql_query($insert_sql)
  or die(mysql_error());

// Redirect the user to the page that displays user information
header("Location: show_user.php?user_id=" . mysql_insert_id());
exit();
?>
```

Your code remains substantially the same. The big change is that now you need a new INSERT statement, and this statement doesn't insert into *users*, but into *images*.

Here's the beauty of this solution, though: you can get every bit of the information you need to put into images from the $_FILES array (which is actually an array of arrays):

```
$insert_sql = "INSERT INTO users (first_name, last_name, email, " .
              "bio, facebook_url, twitter_handle) " .
              "VALUES ('{$first_name}', '{$last_name}', '{$email}', " .
              "'{$bio}', '{$facebook_url}', '{$twitter_handle}');";

// Insert the user into the database
mysql_query($insert_sql)
  or die(mysql_error());

// Insert the image into the images table
$image = $_FILES[$image_fieldname];
$image_filename = $image['name'];
$image_info = getimagesize($image['tmp_name']);
$image_mime_type = $image_info['mime'];
$image_size = $image['size'];
$image_data = file_get_contents($image['tmp_name']);

$insert_image_sql = "INSERT INTO images " .
                    "(filename, mime_type, file_size, image_data) " .
                    "VALUES ('{$image_filename}', '{$image_mime_type}', " .
                    "'{$image_size}', '{$image_data}');";

mysql_query($insert_image_sql);

// Redirect the user to the page that displays user information
header("Location: show_user.php?user_id=" . mysql_insert_id());
exit();
?>
```

There's a lot going on here, and some of it is flat-out confusing, so take this code piece by piece.

First, this code creates a new $image variable that's actually just for convenience:

```
$image = $_FILES[$image_fieldname];
```

This variable makes it easier to deal with all the properties of an image at once. You don't have to continually type $_FILES[$image_fieldname], over and over. This step isn't necessary, but it does make things much more convenient.

Next, you can get the name of the image from this array:

```
$image_filename = $image['name'];
```

Beware: getimagesize Doesn't Return a File Size

Here's where things start to get a little weird. Despite its name, getimagesize does *not* return a numeric file size of the uploaded image. Rather, it returns an array of information about the image such as its MIME type (which you need) and the height and width of the image that you might use to display the image in an HTML page (which you don't currently need).

This might lead you to believe that you should do something like this:

```
$image_size = getimagesize($image['tmp_name']);
```

In fact, that's a problem on two counts: getimagesize returns an array, not a size, and the sizes that getimagesize returns in that array are height and width, not file size.

What you do need from the returned array, though, is the MIME type:

```
$image_info = getimagesize($image['tmp_name']);
$image_mime_type = $image_info['mime'];
```

You also still need the actual file size of the uploaded image. You can get that from a property on the original image-related array:

```
$image_size = $image['size'];
```

The file_get_contents Function Does What You Think It Does

Sometimes a function's name is a bit misleading, such as you just learned with getimagesize. Other times, a function is perfectly named; that's the case with file_get_contents. This function retrieves an object's data in binary form, which is just what you want for the image_data column in your *images* table:

```
$image_data = file_get_contents($image['tmp_name']);
```

INSERTing the Image

Last but not least, you need to build the INSERT query and run it:

```
$insert_image_sql = "INSERT INTO images " .
                        "(filename, mime_type, file_size, image_data) " .
                "VALUES ('{$image_filename}', '{$image_mime_type}', " .
                        "'{$image_size}', '{$image_data}');";

mysql_query($insert_image_sql);
```

Your Binary Data Isn't Safe to Insert...Yet

The code you built in the previous section looks good, but if you run this code, you're likely to see some errors. First, that binary data has all sorts of weird characters on which PHP and MySQL are going to choke. There's always the possibility of running into characters that are a problem, but it's especially true when you're dealing with binary data.

NOTE You can find the finished example code for this section on this book's Missing CD page at *www.missingmanuals.com/cds/phpmysqlmm2e*.

Once again, though, there's a utility function for that.

NOTE You've probably noticed that at nearly every turn, there's a PHP utility function. That's one of the advantages of a language that's fairly mature. Well into versions 4 and 5, PHP has settled, and a robust library exists that contains handy functions like getimagesize and the one you're about to use: mysql_real_escape_string.

The mysql_real_escape_string function escapes any special characters in the string you hand it. This means that you can pass in your $image_data, and then pass the result of mysql_real_escape_string to mysql_query through your INSERT statement. In fact, it's not a bad idea to use this function on any string data you pass in to MySQL:

```
$insert_sql = "INSERT INTO users (first_name, last_name, email, " .
              "bio, facebook_url, twitter_handle) " .
              "VALUES ('{mysql_real_escape_string($first_name)}', " .
                  "'{mysql_real_escape_string($last_name)}', " .
                  "'{mysql_real_escape_string($email)}', " .
                  "'{mysql_real_escape_string($bio)}', " .
                  "'{mysql_real_escape_string($facebook_url)}', " .
                  "'{mysql_real_escape_string($twitter_handle)}');";

// Insert the user into the database
mysql_query($insert_sql);

// Insert the image into the images table
$image = $_FILES[$image_fieldname];
$image_filename = $image['name'];
$image_info = getimagesize($image['tmp_name']);
```

```
$image_mime_type = $image_info['mime'];
$image_size = $image['size'];
$image_data = file_get_contents($image['tmp_name']);

$insert_image_sql = "INSERT INTO images " .
                        "(filename, mime_type, file_size, image_data) " .
               "VALUES ('{mysql_real_escape_string($image_filename)}', ".
                    "'{mysql_real_escape_string($image_mime_type)}', " .
                    "'{mysql_real_escape_string($image_size)}', " .
                    "'{mysql_real_escape_string($image_data)}');";


mysql_query($insert_image_sql);
```

NOTE   You don't need mysql_real_escape_string for the $image_size, because it's a numeric value. However, if you're constantly trying to remember whether input data is a string or a number, you're eventually going to make a mistake and not escape something you should.

To be safe, just escape everything. It's more consistent, and it's another layer of protection. The time it takes PHP to escape that one bit of data is trivial compared to the problems if malicious data goes unescaped.

Printing a String to a Variable

As natural as this code looks, it's got a serious problem. Even though the curly braces surrounding a variable will allow that variable to be printed inside a string (for example, "{$variable}" prints the value of $variable), PHP draws the line at doing actual work inside the curly braces. As such, it won't interpret the call to mysql_real_escape_string.

You have two ways to get around this. The first is the easiest: you could just move the calls to mysql_real_escape_string up into the variable assignments, sort of like this:

```
// Insert the image into the images table
$image = $_FILES[$image_fieldname];
$image_filename = mysql_real_escape_string($image['name']);
$image_info = getimagesize($image['tmp_name']);
$image_mime_type = mysql_real_escape_string($image_info['mime']);
// and so on...
```

This also looks OK, but it's not a good idea. Do you see why?

Think about the function you're calling: it's specifically for getting values set up to work with MySQL. However, what if you want to use $image_filename somewhere else in your script? You've turned this variable into a MySQL-specific version of the file name.

It seems like the original approach—converting the variable by using mysql_real_escape_string as it's going into the actual SQL INSERT statement—is the right one. It allows the variable to just be the image file name, or the image MIME type, and then you convert that into a MySQL-friendly value when that's required.

That seems to indicate there's a need for a way to perform calculations or run functions on values when you're constructing your SQL string—and there is. You usually do so by using sprintf, which is a PHP function that prints to a string. In other words, you construct a string by using any calculations you need and pass all the required information to sprintf. The sprintf function puts everything together and returns a string, which you can then assign to your variable, and boom, you're then ready to pass that variable in to mysql_query.

How does this work? Well, it's a little different than anything you've done so far. Instead of just building the string up via concatenation, you indicate the entire string that you want to create, but every time you come to a spot in the string where you want to include the value of a variable, you put in a special *type specifier*. For example, you use %s for a string type:

```
$hello = sprintf("Hello there, %s %s", $first_name, $last_name);
echo $hello;
```

Suppose $first_name is "John" and $last_name is "Wayne." Running a script with these two lines would give you:

```
Hello there, John Wayne
```

The sprintf function replaces the first %s with the first value after the string, which is $first_name. Then, it replaces the second %s with the second value after the string, $last_name. Finally, the entire string with the values inserted—is assigned to $hello.

What's great about sprintf is that you can perform calculations on variables *before* you pass them to sprintf. The following example might be a bit silly, but the code is perfectly legal:

```
$hello = sprintf("Hello there, %s", $first_name . ' ' . $last_name);
echo $hello;
```

Of course, there are much better ways to use sprintf, like creating a query string and using mysql_real_escape_string in the process:

```
// This replaces the older assignment to $insert_sql
$insert_sql = sprintf("INSERT INTO users " .
                      "(first_name, last_name, email, " .
                      "bio, facebook_url, twitter_handle) " .
            "VALUES ('%s', '%s', '%s', '%s', '%s', '%s');",
            mysql_real_escape_string($first_name),
            mysql_real_escape_string($last_name),
            mysql_real_escape_string($email),
            mysql_real_escape_string($bio),
            mysql_real_escape_string($facebook_url),
            mysql_real_escape_string($twitter_handle));
```

```
// Insert the user into the database
mysql_query($insert_sql)
  or die(mysql_error());
```

This code doesn't do anything noticeably different than your older version. This is because the data being inserted into *users* was probably not a problem in the first place. But now, you can take this same approach and apply it to your insertion into *images*.

```
$insert_image_sql = sprintf("INSERT INTO images " .
                            "(filename, mime_type, " .
                            "file_size, image_data) " .
                    "VALUES ('%s', '%s', %d, '%s');",
                    mysql_real_escape_string($image_filename),
                    mysql_real_escape_string($image_mime_type),
                    mysql_real_escape_string($image_size),
                    mysql_real_escape_string($image_data));

mysql_query($insert_image_sql)
  or die(mysql_error());
```

You can guess what %d means to sprintf: replace that type specifier with a decimal number, like 1024 or 92048. Thus, this code builds up an INSERT, executes it, and escapes your values in the process.

POWER USERS' CLINIC

sprintf Is Your New Best Friend

Most PHP programmers use sprintf initially because it lets them do things like use mysql_real_escape_string on variables before they're inserted into a query string. But those same programmers discover something else, just as you will: using sprintf lets you write a lot more robust and flexible code.

Using sprintf, you can do calculations on your data, escape values, and do just about anything else you want to your data,

as you're inserting into or selecting from your database. You no longer need to calculate things and then assign the results of those calculations to a variable (or, even worse, a new variable, based upon some old variable) and then—and only then—use those variables as part of a SQL construction.

sprintf lets you do all that in a single step. In general, you should use sprintf as your default means of creating SQL strings that are executed as queries against your database.

Now, try this out. Head over to *create_user.php* once again, find a new friend to fill out the form, let her choose an image, and then submit the form. Your new version of *create_user.php* should run, and you'll get to *show_user.php*.

This time you *won't* see the user's profile, because that's not code you've written. In fact, you might see an entirely incorrect user being loaded. You'll fix that soon.

You should, however, be able to dig into your new *images* table and see an entry for the uploaded image:

```
mysql> SELECT image_id, filename FROM images;
+----------+----------------------------------------------------------+
| image_id | filename                                                 |
+----------+----------------------------------------------------------+
|        1 | 7829_1204001948285_1475710666_1190173_2526636_n.jpg      |
+----------+----------------------------------------------------------+
1 row in set (0.43 sec)
```

WARNING You most definitely do *not* want to do a SELECT * here, because you'll get MySQL's attempt to load your actual image data, which might be a few hundred (or a few thousand) kilobytes. But, at least you can see that an image is indeed in your table.

You can also access your table by using phpMyAdmin (see the box on page 55) if you've got that running, and extract a little extra information about your entries in *images*. Figure 10-1 shows you what to expect.

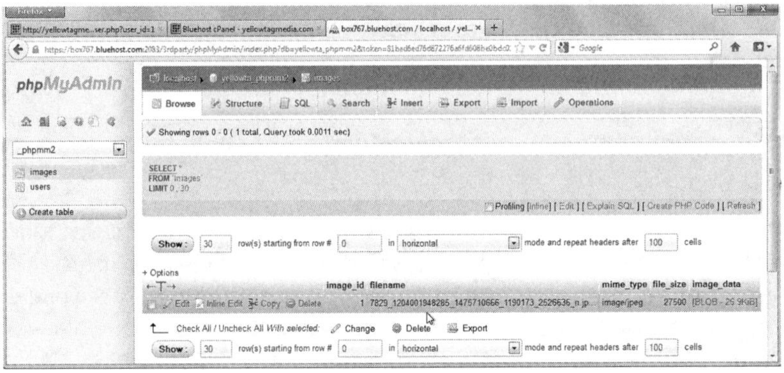

FIGURE 10-1

PhpMyAdmin reports BLOB columns—regardless of what type of BLOB you used—as BLOB and a size. In this case, you can see that the file size, at 27500 bytes, matches up with the size of the data in the BLOB column, which is 26.9 KB. This is a good way to verify that things are working: your script is correctly getting the size of the image it's inserting into your database table.

Getting the Correct ID Before Redirecting

Unfortunately, there's still a problem. You might have noticed something like Figure 10-2 when you got your image insertion working. You could see a blank screen, or even a totally different user, as in this scenario.

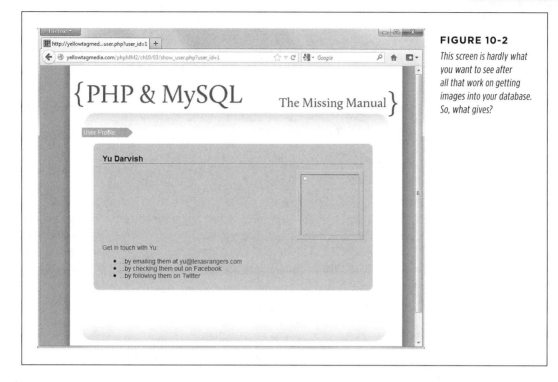

FIGURE 10-2

This screen is hardly what you want to see after all that work on getting images into your database. So, what gives?

This isn't as much of a mystery as it first seems. Here's the last bit of your code from *create_user.php*:

```php
// This replaces the older assignment to $insert_sql
$insert_sql = sprintf("INSERT INTO users " .
                      "(first_name, last_name, email, " .
                       "bio, facebook_url, twitter_handle) " .
               "VALUES ('%s', '%s', '%s', '%s', '%s', '%s');",
               mysql_real_escape_string($first_name),
               mysql_real_escape_string($last_name),
               mysql_real_escape_string($email),
               mysql_real_escape_string($bio),
               mysql_real_escape_string($facebook_url),
               mysql_real_escape_string($twitter_handle));

// Insert the user into the database
mysql_query($insert_sql)
  or die(mysql_error());
```

```
$insert_image_sql = sprintf("INSERT INTO images " .
                            "(filename, mime_type, " .
                            "file_size, image_data) " .
                "VALUES ('%s', '%s', %d, '%s');",
                mysql_real_escape_string($image_filename),
                mysql_real_escape_string($image_mime_type),
                mysql_real_escape_string($image_size),
                mysql_real_escape_string($image_data));
```

```
mysql_query($insert_image_sql)
  or die(mysql_error());
```

```
// Redirect the user to the page that displays user information
header("Location: show_user.php?user_id=" . mysql_insert_id());
exit();
```

What's the problem? It's in that second-to-last line. Remember, mysql_insert_id returns the ID of the *last* INSERT query, which is no longer the INSERT for your *users* table; it's your new INSERT for *images*. The redirect to *show_user.php* is in fact working, but it's sending the ID of the image inserted rather than the user. Fortunately, you can easily fix that:

```
// This replaces the older assignment to $insert_sql
$insert_sql = sprintf("INSERT INTO users " .
                      "(first_name, last_name, email, " .
                      "bio, facebook_url, twitter_handle) " .
                "VALUES ('%s', '%s', '%s', '%s', '%s', '%s');",
                mysql_real_escape_string($first_name),
                mysql_real_escape_string($last_name),
                mysql_real_escape_string($email),
                mysql_real_escape_string($bio),
                mysql_real_escape_string($facebook_url),
                mysql_real_escape_string($twitter_handle));
```

```
// Insert the user into the database
mysql_query($insert_sql);
```

```
$user_id = mysql_insert_id();
```

```
$insert_image_sql = sprintf("INSERT INTO images " .
                            "(filename, mime_type, " .
                            "file_size, image_data) " .
                "VALUES ('%s', '%s', %d, '%s');",
                mysql_real_escape_string($image_filename),
                mysql_real_escape_string($image_mime_type),
                mysql_real_escape_string($image_size),
                mysql_real_escape_string($image_data));
```

```
mysql_query($insert_image_sql);

// Redirect the user to the page that displays user information
header("Location: show_user.php?user_id=" . $user_id);
exit();
?>
```

Try this out again, and you should be back to what you expect: a slightly broken version of *show_user.php*, but broken in the way that you expect (see Figure 10-3).

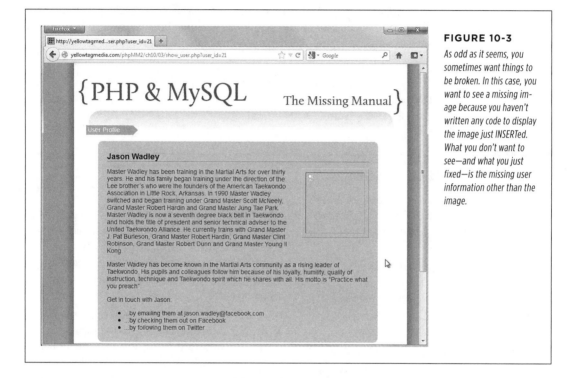

FIGURE 10-3

As odd as it seems, you sometimes want things to be broken. In this case, you want to see a missing image because you haven't written any code to display the image just INSERTed. What you don't want to see—and what you just fixed—is the missing user information other than the image.

Connecting Users and Images

At this point, you have two tables—*users* and *images*—but no connection between them. That's your next challenge. When you load a user from the *users* table and display his profile by using *show_user.php*, how do you determine which image in the *images* table you should display?

Clearly, you need some linkage between those two tables. You already have a unique ID for each entry in *users* (user_id) and in *images* (image_id), which is a good starting place. The question becomes, does a user reference an image, or does an image reference a user?

Here's the fundamental question you'll ask over and over when you're connecting two tables in a database: how are the two tables related? Better still, how are the two objects that your tables represent related?

> **NOTE** You can find the finished example code for this section on this book's Missing CD page at *www.missingmanuals.com/cds/phpmysqlmm2e*.

For example, does a user have an image? Does a user have *lots* of images? In this case, a single user has a single profile image. In database terms, that's called a *one-to-one* (or *1-1*) *relationship*. One user is related to one image. As a result, you can create a new column in your *users* table, and in that column you can store the image_id of that user's profile image. You can make that change to your database like this:

```
mysql> ALTER TABLE users
    ->          ADD profile_pic_id int;
Query OK, 6 rows affected (0.11 sec)
Records: 6  Duplicates: 0  Warnings: 0
```

DESIGN TIME

Foreign Keys and Column Names

The profile_pic_id column in the code above is setting up what's called a *foreign key relationship*. This column is a foreign key because it relates to the key in a different, "foreign" table: *images*.

In most databases, you not only define a column in your table that relates to the referenced table's primary key, you also define a FOREIGN KEY at the database level. That way, your database knows that profile_pic_id is storing IDs that are in the *images* table's image_id column.

You can use foreign keys in MySQL, but you have to use the MySQL InnoDB table engine, which you haven't seen yet. This requires some extra setup, and not all hosting providers support InnoDB. Besides, programmers have been using MySQL without foreign key support for years, so if you write your code properly, you can work around this limitation. If you want to use InnoDB and foreign key support at the database level, start with this command on your tables:

```
ALTER TABLE [table-name]
    ENGINE = InnoDB;
```

Then Google "MySQL foreign keys" and you'll find a wealth of information at your fingertips.

Regardless of whether you use foreign keys through your programming or add support at the database level by using

InnoDB, naming your foreign key columns is a big deal. The typical practice here is to name the foreign key [singular-table-name]_id. For example, for a foreign key connecting *users* to *images*, you'd typically take the singular name of the table you're connecting to—"image" from *images*—and append "_id". This results in get image_id for your foreign key column name.

Why use profile_pic_id in *users*? Because you could very well store more than just profile pictures in *images*. You might store several images for a user, only one of which is a profile picture. You might keep up with user's candid photos, or icons for logging in, or images for companies to which your users connect.

In all of these cases, then, image_id in *users* doesn't provide enough specificity. In these cases—where you're not just setting up a foreign key, but setting up both a foreign key *and* indicating a particular type of usage—using a different name makes sense. For instance, you could end up with a profile_pic_id column in *users*, and then perhaps a company_logo_id in a potential *companies* table, and who knows what other images you'll use? By using profile_pic_id now, you're indicating that you're relating to an image and the specific purpose for which that image is being used.

WARNING You've already made changes to your scripts to accommodate storing images in your database, rather than on your file system. With the ALTER in the preceding example, you're now making the same sort of changes to your database. These changes reflect a deviation in how your application works. To be safe, you want to back things up at this point in your database.

Of course, backing up a script is a lot easier than backing up a database. You might want to give your hosting company a call and see if and how you can backup your database. Or, you can just figure out how to undo these changes if you decide that you want to go back to storing images on your file system.

Either way, you're going to get some PHP and MySQL practice switching between the two approaches. That's a good thing no matter what solution you end up using.

Inserting an Image and then Inserting a User

Once an image is in *images*, you need to get that image's ID and insert it into a user's profile_pic_id column. At the moment, though, your script inserts into *users* before inserting into *images*:

```php
// This replaces the older assignment to $insert_sql
$insert_sql = sprintf("INSERT INTO users " .
                        "(first_name, last_name, email, " .
                        "bio, facebook_url, twitter_handle) " .
                    "VALUES ('%s', '%s', '%s', '%s', '%s', '%s');",
                    mysql_real_escape_string($first_name),
                    mysql_real_escape_string($last_name),
                    mysql_real_escape_string($email),
                    mysql_real_escape_string($bio),
                    mysql_real_escape_string($facebook_url),
                    mysql_real_escape_string($twitter_handle));

// Insert the user into the database
mysql_query($insert_sql)
  or die(mysql_error());

$user_id = mysql_insert_id();

$insert_image_sql = sprintf("INSERT INTO images " .
                            "(filename, mime_type, " .
                            "file_size, image_data) " .
                        "VALUES ('%s', '%s', %d, '%s');",
                        mysql_real_escape_string($image_filename),
                        mysql_real_escape_string($image_mime_type),
                        mysql_real_escape_string($image_size),
                        mysql_real_escape_string($image_data));

mysql_query($insert_image_sql)
  or die(mysql_error());
```

```
// Redirect the user to the page that displays user information
header("Location: show_user.php?user_id=" . $user_id);
exit();
?>
```

At this point, you could look up the ID of the user you inserted using mysql_insert_id and store that in a variable. Then, you could get the image ID by using mysql_insert_id again. Finally, you could update the profile_pic_id column of the new user's row in *users*. That would work, and you'd end up with three different database interactions:

1. **An INSERT to put the user's information into *users*.**

2. **An INSERT to put the image information into *images*.**

3. **An UPDATE to drop the new image's ID into *users*.**

These three steps might not seem like much, but every interaction with your database consumes time and resources. As a general principle, you want to interact with your database as little as possible. That's not to say you don't work with a database; you just don't make three or four calls if you can pull off the same task with one or two.

In this case, you can reduce the number of MySQL interactions from three to two:

1. **INSERT the image into the *images* table (and get the ID of that image in the process).**

2. **INSERT the new user into *users*, and use the image ID you just grabbed as part of the data you put into that INSERT.**

Going from three MySQL interactions to two might sound like a minor issue. Then again, you just cut your database interactions by a third. If you can make fewer calls, do it.

Go ahead and wire up your INSERT statements accordingly:

```
// Get image data

$insert_image_sql = sprintf("INSERT INTO images " .
                             "(filename, mime_type, " .
                              "file_size, image_data) " .
                    "VALUES ('%s', '%s', %d, '%s');",
                    mysql_real_escape_string($image_filename),
                    mysql_real_escape_string($image_mime_type),
                    mysql_real_escape_string($image_size),
                    mysql_real_escape_string($image_data));

mysql_query($insert_image_sql)
  or die(mysql_error());
```

```php
// This replaces the older assignment to $insert_sql
$insert_sql = sprintf("INSERT INTO users " .
                              "(first_name, last_name, email, " .
                              "bio, facebook_url, twitter_handle) " .
                      "VALUES ('%s', '%s', '%s', '%s', '%s', '%s');",
                      mysql_real_escape_string($first_name),
                      mysql_real_escape_string($last_name),
                      mysql_real_escape_string($email),
                      mysql_real_escape_string($bio),
                      mysql_real_escape_string($facebook_url),
                      mysql_real_escape_string($twitter_handle));

// Insert the user into the database
mysql_query($insert_sql)
  or die(mysql_error());

// Redirect the user to the page that displays user information
header("Location: show_user.php?user_id=" . $user_id);
exit();
?>
```

> **NOTE**   There's no additional code here. It's just a wholesale move of the insertion creation and `mysql_query` call related to a user from *before* the image-related code to *after* that code.
>
> But you can remove some code. Now that you have the insertion into *users* coming second, you can go back to using `mysql_insert_id` in your redirection.

From here, it's just a matter of getting the ID from your *images* INSERT and using it in the *users* INSERT. But you know how to do that: you can use `mysql_insert_id` to grab the ID of the row inserted into *images* and then add that to your INSERT for *users*:

```php
// Get image data

$insert_image_sql = sprintf("INSERT INTO images " .
                                    "(filename, mime_type, " .
                                    "file_size, image_data) " .
                            "VALUES ('%s', '%s', %d, '%s');",
                            mysql_real_escape_string($image_filename),
                            mysql_real_escape_string($image_mime_type),
                            mysql_real_escape_string($image_size),
                            mysql_real_escape_string($image_data));

mysql_query($insert_image_sql)
  or die(mysql_error());
```

```php
// This replaces the older assignment to $insert_sql
$insert_sql = sprintf("INSERT INTO users " .
                      "(first_name, last_name, email, " .
                      "bio, facebook_url, twitter_handle, " .
                      "profile_pic_id) " .
              "VALUES ('%s', '%s', '%s', '%s', '%s', '%s', %d);",
                  mysql_real_escape_string($first_name),
                  mysql_real_escape_string($last_name),
                  mysql_real_escape_string($email),
                  mysql_real_escape_string($bio),
                  mysql_real_escape_string($facebook_url),
                  mysql_real_escape_string($twitter_handle),
                  mysql_insert_id());

// Insert the user into the database
mysql_query($insert_sql)
  or die(mysql_error());

// Redirect the user to the page that displays user information
header("Location: show_user.php?user_id=" . mysql_insert_id());
exit();
?>
```

> **NOTE** Remember, because the ID of the image you're inserting into `profile_pic_id` is an int, not a string, you need to use `%d` as your type specifier for `sprintf`. You don't need to include that value in single quotes.

Put everything together, and your updated version of *create_user.php* should look like this:

```php
<?php

require_once '../scripts/app_config.php';
require_once '../scripts/database_connection.php';

$upload_dir = HTTP_WWW_ROOT . "uploads/profile_pics/";
$image_fieldname = "user_pic";

// Potential PHP upload errors
$php_errors = array(1 => 'Maximum file size in php.ini exceeded',
                    2 => 'Maximum file size in HTML form exceeded',
                    3 => 'Only part of the file was uploaded',
                    4 => 'No file was selected to upload.');

$first_name = trim($_REQUEST['first_name']);
$last_name = trim($_REQUEST['last_name']);
```

```php
$email = trim($_REQUEST['email']);
$bio = trim($_REQUEST['bio']);
$facebook_url = str_replace("facebook.org", "facebook.com", trim($_
REQUEST['facebook_url']));
$position = strpos($facebook_url, "facebook.com");
if ($position === false) {
  $facebook_url = "http://www.facebook.com/" . $facebook_url;
}

$twitter_handle = trim($_REQUEST['twitter_handle']);
$twitter_url = "http://www.twitter.com/";
$position = strpos($twitter_handle, "@");
if ($position === false) {
  $twitter_url = $twitter_url . $twitter_handle;
} else {
  $twitter_url = $twitter_url . substr($twitter_handle, $position + 1);
}

// Make sure we didn't have an error uploading the image
($_FILES[$image_fieldname]['error'] == 0)
  or handle_error("the server couldn't upload the image you selected.",
                  $php_errors[$_FILES[$image_fieldname]['error']]);

// Is this file the result of a valid upload?
@is_uploaded_file($_FILES[$image_fieldname]['tmp_name'])
  or handle_error("you were trying to do something naughty. Shame on you!",
                  "Uploaded request: file named '{$_FILES[$image_fieldname]
                  ['tmp_name']}'");

// Is this actually an image?
@getimagesize($_FILES[$image_fieldname]['tmp_name'])
  or handle_error("you selected a file for your picture that isn't an image.",
          "{$_FILES[$image_fieldname]['tmp_name']} isn't a valid image
          file.");

// Name the file uniquely
$now = time();
while (file_exists($upload_filename = $upload_dir . $now .
                                      '-' .
                                      $_FILES[$image_fieldname]['name'])) {
    $now++;
}

// Insert the image into the images table
$image = $_FILES[$image_fieldname];
$image_filename = $image['name'];
```

```php
$image_info = getimagesize($image['tmp_name']);
$image_mime_type = $image_info['mime'];
$image_size = $image['size'];
$image_data = file_get_contents($image['tmp_name']);

$insert_image_sql = sprintf("INSERT INTO images " .
                            "(filename, mime_type, file_size, image_data) " .
                            "VALUES ('%s', '%s', %d, '%s');",
                            mysql_real_escape_string($image_filename),
                            mysql_real_escape_string($image_mime_type),
                            mysql_real_escape_string($image_size),
                            mysql_real_escape_string($image_data));

mysql_query($insert_image_sql)
  or die(mysql_error());

$insert_sql = sprintf("INSERT INTO users " .
                      "(first_name, last_name, email, " .
                      "bio, facebook_url, twitter_handle, " .
                      "profile_pic_id) " .
                "VALUES ('%s', '%s', '%s', '%s', '%s', '%s', %d);",
                mysql_real_escape_string($first_name),
                mysql_real_escape_string($last_name),
                mysql_real_escape_string($email),
                mysql_real_escape_string($bio),
                mysql_real_escape_string($facebook_url),
                mysql_real_escape_string($twitter_handle),
                mysql_insert_id());

// Insert the user into the database
mysql_query($insert_sql)
  or die(mysql_error());

// Redirect the user to the page that displays user information
header("Location: show_user.php?user_id=" . mysql_insert_id());
exit();
?>
```

Try your code out by creating another user. Then, check to see what the last and highest inserted image ID is from your *images* table:

```
mysql> select image_id from images;
+----------+
| image_id |
+----------+
|        2 |
```

```
|         3 |
|         4 |
+-----------+
2 rows in set (0.45 sec)
```

This ID should be the same one that was inserted into your last inserted user in *users*:

```
mysql> select user_id, first_name, last_name, profile_pic_id from users;
+---------+------------+-----------+----------------+
| user_id | first_name | last_name | profile_pic_id |
+---------+------------+-----------+----------------+
|       1 | Yu         | Darvish   |           NULL |
|      10 | David      | Ramirez   |           NULL |
|      19 | Ryan       | Geyer     |           NULL |
|      21 | Jason      | Wadley    |           NULL |
|      24 | Robert     | Powell    |              4 |
+---------+------------+-----------+----------------+
5 rows in set (0.00 sec)
```

You can see that when an image is inserted, the ID of that image is dropped into *users*, which demonstrates that you have a connection between a user and an image.

Joining Tables by Using WHERE

Now that you have a connection between and image and a user, you need a way to get an image for that user. First, utilize the user ID to select the user you want:

```
// Build the SELECT statement
$select_query = sprintf("SELECT * FROM users WHERE user_id = %d",
                        $user_id);
```

This variable is just a sprintf version of code from *show_user.php*. Make this change in your own version of *show_user.php*.

Notice that you get more than just user information, now. You also get the profile_pic_id for that user. This means that you can use this ID to get the image for that user:

```
// Run the query
$result = mysql_query($select_query);
if ($result) {
  $row = mysql_fetch_array($result);
  $first_name     = $row['first_name'];
  $last_name      = $row['last_name'];
  $bio            = preg_replace("/[\r\n]+/", "</p><p>", $row['bio']);
  $email          = $row['email'];
  $facebook_url   = $row['facebook_url'];
  $twitter_handle = $row['twitter_handle'];
  $profile_pic_id = $row['profile_pic_id'];
```

```
$image_query = sprintf("SELECT * FROM images WHERE image_id = %d",
                        $profile_pic_id);
$image_result = mysql_query($image_query);

// Turn $twitter_handle into a URL
$twitter_url = "http://www.twitter.com/" .
                    substr($twitter_handle, $position + 1);
} else {
  handle_error("There was a problem finding your " .
               "information in our system.",
               "Error locating user with ID {$user_id}");
}
```

NOTE   You can remove any code in *show_user.php* that involves the profile image's file path because you're not longer using that approach for dealing with images.

This code works, but it's actually turning what is potentially one step into two. What you're doing here is joining two tables: you have a piece of information—profile_pic_id in *users* and image_id in *images*—that connects the two tables.

■ CONNECT YOUR TABLES THROUGH COMMON COLUMNS

You also have a way to get only certain rows from a table: the WHERE clause. Putting this all together, you can get a user from *users* and an image from *images* where the user's profile_pic_id matches the image's image_id:

```
SELECT first_name, last_name, filename
  FROM users, images
 WHERE profile_pic_id = image_id;
```

Run this in MySQL, and you should see a result like the following example:

```
mysql> SELECT first_name, last_name, filename
    ->   FROM users, images
    ->  WHERE profile_pic_id = image_id;
+------------+-----------+--------------------+
| first_name | last_name | filename           |
+------------+-----------+--------------------+
| Robert     | Powell    | powell-kicking.png |
+------------+-----------+--------------------+
1 row in set (0.44 sec)
```

For the first time, you're connecting your tables together. In a single query, you've *joined* information in one table to corresponding information in another table. That's a big deal!

■ ALIAS YOUR TABLES (AND COLUMNS)

As cool as this query is, it's a bit confusing. Take a look again:

```
SELECT first_name, last_name, filename
  FROM users, images
 WHERE profile_pic_id = image_id;
```

It's obvious that first_name and last_name are columns from *users*. But, unless you really know your database structure, it's not immediately clear where filename comes from. (Of course, you *are* intimately familiar with your database, so you know that filename is a column in *images*.)

The same is true with profile_pic_id and image_id. Both are column names, but which column belongs to which table?

You can make this clear, though, by using table prefixes on your columns. For example, you can convert this query to something a bit more descriptive:

```
SELECT users.first_name, users.last_name, images.filename
  FROM users, images
 WHERE users.profile_pic_id = images.image_id;
```

You'll get the same result, but the query itself is a lot less ambiguous. Still, there's another important fact to keep in mind here: programmers are lazy. Yup, it's true; most programmers would rather type a single character—or at most two—if they can avoid typing five or ten. And SQL is happy to accommodate. You can alias a table by providing a letter or two after the table name and then using that letter as your prefix in the rest of the query:

```
SELECT u.first_name, u.last_name, i.filename
  FROM users u, images i
 WHERE u.profile_pic_id = i.image_id;
```

Once again, there's nothing functionally different about this query, but it's now both clear and succinct: a programmer's best-case situation.

■ Show Me the Image!

At this point, you have all your data, and you can even get the image for a particular user. All that's left is to actually show the image, right?

Yes, but you have an entirely different situation than when you had the image on a file system and just needed to point at that file. In this case, you must load the actual raw image data from your database and then somehow let the browser know, "Hey, this is an image, not just text. Display it like an image." That's not particularly difficult, but it's different from what you've been doing.

> **NOTE** You can find the finished example code for this section on this book's Missing CD page at *www.missingmanuals.com/cds/phpmysqlmm2e.*

Displaying an Image

First, you need a script that can load and display an image. Once that's done, it's easy to reference that display script in *show_user.php*. Therefore, the script is the important piece, with all the new code.

Create a new script, and call it *show_image.php*. You can start out with the basic script shell that all your scripts now have:

```php
<?php

require_once '../scripts/app_config.php';
require_once '../scripts/database_connection.php';

?>
```

■ MAKE A GAME PLAN FOR YOUR SCRIPT

Map out the exact steps that need to happen:

1. **Get an image ID from the request.**

2. **Build a SELECT query from the *images* table by using that image ID.**

3. **Run the SELECT query and get the results.**

4. **Grab what should be the only row from those results.**

5. **Inform the browser that it's about to receive an image.**

6. **Inform the browser what kind of image it's about to receive.**

7. **Give the browser the image data.**

With the exception of these last few steps, you're probably already whirring away, figuring out exactly what sort of code you need to write. But, there's a lot of error handling that has to happen along the way, too:

1. **Ensure that an image ID was sent to the script.**

2. **Ensure that the ID maps to an image in the *images* table.**

3. **Deal with general problems that occur while loading or displaying the image data.**

Again, though, none of this is particularly hard. Time to get to work.

■ GET THE IMAGE ID

First up, you need to get an ID to use for loading the image from the database. This step is also where you can do some initial error handling: if no ID comes in as part of the request, something's gone wrong.

```php
<?php

require_once '../scripts/app_config.php';
```

```php
require_once '../scripts/database_connection.php';

if (!isset($_REQUEST['image_id'])) {
  handle_error("No image to load was specified.");
}

$image_id = $_REQUEST['image_id'];

?>
```

Simple enough, and a lot like code you've written before in *show_user.php*. Once again, handle_error makes dealing with problems, if they do occur, a piece of cake.

■ BUILD AND RUN A SELECT QUERY

Next, you can use your new friend, sprintf, to construct a SQL query, and an older friend, mysql_query, to get a result set:

```php
<?php

// require statements

// Get the image ID

// Build the SELECT statement
$select_query = sprintf("SELECT * FROM images WHERE image_id = %d",
                        $image_id);

// Run the query
$result = mysql_query($select_query);

?>
```

Nothing new here, either.

■ GET THE RESULTS, GET THE IMAGE, AND DEAL WITH POTENTIAL ERRORS

Now, you can grab the data from $result. In the past, you've done that in a few ways. Early on, you looped over all of the rows returned from a query:

```php
if ($return_rows) {
  // We have rows to show from the query
  echo "<p>Results from your query:</p>";
  echo "<ul>";
  while ($row = mysql_fetch_row($result)) {
    echo "<li>{$row[0]}</li>";
  }
```

```
    echo "</ul>";
  } else {
    // No rows. Just report if the query ran or not
    echo "<p>The following query was processed successfully:</p>";
    echo "<p>{$query_text}</p>";
  }
```

NOTE   This code is from way back in Chapter 6 (page 160). Hard to believe how much more advanced your PHP scripts have become in a few short chapters, isn't it?

You also used an if statement if you expected only a single result:

```
if ($result) {
  $row = mysql_fetch_array($result);

  // Deal with the single result
} else {
  handle_error("there was a problem finding your information in our system.",
              "Error locating user with ID {$user_id}");
}
```

This statement assumes that as long as $result is valid, you have a row. Further, it ignores any rows other than the first one, knowing that the SQL query that generated these results can only return a single row.

In *show_image.php*, you want something similar to this latter approach. But it's possible to check and ensure that you have a result without encasing everything in an if:

```
<?php

// require statements
// Get the image ID
// Build and run the query

// Get the result and handle errors from getting no result
if (mysql_num_rows($result) == 0) {
  handle_error("we couldn't find the requested image.",
              "No image found with an ID of " . $image_id . ".");
}

$image = mysql_fetch_array($result);

?>
```

This approach is cleaner because it keeps your code moving along once the error has been dealt with. (For more on why this sequence is more natural, read the box on page 317.)

Sequential Code Is Usually Clearer Code

There's almost always more than one way to accomplish any task in programming. In fact, there are usually multiple good ways to get a job done. But, there's usually a clearest way, and that's what you want to work toward. You want good, working code that's also clear and easy to understand.

Writing clear code becomes harder as your code grows more complex. You often have multiple decision points (with `if` statements), error handling, loops, and all sorts of other constructs that take your code all over the place. Because of all this complexity, you want to make as much of your code as you can *sequential*. In other words, you want to be able to read that code more or less from beginning to end and be able to follow the flow.

With that in mind, take a look again at the earlier code from *show_user.php*:

```
if ($result) {
  $row = mysql_fetch_array($result);

  // Deal with the single result
} else {
  handle_error("there was a problem find-
```

```
ing your " .
"information in our system.",
"Error locating user with " .
"ID {$user_id}");
}
```

This code works, and it's even pretty solid. But, is it sequential? Well...sort of. If there's a result, get that result, and work with it. If there's no result, deal with errors. But, what's the *real* sequence of the process?

First, you want to see if there's a result, and if not, handle the error. Then—and only after you're sure it's safe to carry on—you want to work with the results and continue with the script. Thinking along that line, the `else` at the end handling the error is out of sequence. It's something you want to deal with *before* going on to work with the row.

That's why the newer sequence in *show_image.php* on page 316, in which errors are handled and *then* the results are used, is a better solution for your code's readability. Same functionality, but easier to understand and maintain.

■ TELL THE BROWSER WHAT'S COMING

You have the information you want from *images*, but you can't just toss that to the browser. Well, you *could*, but the browser would become confused. It's used to dealing with HTML; but raw binary data is something else altogether.

There are a couple of things about which you need to apprise the browser:

- What kind of content is coming? This information is passed to the browser through a MIME type. It is usually something like *text/html* or *text/xml*, or in the case of images, *image/jpeg* or *image/gif* or *image/png*.

- If that type is binary—as images are—what amount or size of information is coming? The browser needs to know so it can figure out when it's done receiving information.

You already have the tools you need to communicate with the browser. Remember this line from page 248?

```
header("Location: " . HTTP_WWW_ROOT . "scripts/show_error.php?" .
       error_message={$user_error_message}&" .
       system_error_message={$system_error_message}");
```

This line communicates directly to the browser. It's sending a header called Location to the browser. The value of that header is a location, a URL, and the browser knows that when it gets a Location header, go to the URL specified by the header's value.

The PHP header function is the mechanism by which you can speak directly to the browser. As for the two pieces of information you need to send—the content type and the size of that content—browsers have specific headers for both:

- **Content-type** Use this to alert a browser to what the MIME type is of the content you're about to send.

- **Content-length** Use this to provide the size (the "length" in bytes) of the information you're about to send.

At this point, you have both of these pieces of information in your *images* table, in the mime_type column and the file_size column.

Put all this together, and you have two lines of code to add to *show_image.php*:

```php
<?php

// require statements
// Get the image ID
// Build and run the query
// Get the result and handle errors from getting no result

// Tell the browser what's coming with headers
header('Content-type: ' . $image['mime_type']);
header('Content-length: ' . $image['file_size']);

?>
```

That's it. The browser expects a certain type of information (in your case, *image/jpeg* or *image/gif* in most cases), it knows the size of the information and now it just needs the actual information itself.

WARNING   As with other headers you've sent (such as the Location header, which causes a redirect), you must send headers before any other output. Therefore, ensure that *show_image.php* doesn't echo or spit out any HTML before it calls header.

■ SEND THE IMAGE DATA

All that's left is one easy step. You need to set up an echo statement to send the image to the browser:

```php
<?php

// require statements
// Get the image ID
// Build and run the query
// Get the result and handle errors from getting no result
// Tell the browser what's coming with headers

echo $image['image_data'];

?>
```

That's it. This data is not a string of text; it's the raw binary information pulled from a BLOB column in your *images* table, sent out bit by bit. But the magic isn't in this line. The magic is you telling the browser that this is a certain kind of information and a certain size. Those details let the browser know, "This is an image coming. Treat it like one."

Handling Errors with `try` and `catch`

At this point, you've knocked out your list of things to do to show an image:

1. **Get an image ID from the request.**

2. **Build a SELECT query from the *images* table using that image ID.**

3. **Run the SELECT query and get the results.**

4. **Grab what should be the only row from those results.**

5. **Inform the browser that it's about to receive an image.**

6. **Tell the browser what kind of image it's about to receive.**

7. **Give the browser the image data.**

All done; excellent. And, the script is short, too; clean and easy to follow. That's a win by every account.

You've also taken care of most of your error handling:

1. **Ensure that an image ID was sent to the script.**

2. **Ensure that the ID maps to an image in the *images* table.**

3. **Deal with general problems that occur while loading or displaying the image data.**

The first two are done, but what about those so-called general problems? What happens if, for example, there's an error sending the Content-type header? Or perhaps sending the Content-length header? And what about echoing out the image data? Doesn't that seem like something that can go bad? What if the image data is corrupt, or something happens in pulling data from the result set, or if the browser can't handle a particular type of image that your script tries to send?

In all of these cases, you receive an error that's unaccounted for. And when you have these general sort of errors—errors that don't fit into the black-and-white, "I can check ahead of time and make sure there's no problem" mold—you need a way to deal with them.

The rub here is that you can't pin these things down. You need a way to say, "While this entire chunk of code is running, if a general problem happens, do this…" The good news is that you have a "do this" in handle_error. PHP provides a way to do just this with something called a try/catch block.

The try part of a try/catch block defines a segment (a block) of your error-prone code to which you would like to pay special attention. Essentially, you're saying, "Try this code." The catch path of the try/catch block is run only if an error occurs. If anything goes wrong within the try block, the catch part of the block runs.

Not only that, but in the catch, an object is handed off: an Exception. This Exception has information about what went wrong, so you can report on that—say to a custom function such as handle_error.

To put this into place in *show_image.php*, first, surround all your error-prone code with a try and curly braces, like this:

```php
<?php

require_once '../scripts/app_config.php';
require_once '../scripts/database_connection.php';

try {
  if (!isset($_REQUEST['image_id'])) {
    handle_error("No image to load was specified.");
  }

  $image_id = $_REQUEST['image_id'];

  // Build the SELECT statement
  $select_query = sprintf("SELECT * FROM images WHERE image_id = %d",
                          $image_id);

  // Run the query
  $result = mysql_query($select_query);

  // Get the result and handle errors from getting no result
  if (mysql_num_rows($result) == 0) {
    handle_error("we couldn't find the requested image.",
                 "No image found with an ID of " . $image_id . ".");
  }

  $image = mysql_fetch_array($result);
```

```php
    // Tell the browser what's coming with headers
    header('Content-type: ' . $image['mime_type']);
    header('Content-length: ' . $image['file_size']);

    echo $image['image_data'];
}
?>
```

Whenever anything goes wrong, the PHP interpreter will throw out an Exception object, reporting the problem, and then go to the catch block:

```php
<?php

require_once '../scripts/app_config.php';
require_once '../scripts/database_connection.php';

try {
  // code that may cause an error
} catch (Exception $exc) {
}
?>
```

You can see that this line almost looks like a function: the catch code takes control, and it receives an Exception object. $exc is the variable name of the exception, so you can reference that exception if you need to.

Finally, you should do something useful in this catch block:

```php
<?php

require_once '../scripts/app_config.php';
require_once '../scripts/database_connection.php';

try {
  // code that may cause an error
} catch (Exception $exc) {
  handle_error("something went wrong loading your image.",
               "Error loading image: " . $exc->getMessage());
}
?>
```

With this code, anytime there's an error, handle_error comes to the rescue. As usual, you pass handle_error a friendly string as well as some extra information for the programmers who might be looking on. In this case, that message comes from exc, and the getMessage method. An object in PHP doesn't have functions; it has methods. You reference a method by using ->, that weird arrow character you first met on page 109.

When this code runs, it reports any error that might have occurred and stops PHP
from trying to continue on in the try block.

Here's what you should have for *show_image.php*:

```php
<?php

require_once '../scripts/app_config.php';
require_once '../scripts/database_connection.php';

try {
  if (!isset($_REQUEST['image_id'])) {
    handle_error("No image to load was specified.");
  }

  $image_id = $_REQUEST['image_id'];

  // Build the SELECT statement
  $select_query = sprintf("SELECT * FROM images WHERE image_id = %d",
                          $image_id);

  // Run the query
  $result = mysql_query($select_query);

  // Get the result and handle errors from getting no result
  if (mysql_num_rows($result) == 0) {
    handle_error("we couldn't find the requested image.",
                 "No image found with an ID of " . $image_id . ".");
  }

  $image = mysql_fetch_array($result);

  // Tell the browser what's coming with headers
  header('Content-type: ' . $image['mime_type']);
  header('Content-length: ' . $image['file_size']);

  echo $image['image_data'];
} catch (Exception $exc) {
  handle_error("something went wrong loading your image.",
               "Error loading image: " . $exc->getMessage());
}
?>
```

All that's left is some testing to verify that things work.

Test, Test, Always Test

First, start MySQL and find an image that's been inserted. Make a note of that
image's ID.

```
mysql> select image_id, filename from images;
+----------+----------------------------------------------------+
| image_id | filename                                           |
+----------+----------------------------------------------------+
|        2 | 7829_1204001948285_1475710666_1190173_2526636_n.jpg |
|        4 | powell-kicking.png                                 |
+----------+----------------------------------------------------+
2 rows in set (0.00 sec)
```

Next, open your browser and type the URL for *show_image.php*, but don't press
Enter; if you do, you should get the error shown in Figure 10-4 because you didn't
supply an ID.

FIGURE 10-4

*It's not completely neces-
sary, but it's probably a
good idea to even test
your errors. In this case,
by not specifying an
image ID, you're verifying
that errors are handled
properly, and in particular
that the case where no
image ID is provided is
handled.*

Now, add the image ID to the URL like this: *show_image.php?image_id=4*. Put that
in your browser's address bar (along with the rest of your domain name and path),
and you should see something similar to Figure 10-5.

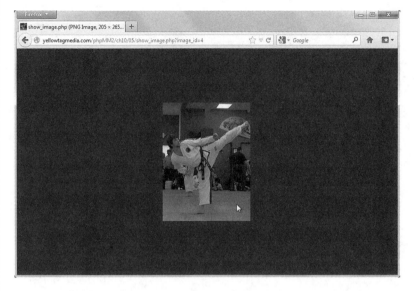

FIGURE 10-5

This is what all this work is about: getting a browser to show an image. In fact, this is a lot like right-clicking an image on another web page, and selecting View Image. It shows you just the image, without any other text.

Embedding an Image Is Just Viewing an Image

Finally, it's back to *show_user.php*. Remember, *show_image.php* was actually a bit of a diversion. It's a necessary one, but the point isn't a script that displays an image. Instead, it's a script that displays a user, and that just happens to mean you have to show that user's image. But, you have all the work done now to make this happen, so *show_user.php* is back into the fold, ready for you to piece it all together.

> **NOTE** You can find the finished example code for this section on this book's Missing CD page at *www.missingmanuals.com/cds/phpmysqlmm2e*.

All You Need Is an Image ID

Your first thought might be to rewrite that SQL query that grabs an entry from *images* based on a user from *users*:

```
SELECT u.first_name, u.last_name, i.filename
  FROM users u, images i
 WHERE u.profile_pic_id = i.image_id;
```

But, do you need to do this? No, because all that *show_image.php* requires is an image ID, and you have that in the *users* table, in profile_pic_id. You don't need to do a join on *users* and *images*.

As a result, when you're getting the results from your SQL query, you just need to grab the profile image ID:

```php
<?php

require_once '../scripts/app_config.php';
require_once '../scripts/database_connection.php';

// Get the user ID of the user to show
// Build the SELECT statement
// Run the query

if ($result) {
  $row = mysql_fetch_array($result);
  $first_name     = $row['first_name'];
  $last_name      = $row['last_name'];
  $bio            = preg_replace("/[\r\n]+/", "</p><p>", $row['bio']);
  $email          = $row['email'];
  $facebook_url   = $row['facebook_url'];
  $twitter_handle = $row['twitter_handle'];
  $image_id       = $row['profile_pic_id'];

  // Turn $twitter_handle into a URL
} else {
  handle_error("there was a problem finding your information in our system.",
               "Error locating user with ID {$user_id}");
}
?>

<!-- HTML -->
```

> **NOTE** This line of new code replaces the older line with which you grabbed the URL to the image, in the version that stored just a path to the image in your *users* table.

A Script Can Be an Image src

With this ID, you're ready to deal with the missing image. However, what's about to happen might seem a bit odd, so some explanation is in order.

Think about your typical HTML <img> element:

```html
<img src="/images/powell_kicking.jpg" />
```

What's really happening here? The `<img>` tag itself informs the browser to expect an image, and the `src` attribute provides the browser with the location of that image. But, that location will just trigger another browser request—in this case, to *images/ powell_kicking.jpg*. And, what does the browser get from that location? A bunch of bits that makes up the image *powell_kicking.jpg*.

Yet, there's nothing magical about *powell_kicking.jpg*, or that URL. It's just a location, and as long as that location returns an image to the browser, the image is displayed. Thus, it's perfectly okay to supply anything to the `src`, as long as that anything returns an image. You might supply it, for example, a script that displays an image. You might just hand it something like this:

```
<img src="show_image.php?image_id=4" />
```

Because *show_image.php* with a valid ID returns an image, the browser happily displays that image in place of the `<img>` tag in your web page.

From here, it's a breeze to change your HTML in *show_user.php* to do just this:

```php
<?php
  // Lots of PHP goodness
?>
<html>
 <head>
  <link href="../css/phpMM.css" rel="stylesheet" type="text/css" />
 </head>

 <body>
  <div id="header"><h1>PHP & MySQL: The Missing Manual</h1></div>
  <div id="example">User Profile</div>

  <div id="content">
    <div class="user_profile">
      <h1><?php echo "{$first_name} {$last_name}"; ?></h1>
      <p><img src="show_image.php?image_id=<?php echo $image_id; ?>"
              class="user_pic" />
        <?php echo $bio; ?></p>
      <p class="contact_info">Get in touch with <?php echo $first_name; ?>:
</p>
      <ul>
        <!-- Connect links -->
      </ul>
    </div>
  </div>
  <div id="footer"></div>
 </body>
</html>
```

That's all there is to it! The src attribute of your `<img>` tag is now a link to your script, with the correct ID. When you take all of *show_user.php* together, you should have something like this:

```php
<?php

require_once '../scripts/database_connection.php';

// Get the user ID of the user to show
$user_id = $_REQUEST['user_id'];

// Build the SELECT statement
$select_query = sprintf("SELECT * FROM users WHERE user_id = %d",
                        $user_id);

// Run the query
$result = mysql_query($select_query);
if ($result) {
  $row = mysql_fetch_array($result);
  $first_name     = $row['first_name'];
  $last_name      = $row['last_name'];
  $bio            = preg_replace("/[\r\n]+/", "</p><p>", $row['bio']);
  $email          = $row['email'];
  $facebook_url   = $row['facebook_url'];
  $twitter_handle = $row['twitter_handle'];
  $image_id       = $row['profile_pic_id'];

  $image_query = sprintf("SELECT * FROM images WHERE image_id = %d",
                         $profile_pic_id);
  $image_result = mysql_query($image_query);

  // Turn $twitter_handle into a URL
  $twitter_url = "http://www.twitter.com/" .
                  substr($twitter_handle, $position + 1);

} else {
  handle_error("There was a problem finding your " .
               "information in our system.",
               "Error locating user with ID {$user_id}");
}

?>
```

```html
<html>
 <head>
  <link href="../../css/phpMM.css" rel="stylesheet" type="text/css" />
 </head>

 <body>
  <div id="header"><h1>PHP & MySQL: The Missing Manual</h1></div>
  <div id="example">User Profile</div>

  <div id="content">
    <div class="user_profile">
      <h1><?php echo "{$first_name} {$last_name}"; ?></h1>
      <p><img src="show_image.php?image_id=<?php echo $image_id; ?>"
             class="user_pic" />
        <?php echo $bio; ?></p>
      <p class="contact_info">Get in touch with <?php echo $first_name; ?>:
</p>
      <ul>
        <li>...by emailing them at
          <a href="<?php echo $email; ?>"><?php echo $email; ?></a></li>
        <li>...by
          <a href="<?php echo $facebook_url; ?>">checking them out
             on Facebook</a></li>
        <li>...by <a href="<?php echo $twitter_url; ?>">following them
             on Twitter</a></li>
      </ul>
    </div>
  </div>
  <div id="footer"></div>
 </body>
</html>
```

You can see the final result in Figure 10-6.

Nice work! Whoever thought before you closed this chapter that you'd be manually loading bits and bytes from a database and displaying them as an image on demand?

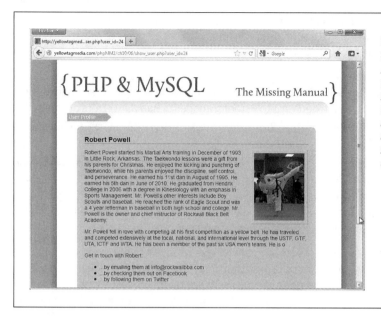

FIGURE 10-6

This reward has been a long time coming. Just a few hundred lines of code ago, you were referencing an image on a file system. Cool, yes; but loading an image from a database? That's something else altogether. Now, you have a new script, a new approach, and yet another way to show a user's smiling face (or perhaps, his cat's face) in full color.

Knowledge Is Power

Couldn't I have learned this code in, say, a quick online tutorial?

If you've spent much time on the Internet, you know what a force Google is. Spend just a few minutes on its search engine and you'll find at least 20 or 30 tutorials on image uploads, in PHP, for both storing paths to the image in your database and for storing the images themselves in your database. Heck, there are even frameworks that take care of all this programming for you!

So, why is it worth plowing through some of the trickiest PHP material you've run across yet, just to do this yourself? There are two important reasons why this sort of code—and in fact this exact code—is important not for you to just type into your editor, but to actually understand.

First, you can do *lots* of things using frameworks floating around on the Internet. And, truth be told, many of the frameworks, especially when you get them from reputable sources, do what your code would do, better, faster, and with greater efficiency. But that doesn't mean it's not important to understand what's

going on. In fact, once you understand how this code works, you're *much* better prepared to make good choices about which frameworks to use, and why those frameworks might be better than writing your own...*after* you've written your own and are ready to move to a more advanced usage.

Second, as you write more and more web applications, you'll often find your needs are more and more specific. Sure, you need image uploading, but you need it with some particular wrinkle or tweak specific to your application. Maybe you only want to accept JPGs and not GIFs; or you want to impose a server-side restriction on size, rather than relying on the HTML input field that sets a maximum size.

If you have no idea how this sort of code works, you're not equipped to make adjustments like this. Whether it's your code or someone else's, you need to be able to make those sort of adjustments that personalize a piece of code. That requires knowledge, and knowledge comes from trying things out for yourself.

■ So, Which Approach Is Best?

Here you are, with two totally different approaches to getting users' images into your database (or at least the paths to those images). In fact, you've probably spent as much time working through this code as any other code you've run across in your PHP journey. Now, one question begs to be answered: which approach is best?

The most accurate answer to that is, "It depends." Or maybe, "It's up to you." Those are frustrating answers and probably completely dissatisfying. That's because the sort of questions you're getting into—storing images or handling errors or interacting with other frameworks and other people's code—you're not always going to have clear "right" answers.

For example, you have to consider questions like the following: Do you have a particularly small file system with which to work? Are you charged based on the space your web server's files take up? Is that charge greater or lesser than the charges you're assessed for the size of your database? Is your database locally accessible and blistering fast? Or, is it a slow connection to another machine?

Yet, at the end of the day, you sometimes have to say, "I'm not sure...I just like this approach better...or that approach better." That's okay. You might just need to pick something, try it out, and get moving. There are plenty of cases in which the only real *wrong* solution is to wait around analyzing the options for hours (days! weeks!) instead of moving forward.

OK, If You Insist on an Answer...

If you're not sure, store your images on a file server, and store just the path to that image in your database. The fact is, although you can write good code that both stores an image in a database and displays that image, it's a lot tougher to do things right. Every time a SELECT runs against your *images* table and grabs the contents of the image_data column, you're selecting the entire size of that image's data. You might have 100 rows each with an image of an average size of 1 MB and 100 MB of image data clogging up your network and database traffic. When in doubt, you'll probably stick with a path in your database, like the example in Chapter 9. But now, you have a firm handle on just what goes on with images, whether they're stored in the database or not.

FREQUENTLY ASKED QUESTION

Back on the Path

So how do I get my database back in order?

All things being equal, going with images stored on the file system is the better solution. (To be clear, though, all things are *never* equal!) Because that's a good default option, the examples in the rest of this book will assume that's your setup. So how do you get back to that solution?

First, you should have backed up your scripts. If you didn't, you might want to redownload the sample files again from the Missing CD page (*www.missingmanuals.com/cds/phpmysqlmm2e*), and use the versions that don't store images in the database.

Second, you need to remove the `profile_pic_id` column in your *users* table. Here's the SQL to make that change:

```
ALTER TABLE users
        DROP COLUMN profile_pic_id;
```

You can then delete the *images* table easily enough:

```
DROP TABLE images;
```

That's it. You're back in action.

Listing, Iterating, and Administrating

For quite a while now, you've been focusing on some basic details: a user, the user's information, and as an extension of that information, the user's profile picture. You've become familiar with PHP and MySQL, figured out not just one but two ways to deal with one of the most common PHP issues—image loading—and you've managed to keep things looking good throughout. These aren't small accomplishments; they're very much big ones.

As a user, you can set up a profile and specify some basic information. If you're an administrator, you might want to see how many users are in your system, delete a malicious user, or update a picture because it's not quite socially palatable. You can do all that through your MySQL command line, but in the real world of web applications, most administrators aren't keeping a MySQL terminal running in the corner of their monitor.

Instead, they have administrative interfaces. They can list all the users in a system; check some boxes here and there and mass delete users; and see any user they want, all through a nice, clean web interface. You can give your web application the same nice features.

When you start thinking about an administrative interface, you run into all sorts of interesting problems. You need to use different types of SQL queries. You have to mix together a lot more PHP and MySQL with your HTML because you'll have to list every user from the database, one at a time. You have to deal with DELETE statements and a lot more WHERE statements.

In this chapter, you'll take everything you know and push further. There are not many radically new techniques to learn, but there are lots of important variations on what you already do know. So why wait any longer, or settle for MySQL as your admin interface? Time to set up a better, more visual way to keep up with your users.

NOTE If you are just salivating for something completely new and different, work through this chapter in anticipation of the next. There, you'll secure all these nice administrative pages, and then you will need—and learn—a whole new bag of tricks.

■ Thinking about What You Need as an Admin

As usual, the first step is to lay out what you need and rough out the broad strokes of how things look and interact. You can start with a few bullet points, figure out the screens you're going to need, and throw together some mock-ups, either in HTML or even a tool such as Photoshop.

Because your app is straightforward, all you'll need for the moment is the following:

- A form that lists all the users in the system

- A link to each user's profile page

- The ability to delete a user

- The ability to update or change a user's information

- A means of giving other users administrative privileges

That last one is going to take quite a bit of work and create some unique headaches with which you'll have to deal, so let's save it for a bit later (that is, the next chapter). But you can get started on the rest, right now.

NOTE You can find the finished example code for this section on this book's Missing CD page at *www .missingmanuals.com/cds/phpmysqlmm2e*.

(User Interface) Brevity Is Still the Soul of Wit

You could build up a complex system of pages that let you manage all these inter-actions. *show_user.php* could figure out if you're an admin and selectively show a Delete button; you could build up an entire administrative menu, in fact. Then again, sometimes the simple things are the best things. On top of that, the Web rewards fewer clicks as a general rule. If you *can* provide a single page that accommodates the major required functionality, you probably should *keep* things to just that single page.

In this case, you keep it concise. You can list users in a simple sequence, turn the name of each user into a link to her profile page, and even add a delete button after each user. You'll still have to deal with changing a user's information, but three items on one form is a good start.

Figure 11-1 shows an example of what your admin page might look like.

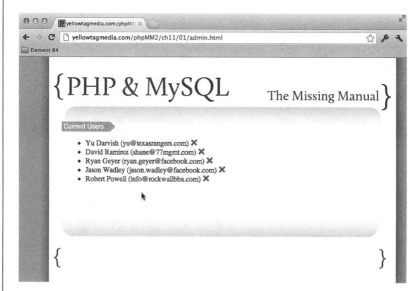

FIGURE 11-1

This design isn't going to win any awards. The delete image needs to be better aligned, the little default bullets look cheesy, and as a whole, this page is in need of some serious help. But you can handle that later. Right now, this mock-up gives you some idea of what you need to get started, and that's all you need at this stage: a starting point and a blueprint.

Looking at the HTML for this page is instructive. You can immediately see that there's a lot of duplication, and PHP is good at reducing duplication:

```html
<html>
 <head>
  <link href="../css/phpMM.css" rel="stylesheet" type="text/css" />
 </head>

 <body>
  <div id="header"><h1>PHP & MySQL: The Missing Manual</h1></div>
  <div id="example">Current Users</div>

  <div id="content">
   <ul>
    <li>
     <a href="show_user.php?user_id=1">Yu Darvish</a>
     (<a href="mailto:yu@texasrangers.com">yu@texasrangers.com</a>)
     <a href="delete_user.php?user_id=1">
       <img class="delete_user" src="../images/delete.png" width="15" />
     </a>
```

```
   </li>
   <li>
    <a href="show_user.php?user_id=10">David Ramirez</a>
    (<a href="mailto:shane@77mgmt.com">shane@77mgmt.com</a>)
    <a href="delete_user.php?user_id=10">
      <img class="delete_user" src="../images/delete.png" width="15" />
    </a>
   </li>
   <li>
    <a href="show_user.php?user_id=19">Ryan Geyer</a>
    (<a href="ryan.geyer@facebook.com">ryan.geyer@facebook.com</a>)
    <a href="delete_user.php?user_id=19">
      <img class="delete_user" src="../images/delete.png" width="15" />
    </a>
   </li>
   <li>
    <a href="show_user.php?user_id=21">Jason Wadley</a>
    (<a href="jason.wadley@facebook.com">jason.wadley@facebook.com</a>)
    <a href="delete_user.php?user_id=21">
      <img class="delete_user" src="../images/delete.png" width="15" />
    </a>
   </li>
   <li>
    <a href="show_user.php?user_id=24">Robert Powell</a>
    (<a href="info@rockwallbba.com">info@rockwallbba.com</a>)
    <a href="delete_user.php?user_id=24">
      <img class="delete_user" src="../images/delete.png" width="15" />
    </a>
   </li>
  </ul>
 </div>
 <div id="footer"></div>
</body>
</html>
```

Wish Lists Are Good, Too

So far, you've gone directly from a mock-up to code. That's not altogether bad, but it does mean that when you bring that mock-up to life in code, anything you want to add is a bit of a mystery. Will it work well with the way you've built your pages and scripts? Or, will you have to do some redesign to get your new ideas into your existing framework?

Obviously, you could spend some serious time with your mock-ups. You could get those little red Xs just right, and you could nail down spacing; you could basically spend significant time in Photoshop. Of course, nothing in HTML and CSS ever looks just like a Photoshop mock-up, but you could get things close. However, you don't want to spend a *lot* of time on the front end before you've done any code. Decisions you make as you work on your code might affect future decisions and functionality.

The answer? Create a short list of features you hope to implement in the future. This doesn't need to be anything fancy; a text document or even something on your iPad or iPhone sitting next to your workstation are all fine. Then, add to or update that list as you go and as features and functionality change. Hopefully, just having these "next version" features handy will help you think clearly about how decisions you make today might help you—or hurt you—when you get around to writing more code tomorrow, next week, or next month.

For now, here are just a few things that might be nice to add once the basic functionality is in place:

- Improve the user interface, setting up the different "columns" of data in a more intuitive fashion and getting those delete "X" buttons to align.

- Add user profile pictures so that you can get a little better graphical view of each user in the admin interface.

- Allow for multiple user selection and deletion on one screen.

- Add a confirmation dialog box or pop-up message when a user is selected for deletion to avoid accidental deletions.

You can add your own ideas to this list, but this is certainly a good starting point. Maybe you'll code these up, and maybe you won't, but now at least you can make decisions that will help allow for these features, rather than get in the way of them.

> **NOTE** Sometimes, no matter how well you plan ahead, current features require you to make decisions that are going to make wish list features harder down the road. That's okay. It's much more important you get the things you need to get done *now* completed on time.

■ Listing All Your Users

First things first: before you can add delete buttons and profile pictures and worry about alignment, you need a list of all your users. This isn't too hard; all you need is a simple SQL query. You could do something like this:

```
SELECT *
  FROM users;
```

Of course, that's a bit of a brute force approach. There's some refinement you can make to improve performance, make your code clearer, and generally be a good PHP and MySQL citizen. Again, first things first: you should get that query into shape.

> **NOTE** You can find the finished example code for this section on this book's Missing CD page at *www.missingmanuals.com/cds/phpmysqlmm2e.*

SELECTing What You Need (Now)

The thing about SELECT * is that it retrieves everything in a table. Even worse, if you're joining tables, it retrieves everything in *all* the tables that are joined. In the case of the *users* table, that's not a particular problem, because there's not much to it. Here are all the columns you're going to grab with a SELECT *.

```
mysql> describe users;
+----------------+----------------+------+-----+---------+----------------+
| Field          | Type           | Null | Key | Default | Extra          |
+----------------+----------------+------+-----+---------+----------------+
| user_id        | int(11)        | NO   | PRI | NULL    | auto_increment |
| first_name     | varchar(20)    | NO   |     | NULL    |                |
| last_name      | varchar(30)    | NO   |     | NULL    |                |
| email          | varchar(50)    | NO   |     | NULL    |                |
| facebook_url   | varchar(100)   | YES  |     | NULL    |                |
| twitter_handle | varchar(20)    | YES  |     | NULL    |                |
| bio            | varchar(1000)  | YES  |     | NULL    |                |
| user_pic_path  | varchar(200)   | YES  |     | NULL    |                |
| profile_pic_id | int(11)        | YES  |     | NULL    |                |
+----------------+----------------+------+-----+---------+----------------+
9 rows in set (0.10 sec)
```

NOTE Depending on how closely you've been following along, you might have the `user_pic_path` column, but not the `profile_pic_id`. In fact, that's probably where you want your database to be, so you don't have to worry about a foreign key with an *images* table that you're no longer using.

You can get rid of that column with this:

```
ALTER TABLE users
    DROP COLUMN profile_pic_id;
```

Before moving on, take a look back again at Figure 11-1. You don't need all this information. Realistically, you need `first_name`, `last_name`, the `user_id` for a hyperlink to *show_user.php*, and the user's email. That SELECT * is grabbing several unnecessary columns: `facebook_url`, `twitter_handle`, `bio`, and `user_pic_path`.

Why is this a big deal? Every time you select all the entries from the *users* table, you're getting one more row. And every column in that row is space, bandwidth on your network, and resources. Suppose that you have 100 users, or 1,000 users, or 10,000 users, each with 20-paragraph bios. Just by *not* selecting * (and thereby *not* selecting bio) from *users*, you're saving a lot of traffic and resource consumption. Getting only the information you need saves time and resources, especially over the life of your application. (For more detail on deciding what to select, see the box on page 339.)

All you need is a few of the columns from *users*:

```
SELECT user_id, first_name, last_name, email
  FROM users;
```

Look Ahead (But Not Too Far)

What if I know I eventually want to use more columns from my table, just not in the current incarnation of my admin page. Should I SELECT what I'll need later, too?

Here's one of those situations for which looking ahead creates a dilemma. It would be nice to add profile pictures of users to the admin page, and you already know there's a column with the path to those pictures in *users*: user_pic_path. Because you're going to want that down the line, you might be tempted to SELECT that column now.

On the one hand, it would be nice to have a SELECT that's already set up for a future feature that you know you'll want. On the other hand, you're not implementing that feature yet; it's just that you'd have the data available when you *do* write that code.

In general, you should think about the implications of what you're doing on future features, but focus on *writing* code that solves current problems, not future ones. Think about how slippery a slope this can become. You might start selecting the bio because one day you want to excerpt that on the admin page; you might go ahead and select social information to build more links to contact the user. Before you know it, you're back to a SELECT * and grabbing far more information than you're actually using.

The good news is that you know it will be easy to add functionality (such as grabbing a user's picture) when the time comes. It's a simple change to your SELECT. So, stop there, and focus on writing code for existing work. Leave future work for the future.

If at some point in your programming career you want to start charging for your work, you'll have to start quoting estimates. You'll have to consider how long (in hours or days) will it take you to implement each feature that your customer wants. You typically bill at least partly based on these estimates, so this is important stuff. If you start calculating based on current and future functionality, those estimates stop making much sense. You end up overcharging, or worse, undercharging because you're not doing one thing at a time.

Building a Simple Admin Page

Now that you've configured a good SELECT statement, it's time to create another script. Before you do that, though, there's another important decision to make: what to call this script. The name *admin.php* might seem like a good idea because it's for your admin page, but take a moment to think through the implications of that choice.

Look back at the other script names you've used:

- *create_user.php* creates a new user
- *show_user.php* shows a user for a given user ID
- *app_config.php* configures your application
- *database_connection.php* connects to your database

Each of these names describes what the script does. That's very helpful because it's immediately clear how to use these scripts and even how they might interact. For example, if you were looking at these scripts for the first time, you would probably conclude that *create_user.php* creates a user and then likely hands over control to *show_user.php*.

What does this script *do*? Well, it lists all the users. Using the same naming logic as other scripts, *show_users.php* (note the plural "users" here) is a better, more descriptive name. Remember, listing and deleting users isn't the only administrative function you're going to have. What if you eventually need to add a form and script so that an admin can change a user's password? You'll need to come up with a name for that script, and *admin.php* still won't be specific enough.

Start a new file, call it *show_users.php*, and begin by selecting all the users, with just the information you need:

```php
<?php

require_once '../scripts/app_config.php';
require_once '../scripts/database_connection.php';

// Build the SELECT statement
$select_users =
  "SELECT user_id, first_name, last_name, email " .
  "  FROM users";

// Run the query
$result = mysql_query($select_users);
?>
```

NOTE   Because you're not inserting anything into the SELECT query, there's no reason to use `sprintf`. You can just create the query directly with a string.

You should also go ahead and set up the shell of the HTML page (the parts that you know won't be generated by your script):

```php
<?php
// Get all the users
?>

<html>
 <head>
  <link href="../css/phpMM.css" rel="stylesheet" type="text/css" />
 </head>

 <body>
  <div id="header"><h1>PHP & MySQL: The Missing Manual</h1></div>
  <div id="example">Current Users</div>

  <div id="content">
   <ul>
     <!-- All the users will go here, in <li> tags. -->
   </ul>
```

```
    </div>
    <div id="footer"></div>
  </body>
</html>
```

There's not much to see yet, but you can still test to verify that you don't have any errors in your PHP or HTML. Figure 11-2 shows the empty—but errorless—*show_users.php* in action.

FIGURE 11-2

Even when there's nothing to see on a page, there might be things you don't want to see. Here, you can ensure that no errors occurred while connecting to your database or executing your SELECT statement. It's worth a few minutes to test at every stage of development. When you're creating a new script, test even more.

Iterating Over Your Array

Now, you need to fill in a list item (`<li>`) for every user. You can build up the entire HTML string by using `sprintf` again:

```
$user_row = sprintf(
  "<li><a href='show_user.php?user_id=%d'>%s %s</a> " .
  "(<a href='mailto:%s'>%s</a>) " .
  "<a href='delete_user.php?user_id=%d'><img " .
    "class='delete_user' src='../images/delete.png' " .
    "width='15' /></a></li>",
  // information to fill in the values);
```

> **NOTE** There's not a significant advantage here to using `sprintf` over a string via quotation marks and curly braces with variables within those braces. Still, once you start using `sprintf`, you'll often find you use it almost everywhere you need to insert variables within strings. It becomes a default tool, and it's quite a handy tool at that.

That's a big string, but ultimately, it should result in something like this:

```
<li><a href="show_user.php?user_id=21">Jason Wadley</a>
  (<a href="jason.wadley@facebook.com">jason.wadley@facebook.com</a>)
```

```
<a href="delete_user.php?user_id=21">
  <img class="delete_user" src="../images/delete.png" width="15" />
</a></li>
```

All you need to do now is to loop over each result from your query. But that's easy; you've done that before with code like this:

```
while ($row = mysql_fetch_row($result)) {
  echo "<li>{$row[0]}</li>";
}
```

Then, of course, you can get each piece of data in the returned query with this:

```
while ($row = mysql_fetch_row($result)) {
  echo "<li>{$row['col_name']}</li>";
}
```

This statement gets a specific value—whatever is associated with col_name—from $row.

If you make that specific to your *users* table and the columns that you know are being returned and then insert *that* into your HTML, you end up with this:

> **NOTE** The following HTML refers to a script that's not yet been written: *delete_user.php*, which is coming up soon. You're working in anticipation of what other work you know you have to complete.

```
<?php
  // Get all the users
?>
<html>
 <head>
  <link href="../css/phpMM.css" rel="stylesheet" type="text/css" />
 </head>

 <body>
 <div id="header"><h1>PHP & MySQL: The Missing Manual</h1></div>
 <div id="example">Current Users</div>

 <div id="content">
  <ul>
    <?php
      while ($user = mysql_fetch_array($result)) {
        $user_row = sprintf(
          "<li><a href='show_user.php?user_id=%d'>%s %s</a> " .
          "(<a href='mailto:%s'>%s</a>) " .
          "<a href='delete_user.php?user_id=%d'><img " .
            "class='delete_user' src='../images/delete.png' " .
            "width='15' /></a></li>",
```

```
            $user['user_id'], $user['first_name'], $user['last_name'],
            $user['email'], $user['email'], $user['user_id']);
        echo $user_row;
      }
    ?>
    </ul>
  </div>
  <div id="footer"></div>
  </body>
  </html>
```

That's a long `sprintf`, but take a second look. You're simply putting a lot of things together; there's nothing here particularly tricky or difficult.

POWER USERS' CLINIC

Your HTML Is Getting Dangerously Cluttered

Something is subtly happening as you write more and more complex PHP. Early on, you had scripts that were all PHP and perhaps used echo to throw out a few lines of text. Then, you started writing scripts that had a block of PHP at the beginning and a bunch of PHP at the end. Then, there were scripts that inserted a little PHP here and there into the HTML at the end of the script.

Now, you have *show_users.php*. There's a block of PHP, some HTML, and then it gets messy. You have PHP that does a good bit of HTML printing. Now, you could probably write that same bit of output that churns out HTML and then has lots of tiny PHP bits inserted here and there, but it's basically the same

issue. No matter how you cut it, you're going to end up with a real mixture of HTML and PHP.

You've just found one of the real dangers of PHP: you're going to end up mixing your code and your markup frequently. As you start this sort of mixing, the separation between your code and your *view*—the markup that displays something to your user—becomes thin, if not non-existent. It's easy to just drop a big block of PHP in the middle of some HTML, but in this case, easy isn't good. As much as you can, keep the bulk of your PHP at the beginning of your script, and then just insert data as you need it.

You're ready to see how things look. Pull up *show_users.php* and verify that everything is where it belongs. Figure 11-3 shows you what you're going for. Granted, your page is still not a work of art, but it's a significant step forward. Click any of the users, and ensure that you're taken to the correct *show_user.php* for that user, as shown in Figure 11-4.

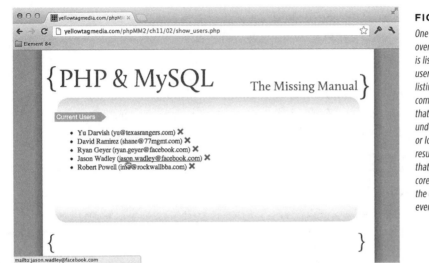

FIGURE 11-3

One of the things you'll do over and over in PHP apps is list things. Whether it's users, groups, or products, listing is just one of those common tasks. This means that you really need to understand how to iterate, or loop, over a list of results from SQL. Master that, and you've got the core to about a third of all the common things you'll ever do in PHP web apps.

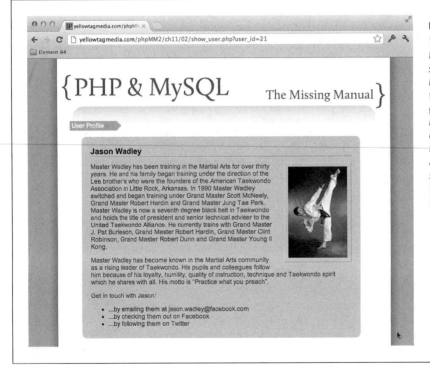

FIGURE 11-4

You're probably still getting used to scripts calling scripts, which in turn build links to other scripts. Take your time because you're going to be doing this a lot in your PHP programming career. Believe it or not, there are large-scale PHP apps that don't use any straight HTML files at all. WordPress, for example, is 100 percent PHP.

Deleting a User

In programming, a new problem often presents new challenges; new techniques that must be grasped; new language features that must be absorbed. Those are fun times, but they can also be frustrating. Your pace slows to a crawl, and it's often at least a few hours—and sometimes a few days—before it seems like you make real progress. Then, there are times that your accumulated pile of tricks, knowledge, and experience stand higher than the new task, which is where you are now. This is one of those easy tasks: deleting a user.

NOTE   You can find the finished example code for this section on this book's Missing CD page at *www*
.missingmanuals.com/cds/phpmysqlmm2e.

Surveying the Individual Components

You already know the query for deleting a user from the *users* table:

```
DELETE FROM users;
```

Add to this a WHERE clause to target a particular user:

```
DELETE FROM users
        WHERE user_id = [some_user_id];
```

Nothing new here. But, how do you get that user_id? Well, you can get it from whatever script calls your script. And you already have that in place in *show_users.php*:

```
<?php
  while ($user = mysql_fetch_array($result)) {
    $user_row = sprintf(
      "<li><a href='show_user.php?user_id=%d'>%s %s</a> " .
      "(<a href='mailto:%s'>%s</a>) " .
      "<a href='delete_user.php?user_id=%d'><img " .
        "class='delete_user' src='../images/delete.png' " .
        "width='15' /></a></li>",
      $user['user_id'], $user['first_name'], $user['last_name'],
      $user['email'], $user['email'], $user['user_id']);
    echo $user_row;
  }
?>
```

Once this code is converted to HTML, you'll get this:

```
<a href='delete_user.php?user_id=22'>...</a>
```

This should look similar to something you've done before, when you sent a user_id to the *show_user.php* script:

```
// Redirect the user to the page that displays user information
header("Location: show_user.php?user_id=" . mysql_insert_id());
```

NOTE   This code was in *create_user.php* (page 214). The user was redirected after her information was stored in the database.

Once you've grabbed a user_id and deleted the user, you can just redirect back to your *show_users.php* script, which will re-SELECT from *users*, but this time, the deleted user will simply be gone. Perfect!

Putting It All Together

At this point, it's just a matter of retyping various bits from your other scripts and changing a few things here and there. The result? *delete_user.php*, shown here:

```php
<?php

require_once '../scripts/app_config.php';
require_once '../scripts/database_connection.php';

// Get the user ID of the user to delete
$user_id = $_REQUEST['user_id'];

// Build the DELETE statement
$delete_query = sprintf("DELETE FROM users WHERE user_id = %d",
                            $user_id);

// Delete the user from the database
mysql_query($delete_query);

// Redirect to show_users to re-show users (without this deleted one)
header("Location: show_users.php");
exit();
?>
```

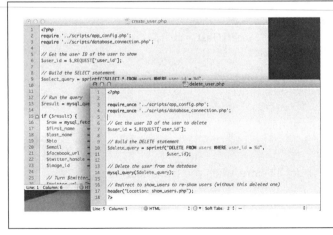

FIGURE 11-5

If you have the screen real estate, there's nothing better than being able to see two pieces of code side by side when you're cutting, copying, and pasting. You don't have to remember anything; it's all right there in front of you. And an editor like TextMate even gives you some nice visual clues like syntax highlighting. Your chances of making a mistake in this setup go way, way down.

Real Programmers Cut and Paste All the Time

In *delete_user.php*, you've written your first script that involves almost a complete reuse of code that you've already written. But this code doesn't really belong in *app_config.php*, so it's not a case where you need to abstract out bits of code here and there and put them into utility functions, as was the case with handling errors or setting up database connections.

At this point, if you've read many programming books, you're ready for a tongue-lashing, or at least some mild finger-wagging: don't cut and paste! Cutting and pasting code is evil; cutting and pasting code will lead to annoying, difficult-to-find mistakes; cutting and pasting will cause you to gain 10 pounds and hamper your sex life. (Well, maybe not that last one.)

Despite all the warnings, every programmer who spends more than a few hours a day writing code knows the shortcut keys to copy, cut, and paste and uses them liberally. If they're making their living coding, they probably know the shortcuts not just on a Mac or in Windows, but in emacs and vi and any other editor they might use.

So, why all the dire warnings? It's true, some of the hardest bugs to track down are the ones caused by cutting, copying, and pasting code and the little inconsistencies introduced as a result. For example, in one bit of copied code a variable might be called $insert_sql and in another it's called $insert_query.

Things go haywire, PHP doesn't always do a great job reporting what the problem is, and you're left to sort out the mess. Realistically, though, that's not a copying and pasting problem; that's an inconsistency-in-naming-variables problem.

So, here come the common-sense warnings:

- Know that you're adding risk when you copy, cut, or paste. Be careful and take your time.

- When possible, cut and copy from as few sources as possible. You're less likely to end up with mismatches between variable names and the like.

- Consider having two windows open (see Figure 11-5 on preceding page) or two tabs open (Figure 11-6) and moving between them, rather than copying, closing a file, opening the new file, and pasting. This arrangement makes it easier to compare code; you can simply move back and forth between open windows.

- *Immediately* test your code after you've pasted something. That way, you catch potential errors quickly and can track them down while you still remember which code you just dropped in.

That's it! Keep those things in mind, and don't be afraid to cut and paste. They're important tools in your arsenal.

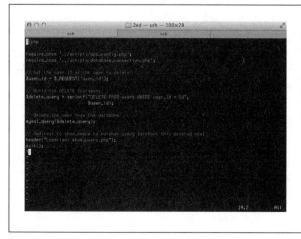

FIGURE 11-6

If you're pressed for screen space or just like things a little more compact, using tabs in your editor (Terminal on the Mac is shown here) is a poor man's version of keeping two windows open. You still have to keep a bit more context in your head, but it's far better than closing one file, opening another, and so on. You can copy in one window, tab to the second window, and then paste.

So try it out. You already have *show_users.php* with the correct links; open it, and pick an unlucky user to delete. Click the "X" icon, and you should get back something like Figure 11-7—which looks just like Figure 11-3, minus poor David Ramirez. (Don't worry, he'll write another heart-breaking sad song about his deletion if he finds out.)

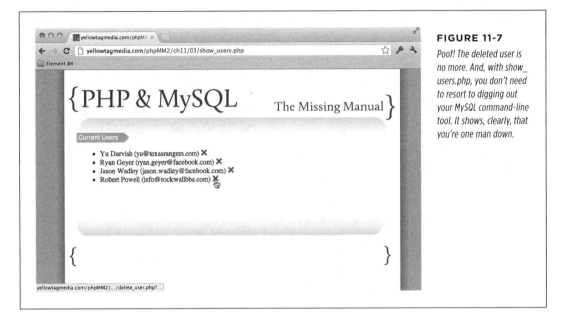

FIGURE 11-7

Poof! The deleted user is no more. And, with show_users.php, you don't need to resort to digging out your MySQL command-line tool. It shows, clearly, that you're one man down.

Deleting Users Shouldn't Be Magical

The functionality that you have in place for deleting users is perfect. There are no hitches, no pauses, nothing but a quick request to *delete_user.php*, a deletion in your database, and a return to *show_users.php*. And that perfection—that minimal pause and nothing else—is exactly why you're not at all done with deleting users.

Deletion is a big deal. You're trashing information, never to be heard from again. What's really concerning is that you're doing it based on one mouse click, with no further warning or second thought. That's a problem.

In fact, think about your own web usage. Have you ever managed to delete anything with one click? Most of the time, you're inundated by pop-up windows asking, "Are you sure?" and "You'll never get to use this file again" and even "Be careful! Your information will be gone forever!" All these warnings are a nuisance, but they're there to prevent you from accidentally deleting something that you can never get back.

With that in mind, you need to add a little more to the deletion process. You must give the user a chance to rethink her decision before you pass things on to *delete_user. php*. So, it's back to *show_users.php*.

■ START WITH A LITTLE JAVASCRIPT

When it comes to things like confirmation boxes, you're firmly in the world of browsers and clients. Although you could build some sort of confirmation in PHP, it wouldn't be pretty. You'd essentially need to send a request to the server for deletion; the server would run a PHP script that creates a new HTML form and asks for confirmation; the browser would return that to the user, and the user would click "OK." Then, another request would go to the browser, at which point you'd finally get to perform deletion.

Even if you used Ajax to avoid lots of page refreshing, this is way too much server interaction for a simple confirmation. That's especially true because JavaScript offers you a built-in, all-client means of doing this by using `confirm`.

Open *show_users.php* and add some JavaScript:

```php
<?php

// SELECT all users
?>


<html>
 <head>
  <link href="../css/phpMM.css" rel="stylesheet" type="text/css" />
  <script type="text/javascript">
    function delete_user(user_id) {
      if (confirm("Are you sure you want to delete this user?" +
                  "\nThere's really no going back!")) {
        window.location = "delete_user.php?user_id=" + user_id;
      }
    }
  </script>
 </head>
 <body>
   <!-- HTML body -->
 </body>
</html>
```

In a nutshell, you're simply creating a function that asks for user confirmation before passing control over to *delete_user.php*. There's a little extra work involved here because the user_id has to be passed to this function, which then shuffles it along to *delete_user.php* by using the JavaScript version of a redirect: `window.location`.

> **NOTE**   If this code freaks you out a bit, or if you're rusty on your JavaScript, check out *JavaScript: The Missing Manual* by David Sawyer McFarland (O'Reilly Media). It's a really solid JavaScript book that will break this and a lot more JavaScript down. In fact, it might be the perfect complement to a PHP book: it covers what you need on the client side to let your server-side scripts run smoothly and without error.

For now, if you feel unsettled by the use of JavaScript in this page—rather than it being referenced through an external JavaScript file—read the box on page 350.

In or Out JavaScript

Isn't it evil not to use an external file for JavaScript functions ?

Almost as common as the scolding you'll get for copying and pasting is the admonition to never, ever use JavaScript in the head of your page such as this code from page 349:

```
<head>
  <link href="../css/phpMM.css"
        rel="stylesheet" type="text/css"
/>
  <script type="text/javascript">
    function delete_user(user_id) {
// code for confirmation
//   and redirection
    }
  </script>
</head>
```

In fact, most books deal with the problem a bit like this:

1. Learn how to write a little JavaScript.
2. Learn how to write some cool JavaScript.
3. Now that you're "advanced," set up that JavaScript as external files.
4. Teach all your beginner JavaScript friends to do the same.

Sounds reasonable, but take a look at the source for pages like Amazon.com, Google, or Apple. Every one of these Web giants

has `<script>` tags that have code in the head of the page! Surely, the high-paid folks at powerhouses such as these know what they're doing. The truth is that there are plenty of times when you want some well-placed JavaScript in the head of your page. Most notably, this is true for JavaScript that is specific *to that page on which you're working.*

If you have utility functions, such as creating generic dialogs in jQuery (stay tuned for more on that) or handling validation for certain data types, put those things in a script file and reference it in all your pages. That's the same sort of thing that you've done with a site-wide CSS file as well as on the server, with *app_config.php* and *database_connection.php.*

But, `delete_user`, the JavaScript function you just wrote, is only useful for this one page. It doesn't belong in a site-wide utility script, and only adds to the clutter if that's where you put it. You could create external scripts for every page on your site, but that would be way too much of a mess.

That's not to say you should have lots of JavaScript littering your page, stuck between `<p>` elements and in the crevices between adjacent `<td>` tags. Just don't be scared to write some JavaScript in your page. Just like copy-and-paste, it's a tool for you to use wisely and judiciously.

■ FINISH WITH A CHANGE IN LINKING

You have your JavaScript in place, and now it's time for the big finish: just change the link that previously went directly to *delete_user.php* in your page to call your new JavaScript function:

```php
<?php
  while ($user = mysql_fetch_array($result)) {
    $user_row = sprintf(
      "<li><a href='show_user.php?user_id=%d'>%s %s</a> " .
      "(<a href='mailto:%s'>%s</a>) " .
```

```
        "<a href='javascript:delete_user(%d);'><img " .
          "class='delete_user' src='../images/delete.png' " .
          "width='15' /></a></li>",
       $user['user_id'], $user['first_name'], $user['last_name'],
       $user['email'], $user['email'], $user['user_id']);
     echo $user_row;
   }
 ?>
```

Try it out, and you'll finally get a handy warning before you push Master Jason Wadley down the deletion black hole, as shown in Figure 11-8.

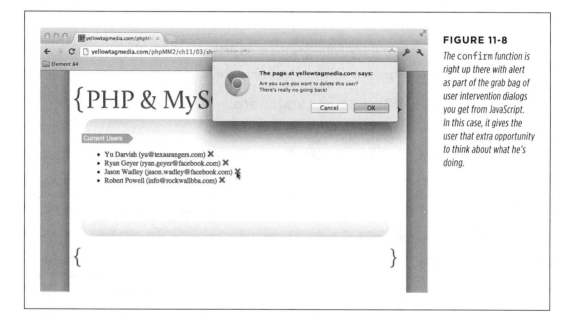

FIGURE 11-8

The confirm *function is right up there with* alert *as part of the grab bag of user intervention dialogs you get from JavaScript. In this case, it gives the user that extra opportunity to think about what he's doing.*

▓ Talking Back to Your Users

The addition of an alert confirmation box goes a long way on the front end of deletion. It lets a user think twice about removing data and provides a mechanism to cancel the operation if she's dissatisfied or concerned. Yet, that's only half of the equation; not only do you need to confirm that deletion is indeed the intent, but then you need to verify that deletion was in fact accomplished.

Obviously, for you, the programmer, you've written code, you've run the code, and you might have even gone back to the database and done your own manual SELECT to ensure that results were deleted in *delete_user.php*. And, as expected, the user is gone from *show_users.php*.

For a user, that's not enough. Just as she will often want to confirm a deletion *before* the deletion goes through, she usually wants to know—beyond any shadow of doubt—that the deletion *has* gone through. This means that at the end of the process, she gets some sort of message that confirms what just transpired. Your flow should look something like this:

1. **A user selects another user to delete by clicking the red "X" in *show_users* .php next to that user.**

2. **The user confirms that the deletion is intended.**

3. ***delete_user.php* handles the deletion of the selected user.**

4. **A message something like, "Yup, they're gone, gone, gone." is supplied to the user.**

5. ***show_users.php* displays the users list again, minus the deletion.**

It's step 4 here that's new and requires a little thought.

redirect **Has Some Limitations**

Just looking at this flow, it seems like the natural place to handle confirmation—and display a post-deletion confirmation pop-up window—is within *delete_user.php*. That's the script that handles deletion, and it also comes before *show_users.php* lists all the users again.

For example, you might present a status message or display an alert pop-up window once deletion is complete. But, take a look at the last line from *delete_user.php*:

```
header("Location: show_users.php");
```

Redirection in PHP is done by using HTTP headers, which means that this line sends the browser a raw Location header. The browser gets the Location header and moves the HTTP response to the URL specified. No big deal, and it works great.

But (and this is a big but), header can only be called before PHP sends any output. You can't use echo or HTML, blank lines, or anything else in a file. The browser can only get the headers, and then it shifts the request. So in reality, you can't send anything before calling header, and once you've called header, you're not supposed to send anything after that. Of course, bugs are made when things that *shouldn't* happen *do* happen, and that's why every call to a Location header is followed by that little exit() statement to ensure that nothing else tries to execute.

In other words, a script like *delete_user.php* can do work on the database and other PHP objects, but it can't do any output. It just deletes a user and then redirects output to a view script, like *show_users.php*. Therefore, you have to figure out a way to interact with *show_users.php* and let that script handle letting the user know that a deletion's gone down.

Model-View-Controller (Well, Sort Of...)

You're starting to see an important web application pattern. This pattern is called the MVC pattern, which stands for "model-view-controller." In this pattern, you have three categories of operation: models, views, and controllers. In a strict MVC pattern, these three categories never overlap.

First, there's the *model*, which interacts with the database. The model represents—or *models*—your app's information. In your application, a script like *delete_user.php* uses MySQL directly. In a more formal MVC approach, you'd have PHP objects like *User.php* with methods such as delete() or remove(). So you might write code like this:

```
User user_to_delete = User.find_by_
id($user_id);

user_to_delete.delete();
```

This example is a little beyond what you're doing. Still, you can see that the model part of MVC is what interacts with the database. For your code, you don't have a clear model, but you're doing plenty of database interaction.

Second, there's the *view*; this is what displays the information to the user. In your app, scripts like *show_user.php* and *show_users.php* are, to some degree, views. They're full of HTML and information. The reason they're only views "to some degree" is that they also share some controller behavior.

Controllers are the third category in an MVC architecture. A controller directs traffic. It uses the model to get information from the database or data store, and it passes that information along to view classes or scripts that display that information. Your *delete_user.php* script is a lot like a controller. Even though it directly accesses the database rather than using a model, it does something and then hands off control to a view, *show_users.php*.

In most PHP web applications, you won't have a strict MVC setup. In fact, it's quite a lot of work to go full-on MVC with PHP. You usually have a more hybrid approach, where controller-oriented scripts like *delete_user.php* hand off information to view-oriented scripts like *show_users.php*. But *delete_user.php* also has aspects of a model, in that it talks directly to the database. Additionally, *show_users.php* has aspects of a controller and a model, because it figures out what to show, and it grabs information directly from the database.

So, if you can't do pure MVC in PHP, why present this entire box about it? Two good reasons. First, you'll hear about MVC all the time, and you'll be a lot more popular at the geeky water cooler or your buddy's *Lord of the Rings* costume party if you can relate what you're doing on the Web to MVC and what your friends might be doing. And second (and possibly a bit more useful), if you can identify what your scripts do, you'll often be able to figure out more quickly how to do those things.

In the case of *delete_user.php*, you see that it's mostly a controller. Thus, makes perfect sense to hand some information to a script that's mostly a view, like *show_users.php*, and let that script handle display of that information to the user.

So, *delete_user.php* needs to provide a message (because it knows that deletion has occurred) but it must let something else handle the actual display. Therefore, you can add a message to your redirect. Go ahead and connect this new message to a new request parameter, success_message, at the end of *delete_user.php*:

```php
<?php

// require code
// Get the user ID of the user to delete
// Build the DELETE statement
// Delete the user from the database
```

```
// Redirect to show_users to re-show users (without this deleted one)
$msg = "The user you specified has been deleted.";
header("Location: show_users.php?success_message={$msg}");
exit();
?>
```

> **NOTE** If you're already thinking that it might be nice to have an `error_message` parameter, too, you're on the right track.

Even before you go back to working on your view code in *show_users.php*, you can test this out. Visit *show_users.php*, delete a user, and then look closely at the browser bar when you're taken back to *show_users.php*. You should see the `success_message` request parameter with the value set to your message, as shown in Figure 11-9.

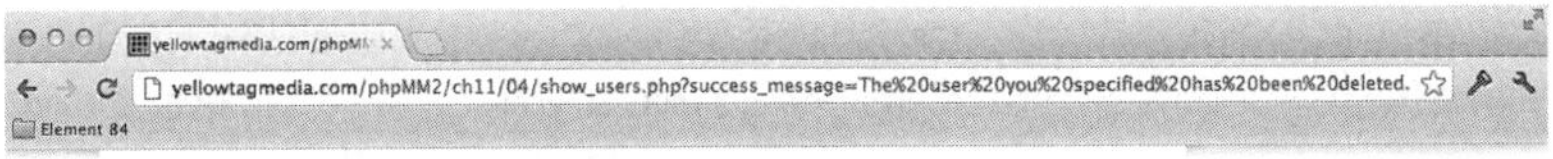

FIGURE 11-9

The message that delete_user.php appended to the URL sent to the browser contains a handy value: the exact text you'd want to see in a nice alert or status message. That's perfect; now you can have your view code handle displaying that message to your user, and you're in great shape.

JavaScript alert Redux

Here you are, back to *show_users.php*, and you have an incoming message.

> **NOTE** Actually, you *potentially* have an incoming message. When *show_users.php* is called normally, it does *not* have a message. It's only when it's the target of a redirect after deletion (or some similar operation) that it has information coming via request parameters.

What needs to happen when that message is received? Probably the easiest option is to go back to JavaScript and use an alert dialog box. This is the equivalent of the confirmation dialog box you used before deletion (page 349), so it's a nice symmetry.

■ AN ALL-JAVASCRIPT APPROACH

One approach would be to write a JavaScript function that you can add to *show_
users.php*. JavaScript doesn't directly support reading request parameters, so you'd
have to do a little parsing to get at them. You'd need something that uses regular
expressions to pick apart the `window.location.href` property, which is the URL
the browser has:

```
function get_request_param_value(param_name) {
  param_name = param_name.replace(/[\[]/,"\\\[").replace(/[\]]/,"\\\]");
  var regexS = "[\\?&]" + param_name + "=([^&#]*)";
  var regex = new RegExp(regexS);
  var results = regex.exec(unescape(window.location.href));
  if (results == null)
    return "";
  else
    return results[1];
}
```

NOTE   This code might not make much sense to you right now, and that's OK. But if you take a few minutes
to work through it line by line, you'll step up your JavaScript game significantly. It also demonstrates once again
that although regular expressions can look weird at first, they're an essential part of your programming toolkit. And
just think, every bit of what you learned about regular expressions in this PHP book translates over to JavaScript.

You could then call this function in the following way to get at the `success_message`
parameter (probably in another JavaScript function):

```
msg = get_request_param_value("success_message");
if (msg.length > 0) {
  // let the user know
}
```

Then (after uncrossing your eyes from all the forward and backslashes in get_
request_param_value), you could issue an alert:

```
msg = get_request_param_value("success_message")
if (msg.length > 0) {
  alert(msg);
}
```

There's certainly nothing wrong with that approach. It works fine, and you'll see
something similar to the message shown in Figure 11-10 if you add this code in to
the head section between script tags in *show_users.php*.

FIGURE 11-10

The gray background you see here is an artifact of where alert *is called. You'd probably want to improve the user experience further by not running the* alert *until the document loads. You can use the* window .onload *property, the* onload *event on body, or jQuery's various ways to run code on document load and achieve a much better user experience.*

Before you start wondering how to piece all this together, though, there might just be a better way.

YOUR PHP CONTROLS YOUR OUTPUT

The all-JavaScript approach discussed in the previous section makes a subtle but important assumption: the page—the HTML, CSS, and JavaScript delivered to the user via his browser—has to make all the decisions about what to do, what to show, and how to act. This means that there's JavaScript that must figure out whether the success_message parameter was passed along, JavaScript to parse the request URL and find the value of that parameter, and JavaScript that conditionally displays an alert.

Here's the thing: *show_users.php* isn't limited in the same way that the page it outputs is. Just because the HTML and JavaScript that's ultimately output is unaware of whether there's a request parameter doesn't mean that your script that *generates* that output is unaware. In fact, it's simple to get a request parameter in *show_users .php*; you've done it tons of times:

```
$msg = $_REQUEST['success_message'];
```

In that one line, you've eliminated all of this JavaScript:

```
function get_request_param_value(param_name) {
  param_name = param_name.replace(/[\[]/,"\\\[").replace(/[\]]/,"\\\]");
  var regexS = "[\\?&]" + param_name + "=([^&#]*)";
```

```
  var regex = new RegExp(regexS);
  var results = regex.exec(unescape(window.location.href));
  if (results == null)
    return "";
  else
    return results[1];
}
```

That's a win by any measure of accounting.

Here's something big to sink your teeth into: you're in control of what goes to the client. Your script can make decisions about what to output. As a result, in your PHP, you can do something like this:

```php
// See if there's a message to display
if (isset($_REQUEST['success_message'])) {
  $msg = $_REQUEST['success_message'];
}
```

That's all taking place on the server, before you've done any output. Then, if you have a message to show—and only if you have a message to show—you can simply add a few lines of JavaScript into your HTML output:

```php
<script type="text/javascript">
  function delete_user(user_id) {
    if (confirm("Are you sure you want to delete this user?" +
                "\nThere's really no going back!")) {
      window.location = "delete_user.php?user_id=" + user_id;
    }
  }

<?php if (isset($msg)) { ?>
    window.onload = function() {
      alert("<?php echo $msg ?>");
    }
<?php } ?>
  </script>
```

Put all this together, and here's the new, improved *show_users.php*:

```php
<?php

require_once '../scripts/app_config.php';
require_once '../scripts/database_connection.php';
```

```php
// Build the SELECT statement
$select_users =
  "SELECT user_id, first_name, last_name, email " .
  "  FROM users";

// Run the query
$result = mysql_query($select_users);

// See if there's a message to display
if (isset($_REQUEST['success_message'])) {
  $msg = $_REQUEST['success_message'];
}
?>

<html>
 <head>
  <link href="../css/phpMM.css" rel="stylesheet" type="text/css" />
  <script type="text/javascript">
    function delete_user(user_id) {
      if (confirm("Are you sure you want to delete this user?" +
                 "\nThere's really no going back!")) {
        window.location = "delete_user.php?user_id=" + user_id;
      }
    }

<?php if (isset($msg)) { ?>
    window.onload = function() {
      alert("<?php echo $msg ?>");
    }
<?php } ?>
  </script>
 </head>

 <body>
  <div id="header"><h1>PHP & MySQL: The Missing Manual</h1></div>
  <div id="example">Current Users</div>

  <div id="content">
   <ul>
     <?php
       while ($user = mysql_fetch_array($result)) {
         $user_row = sprintf(
           "<li><a href='show_user.php?user_id=%d'>%s %s</a> " .
           "(<a href='mailto:%s'>%s</a>) " .
           "<a href='javascript:delete_user(%d);'><img " .
             "class='delete_user' src='../images/delete.png' " .
```

```
            "width='15' /></a></li>",
        $user['user_id'], $user['first_name'], $user['last_name'],
        $user['email'], $user['email'], $user['user_id']);
      echo $user_row;
    }
  ?>
  </ul>
  </div>
  <div id="footer"></div>
  </body>
</html>
```

NOTE   At this point, it might be getting hard to keep up with all the changes to *show_user.php* and *show_users.php* as well as *app_config.php*. If you find yourself getting some weird errors or unusual results, you might want to hop over to *www.missingmanuals.com/cds/phpmysqlmm2e* and download this chapter's examples. That will get you a clean, current set of files that are up to date, and you can focus on new changes, rather than old debugging.

What you've done here is a big accomplishment in PHP programming. Instead of relying on your output to make complicated decisions, you're making most of the decisions in your PHP and then tailoring your output as a result. Thus, one script—depending on the decisions it makes—might push out two, three, four, or even more variations of the same output.

First, then, take your script out for a test drive. If you still have a browser up with a URL like *yellowtagmedia.com/phpMM/ch11/show_users.php?success_message=The%20 user%20you%20specified%20has%20been%20deleted*, just reload that page to get the new changes to *show_users.php*. You should see a nice pop-up window with the message passed through the URL, as shown in Figure 11-11.

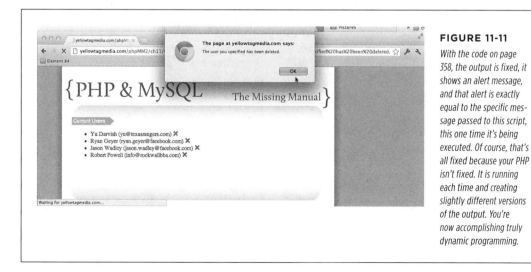

FIGURE 11-11

With the code on page 358, the output is fixed, it shows an alert message, and that alert is exactly equal to the specific message passed to this script, this one time it's being executed. Of course, that's all fixed because your PHP isn't fixed. It is running each time and creating slightly different versions of the output. You're now accomplishing truly dynamic programming.

Take a look at this page's source code to see what's so cool about it. Figure 11-12 shows that there's a hard-coded alert for the message passed along. Change the message in the request URL, and you'll see the HTML change to match.

FIGURE 11-12

You'd never know that this source is perfectly matched to this particular message. It simply looks like there's an alert that triggers every time you access show_users.php. However, that's not true; what is true is that every time you access show_users.php, you actually get a different variant of this basic HTML page.

Now, delete all of the request parameters from *show_users.php* in your URL bar and then go to the page again. The alert box should go away, and so should the JavaScript in the HTML page that *show_users.php* generates. Figure 11-13 shows the resulting source code: the `window.onload` function has vanished.

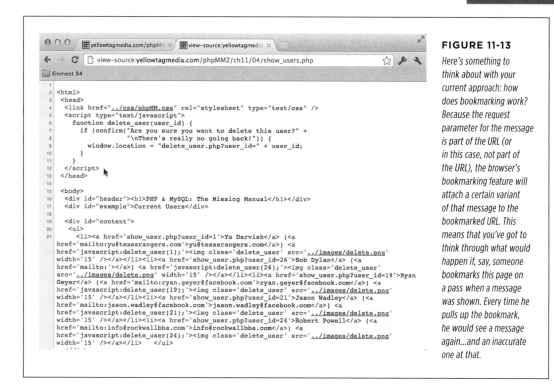

FIGURE 11-13

Here's something to think about with your current approach: how does bookmarking work? Because the request parameter for the message is part of the URL (or in this case, not part of the URL), the browser's bookmarking feature will attach a certain variant of that message to the bookmarked URL. This means that you've got to think through what would happen if, say, someone bookmarks this page on a pass when a message was shown. Every time he pulls up the bookmark, he would see a message again...and an inaccurate one at that.

alert Is Interruptive

You have a nice bookend of notifications now. A confirmation box requires a user's OK before deleting a user, and another alert informs her once that deletion's done. So, from a functional point of view, you're ready to move on.

This is one of those moments when you have to move a bit beyond web programming and start thinking about web design, or better, web *usability*. Usability is just a high-end way of saying, "What's the user experience like?"

> **NOTE** You'll also often hear terms like UX (for user experience) and UI (user interface) in this discussion. To some degree, the two terms aren't that different, although a UX designer might get ruffled if you confused her with a UI designer. Still, the basic goal is the same: create a natural, compelling online experience for a user. You're taking into account not just functionality, but aesthetics, accessibility, and overall feel of a website or web application.

With regard to deleting a user deleting a user, you're doing well. Although you might use something like jQuery to present a better looking dialog box, you're doing all the right things: interrupting the user to ensure that she truly wants to delete a user, and you're requiring a double-action (click once to select delete; and click once more to ensure that's the intention).

> **NOTE** If you'd like a prettier jQuery-style dialog and confirmation box, check out jQuery UI and its dialog boxes at *www.jqueryui.com/demos/dialog*. In particular, look at the option for a *Modal* confirmation window. It'll take you 10 minutes to download and install jQuery UI and another 5 to move from your `confirm` call to a call to the jQuery confirmation dialog. But those 15 minutes are worth it.

What about *after* deletion? Yes, you need to let the user know that the deletion has occurred. But, do you need to effectively shut them down until she clicks OK? Ideally, you'd let her know about deletion, but make it a little less interruptive.

And that's a general principle for web usability: if you're going to make your user take her hands off the keyboard and click a button, make sure it's worth her while. In this case, there's a risk you're being annoying. "Why do I have to click again? I just clicked twice to delete the user in the first place!"

◼ Standardizing on Messaging

There's another issue to consider: Is a success message the only type of message you might need to display? What if you have an error that doesn't rise to the level of requiring `handle_error`? What if you need a status message, perhaps something like "Please log in before attempting to delete a user."

> **NOTE** Logging in before deleting a user? Hmmm...that does sound like a good idea. You'll get to that in Chapter 13.

These are all similar cases: you want to present a message to the user, but you don't want to interrupt his flow. You want to add content to the page, but JavaScript's `alert` and `confirm` aren't the best choices.

Additionally, you'd ideally make this a generic functionality. You don't want every script to have to output 5 or 10 lines of code. It would be nice to have your output do something like this:

```
<body>
  <?php display_messages($_REQUEST); ?>

  <!-- All the rest of the HTML output you want -->
</body>
```

Then, this function would simply "take care of things," whatever that ends up being. For example, for a success message, you might get a banner message across the top of a page, as shown in Figure 11-14.

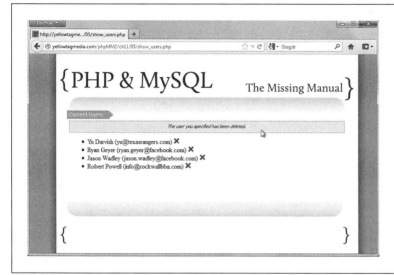

FIGURE 11-14

This page won't win any design awards, but that's what you have designers for. They take rough ideas from programmers and give them subtle style and grace. The advancement here is in how non-intrusive this message is. It communicates with the user without making him click or confirm anything.

The HTML for success messages is simple:

```
<div id="messages">
  <div class="success">
    <p>The user you specified has been deleted.</p>
  </div>
</div>
```

Errors could be shown in similar fashion, à la Figure 11-15.

FIGURE 11-15

Here's an error message that certainly doesn't cross the threshold of needing its own error page. It lets the user know something he'll probably need to correct. You could see a similar style error used for validation—although most good JavaScript validation frameworks will take care of that for you. Still, it's nice to know that you now have multiple ways to report errors, depending upon the severity of the individual error.

NOTE You might have noticed that these rough mock-ups are done with *create_user.html* and *show_users.php*. Those were simply the handiest pieces of HTML and PHP when it came to trying out a look for these messages. It's not relevant what page you use for testing these things out. Remember, the goal is to have every page automatically display, or not display, messages sent to it.

Here's the HTML for the error. It's identical to the success message with a different class on the inner <div>:

```
<div id="messages">
  <div class="error">
    <p>The name you entered is already registered.</p>
  </div>
</div>
```

Building a New Utility Function for Display

Once again, it's back to thinking generic. Rather than worrying about the specific success message passed into *show_users.php* by *delete_user.php*, what's the more general form of a success message?

It's something like this:

```
<div id="messages">
  <div class="success">
    <p>$msg</p>
  </div>
</div>
```

That's not real PHP, of course; you'd really want to do this:

```
<div id="messages">
  <div class="success">
    <p><?php echo $msg; ?></p>
  </div>
</div>
```

That's easy! You just need a new function that takes in the message:

```
function display_success_message($msg) {
  echo "<div id='messages'>\n";
  echo " <div class='success'>\n";
  echo "  <p>{$msg}</p>\n";
  echo " </div>\n";
  echo "</div>\n\n";
}
```

The Right to Readability

What about `sprintf`*? And, why the* *n's?*

There are about as many ways to write a function like `display_success_message` as there are letters in the alphabet. You could use `sprintf` to insert the message. You could combine the multiple `echo` calls into a single line (using `echo` or `sprintf`). You could output raw HTML and interrupt that HTML with PHP by using `<?php` and `?>`. In each case, your solution would be just fine.

The \n's are another curiosity. They're just to make the viewed source a little cleaner. Without them, the output would look something like this:

```
<div id='messages'> <div class='success'>
<p>{$msg}</p> </div></div>
```

It would be just one big line of HTML. With the line feeds, the user sees nothing different. HTML doesn't care a bit about those feeds. But if you viewed the source, you'd see a much nicer bit of HTML:

```
<div id='messages'>
 <div class='success'>
  <p>{$msg}</p>
```

```
 </div>
</div>
```

Are the \n's necessary? Not at all. Do they help the user? Nope. But, they definitely do make debugging and readability a bit simpler. So, should you use them or not, and do they go with `echo`, or `sprintf`, or both?

You're at the place in your PHP journey where style and personal preference are more important than right and wrong. You can use `sprintf` everywhere, for queries and output and everything in between. You can use `echo` for output and `sprintf` for queries. Or, more likely, you'll use whatever comes to mind when you're writing the particular script you're writing.

The same is true with \n and line feeds. Sometimes you'll work hard so that the HTML output is nice and clean and easy to read. Other times, you'll realize that you could spend hours trying to get things to look good for that rare person who Views Source. (Then again, you're that rare person, so sometimes the effort makes perfect sense.)

As it stands, this function works well. How about error messages? You could use something similar:

```php
function display_error_message($msg) {
  echo "<div id='messages'>\n";
  echo " <div class=error>\n";
  echo "  <p>{$msg}</p>\n";
  echo " </div>\n";
  echo "</div>\n\n";
}
```

Look closely: both of these are outputting the messages <div>. That's no good. You need something that can handle *both* error types. Then, that sort of "parent" function can pass the individual messages to smaller functions, each of which handles success *and* errors:

```php
function display_messages($success_msg, $error_msg) {
  echo "<div id='messages'>\n";
  display_success_message($success_msg);
```

```
    display_error_message($error_msg);
    echo "</div>\n\n";
  }

  function display_success_message($msg) {
    echo " <div class='success'>\n";
    echo "  <p>{$msg}</p>\n";
    echo " </div>\n";
  }

  function display_error_message($msg) {
    echo " <div class='error'>\n";
    echo "  <p>{$msg}</p>\n";
    echo " </div>\n";
  }
```

That looks better. But again, look closely. Does it seem like you might be seeing double?

Duplicate Code Is a Problem Waiting to Happen

The problem with the code you just completed is a bit subtle, which is why it can be so nasty. Look how close these two functions are to each other:

```
  function display_success_message($msg) {
    echo " <div class='success'>\n";
    echo "  <p>{$msg}</p>\n";
    echo " </div>\n";
  }

  function display_error_message($msg) {
    echo " <div class='error'>\n";
    echo "  <p>{$msg}</p>\n";
    echo " </div>\n";
  }
```

That's a *lot* of identical code all for just one change—in this case, the class of the <div> in each. Anytime you see code that's this similar, you should immediately be thinking "Uh oh. That's fragile code." That's something you want to avoid. For a much more stern lecture on why this is important, see the box on page 367.

Writing DRY Code

As you progress further into programming, you'll hear people talking about "dry code," or "drying up your code." Both of these expressions are using DRY as an acronym, which stands for "Don't Repeat Yourself." So far in this book, you've been doing a good job of that. Remember back in Chapter 5 (page 133) when you moved some basic application-wide constants into *app_config.php*? You avoided repeating those constants (or yourself) in multiple files. You put them in a single place, and then all your other scripts referenced that single place.

The same was true of *database_connection.php* (page 140). Again, instead of repeating your connection code over and over, you pulled that code out of multiple places and located

it in a single place. That's DRYing up your code: making it DRY, and removing duplicate code whenever and wherever possible.

With `display_success_message` and `display_error_message`, you're at a more microscopic level. It's just three lines of code, right? Still, if you can write those three lines of code in one place and reference them in two, you've improved your overall project. You've ensured that if you need to change how messages are output, you have just one place to investigate rather than two. This is good programming, it results in DRY code, and all your peers will think you're cool. (Well, maybe not that last bit, but you *will* be cool...even if they don't realize it.)

Because there's so much repeated code, you can consolidate these functions:

```php
function display_message($msg, $msg_type) {
  echo " <div class='{$msg_type}'>\n";
  echo "  <p>{$msg}</p>\n";
  echo " </div>\n";
}
```

That's much better. It's clear, succinct, and very DRY. In fact, you can take things even further and define the allowed message types as constants to make your code even neater:

```php
define("SUCCESS_MESSAGE", "success");
define("ERROR_MESSAGE", "error");

function display_messages($success_msg, $error_msg) {
  echo "<div id='messages'>\n";
  display_message($success_msg, SUCCESS_MESSAGE);
  display_message($error_msg, ERROR_MESSAGE);
  echo "</div>\n\n";
}

function display_message($msg, $msg_type) {
  echo " <div class='{$msg_type}'>\n";
  echo "  <p>{$msg}</p>\n";
  echo " </div>\n";
}
```

Using this, you don't have to remember whether the message type for an error was "ERROR" or "error" or "errors" or something else altogether. The constant handles that mapping for you.

You can start to put this all together. Create a new script and call it *view.php* in your *scripts/* directory, alongside *app_config.php* and *database_connection.php*. Then, drop in all of the following code, along with a require_once for the obligatory *app_config.php*:

```php
<?php

require_once 'app_config.php';

define("SUCCESS_MESSAGE", "success");
define("ERROR_MESSAGE", "error");

function display_messages($success_msg, $error_msg) {
  echo "<div id='messages'>\n";
  display_message($success_msg, SUCCESS_MESSAGE);
  display_message($error_msg, ERROR_MESSAGE);
  echo "</div>\n\n";
}

function display_message($msg, $msg_type) {
  echo " <div class='{$msg_type}'>\n";
  echo "  <p>{$msg}</p>\n";
  echo " </div>\n";
}

?>
```

> **NOTE** You're not actually using anything from *app_config.php* in *view.php*. Still, because that's where all your core information resides, it's probably a good bet that you'll need information from it sooner or later. Might as well require_once it now so that it's available.

View and Display Code Belongs Together

You now have another script: *view.php*. Remember, you're creating not just utility code but nicely organized code. Even though you could put display_messages and display_message in *app_config.php*, that's not good organization.

Taking time now to build groups of functions in scripts that are usefully named is well worth your while. When you're writing a script like *show_users.php* that handles display, you immediately know you can include *view.php* and get helpful functions. On the other hand, in a script like *delete_user.php* that doesn't do any display, you can skip *view.php*.

NOTE Of course, this same principle is true of *database_connection.php*. If you don't need a database connection, you don't need to `require_once` *database_connection.php*. If you do, well, then you do. It becomes simple when you have scripts that are organized and named according to their function.

■ Integrating Utilities, Views, and Messages

You're finally ready to put all of this together. Let's revisit *show_users.php* and the less refined messaging that started the entire journey that led to *view.php*:

```
<head>
  <link href="../css/phpMM.css" rel="stylesheet" type="text/css" />
  <script type="text/javascript">
    function delete_user(user_id) {
      if (confirm("Are you sure you want to delete this user?" +
                  "\nThere's really no going back!")) {
        window.location = "delete_user.php?user_id=" + user_id;
      }
    }

<?php if (isset($msg)) { ?>
    window.onload = function() {
      alert("<?php echo $msg ?>");
    }
<?php } ?>
  </script>
</head>
```

This code is no longer needed, so you can remove it, now and forever. Time to get a lot more elegant.

Calling Repeated Code from a View Script

First, add in the `require_once` for your new view-related function script:

```
<?php

require_once '../scripts/app_config.php';
require_once '../scripts/database_connection.php';
require_once '../scripts/view.php';

// and so on...

?>
```

Next, add a call to the display_messages function in your HTML:

```
<body>
    <div id="header"><h1>PHP & MySQL: The Missing Manual</h1></div>
    <div id="example">Current Users</div>
    <?php display_messages($msg); ?>
```

There's a bit of a problem here. display_messages takes two parameters: a success message and an error message. Therefore, you need some way to pass in an empty message, and then display_messages needs to handle an empty message on the receiving end.

By whatever means the issue with errors is resolved, this structure should become a standard part of all your HTML. Anytime you're displaying HTML, you want to allow for message handling. That means you're back to repeat code: every single view-related script has started out with the same basic HTML (although occasionally you've needed to insert some JavaScript, as in *show_users.php*):

```
<html>
 <head>
  <link href="../css/phpMM.css" rel="stylesheet" type="text/css" />
  <script type="text/javascript">
    function delete_user(user_id) {
      if (confirm("Are you sure you want to delete this user?" +
                "\nThere's really no going back!")) {
        window.location = "delete_user.php?user_id=" + user_id;
      }
    }
  </script>
 </head>
```

Now, you have your body tag, the same header—more repeated code—and then a page title. Also, you have messages to display. Here's another chance to take code that you've been typing into your scripts, over and over, pull that repeated code out, and then drop it into yet more utility functions. Your *view.php* script is about to get a lot bigger and a lot more useful.

Flexible Functions Are Better Functions

You now have a list of interrelated things with which you must manage, most of which involve updates to *view.php*:

- display_messages should handle empty or non-existent messages for the success and the error message. If either message isn't set, the <div> related to that message shouldn't be output.

- You need a new function—call it display_header—that handles outputting the head section of each page's HTML. This function should take in JavaScript that can be added to the document's head, but should also handle the case in which there's no extra JavaScript needed.

- You need another new function—call this one display_title—that prints out the page title; the page's subtitle, which is passed in by each script; and any message, which also should be passed in by the calling script.

None of these functions are particularly difficult, so it's time to get back to work.

■ USE DEFAULT ARGUMENT VALUES IN DISPLAY_MESSAGES

Returning to *view.php*, display_messages needs to be able to accept a non-value for a message. Recall from Chapter 5, on page 125, that in PHP, this is handled by the special keyword NULL, which means "non-value."

NOTE   You'll see NULL in nearly every programming language, although usually with slight variations. For example, in Ruby, it's nil; In Java, it's null; PHP uses NULL, as does C++. They always mean the same thing, though: the absence of a value.

Now, because NULL is a non-value, you can't compare it to a value. So, this code doesn't make sense in PHP:

```
if ($value == NULL) // do something
```

What you need to use is another PHP helper, is_null. You pass a value to is_null, and PHP informs you about what you have.

Now, it's possible to make an update to display_messages. If a message passed in is NULL, there's no need to call the individual display_message for that type of message:

```
function display_messages($success_msg, $error_msg) {
  echo "<div id='messages'>\n";
  if (!is_null($success_msg)) {
    display_message($success_msg, SUCCESS_MESSAGE);
  }
  if (!is_null($error_msg)) {
    display_message($error_msg, ERROR_MESSAGE);
  }
  echo "</div>\n\n";
}
```

There's just one thing missing: what if a script—like *show_users.php*—doesn't have a value to pass in for $error_msg or $success_msg? In these cases, you want display_messages to have a *default* value. This is a value that's used if nothing else is passed in.

You can assign the default value for function's argument like this:

```
function do_something(this_value = "default value") {
  // do something with this_value
}
```

Thus, for display_messages, the default values should be NULL (no value):

```php
function display_messages($success_msg = NULL, $error_msg = NULL) {
  echo "<div id='messages'>\n";
  if (!is_null($success_msg)) {
    display_message($success_msg, SUCCESS_MESSAGE);
  }
  if (!is_null($error_msg)) {
    display_message($error_msg, ERROR_MESSAGE);
  }
  echo "</div>\n\n";
}
```

Your display_messages function is finally ready for use by the other functions you need to add to *view.php*.

■ OUTPUT A STANDARD HEADER WITH HEREDOC

Next, you need to deal with the standard HTML output for a page in your app. That's basically the opening <HTML>, the <title>, the <head>, and any page-specific JavaScript that needs to be added. Of course, with *view.php* in place, your knowledge of functions, default arguments, and everything else you've already done, this step should be a piece of cake.

You can create a new function, and because it's possible that some scripts need to pass in JavaScript to add to the <head> section, but others might not, using a default value for a function argument is again the way to go:

```php
function display_head($page_title = "", $embedded_javascript = NULL) {
```

This function, by the way, sets a default value for the $page_title, too. That's not completely necessary, but again, it's a bit of extra protection. This way, if someone calling this function forgets to send in the title, the HTML output can be constructed regardless.

The body of this function is just some echo work and a conditional for the potential JavaScript:

```php
function display_head($page_title = "", $embedded_javascript = NULL) {
  echo "<html>";
  echo " <head>";
  echo " <title>{$page_title}</title>";
  echo ' <link href="../css/phpMM.css" rel="stylesheet" type="text/css" />';
  if (!is_null($embedded_javascript)) {
    echo "<script type='text/javascript'>" .
        $embedded_javascript .
        "</script>";
  }
  echo " </head>";
}
```

Notice that the link line uses single quotes around the HTML. This is so you can use double-quotes for the href, rel, and type attributes. Unfortunately, you're going to have to either use multiple quote styles like this or escape a lot of your quotes with \" and \'. Neither solution is particularly pretty, so pick your own poison (see the box on page 158).

Of course, programmers aren't used to limitations like this, and you should immediately be thinking, "Wait a second. I'm a programmer. Why am I stuck with two bad solutions?" Well, you're not. What you need is a way to deal with multiline strings, and PHP doesn't disappoint. In fact, multiline strings are such a common issue in PHP that it gives you a couple of ways to deal with them.

The most common solution is to use something called *heredoc*. The heredoc method gives you a way to mark the beginning and the end of a piece of text. Everything between those beginning and end markers is treated as text, without you needing to surround things in quotation marks.

You start a string of heredoc by inserting three less-than signs (<). You then add a sequence that you'll use to mark the end of the string:

```
$some_text = <<<EOD
```

In this example, you're saying, "I'm starting some text and the text will end when you run across EOD."

> **NOTE** You can use any ending sequence you want. The most typical choices are EOD and EOT, though, so it's best to stick with these unless you have a good reason for going with a different sequence.

Having done this, you can put as much text as you want in the string. You can use multiple lines, single quotes, double quotes, and even the {$var_name} syntax. It's all fair game:

```
<html>
 <head>
  <title>{$page_title}</title>
   <link href="../css/phpMM.css" rel="stylesheet" type="text/css" />
 </head>
```

Finally, you end the text with your end sequence:

```
EOD;
```

All together, you get this:

```
$some_text = <<<EOD
<html>
 <head>
  <title>{$page_title}</title>
   <link href="../css/phpMM.css" rel="stylesheet" type="text/css" />
 </head>
EOD;
```

You *cannot* indent the ending sequence. It must be the first thing on a line, all by itself, with no spacing before it. Thus, this code will not be treated as an ending sequence:

```
  EOD;
```

Just as dangerous is having whitespace after the ending sequence. There's no way to illustrate that in a book, or course, but even a single space after the closing semicolon will do you in.

The best way to recognize these things is to watch out for the dreaded "unexpected T_SL" error. That's usually PHP's ultra-cryptic way of letting you know that you have whitespace where it doesn't belong, either before or after the ending sequence, in most cases.

Put all of this together, and you can clean up the look of display_head quite a bit:

```
function display_head($page_title = "", $embedded_javascript = NULL) {
  echo <<<EOD
<html>
 <head>
 <title>{$page_title}</title>
 <link href="../css/phpMM.css" rel="stylesheet" type="text/css" />
EOD;
  if (!is_null($embedded_javascript)) {
    echo "<script type='text/javascript'>" .
         $embedded_javascript .
         "</script>";
  }
  echo " </head>";
}
```

Go ahead and add this into your *view.php* script now.

You probably noticed that in this version of display_head, there was no need to assign the string created by using heredoc to a variable. You can directly output the multiline string and save a step. The result is actually a hodgepodge of echo, heredoc, conditional logic, and potentially some JavaScript. Nonetheless, it's becoming increasingly easy to read, and that's a good thing.

■ UPDATE YOUR SCRIPT(S) TO USE DISPLAY_HEAD

Now, you can head back to *show_users.php* (and *show_user.php* if you like) and remove lots of HTML. Replace the HTML for the head of your document with a call to display_head. While you're at it, you might want to use a little more heredoc in the process, particularly in *show_users.php*, which sends some JavaScript to be embedded:

```php
<?php
// code to get all the user data
?>

<?php
  $delete_user_script = <<<EOD
function delete_user(user_id) {
  if (confirm("Are you sure you want to delete this user? " +
              "There's really no going back!")) {
    window.location = "delete_user.php?user_id=" + user_id;
  }
}
EOD;
  display_head("Current Users", $delete_user_script);
?>

  <body>
    <div id="header"><h1>PHP & MySQL: The Missing Manual</h1></div>
    <div id="example">Current Users</div>
    <?php display_messages($msg); ?>

    <!-- Remaining HTML markup -->
  </body>
</html>
```

> **NOTE** You could just as easily keep all of the PHP that gets the users in the same `<?php ?>` block as the code that calls `display_head`. That's up to you. Some programmers prefer to keep the data gathering and the actual view display separate, and some prefer to avoid duplicating `<?php`. The choice is yours.

This code uses heredoc, so creating a string of JavaScript to pass to `display_head` doesn't involve lots of escaping single or double quotes. In fact, you'll find that heredoc is almost as handy to have around as `sprintf` (page 298), and you'll use both liberally for outputting HTML or other long stretches of text.

There's still the issue of displaying messages, but before you get to that, try out your changes to *show_users.php*. You should see something like Figure 11-16.

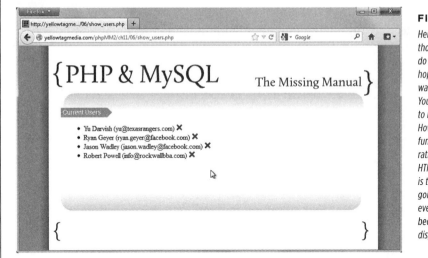

FIGURE 11-16

Here's another one of those cases for which you do a lot of work and then hope that things look the way they always have. You want show_users.php to look like it always has. However, it's now using functions in view.php rather than outputting HTML itself. The result is that this header is going to look exactly like every other page header because they're all using display_head now.

Standardizing and Consolidating Messaging in the View

All that's left is messaging. You have a display_messages function, but it's not integrated into the HTML that's typically around those messages. Just as display_head output HTML with some potential embedded JavaScript, the first part of your page should output some standard HTML, the page title (again), and potentially success and error messages. The final output should look a bit like this:

```
<html>
 <head>
  <title>Current Users</title>
  <link href="../css/phpMM.css" rel="stylesheet" type="text/css" />
  <script type='text/javascript'>function delete_user(user_id) {
  if (confirm("Are you sure you want to delete this user? " +
            "There's really no going back!")) {
    window.location = "delete_user.php?user_id=" + user_id;
  }
}</script>
 </head>
 <body>
  <div id="header"><h1>PHP & MySQL: The Missing Manual</h1></div>

  <div id="example">Current Users</div>
  <div id='messages'>
  <div class='success'>
```

```
  <p>The user you specified has been deleted.</p>
 </div>
</div>
```

```
  <div id="content">
    <!-- HTML content -->
  </div>
 </body>
</html>
```

This is a piece of cake now. Go ahead and create display_title in *view.php*:

```
function display_title($title, $success_msg = NULL, $error_msg = NULL) {
echo <<<EOD
 <body>
  <div id="header"><h1>PHP & MySQL: The Missing Manual</h1></div>
  <div id="example">$title</div>
EOD;
  display_messages($success_msg, $error_msg); ?>
}
```

How easy is that? You'd call this like so, say in *show_users.php*:

```
display_title("Current Users", $msg);
```

But, you already know how messages come across: through request parameters, accessible via $_REQUEST. So, why worry about whether they're set in your view? Just pass them in to display_title, even if the values are NULL:

```
display_title("Current Users",
              $_REQUEST['success_message'], $_REQUEST['error_message']);
```

> **NOTE** You can also remove the code in *show_users.php* that gets the success_message request parameter from $_REQUEST explicitly, because that's now handled by this new call to display_title.

Things are looking good: display_head and display_title are both great, and you already have calls to display_head in place. However, before you go adding in a call to display_title in all your scripts, take a moment to think about what you've done (and read the box on page 378).

Building a Function to Call Two Functions

Remember, the idea here was to create another function, display_title, to handle outputting the starting portion of every HTML page's body. But now that you have that function, there are a few things to think about:

- The HTML from display_title will *always* directly follow the HTML output from display_head.

- The title used in display_head should typically match the title used in display_title.

So, if this HTML always follows the HTML from display_head, and the title in both is the same, why are there two calls? In your scripts, you'd always have something like this:

```php
<?php

// Code like crazy

?>

<?php display_head($title, $javascript);  ?>
<?php display_title($title,
                    $_REQUEST['success_message'], $_REQUEST['error_message']);
?>

<!-- More HTML -->
</html>
```

But are two calls necessary? Wouldn't the following be cleaner:

```php
<?php

// Code like crazy

?>
```

```php
<?php page_start($title, $javascript,
                 $_REQUEST['success_message'], $_REQUEST['error_message']) ?>

  <!-- More HTML -->
</html>
```

Not only is this a simpler call, but now you don't need to pass in $title twice. It goes in a single time and is applied across all the opening HTML.

Doing it this way, you don't need to start messing around with display_title, display_head, or display_messages. Instead, just build a function for your script to call that handles all the smaller functions:

```php
function page_start($title, $javascript = NULL,
                    $success_message = NULL, $error_message = NULL) {

  display_head($title, $javascript);
  display_title($title, $success_message, $error_message);
}
```

> **NOTE** Put this function in *view.php*, along with all your other display functions.

Just Pass That Information Along

What's left? Removing calls to display_head; avoiding another call to display_title; and finally, one call to rule them all. In fact, take a look at the new, improved *show_users.php*. This script is shorter and a lot clearer. Even with the bit of indentation clutter that heredoc introduces, this is a pretty sleek script:

```php
<?php

require_once '../scripts/app_config.php';
require_once '../scripts/database_connection.php';
require_once '../scripts/view.php';

// Build the SELECT statement
$select_users =
  "SELECT user_id, first_name, last_name, email " .
  "  FROM users";
```

```php
// Run the query
$result = mysql_query($select_users);

// Display the view to users
  $delete_user_script = <<<EOD
function delete_user(user_id) {
  if (confirm("Are you sure you want to delete this user? " +
              "There's really no going back!")) {
    window.location = "delete_user.php?user_id=" + user_id;
  }
}
EOD;
  page_start("Current Users", $delete_user_script,
              $_REQUEST['success_message'], $_REQUEST['error_message']);
?>
  <div id="content">
   <ul>
     <?php
       while ($user = mysql_fetch_array($result)) {
         $user_row = sprintf(
           "<li><a href='show_user.php?user_id=%d'>%s %s</a> " .
           "(<a href='mailto:%s'>%s</a>) " .
           "<a href='javascript:delete_user(%d);'><img " .
             "class='delete_user' src='../images/delete.png' " .
             "width='15' /></a></li>",
           $user['user_id'], $user['first_name'], $user['last_name'],
           $user['email'], $user['email'], $user['user_id']);
         echo $user_row;
       }
     ?>
   </ul>
  </div>
  <div id="footer"></div>
 </body>
</html>
```

At this point, take it out for a spin. Verify that error messages work. Confirm that success messages work. Change your other scripts to also use page_start. You can even add more functions to *view.php*. Maybe you want a page_end that outputs the closing <div>, the footer, and some contact text. You could add a sidebar function.

With this modular approach, you can do anything you want. Well, except for controlling just who gets to delete users. That's a problem for the next chapter.

Two Functions Are Better Than One...Kinda

One of the things you've seen over and over is this idea of moving smaller and smaller bits of code into their own functions. This means that you have a little bit of HTML in a function in *view.php*. You have *database_connection.php* doing database connection, and even though it doesn't define a custom function, it's basically called like a function through `require_once`. The same has been true a number of times: take small pieces of behavior or functionality and put them into small, easy-to-call functions.

It might be easy to think that the goal is lots of individual function calls. That's partially true. What is true is that you want lots of building blocks that you can assemble into bigger useful pieces. But, when it comes to using those functions, do you really want to make 20 or 30 individual calls?

Probably not.

Instead, you'll likely want to make as few function calls as you need in your scripts...at least in the ones with which the user interacts. Therefore, it's preferable to call something like this:

```
display_page($title, $javascript, $content);
```

than this:

```
display_head($title, $javascript);

display_messages($msg);

display_content($content);

display_footer();
```

Of course, the way you get around this isn't to reverse field and throw all your code across ten functions into one. But it might be that you want one function that then calls these functions for you. That's still using building blocks, but it's reducing the number of things your top-level scripts need to do to get things working properly.

Just think about it: is it easier to remember to call `display_page`, and then have to look up the arguments to pass, or is it easier to remember to call `display_head`, and then `display_messages`, and then `display_content`, and then...what was that next one again? Of course, it's easier to make the one function call.

That's why you want to move toward a hybrid of small functions with groupings or higher-level functions that assemble those small functions in useful ways. Your scripts should make simple calls rather than lots of calls. And then, those simple calls can do whatever is needed, even if that means calling lots of smaller functions behind the scenes.

The result should be simpler, easier-to-read code. As a bonus, you'll also get a nice set of functions that you can combine in a variety of useful ways.

Security and the Real World

Authentication and Authorization

Something important arises at just about this point in your application design and creation. You have four, five, maybe more core pieces of functionality in place to add users, upload photos, and so on. You have a few tables set up in which to store data. You have most of your application's central components built, and even though it's still a simple application, you have a sense of where you're going. And then, in the previous chapter, you added a new piece of functionality: the ability to delete users. It seems like just another feature; just another user requirement to tick off the list. But, wait a second...deleting users? Is that something that you want to offer to all of your users? Of course not. That's an administrative feature. (You might even remember from page 339 that an early candidate for the name of *delete_user.php* was *admin.php*.)

An administrator, of course, is someone who has the responsibility—and more importantly, the capability (and authority)—to manage user accounts and take care of the application on an overarching level. Unfortunately, your application doesn't know that yet. As far as it's concerned, there's no such thing as an administrator. Right now, anyone can hop over to *delete_user.php* and nuke poor Ryan Geyer, or Robert Powell, or whoever else has signed up through *create_user.html*, with nothing more than a confirmation box standing between them and digital oblivion. What's worse, that tempting little red "X" is visible to anyone who goes to *show_users.php*.

With the addition of this one piece of functionality, you to realize you need several other things, and you need them soon. Here's the quick list of problems that you need to solve:

- Viewing all users (done)

- Deleting users (you have this, with way too much freedom)

- A way to identify users on your system (you kind of have this, through *create_user.html*, but there's no way for users to log in and out right now)

- A way to indicate that a user is an administrator

- A way that users can log in and verify who they are (for example, with a password)

- A way to only show certain functionality—like deleting a user—if the person who is viewing the functionality is an administrator

Your system needs *authentication*—a way to let it know who's who. Users should be required to log in, and then your system should know whether the user is a certain type, like an administrator. Based on that type, the user sees (or doesn't see) certain things. This selective display of resources is authentication's bed fellow, *authorization*. These two terms are often confused for one another, or even casually used interchangeably.

> **NOTE** There are people that would rather be tarred and feathered than mistake authentication for authorization, or vice versa. Then again, those people probably have separate sock drawers for each color they own. It's good to know the difference, but you don't have to sweat the details.

It's certainly not surprising that you need to add these features. Logging in is common to almost every site you regularly visit online, not just Twitter and Facebook. Even YouTube and Google give you more sophisticated options when you create and log in to a user account. All of them use authentication to establish who is who. It's time that your application joined the party.

■ Basic Authentication

Authentication, like everything else, can be done simply or with tremendous complexity. Also, like nearly everything else, it's best to start with the basics and add complexity as needed. For a simple application, you don't need thumbprint readers and lasers scanning a user's face. (Granted, it might be fun, but it's not necessary. James Bond almost certainly isn't going to fill out your *create_user.html* form.)

> **NOTE** You can find the finished example code for this section on this book's Missing CD page at *www.missingmanuals.com/cds/phpmysqlmm2e*.

Using HTTP Headers for Basic Authentication

Basic authentication, also known as *HTTP authentication*, is a means of supplying a user name and password in a web application through HTTP headers. You've already worked with headers a bit. Remember this bit of code from *scripts/app_config.php* (page 249)?

```
function handle_error($user_error_message, $system_error_message) {
  header("Location: " . get_web_path(SITE_ROOT) .
        "scripts/show_error.php" .
        "?error_message={$user_error_message}" .
        "&system_error_message={$system_error_message}");
}
```

This handle_error function is using an HTTP header—the Location header—to send a redirect to the browser. You've also used the Content-type and Content-length headers in displaying an image in *show_image.php* (page 318):

```
header('Content-type: ' . $image['mime_type']);
header('Content-length: ' . $image['file_size']);
```

With basic authentication, there are a couple of other HTTP headers you can send. The first doesn't have a key value such as Content-type or Location. You simply send this:

```
HTTP/1.1 401 Unauthorized
```

When a browser receives this header, it knows that a requested page requires authentication to be displayed. 401 is a special status code, along with lots of others, that informs the browser about the request. 200 is the code used to indicate "Everything is OK," for example, and 404 is the HTTP error code for "Not Found."

NOTE You can read up on all the HTTP status codes at *w3.org/Protocols/rfc2616/rfc2616-sec10.html*. Anything from 400 up indicates an error of some kind.

It's one thing to tell the browser that access to a page is restricted, but at some point you'll want to make that page *unrestricted*. The answer is to send a second header:

```
WWW-Authenticate: Basic realm="The Social Site"
```

This header WWW-Authenticate alerts the browser that authentication needs to happen. Specifically, the browser should pop up a dialog box and ask for some credentials.

You specify what type of authentication to require; in this example, it's Basic. Then, you identify a realm to which that authentication should be applied. In this case, it's "The Social Site". As long as different pages use this same realm, authentication to one of those pages applies to other pages in that same realm.

Basic Authentication Is...Well, Basic

It's time to apply authentication to your own application. Open your *show_users .php* script.

NOTE As usual, you might want to think about making a backup of this script, or copying all your scripts into a new *ch12/* directory. That way you have all your older, working scripts to fall back on in case something goes wrong.

Enter these two header lines near the top of the script:

```php
<?php

require_once '../scripts/app_config.php';
require_once '../scripts/database_connection.php';
require_once '../scripts/view.php';

header('HTTP/1.1 401 Unauthorized');
header('WWW-Authenticate: Basic realm="The Social Site"');

// Build the SELECT statement
$select_users =
  "SELECT user_id, first_name, last_name, email " .
  "  FROM users";

// Remaining PHP

?>
```

Navigate over to *show_users.php*. You should see a nice pop-up window asking you to log in, like Figure 12-1. Well, it's not *that* nice, but it does the trick. Basic authentication, pure and simple.

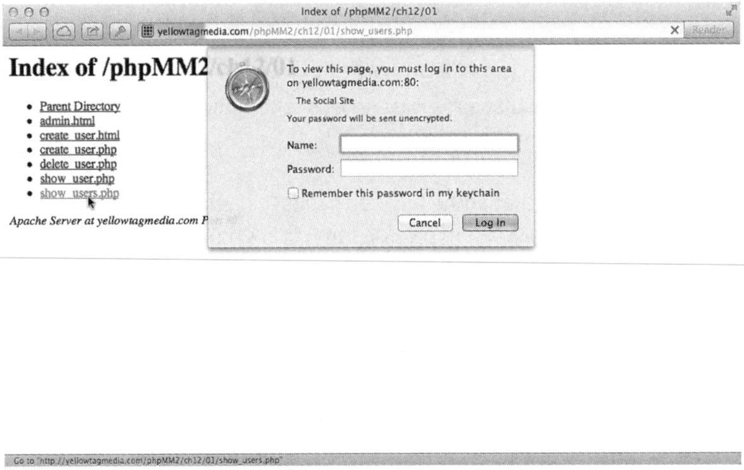

FIGURE 12-1

It's battleship gray, it's forbidding, it's terse. In other words, it's everything you could want a fence around your application to be. However, you almost never see forbidding and terse these days in web applications, so this is just the first in a series of steps toward the current professional standard in authentication.

WARNING   If your web server is using a *.htaccess* file (popular particularly on Apache web servers) to restrict certain directories from web access, you could have problems here. *.htaccess* doesn't always play nicely with PHP's basic authentication. Your best bet would be to call your provider and ask it to not use any *.htaccess* files on the directories in which you're working.

The Worst Authentication Ever

With the addition of the two headers on page 388, there's still a gaping hole in your security. Navigate to *show_users.php* if you're not there already, and leave both the Name and Password fields blank. Then, simply click Cancel. Figure 12-2 shows the result.

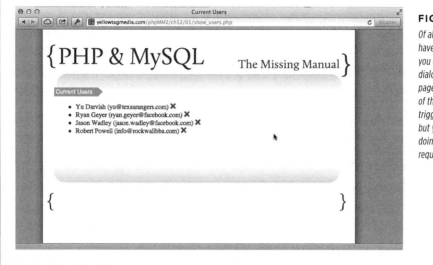

FIGURE 12-2

Of all things you might have expected to see when you canceled out of a login dialog box, the secure page probably wasn't one of them. So far, you're triggering a login request, but you're not actually doing anything with that request.

As if that's not enough, enter *any* user name and password and then click Log In. There you go: Figure 12-2 again. In fact, spend some time trying to get anything other than the normal *show_users.php* page. You won't be able to.

Pretty poor security, isn't it? Canceling should *not* take you on to the supposedly secure page. What you need to do is get the user name and password, check them against acceptable values, and *then* show the page. In every other case, the user should not see *show_users.php*.

Getting Your User's Credentials

To check the user name and password against any values, you need to make some changes to your script. Your current code doesn't extract those values, let alone compare them against any other values. There's clearly some work to do here.

Fortunately, because HTTP authentication is defined in a standard way, it's easy for PHP to interact with users who enter their credentials into a basic authentication pop-up dialog box. In fact, PHP gives you access to both the user name and password entered via two special values in a superglobal variable you've used before, $_SERVER:

- $_SERVER['PHP_AUTH_USER'] gives you the entered user name.
- $_SERVER['PHP_AUTH_PW'] gives you the entered password.

NOTE $_SERVER is used in *app_config.php* to define the SITE_ROOT constant as well as in the get_web_path utility function.

You might expect your flow to proceed something like this:

1. **At the beginning of a script, send the HTTP headers that trigger authentication.**

2. **Once the authentication code is complete, check $_SERVER['PHP_AUTH_USER'] and $_SERVER['PHP_AUTH_PW'] for values and compare those values to some constants or a database.**

3. **Decide whether to let the user see the content your script normally outputs.**

That makes a lot of sense, but turns out to be wrong. Here's what really happens:

1. **Your script is called.**

2. **Authentication headers (actually, a header that says a user is unauthorized and should be allowed to sign in) are sent.**

3. **Once the user enters in a user name and password, the browser *recalls* your script from the top once again.**

Clearly, you need to determine if there are any available credentials *before* authentication headers are sent. If there are credentials, check them against allowed values. Finally, if the credentials don't match or don't exist, *that's* when you send the authentication headers.

Once again, then, isset (page 235) becomes your friend. Start with code like this:

```php
if (!isset($_SERVER['PHP_AUTH_USER']) ||
    !isset($_SERVER['PHP_AUTH_PW'])) {
  header('HTTP/1.1 401 Unauthorized');
  header('WWW-Authenticate: Basic realm="The Social Site"');
}
```

Yet, all this does is pop up the login box if the user name and password haven't previously been set. It still allows access to your page through a couple different avenues. So you need to not only pop up a login box, but also ensure that any preset user names and passwords match an allowed set of values.

Cancel Is Not a Valid Means of Authentication

Before you deal with checking user names and passwords, though, there's something more pressing to deal with. Even worse than accepting any credentials is accepting a click of the Cancel button.

This situation is easy to deal with, albeit not intuitively. Here's your code right now:

```php
if (!isset($_SERVER['PHP_AUTH_USER']) ||
    !isset($_SERVER['PHP_AUTH_PW'])) {
```

```
    header('HTTP/1.1 401 Unauthorized');
    header('WWW-Authenticate: Basic realm="The Social Site"');
}
```

The login dialog box is prompted by the two calls to the header:

```
header('HTTP/1.1 401 Unauthorized');
header('WWW-Authenticate: Basic realm="The Social Site"');
```

When a user clicks Cancel, your PHP continues to run, directly from after the second header line:

```
header('HTTP/1.1 401 Unauthorized');
header('WWW-Authenticate: Basic realm="The Social Site"');
// This line is run if Cancel is clicked
```

Taking the simplest possible path, you could simply bail out of the script:

```
if (!isset($_SERVER['PHP_AUTH_USER']) ||
    !isset($_SERVER['PHP_AUTH_PW'])) {
  header('HTTP/1.1 401 Unauthorized');
  header('WWW-Authenticate: Basic realm="The Social Site"');
  exit("You need a valid username and password to be here. " .
      "Move along, nothing to see.");
}
```

That way, if a user clicks Cancel, the script runs the exit command—which is a lot like die—and bails out with an error message, as shown in Figure 12-3.

FIGURE 12-3

With the exit code above, if a user tries the ever-so-clever Cancel-without-signing-in trick, your script handles the situation. Then again, this method is rather crude, and doesn't exactly live up to your application's standard in user-friendly views and web pages. You'll be able to improve this, but not until the next chapter.

Getting Your User's Credentials

Let's get back to seeing what your user actually supplies to the login dialog box. Remember, the flow here isn't what you might expect. Once the user has entered a user name and password, your script is basically recalled. It's almost as though the server is giving you a free while loop, similar to this:

```
while (username_and_password_are_wrong) {
  ask_for_username_and_password_again();
}
```

> **NOTE** This isn't actually running, working PHP. It's something called *pseudocode*. For more on what pseudocode is—and why it's your friend—check out the following box.

UP TO SPEED

Pseudocode: The Code Before You Write Code

Lots of times you'll find that you need a happy medium before writing full-on working code—syntactically accurate, debugged, ready to run—and scribbling a list of steps to follow in a notebook. You want to think about the details of how things will work without getting bogged down by minutiae of syntax. As a bonus, pseudocode is language-neutral, so you can write pseudocode and later implement that code in any programming language you choose.

That said, when you write pseudocode, you usually know which language you have in mind and use that syntax. For example, if you're writing pseudocode that you'll eventually turn into PHP, you might use an if, a while, an else, and throw in curly braces or angle brackets. That's why this

```
while (username_and_password_are_wrong) {
  ask_for_username_and_password_again();
}
```

is a great example of pseudocode that will later become PHP. But, in the case below, it's not helpful to type out all the $_SERVER stuff, because it's long, full of little commas and apostrophes, and you already know the basic idea. So,

whether you're explaining to a coworker what you're doing or just planning out your code, this is a perfectly good stand-in:

```
while (username_and_password_are_wrong) {
```

In your head, you might be translating that to something like this:

```
if (($_SERVER['PHP_AUTH_USER'] != VALID_
USERNAME) ||

    ($_SERVER['PHP_AUTH_PW'] != VALID_
PASSWORD)) {
```

What will you do once you make that determination? Something...you're not sure what yet. You know basically what has to happen, but the details are still up in the air. That leaves you with this:

```
ask_for_username_and_password_again();
```

It's clear, it's understandable, but it's not bogged down by PHP semantics. It's pseudocode. It's great for getting an idea going, or communicating about code. It's also great for a situation like this in which something tells you the way you're doing things might need to change. And, if change is coming, the less work you put into a solution that isn't permanent, the better.

Right now, you have an if statement that confirms whether the user name and password have been set. If not, send the headers, and if Cancel is clicked, bail out.

```
if (!isset($_SERVER['PHP_AUTH_USER']) ||
    !isset($_SERVER['PHP_AUTH_PW'])) {
```

```
    header('HTTP/1.1 401 Unauthorized');
    header('WWW-Authenticate: Basic realm="The Social Site"');
    exit("You need a valid username and password to be here. " .
        "Move along, nothing to see.");
}
```

In an else part of this script (yet to be written) you could check the user name and password against the acceptable values. If they match, display the output from *show_users.php*. If not, you want to resend the headers that cause the browser to prompt the user to log in again. Therefore, you want something like this:

```
if (!isset($_SERVER['PHP_AUTH_USER']) ||
    !isset($_SERVER['PHP_AUTH_PW'])) {
  header('HTTP/1.1 401 Unauthorized');
  header('WWW-Authenticate: Basic realm="The Social Site"');
  exit("You need a valid username and password to be here. " .
      "Move along, nothing to see.");
} else {
  if (($_SERVER['PHP_AUTH_USER'] != VALID_USERNAME) ||
      ($_SERVER['PHP_AUTH_PW'] != VALID_PASSWORD)) {
    header('HTTP/1.1 401 Unauthorized');
    header('WWW-Authenticate: Basic realm="The Social Site"');
    exit("You need a valid username and password to be here. " .
        "Move along, nothing to see.");
  }
}
```

NOTE Technically, the if block is supplying an incorrect message to exit. That exit deals with the case in which the user pressed Cancel rather than entering a wrong user name and password. As a rule, though, you want to provide minimal information to users on security failures, so a generic "one size fits all" message is the better approach here.

Given that, you can actually consolidate things a bit. Whether the user has never attempted to log in, or incorrectly entered her user name or password, the script needs to send HTTP headers to force authentication. It's only if the user has entered information and it matches the appropriate values that the rest of the page's action should be taken and the output should be displayed. Thus, what you really want is this:

```
if (!isset($_SERVER['PHP_AUTH_USER']) ||
    !isset($_SERVER['PHP_AUTH_PW']) ||
    ($_SERVER['PHP_AUTH_USER'] != VALID_USERNAME) ||
    ($_SERVER['PHP_AUTH_PW'] != VALID_PASSWORD)) {
  header('HTTP/1.1 401 Unauthorized');
  header('WWW-Authenticate: Basic realm="The Social Site"');
  exit("You need a valid username and password to be here. " .
      "Move along, nothing to see.");
}
```

Go ahead and add this code to your version of *show_users.php*. Then, go up to the top of *show_users.php*—make sure it's before your new if statement—and add a few new constants:

```php
<?php

require_once '../scripts/app_config.php';
require_once '../scripts/database_connection.php';
require_once '../scripts/view.php';

define(VALID_USERNAME, "admin");
define(VALID_PASSWORD, "super_secret");

if (!isset($_SERVER['PHP_AUTH_USER']) ||
    !isset($_SERVER['PHP_AUTH_PW']) ||
    ($_SERVER['PHP_AUTH_USER'] != VALID_USERNAME) ||
    ($_SERVER['PHP_AUTH_PW'] != VALID_PASSWORD)) {
  header('HTTP/1.1 401 Unauthorized');
  header('WWW-Authenticate: Basic realm="The Social Site"');
  exit("You need a valid username and password to be here. " .
      "Move along, nothing to see.");
}
```

Try visiting *show_users.php* again and typing *admin* and *super_secret* for the user name and password, respectively, as shown in Figure 12-4. You should be greeted by the normal *show_users.php* view (see Figure 12-5). Otherwise, you'll just get the authentication pop-up over and over. (If that "over and over" bothers you, you've got the right idea; see the box on page 395.)

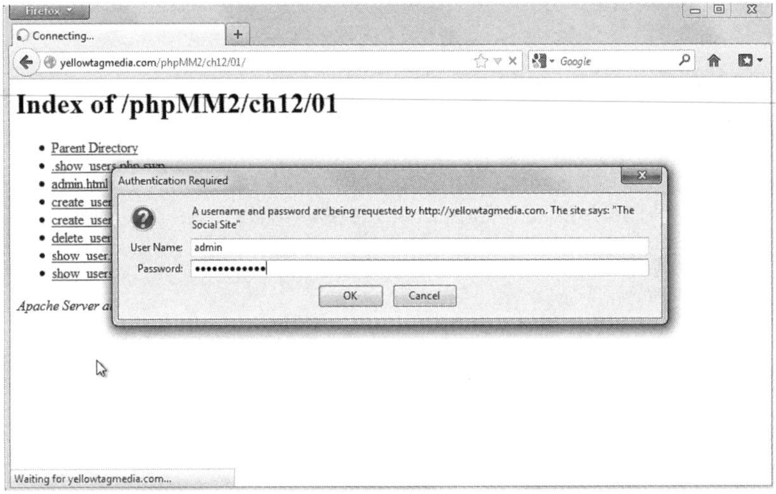

FIGURE 12-4

Finally, entering a user name and password actually matters. The browser responds to your headers with a login dialog box, and reports the values to PHP through the $_SERVER superglobal variable.

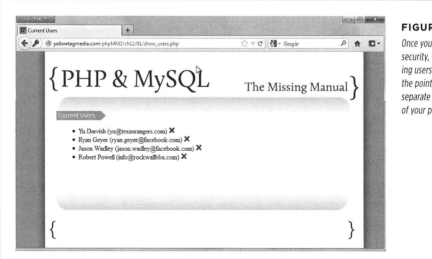

FIGURE 12-5

Once you've made it through security, you're back to seeing users again. And that's the point: authentication is separate from the core content of your pages.

Infinity and Beyond

Isn't an infinite number of login attempts bad?

Yes. Absolutely. Alas, at the moment, that's exactly what you're providing in *show_users.php*: the opportunity to try, over and over and over, to get a valid user name and password. Truth be told, the sample code and patterns you'll see all over the Web for using basic authentication look just like what you have in *show_users.php*.

There certainly are ways to get around this, but they're not as easy as you might hope. Because the browser is making

multiple requests to your script, you'd have to figure out a way to pass the number of requests that have been made to your script from your script. If that sounds tricky, it is.

There are ways to handle multiple requests, and you'll learn about them (although for a much better purpose) in the next chapter on sessions. For now, realize that the basic authentication approach is temporary anyway, and all of this code is a starting point, not an end point.

■ Abstracting What's the Same

Once again, you find yourself with some code in *show_users.php* that probably doesn't belong in *show_users.php*. Why is that? Because the same authorization and authentication you have in *show_users.php* belongs in every other script that should require logging in, such as *delete_user.php*. You don't want to write that code over and over; it becomes just like other repeated code you now have in *app_config. php* and *database_connection.php*. You should take it out of individual scripts and place it somewhere that all your scripts can use.

NOTE You can find the finished example code for this section on this book's Missing CD page at *www. missingmanuals.com/cds/phpmysqlmm2e.*

Another Utility Script: *authorize.php*

Fire up your editor once more; this time, create a file called *authorize.php*. You can start by adding that valid user name/password combination:

```php
<?php

define(VALID_USERNAME, "admin");
define(VALID_PASSWORD, "super_secret");


?>
```

At this point, you'd usually write a function: maybe authorize or get_credentials or something like that. But is that really what you want? Do you want to have to require_once authorize.php, and then explicitly call a function?

More likely, you want to identify scripts that require authorization with a single line:

```php
require_once "../scripts/authorize.php;"
```

Then, ideally, the authorization would all just magically happen for you.

Given that, you *don't* want a function that has to be called. You just want some PHP code in the main part of *authorize.php*. That way, by requiring *authorize.php*, that code runs and handles authentication, and your script doesn't have to do anything to get the benefits of authentication and authorization.

In a lot of ways, authorization here is like having JavaScript inside a set of <script> tags with no function:

```javascript
<script type="text/javascript">
  dashboard_alert("#hits_count_dialog");
  $("#hits_count_dialog").dialog("open");
  query_results_tables();
</script>
```

As soon as a browser encounters that JavaScript, it runs it. The same is true of PHP outside of a function, so you can drop your authorization code right into *authorize.php*:

```php
<?php

define(VALID_USERNAME, "admin");
define(VALID_PASSWORD, "super_secret");
```

```php
if (!isset($_SERVER['PHP_AUTH_USER']) ||
    !isset($_SERVER['PHP_AUTH_PW']) ||
    ($_SERVER['PHP_AUTH_USER'] != VALID_USERNAME) ||
    ($_SERVER['PHP_AUTH_PW'] != VALID_PASSWORD)) {
  header('HTTP/1.1 401 Unauthorized');
  header('WWW-Authenticate: Basic realm="The Social Site"');
  exit("You need a valid username and password to be here. " .
      "Move along, nothing to see.");
}


?>
```

Now, any script that has a require_once for *authorize.php* will cause *authorize.php* to be processed, which in turn will run the authorization code. That, in turn, will ensure that users are either logged in or are forced to log in. So, things look quite nice.

Remove this code from *show_users.php* and add a require_once for *authorize.php*:

```php
<?php

require_once '../scripts/app_config.php';
require_once '../scripts/authorize.php';
require_once '../scripts/database_connection.php';
require_once '../scripts/view.php';

// Authorization code is no longer in this script

// Build the SELECT statement
$select_users =
  "SELECT user_id, first_name, last_name, email " .
  "  FROM users";

// and so on...
?>
```

The next time you go to *show_users.php*, you get a nice login dialog box. But, that's not all this change buys you. Add a similar line into *delete_user.php*:

```php
<?php

require_once '../scripts/app_config.php';
require_once '../scripts/authorize.php';
require_once '../scripts/database_connection.php';

// and so on...
```

To test it out, close out your browser so that any passwords are lost. Then, open your browser again and navigate directly to *delete_user.php*. You'll be greeted with a login dialog box (see Figure 12-6). What's significant about this? Most obviously, all it took was a single line of PHP to add security to another page.

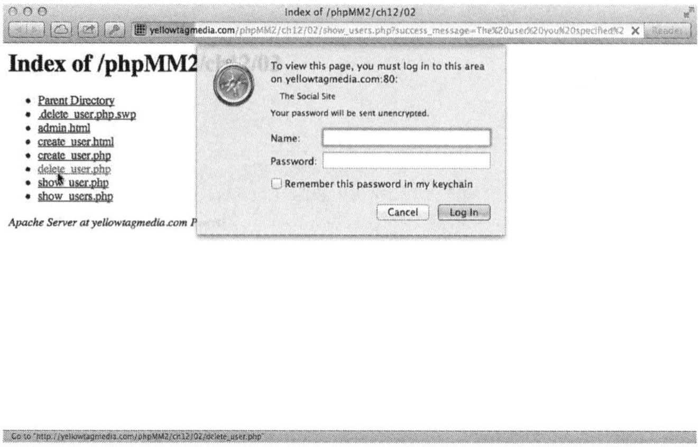

FIGURE 12-6

Once you've made it through security, you're back to seeing users again. That, of course, is the point: authentication is separate from the core content of your pages.

But there's more! If you've logged in, close out your browser again and head over to *show_users.php*. As you'd expect, you need to log in. After you've logged in, click the Delete icon on one of your users. This will take you to *delete_user.php*, and the PHP in *authorize.php* will be triggered. However, because you've already logged in to the realm identified as "The Social Site," you're not prompted to log in again. Remember your code that specifies a realm (page 387):

```
header('WWW-Authenticate: Basic realm="The Social Site"');
```

Any page that uses this realm, in effect, shares credentials with other pages in the same realm. Because you logged in to access *show_users.php*, and that realm is identical to the realm for *delete_user.php*, your delete request goes through without a problem. Figure 12-7 shows the result—no login dialog box in sight.

There's still a glaring problem, though. At this point, it's easy to forget that behind every good script lies a great database. It's a horrible idea to have a PHP script—even a utility script like *app_config.php* or *authorize.php*—contain a few constants defining allowable user names and passwords. Storing bits of information like this is the job of the database; hence the title of the next section.

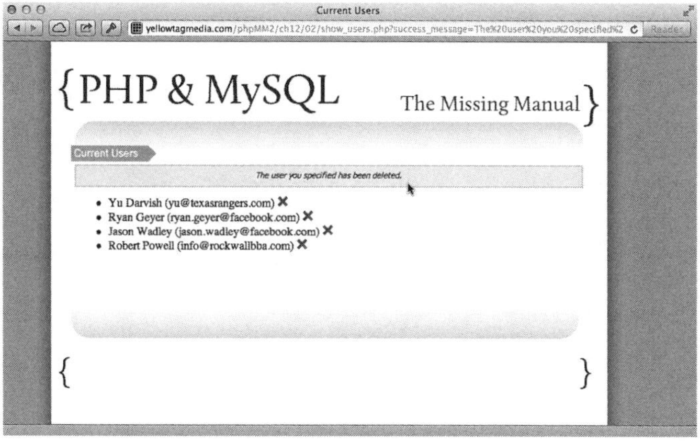

FIGURE 12-7

Sharing credentials works only if the realm is the same for these two pages. That's yet another reason to pull authentication and authorization code out of individual scripts and put it in one single place that's referenced by your other scripts. Your realm will be identical across all those referencing scripts.

Passwords Don't Belong in PHP Scripts

Databases are better for storing passwords because, among other reasons, they're typically more difficult to access than your scripts, which are to some degree web-accessible. Your database, on the other hand, is generally at least a layer further removed from the typical web user. Additionally, your database and SQL require structural knowledge to be useful. Scripts are just files that can be browsed, and often the information in those files is just text. Clearly, a database is a safer place for passwords than *authorize.php*.

NOTE   You can do a few things to make your scripts—especially utility ones—less accessible from the Web. To be certain, you can also make bad decisions that make your database *more* accessible from the Web. But in their default states, scripts are meant to be accessed by a browser, and raw database columns and rows are not, apart from a healthy authentication system.

There's yet another reason to place your passwords into a database: You're already storing user information there. You can connect that information to a password by adding a column. Moreover, as you'll see soon, groups of users aren't far away, either. Before you get too comfortable, though, you need to dig back into MySQL and improve that authentication situation.

NOTE You can find the finished example code for this section on this book's Missing CD page at *www
.missingmanuals.com/cds/phpmysqlmm2e.*

Updating the *users* Table

The first thing you need to do is update *users.* It's been a while since you've been
poking around in there, so here's a refresher as to what you should have at this
point (page 276):

```
mysql> describe users;
+----------------+----------------+------+-----+---------+----------------+
| Field          | Type           | Null | Key | Default | Extra          |
+----------------+----------------+------+-----+---------+----------------+
| user_id        | int(11)        | NO   | PRI | NULL    | auto_increment |
| first_name     | varchar(20)    | NO   |     | NULL    |                |
| last_name      | varchar(30)    | NO   |     | NULL    |                |
| email          | varchar(50)    | NO   |     | NULL    |                |
| facebook_url   | varchar(100)   | YES  |     | NULL    |                |
| twitter_handle | varchar(20)    | YES  |     | NULL    |                |
| bio            | varchar(1000)  | YES  |     | NULL    |                |
| user_pic_path  | varchar(200)   | YES  |     | NULL    |                |
+----------------+----------------+------+-----+---------+----------------+
8 rows in set (0.02 sec)
```

There's nothing wrong here, but there are some omissions: notably a user name
and a password. Those are the two essential pieces of information that your basic
authentication requires.

Use the following to add two columns to your table:

```
mysql> ALTER TABLE users
    ->         ADD username VARCHAR(32) NOT NULL
    ->      AFTER user_id,
    ->         ADD password VARCHAR(16) NOT NULL
    ->      AFTER username;
```

NOTE The AFTER keyword specifies to MySQL exactly where to add a column. This helps to prevent important
columns—and username and password are certainly important columns—from becoming stuck at the end of
a table's structure. You can leave this off, but it tends to make for more organized tables, especially when you're
using DESCRIBE.

Take a moment to verify that these changes are in place now:

```
mysql> describe users;
+----------------+---------------+------+-----+---------+----------------+
| Field          | Type          | Null | Key | Default | Extra          |
+----------------+---------------+------+-----+---------+----------------+
| user_id        | int(11)       | NO   | PRI | NULL    | auto_increment |
| username       | varchar(32)   | NO   |     | NULL    |                |
| password       | varchar(16)   | NO   |     | NULL    |                |
| first_name     | varchar(20)   | NO   |     | NULL    |                |
| last_name      | varchar(30)   | NO   |     | NULL    |                |
| email          | varchar(50)   | NO   |     | NULL    |                |
| facebook_url   | varchar(100)  | YES  |     | NULL    |                |
| twitter_handle | varchar(20)   | YES  |     | NULL    |                |
| bio            | varchar(1000) | YES  |     | NULL    |                |
| user_pic_path  | varchar(200)  | YES  |     | NULL    |                |
+----------------+---------------+------+-----+---------+----------------+
10 rows in set (0.03 sec)
```

Dealing with Newly Invalid Data

As was the case when you added columns before, you now have a table full of invalid rows. Because both user name and password are required (NOT NULL), and
none of the existing rows have values in those columns, all of your table's rows are
in violation of that table's rules.

You can fix this by using some more SQL. For example, to update Jason Wadley,
you'd use something like this:

```
mysql> UPDATE users
    ->     SET username = "jwadley",
    ->         password = "chung_moo"
    -> WHERE user_id = 21;
```

You can confirm that these changes were made, as well:

```
mysql> SELECT user_id, username, password, first_name, last_name
    ->   FROM users
    -> WHERE user_id = 21;
+---------+----------+-----------+------------+-----------+
| user_id | username | password  | first_name | last_name |
+---------+----------+-----------+------------+-----------+
|      21 | jwadley  | chung_moo | Jason      | Wadley    |
+---------+----------+-----------+------------+-----------+
1 row in set (0.00 sec)
```

You should make similar changes to your own *users* table so all the users you've
added have a user name and password.

What's in a (User) Name?

Why not just let people use an email address as the user name? It's easier for them, and it eliminates the need for an additional, new column.

It seems like every time you turn around, a new social website is popping up—a site that you simply *must* join. More and more of those sites are using email addresses as your login name. There's a lot to like about this approach:

- Most people remember their email address more readily than one of 50 different user names floating around.

- Email addresses like *tommy.n@dbc.org* are a lot more readable (and typeable) than a user name like tn1954a.

- It's one less piece of information to store in your database.

So, if that's the way the wind is blowing, why create a user name column in *users*? Why not just use the email address?

First, a lot of people have just as many email addresses as they have user names these days. With GMail, Apple's iCloud, at least one business email, and perhaps a personal domain or two, individuals can still have a hard time remembering which email address to use for login.

Second, plenty of people don't like using their email addresses as their user name. A user name seems more anonymous, whereas your email address is a way to get something into your inbox. It might seem odd, but lots of people are fine with supplying an email as part of signup, but they're not comfortable typing it into a lot of login boxes.

Perhaps the most important reason is that, if an email is the user name, how do you retrieve a user's password? Typically, with a user name system, you require a user to supply his user name when a password is lost as some sort of verification. When the user's email *is* his user name, you need to come up with a different method of verification.

Even though there's nothing wrong with using an email address, it's still a bit better to require a dedicated user name. Besides, fantastic programs like 1Password (*www.agilebits .com/products/1Password*) make it easy for your users (and you) to manage multiple logins. (Seriously, although it might seem a bit pricey at $59.99, go buy 1Password *today*. It's a web-life changer.)

> **NOTE** If something at the back of your neck tickles as you look at the user passwords, that's a good thing. It's a bad idea to store passwords in this way, where anyone with access to your database can see everyone's passwords. Don't worry, though, you're going to fix that before much longer.

Getting an Initial User Name and Password

At this juncture, you've got to go back...way back. Remember *create_user.html*? That was the rather simple HTML form that gathers the user's initial information. To be able to go forward, it needs some improvement: a user name and password field, for starters.

Here's a significantly updated version of *create_user.html*, which adds—among a lot of other things—a field in which new users can enter a user name and two fields that combine to get a password.

```html
<html>
 <head>
  <link href="../css/phpMM.css" rel="stylesheet" type="text/css" />
  <link href="../css/jquery.validate.password.css" rel="stylesheet"
        type="text/css" />
  <script type="text/javascript" src="../js/jquery-1.8.1.min.js"></script>
  <script type="text/javascript" src="../js/jquery.validate.min.js"></script>
  <script type="text/javascript"
          src="../js/jquery.validate.password.js"></script>

  <script type="text/javascript">
    $(document).ready(function() {
      $("#signup_form").validate({
        rules: {
          password: {
            minlength: 6
          },
          confirm_password: {
            minlength: 6,
            equalTo: "#password"
          }
        },
        messages: {
          password: {
            minlength: "Passwords must be at least 6 characters"
          },
          confirm_password: {
            minlength: "Passwords must be at least 6 characters",
            equalTo: "Your passwords do not match."
          }
        }
      });
    });
  </script>
 </head>

 <body>
  <div id="header"><h1>PHP & MySQL: The Missing Manual</h1></div>
  <div id="example">User Signup</div>
  <div id="content">
    <h1>Join the Missing Manual (Digital) Social Club</h1>
    <p>Please enter your online connections below:</p>
    <form id="signup_form" action="create_user.php"
          method="POST" enctype="multipart/form-data">
      <fieldset>
```

```html
      <label for="first_name">First Name:</label>
      <input type="text" name="first_name" size="20" class="required" /><br />
      <label for="last_name">Last Name:</label>
      <input type="text" name="last_name" size="20" class="required" /><br />
      <label for="username">Username:</label>
      <input type="text" name="username" size="20" class="required" /><br />
      <label for="password">Password:</label>
      <input type="password" id="password" name="password"
            size="20" class="required password" />
      <div class="password-meter">
        <div class="password-meter-message"> </div>
        <div class="password-meter-bg">
          <div class="password-meter-bar"></div>
        </div>
      </div>
      <br />
      <label for="confirm_password">Confirm Password:</label>
      <input type="password" id="confirm_password" name="confirm_password"
            size="20" class="required" /><br />
      <label for="email">E-Mail Address:</label>
      <input type="text" name="email" size="30" class="required email" /><br />
      <label for="facebook_url">Facebook URL:</label>
      <input type="text" name="facebook_url" size="50" class="url" /><br />
      <label for="twitter_handle">Twitter Handle:</label>
      <input type="text" name="twitter_handle" size="20" /><br />
      <input type="hidden" name="MAX_FILE_SIZE" value="2000000" />
      <label for="user_pic">Upload a picture:</label>
      <input type="file" name="user_pic" size="30" /><br />
      <label for="bio">Bio:</label>
      <textarea name="bio" cols="40" rows="10"></textarea>
    </fieldset>
    <br />
    <fieldset class="center">
      <input type="submit" value="Join the Club" />
      <input type="reset" value="Clear and Restart" />
    </fieldset>
  </form>
</div>

<div id="footer"></div>
</body>
</html>
```

In addition to the two new fields, this version of the form adds in some jQuery, which is available from *www.jquery.com*. jQuery is a free, downloadable JavaScript library that makes almost everything in JavaScript a lot easier. In addition to the core jQuery library, there are two jQuery plug-ins, which you can see near the top of the code: one for general validation (*jquery.validate.min.js*) and another specifically for password validation (*jquery.validate.password.js*). You can download both of these plug-ins from *www.jquery.bassistance.de*.

Save this updated version of *create_user.html* and check it out. The initial page looks the same (see Figure 12-8), but now you get validation of most of the form fields (Figure 12-9) and a nifty password-strength indicator, too (Figure 12-10).

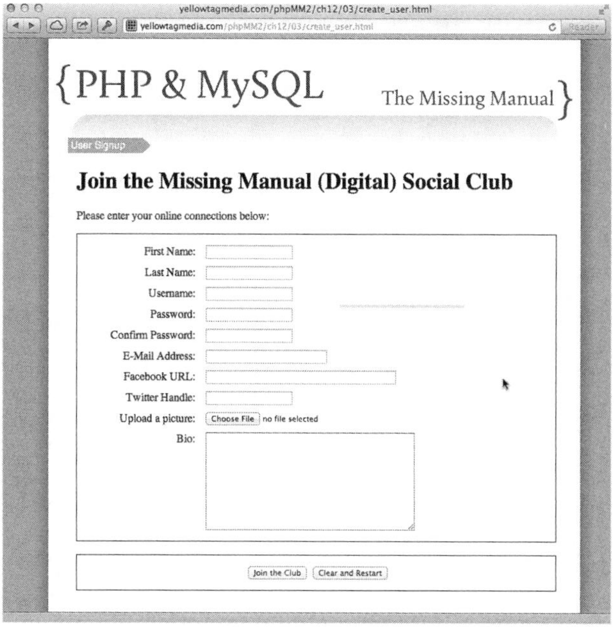

FIGURE 12-8

The new version of create_user.html looks largely the same. It adds a password strength bar, although that's not apparent until the user tries to enter a password. Most important, this form adds in a user name and two places to enter a password: an initial entry, and a place to confirm that entry. Make sure these fields are the "password" type to hide the user's typing, too.

NOTE If you're completely new to jQuery, pick up *JavaScript and jQuery: The Missing Manual* by David Sawyer McFarland (O'Reilly Media). You'll get up to speed on how to use jQuery, and a whole host of reasons—besides the nifty validation plug-ins now used by *create_user.html*—that's why it's worth your time to learn.

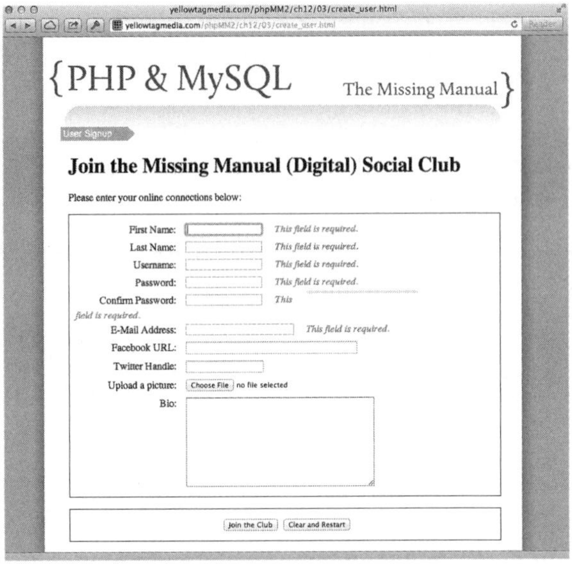

FIGURE 12-9

jQuery and the jQuery validation plug-in makes field validation a piece of cake. With minimal work, you get type validation, length validation, optionally customized error messages, and more. You can also validate emails, zip codes, and phone numbers. All that for a quick download and a few lines of JavaScript.

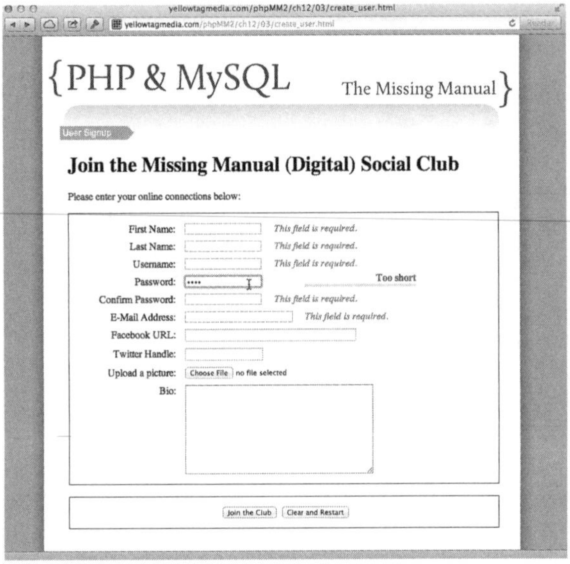

FIGURE 12-10

The password validator is an add-on for the jQuery validation plug-in. It adds a strength indicator that requires "strong" passwords. It's a nice feature, and best of all, it doesn't increase your work load at all. You get all this for free, before data ever makes it to your PHP scripts.

Now, you're getting the right information from your users. It's time to update your PHP to do something with this.

Inserting the User Name and Password

At this point, you can update *create_user.php*, as well. This update is straightforward and certainly requires a lot less work, although the result of these changes is significant.

```php
<?php

require_once '../scripts/app_config.php';
require_once '../scripts/database_connection.php';

$upload_dir = SITE_ROOT . "uploads/profile_pics/";
$image_fieldname = "user_pic";

// Potential PHP upload errors
$php_errors = array(1 => 'Maximum file size in php.ini exceeded',
                    2 => 'Maximum file size in HTML form exceeded',
                    3 => 'Only part of the file was uploaded',
                    4 => 'No file was selected to upload.');

$first_name = trim($_REQUEST['first_name']);
$last_name = trim($_REQUEST['last_name']);
$username = trim($_REQUEST['username']);
$password = trim($_REQUEST['password']);
$email = trim($_REQUEST['email']);
$bio = trim($_REQUEST['bio']);
$facebook_url = str_replace("facebook.org", "facebook.com", trim($_
REQUEST['facebook_url']));
$position = strpos($facebook_url, "facebook.com");
if ($position === false) {
  $facebook_url = "http://www.facebook.com/" . $facebook_url;
}

$twitter_handle = trim($_REQUEST['twitter_handle']);
$twitter_url = "http://www.twitter.com/";
$position = strpos($twitter_handle, "@");
if ($position === false) {
  $twitter_url = $twitter_url . $twitter_handle;
} else {
  $twitter_url = $twitter_url . substr($twitter_handle, $position + 1);
}

// Make sure we didn't have an error uploading the image
($_FILES[$image_fieldname]['error'] == 0)
```

```php
  or handle_error("the server couldn't upload the image you selected.",
                  $php_errors[$_FILES[$image_fieldname]['error']]);

// Is this file the result of a valid upload?
@is_uploaded_file($_FILES[$image_fieldname]['tmp_name'])
  or handle_error("you were trying to do something naughty. Shame on you!",
                  "Uploaded request: file named '{$_FILES[$image_fieldname]
['tmp_name']}'");

// Is this actually an image?
@getimagesize($_FILES[$image_fieldname]['tmp_name'])
  or handle_error("you selected a file for your picture that isn't an image.",
                  "{$_FILES[$image_fieldname]['tmp_name']} isn't a valid image
file.");

// Name the file uniquely
$now = time();
while (file_exists($upload_filename = $upload_dir . $now .
                                      '-' .
                                      $_FILES[$image_fieldname]['name'])) {
    $now++;
}

// Finally, move the file to its permanent location
@move_uploaded_file($_FILES[$image_fieldname]['tmp_name'],
                    $upload_filename)
  or handle_error(
      "we had a problem saving your image to its permanent location.",
      "permissions or related error moving file to {$upload_filename}");

$insert_sql = sprintf("INSERT INTO users " .
                      "(first_name, last_name, username, " .
                      "password, email, " .
                      "bio, facebook_url, twitter_handle, " .
                      "user_pic_path) " .
                      "VALUES ('%s', '%s', '%s', '%s', '%s',
                          '%s', '%s', '%s', '%s');",
                      mysql_real_escape_string($first_name),
                      mysql_real_escape_string($last_name),
                      mysql_real_escape_string($username),
                      mysql_real_escape_string($password),
                      mysql_real_escape_string($email),
                      mysql_real_escape_string($bio),
                      mysql_real_escape_string($facebook_url),
                      mysql_real_escape_string($twitter_handle),
                      mysql_real_escape_string($upload_filename));
```

```
// Insert the user into the database
mysql_query($insert_sql)
  or die(mysql_error());

// Redirect the user to the page that displays user information
header("Location: show_user.php?user_id=" . mysql_insert_id());
?>
```

> **NOTE** Even though only a few lines have changed, this is a good chance for you to check your current version of *create_user.php* (along with *create_user.html*). Make sure they're current, especially with respect to all the changes from Chapters 9 and 10 related to image handling. If you feel your code is hopelessly out of date, you can always download these scripts again from this book's Missing CD page (*www.missingmanuals.com/cds/phpmysqlmm2e*).

As usual, try entering some sample data and confirm that you get a normal *show_user.php* response as a validation that all your changes work. Also, ensure that you do not add *authorize.php* to your scripts list of require_once statements. You can hardly require users to log in to the form with which they tell your application about the user name and password they want to use for those logins.

FREQUENTLY ASKED QUESTION

There's No One Quite Like You

Shouldn't create_user.php verify that no one's already using the requested user name?

Yes. You should put the book down and write that code, right now.

In the current version of *create_user.php*, users are inserted into the database without checking whether their user names are unique. Certainly, you could enforce that at the database level, but then you'd just get a nasty error.

In its simplest form, you could do a SELECT on the desired user name, and if any users are returned, redirect the user to an error page by using handle_error. That's pretty primitive, though. It completely shuts down any flow, and the user—if she doesn't bail from your application completely—will have to enter all of her information into the user sign-in form again.

A better approach would be to convert *create_user.html* to a script, or even roll it into the current version of *create_user.php*. In either case, if the user name is already taken, the user should be redirected back to the sign-in form, with all her previous information filled in, and a message should tell her to try another user name. Then, if you want to move into the deep end of the pool, do everything above, but do it with Ajax so that the sign-in page never reloads.

So, where's the code for this? It's in your head and at your fingertips. At this stage of your PHP journey, you're increasingly ready to tackle problems like this yourself. Use a book or the Web as a resource for new techniques—like authentication in this chapter or sessions in Chapter 14—but you're plenty capable of working out new uses for things you already know on your own.

In fact, tweet a link to your solution to preventing multiple user names to *@missingmanuals* on Twitter or post it on the Missing Manuals Facebook page at *www.facebook.com/MissingManuals*. Free books, videos, and swag are always available for clever and elegant solutions.

Connect *authorize.php* to Your *users* Table

At this point, there's just one glaring hole to plug: *authorize.php*. Right now, there is only one user name and one password accepted, and they're here in this rather silly bit of constant work:

```
define(VALID_USERNAME, "admin");
define(VALID_PASSWORD, "super_secret");
```

Now, however, *authorize.php* has a *users* table from which to pull user names and passwords. Fortunately, fixing up *authorize.php* requires simply stringing together things you've already done. First, remove those two constants and add in require_once for *database_connection.php*, which you'll need for interacting with the *users* table.

```
<?php

require_once 'database_connection.php';

// define(VALID_USERNAME, "admin");          DELETE THIS LINE
// define(VALID_PASSWORD, "super_secret");  DELETE THIS LINE

if (!isset($_SERVER['PHP_AUTH_USER']) ||
    !isset($_SERVER['PHP_AUTH_PW']) ||
    ($_SERVER['PHP_AUTH_USER'] != VALID_USERNAME) ||
    ($_SERVER['PHP_AUTH_PW'] != VALID_PASSWORD)) {
  header('HTTP/1.1 401 Unauthorized');
  header('WWW-Authenticate: Basic realm="The Social Site"');
  exit("You need a valid username and password to be here. " .
      "Move along, nothing to see.");
}

?>
```

That big, burly if statement needs to be trimmed some. The first portion still works; if the $_SERVER superglobal has no value for PHP_AUTH_USER or PHP_AUTH_PW, headers should still be sent to the browser, instructing it to pop up a login dialog box. But now, there's no VALID_USERNAME or VALID_PASSWORD constant to which the user's values should be compared, so that part of the if statement has to go. Here's what should be left:

```
if (!isset($_SERVER['PHP_AUTH_USER']) ||
    !isset($_SERVER['PHP_AUTH_PW'])) {
  header('HTTP/1.1 401 Unauthorized');
  header('WWW-Authenticate: Basic realm="The Social Site"');
  exit("You need a valid username and password to be here. " .
      "Move along, nothing to see.");
}
```

NOTE Everything after the if is effectively an else, even though there's no else keyword. If the body of the if executes, it will call exit, ending the script. As a result, it's only if there is a value for PHP_AUTH_USER and PHP_AUTH_PW in $_SERVER that the rest of the script runs.

The next thing the script needs to do is to get anything the user entered—and if the script gets this far, the user *did* enter something—and compare it to values in the database. This is something you've done a number of times. It's just more sprintf and mysql_real_escape_string, both of which you've used before:

```php
<?php

require_once 'database_connection.php';

if (!isset($_SERVER['PHP_AUTH_USER']) ||
    !isset($_SERVER['PHP_AUTH_PW'])) {
  header('HTTP/1.1 401 Unauthorized');
  header('WWW-Authenticate: Basic realm="The Social Site"');
  exit("You need a valid username and password to be here. " .
      "Move along, nothing to see.");
}

// Look up the user-provided credentials
$query = sprintf("SELECT user_id, username FROM users " .
            " WHERE username = '%s' AND " .
            "      password = '%s';",
        mysql_real_escape_string(trim($_SERVER['PHP_AUTH_USER'])),
        mysql_real_escape_string(trim($_SERVER['PHP_AUTH_PW'])));

$results = mysql_query($query);

?>
```

There's nothing particularly new here; you know how to get the results. But this time, before worrying about the actual values from the response, the biggest concern is seeing whether there *are* any results. If a row matches the user name and password provided, the user is legitimate. (Or, he's borrowed someone else's credentials. And "borrowed" is being used loosely here.)

The first thing to do is to see whether there are any results. If there are none, the script has reached the same point as the earlier version, when the user name and password weren't valid. This means sending those headers again:

```php
if (mysql_num_rows($results) == 1) {
  // Everything's ok! Let this user through
} else {
  header('HTTP/1.1 401 Unauthorized');
```

```
    header('WWW-Authenticate: Basic realm="The Social Site"');
    exit("You need a valid username and password to be here. " .
        "Move along, nothing to see.");
}
```

There's just one more thing to do, and it's a bit of a nicety. Because the user has just logged in, go ahead and let any script that calls *authorize.php* have access to that newly logged-in user:

```
if (mysql_num_rows($results) == 1) {
  $result = mysql_fetch_array($results);
  $current_user_id = $result['user_id'];
  $current_username = $result['username'];
} else {
  header('HTTP/1.1 401 Unauthorized');
  header('WWW-Authenticate: Basic realm="The Social Site"');
  exit("You need a valid username and password to be here. " .
      "Move along, nothing to see.");
}
```

The entire script, new and certainly improved, looks like this:

```
<?php

require_once 'database_connection.php';

if (!isset($_SERVER['PHP_AUTH_USER']) ||
    !isset($_SERVER['PHP_AUTH_PW'])) {
  header('HTTP/1.1 401 Unauthorized');
  header('WWW-Authenticate: Basic realm="The Social Site"');
  exit("You need a valid username and password to be here. " .
      "Move along, nothing to see.");
}

// Look up the user-provided credentials
$query = sprintf("SELECT user_id, username FROM users " .
                 " WHERE username = '%s' AND " .
                 "       password = '%s';",
            mysql_real_escape_string(trim($_SERVER['PHP_AUTH_USER'])),
            mysql_real_escape_string(trim($_SERVER['PHP_AUTH_PW'])));

$results = mysql_query($query);
```

```
   if (mysql_num_rows($results) == 1) {
     $result = mysql_fetch_array($results);
     $current_user_id = $result['user_id'];
     $current_username = $result['username'];
   } else {
     header('HTTP/1.1 401 Unauthorized');
     header('WWW-Authenticate: Basic realm="The Social Site"');
     exit("You need a valid username and password to be here. " .
         "Move along, nothing to see.");
   }

   ?>
```

Test it out. Create a user (or add a user name and password to an existing user in your database), and then close and re-open your browser to reset any saved credentials. Go to *show_users.php* or any other page in which you've required *authorize.php*. You should get a login dialog box, be able to enter database values, and see the page you requested.

■ Passwords Create Security, But Should Be Secure

With your new database-driven login facility, you have lots of new possibilities. First and foremost, you can create groups in the database, and grant users access to certain parts of your application based on their group membership. For example, instead of letting just anyone into *show_users.php*, you can grant access only to users that are members of an administrator's group.

> **NOTE** You can find the finished example code for this section on this book's Missing CD page at *www.missingmanuals.com/cds/phpmysqlmm2e*.

Before you do all of that, take a second look at a sample SQL statement and its results:

```
mysql> SELECT user_id, username, password, first_name, last_name
    ->   FROM users
    ->  WHERE user_id = 45;
+---------+----------+-------------+------------+-----------+
| user_id | username | password    | first_name | last_name |
+---------+----------+-------------+------------+-----------+
|      45 | jroday   | psych_rules | James      | Roday     |
+---------+----------+-------------+------------+-----------+
1 row in set (0.00 sec)
```

Anything odd there? Well, other than James Roday's lousy choice of password. (Sure, Psych is a good show, but it's not exactly a hard-to-crack password.)

All the same, the more glaring issue is that the password just sits there in the database. It's plain-old text. Even if you're new to the world of authentication and authorization, you probably have heard the term *encryption*. Encryption is simply taking a piece of information, usually something valuable like a password, and making it unreadable for the normal mortal. The idea is that other than the user who "owns" a password, nobody—even you, the all-wise, all-knowing programmer—should see a user's password in normal text. What you need is a means of encrypting that password into something unreadable. And, you know what's coming: PHP has a function for that.

Encrypting Text by Using the `crypt` Function

First, you need to convert the password to something that's non-readable. You can do that using PHP's crypt function. This function takes a string (and an optional second parameter you'll need shortly) and produces what looks like gibberish:

```
$encrypted_password = crypt($password);
```

To see this in action, make this change to *create_user.php*:

```
$insert_sql = sprintf("INSERT INTO users " .
                      "(first_name, last_name, username, " .
                      "password, email, " .
                      "bio, facebook_url, twitter_handle, " .
                      "user_pic_path) " .
              "VALUES ('%s', '%s', '%s', '%s', '%s',
                      '%s', '%s', '%s', '%s');",
              mysql_real_escape_string($first_name),
              mysql_real_escape_string($last_name),
              mysql_real_escape_string($username),
              mysql_real_escape_string(crypt($password)),
              mysql_real_escape_string($email),
              mysql_real_escape_string($bio),
              mysql_real_escape_string($facebook_url),
              mysql_real_escape_string($twitter_handle),
              mysql_real_escape_string($upload_filename));
```

Create a new user, allow *create_user.php* to save that user, and then check out that user in your *users* table:

```
mysql> SELECT user_id, username, password, last_name
    ->   FROM users
    ->  WHERE user_id = 51;
+---------+----------+------------------+-----------+
| user_id | username | password         | last_name |
+---------+----------+------------------+-----------+
|      51 | traugott | $1$qzifqLu4$OC88 | Traugott  |
+---------+----------+------------------+-----------+
1 row in set (0.00 sec)
```

That's quite an improvement. In fact, you should probably increase the size of the password field because crypt adds a good bit of length to the originally entered password.

```
ALTER TABLE users
    CHANGE password
        password VARCHAR(50) NOT NULL;
```

NOTE That doubled password field name is intentional. When you're changing a column, you first give the original name of the column. Then, you provide the new column name, the new column type, and any modifiers (like NOT NULL). In this instance, because the original name and new name are identical, you simply double password.

That gets the password *into* your database...but what about getting it out?

crypt Is One-Way Encryption

The crypt function, by definition, is one-way encryption. This means that once a password has been encrypted, it can't be unencrypted. While that presents you some problems as a programmer, it's a good thing for your users. It means that even the administrators of the applications they use can't go digging into databases and pulling out their passwords.

Well, to be accurate, they *can*, but they'll only get an encrypted version. And there's no special formula or magical command that lets them get at the original password. Users are protected. And, ultimately, you, as an administrator, are protected. If you can't get at an encrypted password, for example, you can't very well be blamed for identity fraud.

But, how do you see whether a user has entered a valid password if you can't decrypt their password value in the database?

Easy: you can encrypt his supplied password, and compare that encrypted value to the encrypted value in the database. If the encrypted values match, things are good—and you still haven't seen that user's real password. You want something like this in *authorize.php*, in which passwords are checked:

```
// Look up the user-provided credentials
$query = sprintf("SELECT user_id, username FROM users " .
            " WHERE username = '%s' AND " .
            "       password = '%s';",
        mysql_real_escape_string(trim($_SERVER['PHP_AUTH_USER'])),
        mysql_real_escape_string(
          crypt(trim($_SERVER['PHP_AUTH_PW'])))));
```

WARNING Take your time with all of those closing parentheses. It can get hairy, and the last thing you want is a nasty, hard-to-find bug because you're one parenthesis shy.

At this point, you should be able to try things out. You're encrypting passwords on user creation, and you're encrypting the value to compare with that password on user login.

Unfortunately, try as you might, you're going to be stuck with Figure 12-11—a failed login because the password doesn't match.

So, what gives? Remember that briefly-mentioned second argument to crypt (page 415)? It's called a *salt*. A salt is a key—usually a few characters—that's used in generating the one-way encryption used by functions like crypt. The salt helps ensure the randomness and security of a password, and unless the salt matches, the encrypted password values won't match.

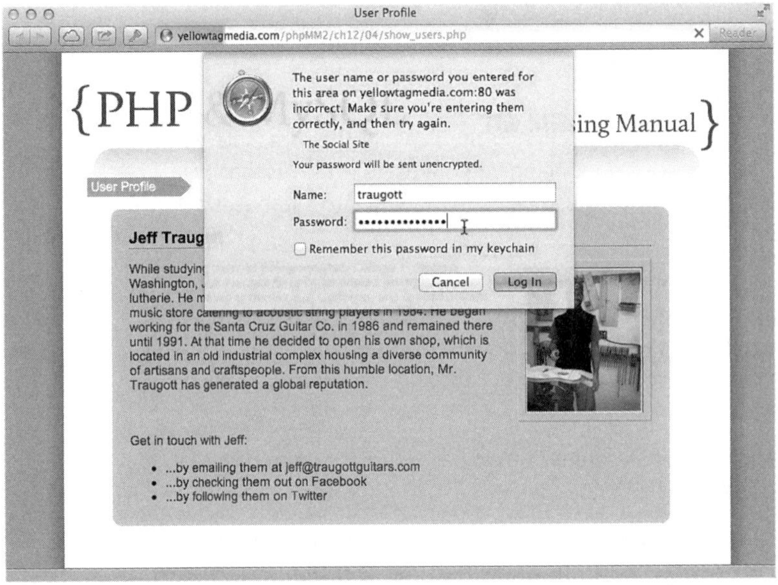

FIGURE 12-11

No, it's not groundhog day. It seems that no matter how many users you create, you'll never get past this forbidding login dialog box. There's one thing missing, and it has to do with the inner workings of crypt.

Encryption Uses Salt

So far, by not providing a salt, you've been letting crypt figure one out on its own. But unless the salt provided in two different calls to crypt is identical, the resulting encryption *will not match*. In other words, calling crypt on the same string two times without providing a salt will give you two different results.

To see it in action, create a simple script called *test_salt.php*:

```php
<?php

$input = "secret_string";
$first_output = crypt($input);
$second_output = crypt($input);
```

```
echo "First output is {$first_output}\n\n";
echo "Second output is {$second_output}\n\n";

?>
```

Run this script in your command-line terminal:

```
yellowta@yellowtagmedia.com [~/www/phpMM/ch11]# php test_salt.php
Content-type: text/html

First output is $1$9Jp.b9bG$6rLQRuAkG34msBkO9MoN51

Second output is $1$n845Ptys$Mv9s11qzZJj/xjSPSj20S0
```

Run it again, and you'll get two different results from those two.

With one change, though, things get back to what you'd expect:

```
<?php

$input = "secret_string";
$salt = "salt";
$first_output = crypt($input, $salt);
$second_output = crypt($input, $salt);

echo "First output is {$first_output}\n\n";
echo "Second output is {$second_output}\n\n";

?>
```

Now, run this updated version and smile at the results:

```
yellowta@yellowtagmedia.com [~/www/phpMM/ch11]# php test_salt.php
Content-type: text/html

First output is sazmIw2D3KJ/M

Second output is sazmIw2D3KJ/M
```

As you can see, you need to ensure that both calls to crypt in your application's scripts use the same salt. Of course, you could just create a new constant, but there's an even better solution: use the user's user name itself as the salt! This actually means you could completely lose your scripts and any constant that defines a salt, and your authentication would still work.

The user name always stays with the password, so you're essentially ensuring that they are truly a united combination.

First, update *create_user.php* (yes, one more time!) to utilize the supplied user name as a salt:

```
$insert_sql = sprintf("INSERT INTO users " .
                        "(first_name, last_name, username, " .
                        "password, email, " .
                        "bio, facebook_url, twitter_handle, " .
                        "user_pic_path) " .
                "VALUES ('%s', '%s', '%s', '%s', '%s',
                        '%s', '%s', '%s', '%s');",
                mysql_real_escape_string($first_name),
                mysql_real_escape_string($last_name),
                mysql_real_escape_string($username),
                mysql_real_escape_string(crypt($password, $username)),
                mysql_real_escape_string($email),
                mysql_real_escape_string($bio),
                mysql_real_escape_string($facebook_url),
                mysql_real_escape_string($twitter_handle),
                mysql_real_escape_string($upload_filename));
```

Now, make the exact same change in *authorize.php*. Remember in this script, the user name comes in through the $_SERVER superglobal:

```
// Look up the user-provided credentials
$query = sprintf("SELECT user_id, username FROM users " .
                " WHERE username = '%s' AND " .
                "       password = '%s';",
            mysql_real_escape_string(trim($_SERVER['PHP_AUTH_USER'])),
            mysql_real_escape_string(
                crypt(trim($_SERVER['PHP_AUTH_PW']),
                    $_SERVER['PHP_AUTH_USER'])));
```

Finally, create a new user (hopefully you're not running out of friends yet!). Then, try to log in by using that user's user name and password.

And voilà! Getting that same old *show_users.php* screen means you've got a lot more than the ability to delete users. It means you've got a solid, working authentication system. Congratulations. You've got one more big hurdle left to overcome—controlling user login with cookies.

Cookies, Sign-Ins, and Ditching Crummy Pop-Ups

I t's time to start winding down. You've gone from seeing PHP as some strange, cryptic arrangement of angle brackets and dollar signs to building your own application, including integration with a MySQL database, authentication, redirection, and a decent set of utility functions. You might not be able to sell your modest application for a million dollars. But you should have a good sense of how to think in PHP, and how scripts are structured to solve problems.

Before you can twist and bend this application and your new skills to other purposes, there are still some lingering issues that you need to handle. A few of these are nice-to-haves; and some are downright necessities if you're going to spend your career writing web applications.

Here are just a few things that you could give your application needs to round out both its usefulness and your skills:

- A better login screen. Nobody likes a bland, gray pop-up dialog box; they want a branded, styled login form.

- Better messaging to indicate whether a user is logged in.

- A way to log out.

- Two levels of authentication: one to get to the main application, and then administrator-level authentication to get to a page like *show_users.php* or *delete_user.php*.

- Some basic navigation. That navigation should change based on a user's login and the groups to which that user belongs.

These are mostly related to the idea of logging in, and that's no accident. Whether it's a good-looking login screen or the ability to group users, you'll probably spend as much time on the authentication and authorization of your web applications as you do on anything else. Even if you have boilerplate code to get a user name and password, most web pages are structured as components that are only selectively accessible. In other words, a web application shows users different things and gives users different functionality based upon their login.

It's time to get a handle on how to store user credentials, move users around your site, and the issues that underlie keeping up with a user's information. You're ready to take your programming into the real world.

Moving Beyond Basic Authentication

Right now, your authentication uses the browser's built-in HTTP capabilities. Unfortunately, as useful as HTTP authentication is, it leaves you with a lame visual; check out Figure 13-1 for the sad reminder.

FIGURE 13-1

The biggest issue with this HTTP login feature isn't its awful look and feel. It's that you don't have as much control as you'll ultimately want. For example, you can't provide a customized message if the user login fails: you have to cause the user to request a page to fire the login headers off. And ultimately, that's way too little control for someone who's comfortable with PHP—and that's definitely you by now.

Keep in mind: other than signing up initially or seeing a generic home page, this HTTP login dialog box is the doorway to much of your application. So any work you do with a top-tier designer; any nice CSS and color scheming; any clever HTML5 and SVG is all lost because it's hidden behind that annoying, gray dialog box. Even worse, when the user doesn't get in, it *keeps* popping up.

But changing that takes more than changing one thing. It's going to require a complete rework of how users access your site.

NOTE You can find the finished example code for this section on this book's Missing CD page at *www.missingmanuals.com/cds/phpmysqlmm2e.*

Starting with a Landing Page

Any site that requires a login has to give users somewhere to land before they hit the login page. To build out your site, you need something simple and effective as a central location for your users to begin. From this starting point they should be able to log in or create a new login.

Here's a simple version of just that. Call it *index.html* so that it can eventually be your site's default landing page:

```
<html>
 <head>
  <link href="../css/phpMM.css" rel="stylesheet" type="text/css" />
 </head>

 <body>
  <div id="header"><h1>PHP & MySQL: The Missing Manual</h1></div>
  <div id="content">
    <div id="home_banner"></div>
    <div id="signup">
      <a href="create_user.html"><img src="../images/sign_me_up.png" /></a>
      <a href="signin.html"><img src="../images/sign_me_in.png" /></a>
    </div>
  </div>

  <div id="footer"></div>
 </body>
</html>
```

You can see what the page looks like in Figure 13-2.

Signing up users is easy: just point them over to *create_user.html* and let the work you've already done take effect. But that link to *signin.html* creates a new set of questions to answer, first and foremost among them: What exactly needs to happen there to sign a user in?

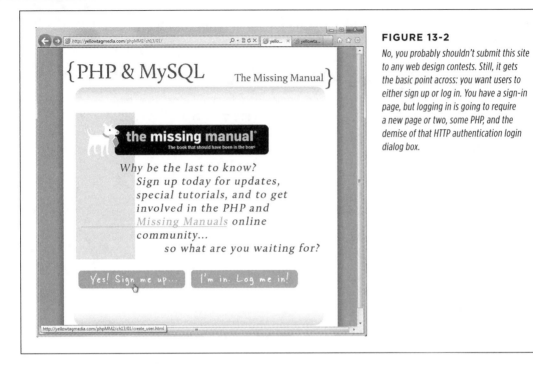

FIGURE 13-2

No, you probably shouldn't submit this site to any web design contests. Still, it gets the basic point across: you want users to either sign up or log in. You have a sign-in page, but logging in is going to require a new page or two, some PHP, and the demise of that HTTP authentication login dialog box.

Taking Control of User Sign Ins

Obviously, there needs to be a form into which users can enter information. And the way things have been going, that form should submit to a script, which checks the user name and password. Already, that's different from what you have: currently, authentication happens as a sort of side effect of requesting a page that requires *authorize.php*. So far, there's no explicit login form, but now there needs to be one.

Then, this script that receives information from the form login has to check the user's credentials. That's easy; *authorize.php* already does that, and even though it currently uses $_SERVER, it's easy to change to accept input from a sign-in form. Wait, though, here's another wrinkle: if the credentials aren't good, then you need to display the sign-in form again, preferably with the user's original input for user name, or at a minimum, a message stating that there was an error logging in.

> **NOTE** There's nothing as frustrating as a login form that sits staring blank-faced at you, never telling you that it's received your credentials and that they were rejected. User feedback is critical in any good login system.

So here's the basic flow:

1. **Sign-in form (HTML): Takes in the user name and password.** Submits to...

2. **Authentication script (PHP): Verifies the user name and password against the database.** If there's a match take the user to a secure page, like the user's profile (*show_user.php*), and let her know that she's logged in. If her credentials are not valid, take her back to...

3. **Sign-in form (HTML)**

Here's a problem: How can an HTML form display an error message on a particular condition or pre-insert the contents of a user name field?

Having that sign-in form as HTML limits you, not on its initial display, but for the situation in which there's a login failure. It's then that you want PHP on your side.

The obvious solution is to convert the sign-in page to PHP, and you'd end up with a flow like the following (the changes are highlighted in bold Italic):

1. **Sign-in form (PHP): Takes in the user name and password.** Submits to...

2. **Authentication script (PHP): Verifies the user name and password against the database.** If there's a match take her to a secure page, like the user's profile (*show_user.php*), and let her know that she's logged in. If her credentials are not valid, take her back to...

3. **Sign-in form (PHP): *Now this form displays a customized error and reloads the user name.***

Why not take this even further? What if instead of two scripts, you had a single script that submitted to itself, and either redirected the user on successful login, or displayed itself again if the login was unsuccessful? (If the idea of a script submitting to itself sounds like something you'd see in the movie *Inception*, see the box on page 424.)

By the way, you'll need to make a quick change to your site's new home page before you forget. Because you're using a script not just for processing logins, but for creating the login page itself, do that now before you're neck deep into PHP:

```html
<html>
 <head>
  <link href="../css/phpMM.css" rel="stylesheet" type="text/css" />
 </head>

 <body>
  <div id="header"><h1>PHP & MySQL: The Missing Manual</h1></div>
  <div id="content">
    <div id="home_banner"></div>
    <div id="signup">
      <a href="create_user.html"><img src="../images/sign_me_up.png" /></a>
      <a href="signin.php"><img src="../images/sign_me_in.png" /></a>
    </div>
  </div>
</div>
```

```
<div id="footer"></div>
  </body>
</html>
```

PHP Loves to Self-Reference

Up until now, you've had a strong distinction between forms—created in HTML files—and the scripts to which they submit—PHP. But, you've torn down that distinction in view pages. You have lots of scripts that do some programming—logging in a user; getting all the current users; or looking up a particular user—and then outputting a bunch of HTML.

Why not blow that distinction away in forms, too?

A script could output a form and set the action of that form as itself. Then, when the form is recalled, it would determine whether there's any submitted data. If so, this means that it's receiving a form submission and can do what it needs to programmatically. There's no real magic here; all you need is an if statement that directs traffic. Inside that if, you could even output a completely different page, perhaps letting the user know that his data has been accepted.

What if there's no submission data? Well, then it's just a normal initial request for the form, so the form should be shown. But you get some nice benefits here, too. You can check whether there might be error messages or existing data from a previous submission, and drop those values right into your form.

This technique is extremely common in PHP. It's something with which you want to become comfortable. Even though it's a bit of heavy lifting the first few times, you'll soon find that in a PHP-driven application, there are very few times when you're *not* going to use a PHP script. Forms, error pages, login pages, even welcome pages...you'll get hooked on having the ability to use PHP and be hard-pressed to go back.

At this point, you might be dying inside—well, that is if you love or have bought into the Model-View-Controller (MVC) pattern, that is. HTML inside a script that submits to itself means you've completely eradicated a wall (or even a large overgrown hedge) between the model, the view, and the controller. But as you've already seen, you're not going to get a true MVC pattern working well in PHP, anyway. You can get an approximation (and don't shy away from that approximation), but you're just not going to get the really clean separation that's possible in languages like Ruby or Java (and you can still make just as big a mess in those languages, in case you were wondering).

Given that, you might need to simply accept that PHP is often going to cause you to sacrifice really clean MVC at the altar of getting things done.

From HTTP Authentication to Cookies

Before you can dive into writing this sign-in script—call it *signin.php*—there's another glaring issue to work out. How do you actually let the user log in? By abandoning that HTTP login dialog box, you're taking logging into your own hands.

Getting the user name and password and checking them against the database is not a big deal. You can do that; and you will do that in *signin.php*. The big problem, however, is keeping that information around. With HTTP authentication, the browser kept up with all your pages being in one realm and whether the user was logged into that realm. As a result, after logging in and accessing *show_users.php*, a user did not have to log in to get to *delete_user.php*; she would already have done that for another page in the same realm.

This is where cookies come into play.

NOTE Here's where you usually get the obligatory baked-goods joke. *Cookies* is a strange term, one that refers back to something called *magic cookies*. That was a term old-school Unix hackers used for little bits of data passed back and forth between programs.

Well, it stuck, so if you're new to cookies in the programming world, feel free to snicker as you read the rest of this chapter.

■ WHAT IS A COOKIE?

A cookie is nothing magical at all. It's simply a means by which you can store a single piece of information on your user's computer. A cookie has a name, a value—that single piece of information—and a date on which the cookie expires. When the cookie expires, it's gone; you can no longer retrieve the value.

You can have a cookie with a name "username" and a value "my_username," and perhaps another cookie named "user_id" with a value of "52." Then, your scripts can check whether there's a "username" cookie, and if so, assume the user's logged in. In the same manner, your login script can set a "username" cookie.

In other words, other than setting the cookie in the first place, you get the same sort of effect as you were getting with basic authentication. Of course, creation of cookies is within your control, so you can create them with your own form, delete them with your scripts (say, on a user logout), and issue messages based on the status of cookies.

WARNING Although you can control the creation of cookies, your users can easily modify them, delete them, and even create cookies of their own. Because of that, cookies aren't ideal for the sort of information you're storing in them for our purposes here: secure user name and passwords.

That's why there's a Chapter 14. Have no fear; even though you'll change the manner in which you use cookies, everything you're learning here will be important in your final authentication solution. Besides, there are plenty of times when cookies are helpful, and they'll be a staple of your programming toolkit.

■ CREATE AND RETRIEVE COOKIES

You're almost ready to jump into scripting again, and that's where all the fun is. (It's certainly not as much fun reading about code as it is writing code.) All that's left is to learn how to write cookies and then look them up and get their values. Thankfully, PHP makes this as simple as working with the superglobals with which you've already become accustomed: $_SERVER and $_REQUEST.

To set a cookie, you simply call setcookie and supply the cookie's name and value:

```
setcookie("username", "my_username");
```

Once a cookie is set, you retrieve the value you just set with the $_COOKIE superglobal:

```
echo "You are signed in as " . $_COOKIE['username'] . ".";
```

It's that simple. Sure, there are some wrinkles here and there, and you'll add a bit of nuance to your cookie creation, but if you have setcookie and $_COOKIE down, you're ready to roll.

> **NOTE** One of those nuances that you might already be thinking about is the cookie's expiration value. You can pass that as a third value to setcookie, but for now, don't concern yourself with it.

■ Logging In with Cookies

You know what cookies are, and you know the flow of the sign-in form. Now, it's time to write some code. Create *signin.php* and start with the basic outline:

```php
<?php

require_once '../scripts/database_connection.php';
require_once '../scripts/view.php';

// If the user is logged in, the user_id cookie will be set
if (!isset($_COOKIE['user_id'])) {

  // See if a login form was submitted with a username for login
  if (isset($_REQUEST['username'])) {
    // Try and log the user in
    $username = mysql_real_escape_string(trim($_REQUEST['username']));
    $password = mysql_real_escape_string(trim($_REQUEST['password']));

    // Look up the user

    // If user not found, issue an error
  }

  // Still in the "not signed in" part of the if
  // Start the page, and we know there's no success or error message
  //    since they're just logging in
  page_start("Sign In");
?>

<html>
  <div id="content">
    <h1>Sign In to the Club</h1>
    <form id="signin_form" action="signin.php" method="POST">
      <fieldset>
        <label for="username">Username:</label>
        <input type="text"  name="username" id="username" size="20" />
```

```
        <br />
        <label for="password">Password:</label>
        <input type="password"  name="password" id="password" size="20" />
      </fieldset>
      <br />
      <fieldset class="center">
        <input type="submit" value="Sign In" />
      </fieldset>
    </form>
  </div>
  <div id="footer"></div>
 </body>
</html>

<?php
} else {
  // Now handle the case where they're logged in
  // redirect to another page, most likely show_user.php
}
?>
```

> **NOTE** Did you notice that *database_connection.php* is required for logging the user in but *app_config.php* isn't? You can include *app_config.php* because there's a good chance that you'll need it at some point, but you might also remember that *database_connection.php* actually requires *app_config.php* itself. So, if you require *database_connection.php*, you really get a `require_once` for *app_config.php* for free.

This script is far from complete and has several problems, but it's still a lot of code. Let's take it piece by piece.

> **NOTE** You can find the finished example code for this section on this book's Missing CD page at *www .missingmanuals.com/cds/phpmysqlmm2e.*

Determining Whether the User Is Already Signed In

Even if a user comes to your sign-in page explicitly, you shouldn't make him sign in if he's already in. So the first thing to do (other than a few `require_once` lines) is establish whether the "user_id" cookie is set. If it's not, the user is not logged in, and everything flows from there.

```
<?php

require_once '../scripts/database_connection.php';
require_once '../scripts/view.php';

// If the user is logged in, the user_id cookie will be set
if (!isset($_COOKIE['user_id'])) {
```

Here's your first clue that cookies aren't much different than what you've already been using: you can use isset to see if it's already created and then you just pass in the cookie name. Piece of cake.

Is the User Trying to Sign In?

If the "user_id" cookie isn't set, the user is not logged in. The next thing to check, then, is whether he's *trying* to log in. This would mean that you have some request information. In fact, the user might have filled out the HTML form already (later in this script) and submitted that form back to this script.

However, that's not the same as trying to access this script without any information. In that case, the user should just get the regular HTML sign-in form. As a result you can see whether there's a submission by checking if there's anything in the $_REQUEST superglobal for "username," a field from the sign in form:

```
// See if a login form was submitted with a username for login
if (isset($_REQUEST['username'])) {
  // Try and log the user in
  $username = mysql_real_escape_string(trim($_REQUEST['username']));
  $password = mysql_real_escape_string(trim($_REQUEST['password']));

  // Look up the user

  // If user not found, issue an error
}
```

If there's request data, you can get the user name and password that have been submitted, and (in a moment) look up the user and deal with any problems.

Before you do that, though, there's a nice change you can make. So far, you've been using $_REQUEST for everything. It takes in GET requests—which are requests where information is passed through the URL—and POST requests, like the ones that most of your forms have issued. But, you already know that the only way information should get to this stage is by a submission from your own form, which will use a POST request.

It would probably be better to replace $_REQUEST with a more specific superglobal: $_POST, which only has request data from a POST request.

> **NOTE** As you've probably already guessed, $_POST has a counterpart for GET requests: $_GET. For more detail on the differences, see the box on page 429.

It's a good idea to begin moving toward the more specific $_POST when possible. POST data prohibits parameters on the request URL, and it's generally a bit more secure.

Make that small change to your script:

```
// See if a login form was submitted with a username for login
if (isset($_POST['username'])) {
  // Try and log the user in
  $username = mysql_real_escape_string(trim($_REQUEST['username']));
  $password = mysql_real_escape_string(trim($_REQUEST['password']));

  // Look up the user

  // If user not found, issue an error
}
```

FREQUENTLY ASKED QUESTION

Post It or Get It?

$_REQUEST, $_POST, and $_GET all seem to do the same thing: take in a value. How do I know which one to use?

Ahh, yes, another quibble over which programmers can argue, demonize, and distort. No matter what you hear, there's just no functional difference between $_REQUEST, $_GET, and $_POST in terms of getting request information. $_REQUEST will always have what's in both $_GET and $_POST, but if you know you've got a POST request, you don't gain or lose anything by using $_REQUEST over $_POST.

In fact, not only does $_REQUEST have the combined values from $_GET and $_POST, it has the contents of $_COOKIE in it too (at least by default). Technically, you could do this in *signin.php*:

```
// If the user is logged in, the
//  user_id cookie will be set
if (!isset($_REQUEST['user_id'])) {
```

In other words, you could use $_REQUEST and totally ditch $_GET, $_REQUEST, and $_COOKIE. But, think back to all the programming principles you've been learning: make your code clear and readable; be specific over being just generic; and think about what those who have to work with your code after you will see. For all of those reasons, although $_REQUEST isn't bad, it's often helpful to use $_GET and $_POST and $_COOKIE when that's what you're dealing with.

In the case of *signin.php*, you know you're getting a POST request. Given that, use $_POST when you can. If you know you're getting a GET request, use $_GET. And if you're looking for a cookie, use $_COOKIE. Your code will be clearer and more specific, and most of all, you'll know exactly what it's intended to do.

Displaying the Page

Whether the user got to this page by submitting incorrect credentials or by submitting no credentials at all, she should see a form. You're now ready to display some HTML.

NOTE If the user logs in successfully, your code will need to redirect her elsewhere. Therefore, that code
block that checks user names and passwords needs to eventually forward the user on to another location if her
login is successful.

```php
    // Still in the "not signed in" part of the if
    // Start the page, and we know there's no success or error message
    //    since they're just logging in
    page_start("Sign In");
?>

<html>
  <div id="content">
    <h1>Sign In to the Club</h1>
    <form id="signin_form" action="signin.php" method="POST">
      <fieldset>
        <label for="username">Username:</label>
        <input type="text"  name="username" id="username" size="20" />
        <br />
        <label for="password">Password:</label>
        <input type="password"  name="password" id="password" size="20" />
      </fieldset>
      <br />
      <fieldset class="center">
        <input type="submit" value="Sign In" />
      </fieldset>
    </form>
  </div>
  <div id="footer"></div>
 </body>
</html>
```

Don't miss that opening comment block; it's an important one. This code, including
the HTML, is all still part of the opening if block:

```php
// If the user is logged in, the user_id cookie will be set
if (!isset($_COOKIE['user_id'])) {
```

In other words, all of this HTML is shown if, and only if, the user is not logged in.

There's another small improvement you can make here, in the same vein as using
$_POST instead of $_REQUEST. Take a look at this line:

```php
<form id="signin_form" action="signin.php" method="POST">
```

This line instructs the form to submit to the same script that's generating the form.
There's nothing wrong with it, but what if you were to rename *signin.php*? It might
be a remote possibility, but all the same, it's not unrealistic. (It wasn't that long ago

that you moved away from calling a script *admin.php* and instead went with the more functionally named *delete_user.php* and *show_users.php*.)

Remember that PHP loves this script-submitting-to-script paradigm. In fact, just to make it a bit easier, there's a property in $_SERVER that furnishes the current script name. No, it's not there just for self-referential scripts, but it sure does help. Update *signin.php* to take advantage of $_SERVER['PHP_SELF']:

```
<form id="signin_form"
      action="<?php echo $_SERVER['PHP_SELF']; ?>"
      method="POST">
```

With this addition, the form submits, literally, to itself. A small change, but a good one, and one you'll find yourself coming back to over and over again.

Redirecting as Needed

The only thing left, at least in this pseudocode version, is to redirect the user if she's logged in:

```
<?php
} else {
  // Now handle the case where they're logged in
  // redirect to another page, most likely show_user.php
}
?>
```

You have the basic flow, but there's loads of stuff missing. Time to dig in and start piecing this code into a usable form. (For more advice on how to get started, see the following box.)

POWER USERS' CLINIC

Pseudocode with Comments and Real Code

It might seem strange to think of *signin.php* as it currently exists as pseudocode, but that's just what it is. It's certainly not a complete working script; there are numerous holes through which you could drive a truck. Fortunately, those holes are generally indicated with a helpful, clear comment. Although those comments don't do anything programmatically, they do remind you of *what* you need to do and *where* you need to do it.

Truth be told, pseudocode is often best done in just this way. You're not wasting time writing non-existent function names

like check_the_user_credentials(). But you're accomplishing the same goal with comments like:

```
// Look up the user
```

```
// If user not found, issue an error
```

Those comments are just as useful, and they can stay put as you write code *under* each comment that fills out the script's functionality.

Before you begin, though, you can already get a good idea of this flow. Right now, a non-logged-in user will get the HTML output, without all the PHP that runs when there's a user name coming in through a POST request. As a result, Figure 13-3 is the default view, so to speak.

When you try to submit the form—with a good or bad user name—you get the same form over again. Not so great, but it's a place to start, and you can begin to tackle each individual piece of functionality.

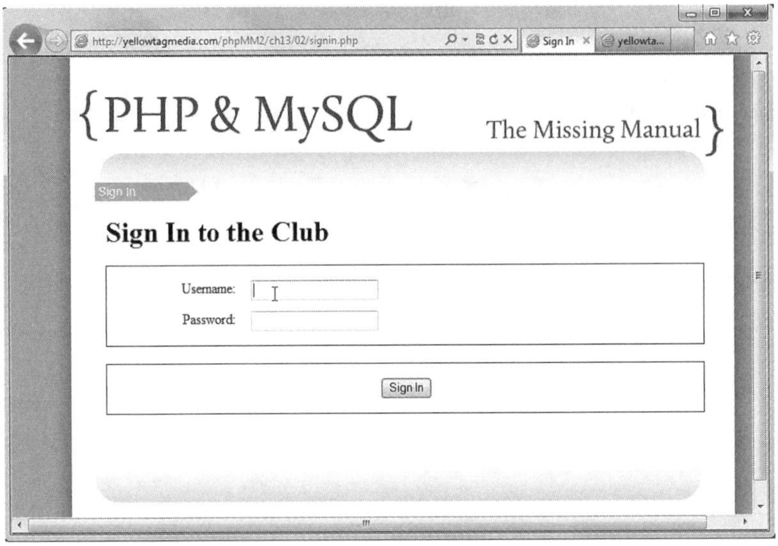

FIGURE 13-3

It might seem a bit odd, but the same PHP script that checks login credentials now grabs them from your users. This is just a simple HTML form, because there's no user_id *cookie and no user name in the POST data.*

Logging In the User

The next bit of code is nothing more than a copy-paste-and-modify job from *authorize.php.* Here's where that script left off:

```php
// Look up the user-provided credentials
$query = sprintf("SELECT user_id, username FROM users " .
                 " WHERE username = '%s' AND " .
                 "       password = '%s';",
              mysql_real_escape_string(trim($_SERVER['PHP_AUTH_USER'])),
              mysql_real_escape_string(
                crypt(trim($_SERVER['PHP_AUTH_PW']),
                    $_SERVER['PHP_AUTH_USER']))));

$results = mysql_query($query);

if (mysql_num_rows($results) == 1) {
  $result = mysql_fetch_array($results);
  $current_user_id = $result['user_id'];
  $current_username = $result['username'];
} else {
  header('HTTP/1.1 401 Unauthorized');
  header('WWW-Authenticate: Basic realm="The Social Site"');
```

```
      exit("You need a valid username and password to be here. " .
          "Move along, nothing to see.");
  }
```

Pretty good, although it all depends on HTTP authentication. Now, you can drop that into *signin.php*, change the successful block to set some cookies, and redirect somewhere useful:

```php
<?php

require_once '../scripts/database_connection.php';
require_once '../scripts/view.php';

// If the user is logged in, the user_id cookie will be set
if (!isset($_COOKIE['user_id'])) {

  // See if a login form was submitted with a username for login
  if (isset($_POST['username'])) {
    // Try and log the user in
    $username = mysql_real_escape_string(trim($_REQUEST['username']));
    $password = mysql_real_escape_string(trim($_REQUEST['password']));

    // Look up the user
    $query = sprintf("SELECT user_id, username FROM users " .
                    " WHERE username = '%s' AND " .
                    "       password = '%s';",
                    $username, crypt($password, $username));

    $results = mysql_query($query);

    if (mysql_num_rows($results) == 1) {
      $result = mysql_fetch_array($results);
      $user_id = $result['user_id'];
      setcookie('user_id', $user_id);
      setcookie('username', $result['username']);
      header("Location: show_user.php");
      exit();
    } else {
      // If user not found, issue an error
    }
  }

  // Still in the "not signed in" part of the if
  // Start the page, and we know there's no success or error message
  //    since they're just logging in
  page_start("Sign In");
?>
```

Open up *signin.php*, and you should see the login form (refer back to Figure 13-3 to ensure that you're on the right page with the right HTML). Use some valid credentials, and you should successfully log in, have a cookie set, and be passed over to *show_user.php* (see Figure 13-4).

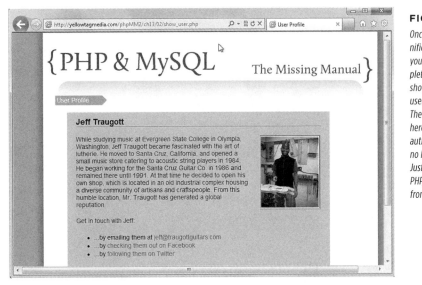

FIGURE 13-4

Once again, victory is signified by getting to a page you've long since completed. Here, it's getting to show_user.php with the user who just logged in. There's no browser magic here (well, not in the authentication bit), and no HTTP authentication. Just good old-fashioned PHP, MySQL, and some help from cookies.

Did you notice anything odd in that last bit of redirection? Here's the line where the redirect is sent to the browser:

```
if (mysql_num_rows($results) == 1) {
  $result = mysql_fetch_array($results);
  $user_id = $result['user_id'];
  setcookie('user_id', $user_id);
  setcookie('username', $result['username']);
  header("Location: show_user.php");
  exit();
} else {
  // If user not found, issue an error
}
```

If no bells are ringing, check out *create_user.php* (page 214). That script creates a user and redirects her to *show_user.php*. Here's the relevant line:

```
header("Location: show_user.php?user_id=" . mysql_insert_id());
```

Here, additional information is sent: the user_id of the user to display, sent as a GET parameter within the request URL. However, in *signin.php*, there's no user_id parameter. Figure 13-4 confirms that things work.

All the same, *show_user.php* expects that information:

```
// Get the user ID of the user to show
$user_id = $_REQUEST['user_id'];
```

So, how does this work in *signin.php*? The answer lies in how $_REQUEST works and what information it contains. For starters, read the box on page 429 if you haven't already. You're setting a cookie in *signin.php*, and that cookie is accessible through the $_COOKIE superglobal. But, $_REQUEST also contains what's in $_COOKIE—along with what's in $_POST and $_GET. As a result, this

```
$user_id = $_REQUEST['user_id'];
```

is actually just as good as the following for getting the value in a cookie:

```
$user_id = $_COOKIE['user_id'];
```

> **NOTE** The obvious question is, "Which should you use: $_COOKIE or $_REQUEST? As usual, it depends. Here, if you switch to $_COOKIE, you'll need to update *create_user.php*. It might be best to leave this as $_REQUEST, at least for now, because it makes *show_user.php* a little more flexible. It accepts request parameters and cookies, and that's a nice thing. Later, if you move to using only cookies, you can update *show_user.php* to use $_COOKIE and be more specific.

Blank Pages and Expiring Cookies

At some point as you're trying things out, you might get a strange response. You enter in *signin.php* in your URL bar, you press enter, and you end up with a blank page, like the one in Figure 13-5.

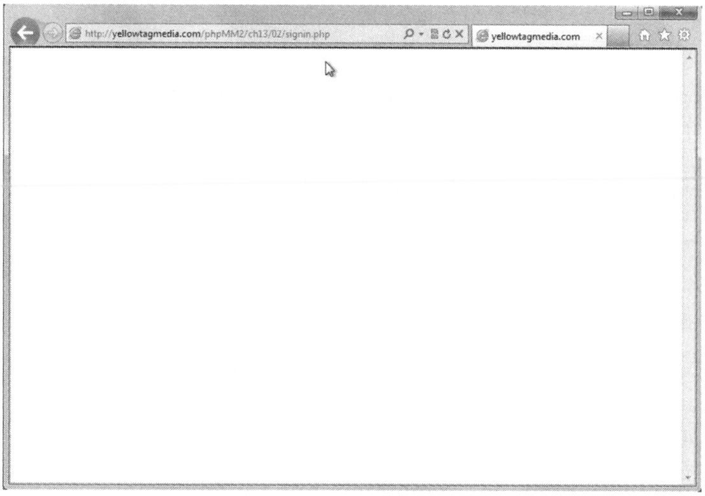

FIGURE 13-5

Nobody said that testing authentication wasn't a hassle. This blank screen actually means that your login and cookie setting are working. Clearly, this can't be right. The answer lies in the fact that you're once again stuck in a loop, as you'll see on the next few pages.

You try it again. You try to reload. You try to clear your cache. Nothing! Finally, you restart your browser, and things start to behave. But no sooner have you signed in through *signin.php* than it's happening again. What's up?

Actually, this is a sign that things are working *correctly*. Remember that in your script, the first conditional checks for a cookie:

```php
// If the user is logged in, the user_id cookie will be set
if (!isset($_COOKIE['user_id'])) {
```

If this cookie is set, the script jumps all the way down to this bit at the bottom of your file:

```php
<?php
} else {
  // Now handle the case where they're logged in
  // redirect to another page, most likely show_user.php
}
?>
```

There's nothing there, so you get a blank browser. You can fix this (kind of) by setting up a default action for users who are sent to *signin.php* and yet are already logged in. In fact, it's the same thing you did earlier for a login: redirect them to *show_user.php*:

```php
} else {
  // Now handle the case where they're logged in
  header("Location: show_user.php");
  exit();
}
```

Now, there's no more blank screen. Your *show_user.php* script picks up on the "user_id" cookie and shows the currently logged-in user. Good, right?

Well, sort of. It still leaves you in an endless loop. It's just that now you're looping on the nice looking *show_user.php* rather than a crummy-looking blank page. You'll need to completely close out your browser to stop the madness—which is exactly as it should be. Just as when you logged in via HTTP authentication, logging in and setting a cookie sets that cookie to exist until the browser is closed.

> **NOTE** The default value for the third parameter of setcookie is "0". This means that the cookie expires at the end of the user's session, which is when the user closes his browser.

If you need to get out of this loop, just close your browser. Be sure to close the program, not just the current tab or window. This will cause a cookie that has a default expiration value to expire.

To set the cookie to last longer (or shorter), just pass a third parameter to setcookie. That third parameter should be expressed in the number of seconds from what Unix and Linux systems call the *epoch*, January 1, 1970, at 0:00 GMT. You usually pass in time, which gives the current time—also in seconds since the epoch—and then add to that. Thus, time() + 10 would be 10 seconds in the future, as reckoned from the epoch.

Here are just a few examples of setcookie with a set expiration time:

```
// Expire in an hour (60 seconds * 60 minutes = 3600)
setcookie('user_id', $user_id, time() + 3600);

// This actually deletes the cookie, since it indicates an
//   expiration in the past
setcookie('user_id', $user_id, time() - 3600);

// The default: expire on browser close
setcookie('user_id', $user_id, 0);
```

You can also supply a time via mktime, which takes an hour, date, second, month, day, and year, and returns the number of seconds since the epoch (again); therefore

```
setcookie('user_id', $user_id, mktime(0, 0, 0, 2, 1, 2021);
```

sets a cookie to expire on February 1, 2021, GMT. That's a little far away, wouldn't you say? In general, the default value is perfectly reasonable. Most users are comfortable signing in again when their browser closes. In fact, many users would *not* be comfortable with their login lasting on and on, potentially in perpetuity.

> **NOTE**   The notable exceptions here are sites like Facebook and Twitter that don't contain a lot of valuable user information. By contrast, most financial sites like banks don't even wait for your browser to close; they'll force your session to expire every 10 minutes or so.

Close your browser, which will terminate your cookies, and open *signin.php* again for some more improvement.

Errors Aren't Always Interruptive

At this juncture, you have a potential error with which you must deal: the else that's run when the user's user name and password don't match that which is in the database:

```
if (mysql_num_rows($results) == 1) {
  // set a cookie and redirect to show_user.php
} else {
  // If user not found, issue an error
}
```

Your typical error handling so far has been via handle_error. But that's no good; you don't want to short-circuit the login process by throwing the user out to an error page. She would have to get back to the login page, try again, and potentially go to the error page yet again.

What you need is a means by which you can show any errors without interrupting the application's overall flow. When something goes badly wrong, handle_error makes perfect sense; a major error deserves to interrupt your application. But here, you need a non-interruptive way to show errors.

You *do* in fact have another way to show errors: the page_start function in *view .php*. Right now, you're calling this function in *signin.php*, but without anything apart from the page title:

```
page_start("Sign In");
```

Back in *view.php* (page 379), you can see the complete set of arguments this method takes:

```
function page_start($title, $javascript = NULL,
                    $success_message = NULL, $error_message = NULL) {
```

Normally, you've been passing in any request parameters as the values for $success_message and $error_message, but that's not a requirement. You can create a new variable called $error_message, fill it with text as your script progresses, and then hand it off to page_start as the HTML output commences.

Here's what you need to add:

```php
<?php

require_once '../scripts/database_connection.php';
require_once '../scripts/view.php';

$error_message = "";

// If the user is logged in, the user_id cookie will be set
if (!isset($_COOKIE['user_id'])) {

  // See if a login form was submitted with a username for login
  if (isset($_POST['username'])) {
    // Try and log the user in

    // Look up the user

    if (mysql_num_rows($results) == 1) {
      $result = mysql_fetch_array($results);
      $user_id = $result['user_id'];
      setcookie('user_id', $user_id);
      setcookie('username', $result['username']);
      header("Location: show_user.php");
      exit();
    } else {
      // If user not found, issue an error
```

```
      $error_message = "Your username/password combination was invalid.";
    }
  }

  // Still in the "not signed in" part of the if
  // Start the page, and pass along any error message set earlier
  page_start("Sign In", NULL, NULL, $error_message);
?>

<!-- Rest of HTML output -->

<?php
} else {
  // Now handle the case where they're logged in
  // redirect to another page, most likely show_user.php
  header("Location: show_user.php");
  exit();
}
?>
```

> **WARNING** Remember, this cookie-based solution is a step toward a final solution, but it is not the final solution itself. In the next chapter, you'll add support for sessions and move information like a user name and user ID out of a user's cookie and onto the server.
>
> Whatever you do, keep reading! You'll need the cookie skills you're learning here, but you'll add session support to those skills in the next chapter. Woe be the PHP programmer who uses cookies, and only cookies, for authentication.

Now visit *signin.php* (or *index.html* and click the Sign Up button). Uh oh! Figure 13-6 reveals there's still a problem somewhere.

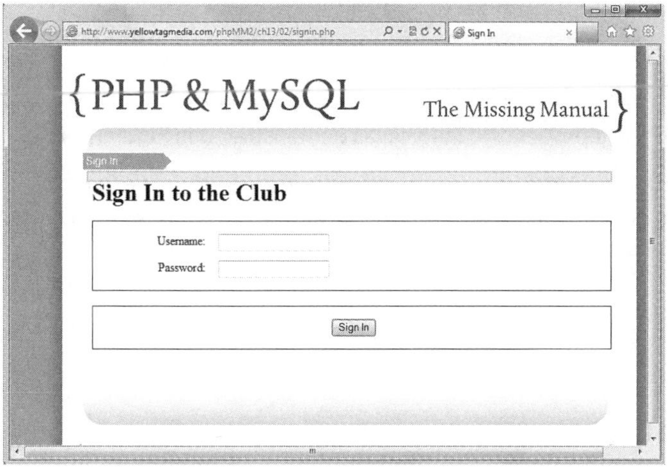

FIGURE 13-6

That's a strange sight: an error-less error. But, because this is probably the second screen all of your users will ever see, it's a big issue. Still, by now, you're probably already thinking about what the problem is and how you'll fix it quickly.

This predicament is typical of application work. You take a function you wrote ages ago—the code in *view.php* that shows an error, in this case—and then use it in a different way later. That's when the bugs appear.

In this case, the problem is that you're calling page_start with $error_message, but in some cases, $error_message is blank. It's an empty string, "", so nothing should be shown. Check out *view.php*, and find display_message:

```php
function display_messages($success_msg = NULL, $error_msg = NULL) {
  echo "<div id='messages'>\n";
  if (!is_null($success_msg)) {
    display_message($success_msg, SUCCESS_MESSAGE);
  }
  if (!is_null($error_msg)) {
    display_message($error_msg, ERROR_MESSAGE);
  }
  echo "</div>\n\n";
}
```

In this case, $error_message *isn't* null. It's an empty string that the if block lets pass, causing a blank error message to appear in a red box: not so good.

The fix is no problem, though. Simply determine whether $error_message is not null, and whether it has a length greater than 0. While you're at it, make the same improvement to the handling of success messages:

```php
function display_messages($success_msg = NULL, $error_msg = NULL) {
  echo "<div id='messages'>\n";
  if (!is_null($success_msg) && (strlen($error_msg) > 0)) {
    display_message($success_msg, SUCCESS_MESSAGE);
  }
  if (!is_null($error_msg) && (strlen($error_msg) > 0)) {
    display_message($error_msg, ERROR_MESSAGE);
  }
  echo "</div>\n\n";
}
```

Now you should see a proper sign in form, as demonstrated in Figure 13-7.

Try to enter an incorrect user name or password, and you should see a nice, clear error that doesn't pull you out of the login process. Figure 13-8 shows this message. Better still, your user can immediately re-enter her information.

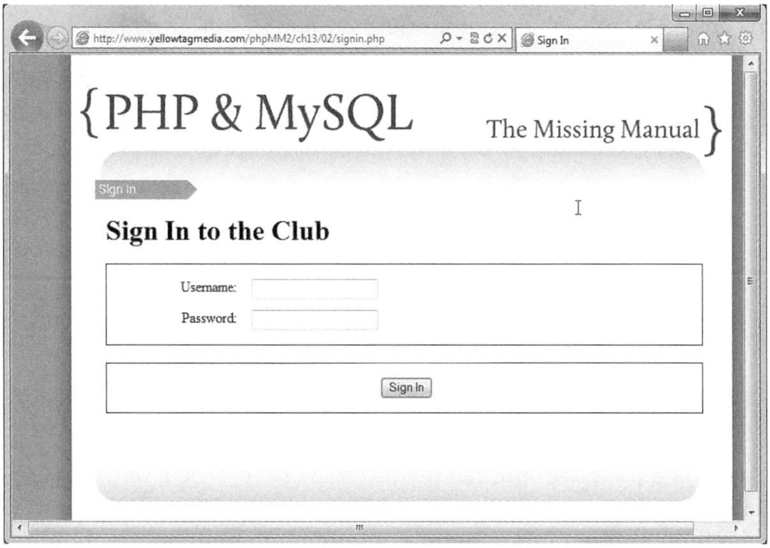

FIGURE 13-7

It makes no sense to present a user with an error the first time she sees the sign in form. But after she's tried an incorrect user name or password, that's when you want to let her know there's a problem.

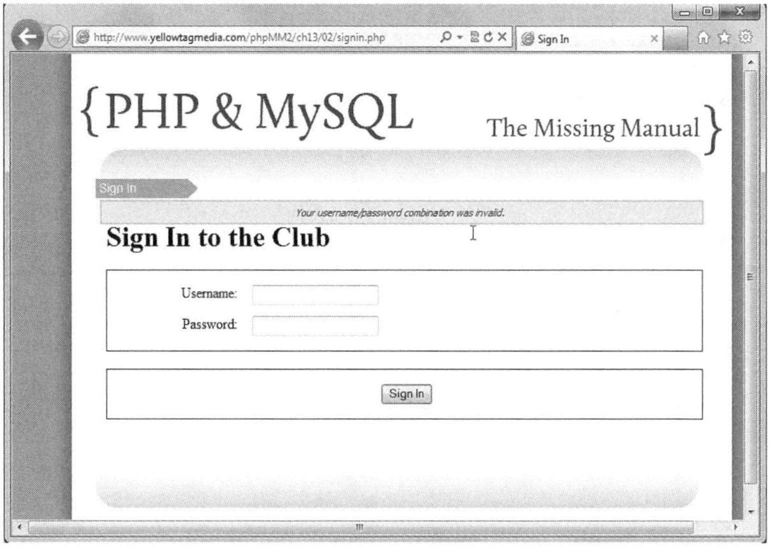

FIGURE 13-8

Now this is a solid non-interruptive error. It's impossible to miss, it creates a change that lets the user know something needs her attention, but it's not over the top. The user can try again...and again...and again.

An Option for Repeat Attempts

At this point, your sign-in page is functionally complete. However, there's one more option that you can provide to your users: reloading their user name on login failure. Some sites do this, and some don't. It's a matter of opinion, but even if you choose not to implement this feature, you should know *how* to implement it.

If you need to display a user name, this means that the user has already submitted the form at least once before. That places you squarely in this portion of *signin.php*:

```php
if (isset($_POST['username'])) {
    // Try and log the user in
    $username = mysql_real_escape_string(trim($_REQUEST['username']));
    $password = mysql_real_escape_string(trim($_REQUEST['password']));

    // and so on...
}
```

The user name has been sent, but the login failed. However, you still have the $username variable ready to display.

Now, move into the HTML. You can set the value of a form field with the value attribute, and you've got the attribute value in $username. Put that together, and you'll end up with something like this:

```html
<label for="username">Username:</label>
<input type="text"  name="username" id="username" size="20"
        value="<?php if (isset($username)) echo $username; ?>" />
```

That's all there is to it. Enter a user name, submit the sign-in page, and you should see an error, but now you'll also see the previously entered user name. Take a look at Figure 13-9 for the details.

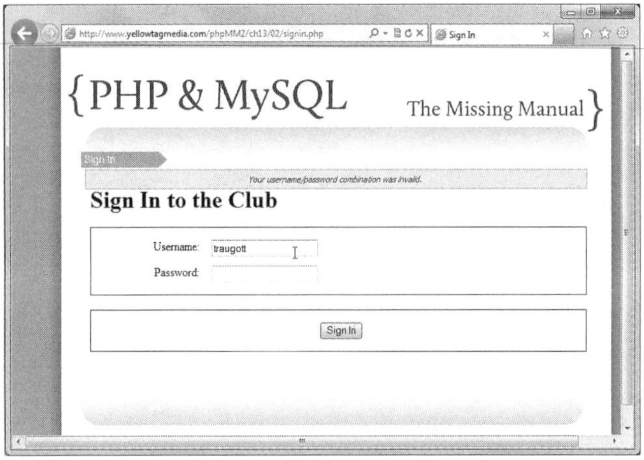

FIGURE 13-9

You'll have to decide for yourself whether you want to reshow previously entered user names. On the one hand, it's a nice feature. On the other hand, though, the user name might be part of the problem. By displaying it again, you might be implying that the user name is correct when it's not.

■ Adding Context-Specific Menus

Menus and navigation deserve a lot more than a brief mention in a chapter. There's a ton of user interface design and usability to discuss; there are the considerations regarding; and there's the ever-raging argument over horizontal versus vertical menus. Still, these are all non-PHP issues. For you, PHP programmer extraordinaire, the concern is building out links and options that change based upon whether a user is logged in.

You already have a sense of this. You can just check the "user_id" cookie:

```
if (isset($_COOKIE['user_id'])) {
  // show options for logged in users
} else {
  // show options for non-logged in users
}
```

That's all there is to it.

> **NOTE** You can find the finished example code for this section on this book's Missing CD page at *www.missingmanuals.com/cds/phpmysqlmm2e*.

Putting a Menu into Place

Go back to *view.php*, which is where all the code that controls the header of your page resides. Having some of your core view code tucked away in scripts that the rest of your pages can reference makes a huge difference. The display_title function handles the first bits of a displayable page right now.

Find that function, and you can add a simple if: if the "user_id" cookie exists, show a profile link to *show_user.php* and a *signout.php* link (more on that in a bit). If he's not signed in, show him a Sign In link. Of course, you can add a Home link that appears regardless:

```
function display_title($title, $success_message = NULL, $error_message = NULL)
{
echo <<<EOD
 <body>
  <div id="header"><h1>PHP & MySQL: The Missing Manual</h1></div>
  <div id="example">$title</div>
  <div id="menu">
    <ul>
      <li><a href="index.html">Home</a></li>
EOD;
  if (isset($_COOKIE['user_id'])) {
    echo "<li><a href='show_user.php'>My Profile</a>";
    echo "<li><a href='signout.php'>Sign Out</a></li>";
  } else {
```

```php
      echo "<li><a href='signin.php'>Sign In</a></li>";
  }
  echo <<<EOD
    </ul>
  </div>
EOD;
  display_messages($success_message, $error_message);
}
```

There's a twofold beauty to this. First, this menu is now available to all scripts via *view.php*. This means that you don't need to go rooting through all your files and insert new HTML and if statements to get a site-wide menu. Second, because you dropped this code into display_title, any of your scripts that already call display_title automatically get the menu code. Nothing to change in those at all.

Also, once again, the fact that $_REQUEST will return anything in $_COOKIE makes this script simple:

```php
if (isset($_COOKIE['user_id'])) {
  echo "<li><a href='show_user.php'>My Profile</a>";
  echo "<li><a href='signout.php'>Sign Out</a></li>";
} else {
  echo "<li><a href='signin.php'>Sign In</a></li>";
}
```

You're not worried about passing a user's ID into *show_user.php*, because there's a cookie set, and you've already seen that *show_user.php* is happy to grab that value through $_REQUEST['user_id'], just as though you'd explicitly passed in a user ID through a request parameter.

FREQUENTLY ASKED QUESTION

Signing Out

Does anyone actually sign out these days?

It's true: unless people are on a financial site—their bank or perhaps a stock trading site—logging and signing out is largely never touched. Most Internet users are not very security conscious, and there's also an expectation that a website will simply remember them when they return later. Signing out would prevent that, so why do it?

There are good reasons to add sign-out capabilities to any app. First, if users are accessing your app on a public computer or shared laptop, you want to ensure that they can protect their credentials by signing out *before* letting anyone else use the computer. Second, just because most users aren't security conscious doesn't mean that none are. Give someone the option to sign out, and if he doesn't avail himself of it, no big deal. If he does, he'll be glad your app gives him that control.

And last but not least, you know how to create cookies. It would be a good thing to know how to delete them, as well. Thus, adding a sign-out link forces you to get a handle on that, too.

To test this out, open your various scripts that display HTML: *show_user.php*, *show_users.php*, and *signin.php*. Each should call page_start rather than display HTML explicitly. Otherwise, you'll lose the menu code that you just added to page_start in *view.php*. Here, for example, is what *show_user.php* should look like:

```php
<?php

require '../scripts/database_connection.php';
require '../scripts/view.php';

// Lots of PHP to load the user ID from a request parameter or
//    a cookie, look up that user, and set some values.

page_start("User Profile");
?>

    <div id="content">
      <div class="user_profile">
        <h1><?php echo "{$first_name} {$last_name}"; ?></h1>
        <p><img src="<?php echo $user_image; ?>" class="user_pic" />
          <?php echo $bio; ?></p>
        <p class="contact_info">Get in touch with <?php echo $first_name; ?>:</p>
        <ul>
          <li>...by emailing him at
            <a href="<?php echo $email; ?>"><?php echo $email; ?></a></li>
          <li>...by
            <a href="<?php echo $facebook_url; ?>">checking him out on
              Facebook</a></li>
          <li>...by <a href="<?php echo $twitter_url; ?>">following him
              on Twitter</a></li>
        </ul>
      </div>
    </div>
    <div id="footer"></div>
  </body>
</html>
```

Now, sign in. You should automatically land on *show_user.php* and see something like Figure 13-10. There's a nice, simple menu on the right that appears, thanks to start_page, display_title, *view.php*, and the cookies you set in *signin.php*.

FIGURE 13-10

The menu at the upper right gives you only three basic options. Still, it's easy to build this script now that you have a basic mechanism for displaying the page for authenticated users, and hiding it for others. You can add all the links and sublinks that your application needs; and as long as they're in the portion of the if block in display_title *that requires a cookie, you're good to go.*

From HTML to Scripts

You might have noticed that even once you've fixed up *show_user.php*, *show_users .php*, and *signin.php*, there are still HTML web pages left in your application. There's *index.html*, the initial page, as well as *create_user.html*. But, these pages don't get the benefit of start_page and *view.php*, because they're HTML, not PHP. For *index .html*, that probably makes sense. The only two places you want users to go is the sign-in page or the sign-up page; both are clearly accessible through those big green buttons.

However, that's not the case with *create_user.html*. Suppose that someone clicks through to that form and then wants to return to the main page. Or, more likely, she might want to sign in rather than sign up. This becomes even more the case as you add other options to the menu, such as an About page. Clearly, *create_user .html* needs that menu.

■ ANY HTML FILE CAN BE CONVERTED TO PHP

In essence, all you have to do is convert *create_user.html* to PHP. You could call it *create_user.php*—apart from the fact that *create_user.php* already exists. So, as a starting point, rename *create_user.html* to *signup.php*. After all, it's a form for signing up users, and the name doesn't clash with any other file names.

```
[~/www/phpMM/ch13]# cp create_user.html create_user.html.orig
[~/www/phpMM/ch13]# mv create_user.html signup.php
```

Then, you can simply cut out the opening HTML and replace it with a PHP-driven call to page_start. You'll have to pass through all that inline validation JavaScript, but that's easy now; you can just use *heredoc*.

```php
<?php

require_once "../scripts/view.php";

$inline_javascript = <<<EOD
    $(document).ready(function() {
      $("#signup_form").validate({
        rules: {
          password: {
            minlength: 6
          },
          confirm_password: {
            minlength: 6,
            equalTo: "#password"
          }
        },
        messages: {
          password: {
            minlength: "Passwords must be at least 6 characters"
          },
          confirm_password: {
            minlength: "Passwords must be at least 6 characters",
            equalTo: "Your passwords do not match."
          }
        }
      });
    });
EOD;
page_start("User Signup", $inline_javascript);
?>

  <div id="content">
    <h1>Join the Missing Manual (Digital) Social Club</h1>
    <p>Please enter your online connections below:</p>
    <form id="signup_form" action="create_user.php"
        method="POST" enctype="multipart/form-data">
      <!-- Form content -->
```

```
      </form>
    </div>

    <div id="footer"></div>
  </body>
</html>
```

This is also a good time to update *view.php* to include the jQuery, validation scripts, and CSS that *signin.php* needs. There's no reason to not make those available to all your site's pages:

```
function display_head($page_title = "", $embedded_javascript = NULL) {
echo <<<EOD
<html>
 <head>
  <title>{$page_title}</title>
  <link href="../css/phpMM.css" rel="stylesheet" type="text/css" />
  <link href="../css/jquery.validate.password.css" rel="stylesheet"
        type="text/css" />
  <script type="text/javascript" src="../js/jquery-1.8.1.min.js"></script>
  <script type="text/javascript" src="../js/jquery.validate.min.js"></script>
  <script type="text/javascript"
          src="../js/jquery.validate.password.js"></script>
EOD;
  if (!is_null($embedded_javascript)) {
    echo "<script type='text/javascript'>" .
        $embedded_javascript .
        "</script>";
  }
  echo " </head>";
}
```

Update your links in *index.html* to reference *signup.php* rather than *create_user.html*:

```
<div id="content">
  <div id="home_banner"></div>
  <div id="signup">
    <a href="signup.php"><img src="../images/sign_me_up.png" /></a>
    <a href="signin.php"><img src="../images/sign_me_in.png" /></a>
  </div>
</div>
```

Take a break to check out the new page—and what should be a new menu. The results are shown in Figure 13-11. This is the "not logged in" version of the menu, so now you've tested both versions.

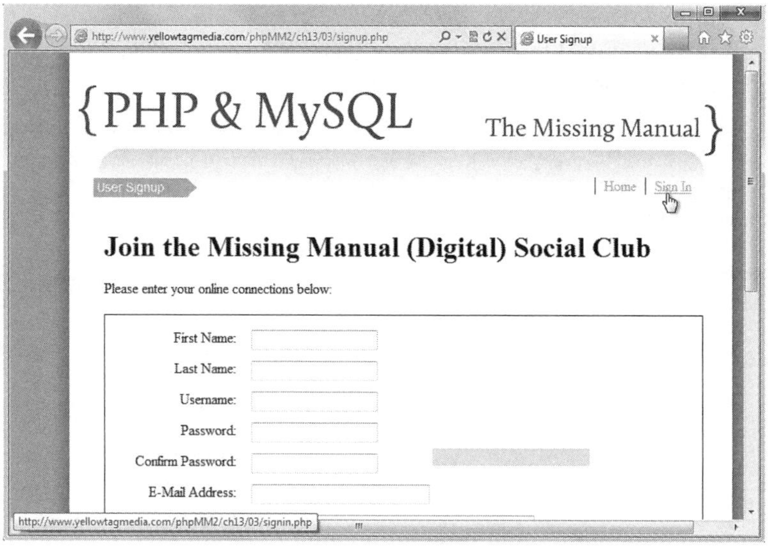

FIGURE 13-11

The menu in its current state doesn't offer a ton of new functionality. Still, lots of users forget they're signed up for a site and need a simple way to get to the sign-in page rather than the sign-up page. In addition, you can add About information, Contact information, and anything else you want that might not require authentication, and it all becomes available to this form now.

■ CHALLENGE: BE SELF-REFERENTIAL WITH USER CREATION

By now, you realize that you don't *need* two scripts to handle user creation. You could create a single script that submits to itself. That lets you not only do the client-side validation already in place with jQuery and JavaScript, but also check user names and emails against the database and return errors if there are duplicates.

At this stage, though, you don't need to see another painfully long code listing. You have all you need to do it yourself. Set this book down and start combining *signin .php* and *create_user.php*. As always, there's swag to be had by tweeting your solution to *@missingmanuals* or hopping on Facebook at *http://www.facebook.com/ MissingManuals.*

Logging Users Out

Your login now works, but don't forget to add logging out. Whether you set your cookie's expiration value to a short few minutes or a long one, always let users control their own authentication. They should be able to log in and log out when they want.

Logging in involves setting a cookie name, value, and optionally, a time for expiration:

```
setcookie('user_id', $user_id);              // Defaut expiration:
setcookie('username', $result['username']); // Log out on browser close
```

Logging out is much the same, but inverted. Just set the cookie's value to an empty value, and set the expiration to a point in the past:

```
// Expire the user_id cookie with a date a year in the past
setcookie('user_id', '', time()-(60*60*24*365));
```

In this case, the value of the cookie's user_id is set to nothing (an empty string), and the expiration date is set to a year in the past.

> **NOTE** Be sure to set the expiration well into the past. That way, if the system time on your server is off by a few minutes or even days, it doesn't affect your code. (Then again, if the system time is more than a year off, well, you have much bigger issues.)

Turning this into a script is awfully simple. Just expire the two cookies your app uses (user_id and username) and redirect the user back to a home page or sign-in page. Create this script and save it as *signout.php*.

```php
<?php

setcookie('user_id', '', time()-(365*24*60*60));
setcookie('username', '', time()-(365*24*60*60));

header('Location: signin.php');
?>
```

Try it out. Visit your app (after closing your browser and clearing any cookies) and sign in as a known user. You should be able to visit *show_user.php*, *show_users.php*, and delete users. That's all working as it should.

> **NOTE** Well, it's kind of working. Any old user shouldn't be able to see all the users and delete users, but you'll fix that shortly.

Now, click the Sign Out link on the menu. You should be redirected to the sign-in page. You also can visit pages that require a user ID, and you'll not see your user's profile. That's good—but the result isn't. Check out Figure 13-12.

Signing out appears to be working, but it's revealed a nasty hole in the app: pages that shouldn't be accessible at all *are* accessible. They just error out, which is arguably worse than just letting unauthorized users see them. No matter how you cut it, there's an issue to be resolved.

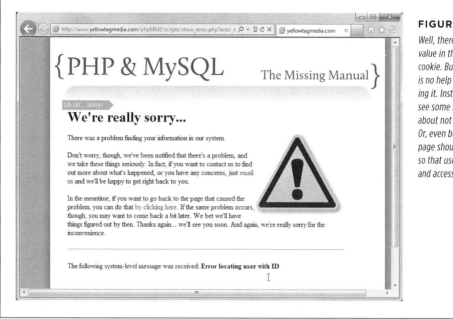

FIGURE 13-12

Well, there's definitely no value in the user_id *cookie. But, this error page is no help to the users seeing it. Instead, they should see some sort of error about not being logged in. Or, even better, the sign-in page should be displayed so that users can sign in and access your system.*

Requiring the Cookie to Be Set

Fortunately, the issue of error pages showing up at the wrong time isn't hard to fix. Earlier, *show_user.php* and other restricted scripts required *authorize.php* (page 396), which did all sorts of database work to determine whether a user could log in, all using basic HTTP authentication. As a result, you got a nice wall around your scripts.

By removing *authorize.php*, it became possible to have *signin.php* handle logins. In the process, though, you knocked down that wall around your other scripts. You need the wall, but you still need to let *signin.php* handle authentication. That's not hard.

First, you can drastically simplify *authorize.php*. Chop it down to do little more than check for a valid cookie:

```php
<?php



if ((!isset($_COOKIE['user_id'])) ||
    (!strlen($_COOKIE['user_id']) > 0)) {
}
?>
```

If there's no cookie, or if the cookie has an empty value, just redirect the user to the sign-in page with a message that explains what's going on:

```php
<?php


if ((!isset($_COOKIE['user_id'])) ||
    (!strlen($_COOKIE['user_id']) > 0)) {
  header('Location: signin.php?' .
         'error_message=You must login to see this page.');
  exit();
}
?>
```

> **WARNING** The exit here is important. Because this code will run and then pass control back to the calling script—*show_user.php*, *delete_user.php*, or whatever else—you need to ensure that those scripts don't continue to try to run. Send the redirect headers and bail out of any further action.

Next, you can add the require_once back in to *show_user.php*, *show_users.php*, and *delete_user.php*.

Test it. Make sure that you're signed out (*signout.php* via the menu link makes that a breeze now). Then, try to access *show_user.php*. You see signs of progress, although things aren't perfect yet. Figure 13-13 is a good start, though.

FIGURE 13-13

Attempts to access secure pages are sent to the sign-in page. That's good, but where's the helpful message? Notice that it's in the request URL, but doesn't show up on the page.

The missing message in Figure 13-13 is due to the fact that there's nothing in *signin .php* that deals with a potential message on the request URL. Happily, you actually have the mechanics for this in place. Open *signin.php* and check out the opening section:

```
require_once '../scripts/view.php';

$error_message = "";

// If the user is logged in, the user_id cookie will be set
if (!isset($_COOKIE['user_id'])) {
```

This is great! You have a variable to hold the error message in place. And, you already have code to display $error_message as an error:

```
// Still in the "not signed in" part of the if
// Start the page, and pass along any error message set earlier
page_start("Sign In", NULL, NULL, $error_message);
```

Now, you just need to see whether there's a request parameter back up at the top rather than automatically assigning $error_message an empty string:

```
<?php

require_once '../scripts/database_connection.php';
require_once '../scripts/view.php';

$error_message = $_REQUEST['error_message'];

// If the user is logged in, the user_id cookie will be set
if (!isset($_COOKIE['user_id'])) {
```

Go ahead and try things one more time. Go to *show_user.php* without having a cookie, and you should see something like Figure 13-14.

FIGURE 13-14

Perfect! Blocked access, a helpful error message, and an immediate chance to sign in. That's just what you want. Things are looking good.

So, what's left? Take a look back at your original list:

- A better login screen. Folks don't like a bland, gray pop-up dialog box; they want a branded, styled login form. **(Done!)**

- Better messaging to indicate whether a user is logged in. **(Done!)**

- A way to log out. **(Done!)**

- Two levels of authentication: one to get to the main application, and then admin-level authentication to get to a page like *show_users.php* and *delete_user.php*. **(Hmmm, nothing here yet at all.)**

- Some basic navigation. That navigation should change based on a user's login and the groups to which the user belongs. **(Sort of done...)**

Take a quick breath and get ready for the home stretch: group-based authentication and the reason that cookies are cool, but maybe not your final authentication destination.

Authorization and Sessions

I t's time to add some refinement to the authentication and navigation systems you built in the last couple of chapters. You've created an attractive login screen as well as added authentication to let users into and out of your application. It's time to go further: *authorize.php* needs to be improved. It should take in a group (or, better, a list of groups) for the user and only allow access if the user is in the permitted group, such as an administrator group.

You also have basic navigation, but again, there are some needed improvements: users in certain groups should see an option to administrate users and get a link to *show_users.php* (in addition to the standard link to *show_user.php*).

And then...there's a problem with cookies. In Chapter 13, you learned how to go beyond basic authentication by using cookies, and that's a good thing. But, there are some very real concerns surrounding a high-end application using cookies, and only cookies, for authentication. In this chapter, you'll do all of the above and more.

■ Modeling Groups in Your Database

Before you can look up the groups to which a user belongs, you need to have some groups in your database. You need a table to store groups and some means by which you can connect a user to a group. Also, you need to be able to connect one user to multiple groups.

There are a few distinct steps here:

1. **Create a table in the database to store groups.**

2. **Map a user to zero, one, or more groups.**

3. **Build PHP to look up that mapping.**

4. **Restrict pages based on any login, or a particular set of groups.**

First things first: It all begins with a database table.

Adding a Groups Table

Creating a new table is a trifling thing for you as a PHP and MySQL programmer. You can easily create a new table, name it (*groups*), give MySQL a few columns, specify which are NOT NULL, and bang; you're quickly past database table creation.

```
mysql> CREATE TABLE groups (
    -> id      INT    NOT NULL AUTO_INCREMENT PRIMARY KEY,
    -> name    VARCHAR(30) NOT NULL,
    -> description VARCHAR(200)
    -> );
Query OK, 0 rows affected (0.03 sec)

mysql> DESCRIBE groups;
+-------------+--------------+------+-----+---------+----------------+
| Field       | Type         | Null | Key | Default | Extra          |
+-------------+--------------+------+-----+---------+----------------+
| id          | int(11)      | NO   | PRI | NULL    | auto_increment |
| name        | varchar(30)  | NO   |     | NULL    |                |
| description | varchar(200) | YES  |     | NULL    |                |
+-------------+--------------+------+-----+---------+----------------+
3 rows in set (0.03 sec)
```

As usual, each group needs an ID and a name. The description column is optional—it's not NOT NULL, which is bad grammar but good database design—and that's all you need.

It's hard to do much testing without some group information, so go ahead and add a few groups into your new *groups* table:

```
mysql> INSERT INTO groups
    ->    (name, description)
    -> VALUES ("Administrators",
    ->    "Users who administrate the entire application.");
Query OK, 1 row affected (0.04 sec)

mysql> INSERT INTO groups
    ->    (name, description)
    -> VALUES ("Luthiers",
    ->    "Guitar builders. They make the instrument that makes the music.");
```

```
Query OK, 1 row affected (0.00 sec)

mysql> INSERT INTO groups
    ->    (name, description)
    -> VALUES ("Musicians",
    ->    "Play what you feel, they say. And they feel it.");
Query OK, 1 row affected (0.00 sec)

mysql> INSERT INTO groups
    ->    (name, description)
    -> VALUES ("Martial Artists",
    ->    "Friendship with these folks is like a kick in the head.");
Query OK, 1 row affected (0.00 sec)
```

> **NOTE** Create whichever groups that pertain to your own users. Just be sure to create an Administrators group. If you call that group something else, swap that group name in whenever this chapter refers to "Administrators."

As usual, test before moving on:

```
mysql> SELECT id, name FROM groups;
+----+-----------------+
| id | name            |
+----+-----------------+
|  1 | Administrators  |
|  2 | Luthiers        |
|  3 | Musicians       |
|  4 | Martial Artists |
+----+-----------------+
4 rows in set (0.01 sec)
```

The Many-to-Many Relationship

Next, establish how you're going to connect users to groups. Before you can start worrying about SQL, you need to think clearly about how these two tables are related. Relationships help you to determine in what manner tables are linked.

▉ ONE-TO-ONE, ONE-TO-MANY, MANY-TO-MANY

You've already seen an example of a one-to-one relationship. For example, when you were storing images in your database (page 303), you had a single entry in *users* that was related to a single entry in *images*. This is a *one-to-one relationship* between *users* and *images*.

With groups, that's not the case. You've already seen that a single user can be in zero groups, one group, or many groups. Certainly Michael Greenfield can be a luthier, musician, and administrator. You might have another user who is in none of those groups.

From that perspective, you have a *one-to-many relationship*: one user can be related to many groups. "Many" doesn't have a strict literal meaning here, either. It means more like "as many as you want." So, "many" can mean 0, 1, 1,000, or anything in between or above.

However, that's only part of the story. You must also consider the point of view of the *groups* table. A group can have many users. For example, the Administrators group might have 4, 5, or 20 users. This means that there's a one-to-many relationship on the groups-to-users side of things as well as on the users-to-groups side.

What you have here is a *many-to-many relationship* between users and groups (or, if you like, between groups and users). One user can be in many groups; one group can have many users. It's a multi-sided relationship, which is a bit more complex to model at the database level but just as important in the real world of data as a one-to-one relationship or a one-to-many relationship.

> **NOTE** A good example of a true one-to-many relationship is a user who might have a gallery of images. A user can have many images, but that user's images can't be related to multiple users. It's a one (user)-to-many (images) relationship.

POWER USERS' CLINIC

Lots of Programmers Are Secretly Math Geeks

It's true: most programmers have at least a little love for math, often buried somewhere deep down. One proof of this is that many programming concepts share naming ideas from math.

For example, you might hear about one-to-one (1-to-1, or even, sometimes, 1:1) relationships. You'll also hear about one-to-many relationships. But, just as often, you'll hear about a 1-to-N relationship. N is a mathematical term; it's usually written as lowercase n in math, but it's more often capital N in programming. That N is just a stand-in for a variable number. So N could be 0, or 1, or some large number.

In that light, then, a one-to-many relationship is the same as a 1:N relationship. It's just that 1:N is a shorter, more concise way to say the same thing. You know that programmers—like you—tend to favor short and concise. So, on database diagrams you'll often see 1:N, which just tells you that relationship between two tables is one-to-many.

And then, of course, you have N:N, which is just saying that many items in one table are related to many items in another. That said, an N:N relationship (and the many-to-many relationship that it represents) is a conceptual or virtual idea. It takes two relationships at the database level in most systems to model an N:N relationship, as you'll see on page 459.

■ JOINS ARE BEST DONE WITH IDS

When you related a user to a profile image, you used an ID. Each image had its own ID, uniquely identifying it. It also had a user_id, which connected the image to a particular user in the *users* table. That made it easy to grab an image for a user by using something like this:

```
SELECT *
 FROM images
 WHERE user_id = $user_id;
```

Or, you can join the two tables like this:

```
SELECT u.username, u.first_name, u.last_name, i.filename, i.image_data
  FROM users u, images i
  WHERE u.id = i.user_id;
```

In both cases, the IDs are the connectors. That works fine in a one-to-one relationship, as it does in a one-to-many relationship. The "many" side just adds a column that references the ID of the "one" side. Therefore, many images all have a user_id column that references a user with the ID 51 (or 2931 or whatever else you have in *users*).

But with users and groups, you don't have a one-to-one or a one-to-many relationship. You have a many-to-many. How do you handle that?

■ USE A JOIN TABLE TO CONNECT USERS WITH GROUPS

It's easy to model a one-to-many relationship by using the ID as a connector. When you're modeling a many-to-many relationship, connecting the IDs is more complex. You need a sort of matrix: a set of user IDs and group IDs that are connected.

Think about the many-to-many relationship. In its simplest form, it's two one-to-many relationships; users and groups have a many-to-many relationship going in each direction. You started with one side: users. Then you figured out it was one-to-many. Then, the other side: groups. Also one-to-many.

You construct a many-to-many relationship at the database level the same way. You have a table like *users* that connects to an intermediary table. Call it *user_groups*, and assume that it has a user_id and a group_id. A user_id might appear in two rows: in the first row along with the ID for the "Administrators" group, and again with the ID of the "Musicians" group. That gives you the one-to-many from *users* to *groups*.

But then you also have the one-to-many from groups to users. The ID for "Administrators" might appear in five different rows within *user_groups*, once for each of the five users to which that group relates.

To give this idea a concrete form, create the following table:

```
mysql> CREATE TABLE user_groups (
    ->    user_id INT NOT NULL,
    ->    group_id INT NOT NULL
    -> );
Query OK, 0 rows affected (0.03 sec)
```

This table becomes a bridge: each row connects one user to one group. So, for "Jeff Traugott" with an ID of 29, and a group "Luthiers" with an ID of 2, you'd add this row to *user_groups*.

```
mysql> INSERT INTO user_groups
    ->    (user_id, group_id)
    -> VALUES (29, 2);
Query OK, 1 row affected (0.02 sec)
```

```
mysql> select * from user_groups;
+---------+----------+
| user_id | group_id |
+---------+----------+
|   29    |    2     |
+---------+----------+
1 row in set (0.00 sec)
```

On their own, the *users* and *groups* tables aren't connected. But this additional table establishes the many-to-many relationship.

Testing Group Membership

To see whether a user is in a group, you need to determine whether there's an entry in *user_groups* with both the ID of the ID you want, and the ID of the group you want.

```
mysql> SELECT COUNT(*)
    -> FROM users u, groups g, user_groups ug
    -> WHERE u.username = "traugott"
    -> AND g.name = "Luthiers"
    -> AND u.user_id = ug.user_id
    -> AND g.id = ug.group_id;
+----------+
| COUNT(*) |
+----------+
|    1     |
+----------+
1 row in set (0.00 sec)
```

Bingo! This query looks a little complex at first blush, but it's straightforward if you walk through it step by step.

First, you use COUNT(*) to return a count on the rows returned from the query. And then there are the three tables involved: *users*, *groups*, and *user_groups*.

```
SELECT COUNT(*)
  FROM users u, groups g, user_groups ug
```

Next, you indicate the name of the user you want (using any column you want; first name, last name, or user name), and the name of the group you want. This will cause exactly one (or zero, if there's no match) row in both *users* and *groups* to be isolated.

```
SELECT COUNT(*)
  FROM users u, groups g, user_groups ug
  WHERE u.username = "traugott"
    AND g.name = "Luthiers"
```

Now, you need to connect those individual rows—each with an ID—to *user_groups*. This is just a regular join. You use the IDs in each table to match up with the ID columns in *user_groups*:

```
SELECT COUNT(*)
 FROM users u, groups g, user_groups ug
 WHERE u.username = "traugott"
  AND g.name = "Luthiers"
  AND u.user_id = ug.user_id
  AND g.id = ug.group_id;
```

This query connects zero or one row in *users* to *user_groups*, which is also connected to zero or one row in *groups*. The result? Either a single row with a COUNT value of 1, meaning that there's a connection from a user in *users* to the group in *groups* you indicated

```
+----------+
| COUNT(*) |
+----------+
|        1 |
+----------+
```

or a row with a COUNT value of 0, meaning there's no connection:

```
mysql> SELECT COUNT(*)
    ->  FROM users u, groups g, user_groups ug
    -> WHERE u.username = "traugott"
    ->  AND g.name = "Administrators"
    ->  AND u.user_id = ug.user_id
    ->  AND g.id = ug.group_id;
+----------+
| COUNT(*) |
+----------+
|        0 |
+----------+
1 row in set (0.05 sec)
```

WARNING Watch out! With this particular expression (using COUNT) you do get a single row each time. The important information is the *value* in the row, not that there *is* a row.

The task now is to turn this into PHP code.

■ Checking for Group Membership

By replacing basic authentication with your own authentication scheme, you have the makings of good, solid authentication. Authentication simply lets users into your application when they log in. They authenticate in some manner that confirms to your system that they are who they say they are.

But now, it's time to add *authorization*: the ability to give access only to certain pages, based on more specific criteria. At its simplest, you do have some level of authorization through *authorize.php* in that you only authorize users who are authenticated. Typically, authorization goes a lot further than that. It's more detailed; you can control access based on, say, group membership.

At this point, you have the users, you have the groups, and you have the connection between the two. You need to enhance *authorize.php* to work these groups into your authorization scheme.

authorize.php Needs a Function

At the moment, *authorize.php* runs automatically when it's required by a script. The code in *authorize.php* isn't in a function; it's just dropped into the body of the PHP file:

```php
<?php

if ((!isset($_COOKIE['user_id'])) || (!strlen($_COOKIE['user_id']) > 0)) {
  header('Location: signin.php?' .
      'error_message=You must login to see this page.');
  exit;
}
?>
```

That's worked fine up until now. But now, you need a means by which you can pass in a group, or a list of groups, to *authorize.php*, and then *authorize.php* has to run through those groups and see whether there's a connection with the current user. That situation—a block of code that should take in a piece of information with which to work—screams "function." There are some other options, but they're less easy to understand and maintain. (If you're curious about those options, check out the box on page 464.)

Create that new function in *authorize.php*. Eventually, it should take an array of groups that allow access. For now, you can set a default value for the parameter the function takes and use that default value to keep the current functionality: allowing access to any authorized user.

```php
<?php

function authorize_user($groups = NULL) {
  // No need to check groups if there aren't cookies set
  if ((!isset($_COOKIE['user_id'])) ||
    (!strlen($_COOKIE['user_id']) > 0)) {
  header('Location: signin.php?' .
      'error_message=You must login to see this page.');
   exit;
  }
}
?>
```

Jump back into *show_user.php* and add an explicit call to this function. You don't
need to pass in any group names. *show_user.php* should be open to any logged-in
user.

```php
<?php

require_once '../scripts/authorize.php';
require_once '../scripts/database_connection.php';
require_once '../scripts/view.php';

// Authorize any user, as long as they're logged in
authorize_user();

// Get the user ID of the user to show
$user_id = $_REQUEST['user_id'];

// Build the SELECT statement

// and so on...
```

Take a moment to test this script. Because the default functionality should be just
what you already have, verify that you can't access *show_user.php* without first
logging in. Enter the URL into your browser, and you should see your sign-in page,
as shown in Figure 14-1.

FIGURE 14-1

*One of the first steps to
any new bit of functionality is to ensure that old
functionality still works.
It's no good to code for
an hour or two adding
new features if you end
up breaking all the old
features in the process.
Test the new stuff, but
start by testing the old
stuff first.*

On Functions and Non-Functions

In *authorize.php*, you've got a function that takes in zero or more groups via a parameter. Yet, that's just one way to handle the issue. There are other approaches: you could, for example, set a variable and then use that variable in the required file.

Take, for example, a simple script like this:

```
<?php

$message = "hello\n\n";

require_once "print.php";
?>
```

You can call this script *test.php*. Suppose, then, that *print.php*, the referenced script, looks like this:

```
<?php

echo $message;

?>
```

When *print.php* is required, it's like the code in *print.php* is inserted in place of the require_once line. When you run this script, PHP essentially sees this:

```
<?php

$message = "hello\n\n";
```

```
echo $message;
?>
```

Run *test.php*, and you'd get this result:

```
yellowta@yellowtagmedia.com [../ch14]# php
test.php
Content-type: text/html

hello
```

You can "pass" information into a required script in this manner.

This approach is perfectly easy to implement, but it's not terribly clear.

Here's what the authorization code would look like:

```
$allowed_groups = array("Musicians",
"Luthiers");
require_once "../scripts/authorize.php";
```

Again, there's nothing overtly wrong here. It's just really unclear that the $groups variable is required before the require_once to *authorize.php*, and that in fact *authorize.php* makes use of that variable. So, although an authorize_user function is a bit clumsy, it's clear and better than the alternative: code that's difficult to understand unless you already know what it does.

Take in a List of Groups

It's time to get to the point of all this work. Start by sending a list of groups—through a PHP array—to authorize_user. You can do this in *show_users.php* and *delete_user.php*, both of which should require the Administrators group for access.

```
<?php

require_once '../scripts/app_config.php';
require_once '../scripts/authorize.php';
require_once '../scripts/database_connection.php';
require_once '../scripts/view.php';
```

```
// Only Administrators can access this page
authorize_user(array("Administrators"));

// Rest of the PHP code and HTML output
```

> **NOTE** The preceding change is shown in *show_users.php*. Make the same change in *delete_user.php* so that it can't be directly accessed.

Using an array is about the simplest means in PHP of getting a list to a function. Currently, in *authorize.php*, you're getting either nothing or a list of allowed group names. So you can start to do some work with those groups.

First, though, if the parameter passed to authorize_user is either an empty list or NULL, you should have the function bail out. There's no need to do any database searching in those two cases.

```php
<?php

function authorize_user($groups = NULL) {
 // No need to check groups if there aren't cookies set
 if ((!isset($_COOKIE['user_id'])) ||
   (!strlen($_COOKIE['user_id']) > 0)) {
  header('Location: signin.php?' .
      'error_message=You must login to see this page.');
   exit;
 }

 // If no groups passed in, the authorization above is enough
 if ((is_null($groups)) || (empty($groups))) {
  return;
 }
}
?>
```

> **NOTE** The empty function takes just about any PHP type and figures out what "empty" means, and then returns either true or false. For an array, empty returns true if there aren't any items in the array.

When you use return, you're instructing PHP to give control back to the calling script. It lets the script run, which means letting the user see the page he requested.

Iterating Over Each Group

Take a step back to the case in which you *do* get a list of groups, as in *show_users .php* and *delete_user.php*. In those cases, *authorize.php* should loop over each group, and for each group, build a SQL query.

Start out by just looping over the $groups array. You can use a for loop, but in this case, there's a better choice: foreach. foreach lets you loop over an array and automatically assign a variable to the current item in the array:

```
$my_array = array("first", "second", "third");
foreach ($my_array as $item) {
 echo $item;
}
```

For $groups, you could set the loop up like this:

```
foreach ($groups as $group) {
 // do a SQL search for the current $group
}
```

Think through what happens inside the loop. You want something similar to the original SQL you used to connect users to groups:

```
SELECT COUNT(*)
 FROM users u, groups g, user_groups ug
 WHERE u.username = "traugott"
  AND g.name = "Luthiers"
  AND u.user_id = ug.user_id
  AND g.id = ug.group_id;
```

This query is actually *more* complex than what you need in *authorize.php*. First, you don't need the *users* table at all. That table is only part of the query to connect a username to a user_id. However, your app already has the user's user_id, so things simplify to this:

```
SELECT COUNT(*)
 FROM user_groups ug, groups g
 WHERE g.name = mysql_real_escape_string($group)
  AND g.id = ug.group_id
  AND ug.user_id = mysql_real_escape_string($_COOKIE['user_id']);
```

> **NOTE** As usual, you'll want to use mysql_real_escape_string to ensure that your database gets clean values. In fact, you might as well get into the habit now: use mysql_real_escape_string on anything that originates in your scripts and is sent to MySQL.

There's another improvement you can make, too. In the preceding query, you'd need to get the result row and see if the value is 0 (no membership) or 1 (membership). But, that's an additional step. Better to just check and see whether there's a result at all. In other words, you want a query that returns a result row only if there's a match; therefore, make another change:

```
SELECT ug.user_id
 FROM user_groups ug, groups g
 WHERE g.name = mysql_real_escape_string($group)
```

```
       AND g.id = ug.group_id
       AND ug.user_id = mysql_real_escape_string($_COOKIE['user_id']);
```

The particular column you select from *user_groups* doesn't matter; you could use ug.group_id, as well. You either get a result when there's a match or you get no result, so that's one less step your code needs to take.

Put this together, and you end up with something like this in your foreach loop:

```
foreach ($groups as $group) {
  // do a SQL search for the current $group
  $query = "SELECT ug.user_id" .
      " FROM user_groups ug, groups g" .
      " WHERE g.name = '" . mysql_real_escape_string($group) . "'" .
      "  AND g.id = ug.group_id" .
      "  AND ug.user_id = " .
          mysql_real_escape_string($COOKIE['user_id']) . "';";
  mysql_query($query);

  // Deal with results
}
```

This query works, and it doesn't require the *users* table. The downside is that you're constructing this string, over and over again. For every group, this string is recreated, and that's wasteful.

Here's where you rekindle your friendship with sprintf (page 298). With sprintf, you can construct a single string, give it an escape character or two, and insert values for each escape character into the string. The string remains unchanged; you're modifying only the data within that string that's variable.

As a result, you can construct the query string outside of the foreach, like this:

```
// Set up the query string
$query_string =
  "SELECT ug.user_id" .
  " FROM user_groups ug, groups g" .
  " WHERE g.name = '%s'" .
  "  AND g.id = ug.group_id" .
  "  AND ug.user_id = " . mysql_real_escape_string($_COOKIE['user_id']);

foreach ($groups as $group) {
  // do a SQL search for the current $group

  // Deal with results
}
```

Then, within the foreach, use sprintf to supply the values to drop into the string for a particular group:

```
// Set up the query string
$query_string =
  "SELECT ug.user_id" .
  " FROM user_groups ug, groups g" .
  " WHERE g.name = '%s'" .
  "  AND g.id = ug.group_id" .
  "  AND ug.user_id = " . mysql_real_escape_string($_COOKIE['user_id']);

foreach ($groups as $group) {
  // do a SQL search for the current $group
  $query = sprintf($query_string, mysql_real_escape_string($group));
  $result = mysql_query($query);

  // Deal with results
}
```

In addition to using sprintf, this code assigns the current user ID—from $_COOKIE—to the string assembled outside of the loop. There's no need to feed that to sprintf, because it won't change as you loop.

Allow, Deny, Redirect

With a solid query in place, it's time to deal with the results. You can check the number of rows to know all you need: if no rows were returned, the user isn't a member of the group indicated by $group, and your loop should continue, going to the next $group in $groups.

If there is a row returned from a query, not only is the user in an allowed group, but authorize_user needs to stop. There's no need to continue looping over $groups; just return control to the calling script so that the PHP and HTML of that script can take over.

And then, the final case: all the groups have been checked, and there's never been a result row. This is the case when the foreach loop ends. If that's the case, it's not okay to send control back to the calling script, because that would be letting the user "in," and that's exactly the *opposite* of what should happen. It's also not appropriate to redirect the user back to the sign-in page. He *is* signed in, at least in most cases; he just doesn't have the right level of permissions to access the current page.

So, what's left? In the simplest case, just use handle_error one more time. You might want to build this out yourself, though. Perhaps you could redirect the user to the last page he viewed and set an error message. Or, you could build a customized page to let the user request permissions for a certain page. No matter how you cut it, though, you're going to be sending him somewhere else; the current page is never shown.

Better, Faster, Easier

Don't all of the queries on page 467 match up a user with the groups she belongs to? Why keep finding different ways to do the same thing?

Yes, they indeed all get the job done. As you've come to realize, though, there are solutions to problems and then there are *better* solutions to problems. When you're working with databases, "better" usually means "faster," and "faster" usually means "less work for the database to do."

In the case of looking up a group and establishing whether a user is a member, there's nothing *functionally* wrong with the following query:

```
SELECT COUNT(*)
  FROM users u, groups g, user_groups ug
 WHERE u.username =
    mysql_real_escape_string(
    $_COOKIE['username'])
AND g.name = mysql_real_escape_
string($group)
   AND u.user_id = ug.user_id
   AND g.id = ug.group_id;
```

You're doing a *lot* more work than you need to. There's an entire extra table involved (*users*) that you can cut out because you already have the user's ID in a cookie.

You can cut down on dealing with results by moving from a COUNT in the SELECT—which will require you to always examine the results in a row—for a column in *user_groups*. With that done, you only need to see if there are rows returned; the values in those result rows become irrelevant.

And, you can improve on general execution time by creating a string only once and using `sprintf` to modify just a small part of that string every time you go to a new group. Again, this is a small improvement, but an important one that's easy to make.

All of these small changes can add up to noticeable improvements in your app. It will simply "feel" more responsive. This is even more important because the authorization script is going to run every time a user visits your page. This means that a script that's sloppy or slower than it needs to be creates a lag in every single page access.

Most users don't like—and many won't put up with—slow-loading sites. This isn't a pause while you secure your user concert tickets or look up shipping information. It's simply them navigating to a new page. A little work on your script to keep things peppy makes a huge difference in your users' experience, especially as you have more and more users accessing your site, which means more and more hits against your database to verify group membership.

Here's a version of *authorize.php* that takes all of this into account:

```php
<?php

require_once 'database_connection.php';
require_once 'app_config.php';

function authorize_user($groups = NULL) {

  // No need to check groups if there aren't cookies set
  if ((!isset($_COOKIE['user_id'])) || (!strlen($_COOKIE['user_id']) > 0)) {
```

```php
  header('Location: signin.php?' .
    'error_message=You must login to see this page.');
  exit;
}

// If no groups passed in, the authorization above is enough
if ((is_null($groups)) || (empty($groups))) {
  return;
}

// Set up the query string
$query_string =
  "SELECT ug.user_id" .
  " FROM user_groups ug, groups g" .
  " WHERE g.name = '%s'" .
  "   AND g.id = ug.group_id" .
  "   AND ug.user_id = " . mysql_real_escape_string($_COOKIE['user_id']);


// Run through each group and check membership
foreach ($groups as $group) {
  $query = sprintf($query_string, mysql_real_escape_string($group));
  $result = mysql_query($query);

  if (mysql_num_rows($result) == 1) {
    // If we got a result, the user should be allowed access
    //   Just return so the script will continue to run
    return;
  }
}

// If we got here, no matches were found for any group
// The user isn't allowed access
handle_error("You are not authorized to see this page.");
exit;
}
?>
```

It's been a long time coming, but you can finally try this out. Ensure that you've got a user in *users* who is a member of Administrators (through *user_groups*) and one who's not. The former should be able to navigate to *show_users.php* without any problems; the latter should be kicked to the error page, as shown in Figure 14-2.

FIGURE 14-2

*You should see this page
as a first step toward
authorization rather than
a last one. Full-page
errors should be serious
things, rarely shown
without a lot of thought,
and in this case you can
come up with a better,
less interruptive way to let
users know that they've
ended up somewhere they
shouldn't be. Take them
back to a page they can
access, if possible.*

Group-Specific Menus

Right now, you can use authorize_user to check a user against a list of groups and
either reject access to a page or allow the user to see a page. That means you have
the logic to handle group-specific menus, but the actual implementation might take
a bit of refactoring.

Take a look at your menu system as it stands, in *view.php*:

```
function display_title($title, $success_msg = NULL, $error_msg = NULL) {
echo <<<EOD
 <body>
 <div id="header"><h1>PHP & MySQL: The Missing Manual</h1></div>
 <div id="example">$title</div>
 <div id="menu">
  <ul>
   <li><a href="index.html">Home</a></li>
EOD;
 if (isset($_COOKIE['user_id'])) {
  echo "<li><a href='show_user.php'>My Profile</a>";
  echo "<li><a href='signout.php'>Sign Out</a></li>";
```

```
} else {
 echo "<li><a href='signin.php'>Sign In</a></li>";
}
echo <<<EOD
 </ul>
 </div>
EOD;
 display_messages($success_msg, $error_msg);
}
```

You can't just drop the authorize_user function in here; it either gives a user access a page or disallows it. It's not a fine-grained tool with which you can check group membership and get back a true or false value.

What you want is something like this:

```
function display_title($title, $success_msg = NULL, $error_msg = NULL) {
echo <<<EOD
 <body>
 <div id="header"><h1>PHP & MySQL: The Missing Manual</h1></div>
 <div id="example">$title</div>
 <div id="menu">
  <ul>
   <li><a href="index.html">Home</a></li>
EOD;
 if (isset($_COOKIE['user_id'])) {
  echo "<li><a href='show_user.php'>My Profile</a>";
  if (user_in_group($_COOKIE['user_id'], "Administrators")) {
   echo "<li><a href='show_users.php'>Manage Users</a></li>";
  }
  echo "<li><a href='signout.php'>Sign Out</a></li>";
 } else {
  echo "<li><a href='signin.php'>Sign In</a></li>";
 }
echo <<<EOD
 </ul>
 </div>
EOD;
 display_messages($success_msg, $error_msg);
}
```

NOTE   You'll also need to add a require_once for *authorize.php* to *view.php* for this to eventually work.

Then, that function would check group memberships and show the Manage Users link to Administrators. In fact, you have all the relevant code already in *authorize_user .php*:

```php
// Set up the query string
$query_string =
  "SELECT ug.user_id" .
  " FROM user_groups ug, groups g" .
  " WHERE g.name = '%s'" .
  "  AND g.id = ug.group_id" .
  "  AND ug.user_id = " . mysql_real_escape_string($_COOKIE['user_id']);

// Run through each group and check membership
foreach ($groups as $group) {
  $query = sprintf($query_string, mysql_real_escape_string($group));
  $result = mysql_query($query);

  if (mysql_num_rows($result) == 1) {
  // If we got a result, the user should be allowed access
  //  Just return so the script will continue to run
   return;
  }
}
```

This code just needs to be adapted to a new function that takes in a user's ID and a group. First, add the following function to *authorize.php* in your *scripts/* directory:

```php
function user_in_group($user_id, $group) {
 $query_string =
  "SELECT ug.user_id" .
  " FROM user_groups ug, groups g" .
  " WHERE g.name = '%s'" .
  "  AND g.id = ug.group_id" .
  "  AND ug.user_id = %d";
 $query = sprintf($query_string, mysql_real_escape_string($group),
                  mysql_real_escape_string($user_id));
 $result = mysql_query($query);

 if (mysql_num_rows($result) == 1) {
  return true;
 } else {
  return false;
 }
}
```

Nothing here is new. This is just a new riff on an old hit: the code you've already got in *authorize.php*, in the authorize_user function.

Get this code in place and then try it out. First, log in as a user who's not in Administrators. Visit a page like *show_user.php*, and your menu options should not have a Manage Users options, as shown in Figure 14-3.

Now, sign out and do exactly the same thing again, this time with an administrative user. Magically—at least from the non-PHP programmer's point of view—a new menu option appears. You can see the Manage Users link in Figure 14-4.

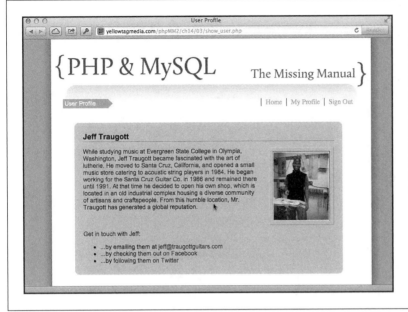

FIGURE 14-3

Ahh, pity the users who aren't Administrators. They see no Manage Users option—but, that's a good thing. You don't want users to see options they can't access. That's the heart of good authorization: as important as it is to control access, it's equally important to avoid letting people see options that they can't use anyway. Out of sight, out of mind.

FIGURE 14-4

Administrators get additional menu options, such as Manage Users, so you have to ensure that they can see those options. One thing to think about, though: you're repeating the "Administrators" group in several places in your script. You might want to think about a constant or even an is_admin function to make remembering how to spell "Administrators" unnecessary.

Refactoring Redux

In the code on page 473, shouldn't authorize_user *call* user_in_group, *because it's using that same code?*

Major refactoring points if you thought of this question, or if it felt a bit like you might be duplicating code in user_in_group, and that bothered you. It's true; there's a lot *similar* (but not quite the same) about the code in user_in_group and the code that iterates over $groups and looks up each group within authorize_user.

One way to take advantage of user_in_group and remove this similar code would be to rework the foreach in authorize_user:

```
// Remove the initial query string before
the loop


// Run through each group and check mem-
bership
foreach ($groups as $group) {
 if (user_in_group($_COOKIE['user_id'],
$group) {
  // Just return so the script will con-
tinue to run
```

```
  return;
 }

}
```

It's true, there's a lot less code, and you've done some nice refactoring. Unfortunately you've actually gone back toward the original code in authorize_user (page 472) from which you were trying to move away. Now, there's a query string created every time through the loop (hidden away within user_in_group). That string is being created over and over, and continually assigned the same user ID with each group in $groups. By moving away from that approach, you (if only in some small ways) sped up the performance of authorize_user.

Here's where you have to make a tough decision. Is the clean, refactored approach here worth the loss in speed that requires some nearly-duplicate code? In the case of a bit of code that's potentially called on most, if not every page—authorize_user—it might be worth not refactoring. That little bit of improved speed times one hundred page views (or one thousand or one million) it starts to seriously add up.

■ Entering Browser Sessions

So far, cookies have been the secret to much of your authentication and authorization success. But, there are many programmers who really, really hate a cookie-only solution to storing a user's information. The biggest issue with cookies is that they are entirely *client-side* entities. This means that anything you store in a cookie resides in that cookie, on the user's computer (the client device).

In your case, the user's ID and user name are stored on your computer. In fact, on most web browsers, you can easily look at your cookies. In Firefox, for example, you can click Preferences, select the Privacy tab, and then click "Remove individual cookies." Figure 14-5 shows the cookies related to your social networking app.

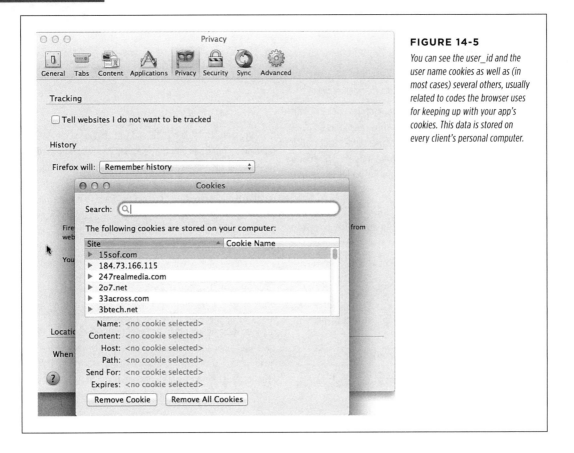

FIGURE 14-5

You can see the user_id and the user name cookies as well as (in most cases) several others, usually related to codes the browser uses for keeping up with your app's cookies. This data is stored on every client's personal computer.

NOTE In Safari for the Mac, cookies are under Safari→Preferences. Click the Privacy tab and then click the Details button. In Chrome, go to Preferences→Under the Hood→Content Settings→All Cookies and Site Data. In Internet Explorer, go to View→Internet Options→General tab, and then under Browser History, select Settings. Then, under Temporary Internet Files And History Settings, select View Files. All of these options get you the same information, although in each case it looks a bit different.

This client-side storage is the main reason some developers don't like cookies. Whether the client computer is a public device in a library in a home there's just something that seems unsafe about leaving what amounts to a system-level value like a user ID on any old computer. After all, that user ID uniquely identifies a user in your database. On top of that, most applications that use cookies add additional information to a client's computer, rather than lessening it. You might speed up user and group searches by storing cookies with the user's groups (or the IDs of those groups) in cookies; you might store personal information you don't want to constantly look up in cookies.

All of this information ends up residing on your users' computers until those cookies expire. So, what's a security-conscious programmer to do? Keep user IDs and similar information on the server, not the client side.

Sessions Are Server-Side

Sessions are generally considered the answer to the vulnerability of cookies. Sessions are similar to cookies in that they can store information. However, sessions have two big differences:

- Sessions are stored on the server rather than the client computer. People can't view session data in a browser because there's nothing to view, except perhaps a non-readable ID that connects a particular browser with a session.

- Because sessions are stored on the server, you can use them to store much bigger chunks of data than cookies. You can store a user's profile picture on the server in a session, for example, and not worry about taking up space on a user's computer.

Because you're not storing potentially sensitive information on the user's computer, many programmers prefer sessions.

Sessions Must Be Started

The biggest change in dealing with sessions isn't lots of new syntax. In fact, you'll quickly see that changing from using cookies to sessions is pretty simple. But there's one significant difference: before you can do any work with sessions, you must call session_start:

```
// Start/resume sessions
session_start();

// Now do work with session information
```

If you're already thinking you can call session_start in *signin.php*, you're right. That's exactly where you should first call session_start:

```
<?php

require_once '../scripts/database_connection.php';
require_once '../scripts/view.php';

$error_message = $_REQUEST['error_message'];

session_start();

// Rest of PHP and HTML...
```

Calling session_start here kicks off the PHP machinery that makes sessions available.

From $_COOKIE to $_SESSION

This is where it gets easy: instead of using the superglobal $_COOKIE, you use the superglobal $_SESSION. Yes, it's that easy; simply make this change in *signin.php*:

```php
<?php

require_once '../scripts/database_connection.php';
require_once '../scripts/view.php';

$error_message = $_REQUEST['error_message'];

session_start();

// If the user is logged in, the user_id in the session will be set
if (!isset($_SESSION['user_id'])) {
 // and so on...
```

Then, there's one other small change. With sessions, you don't use setcookie. Instead, you directly set values in $_SESSION, providing a key and a value:

```php
if (!isset($_SESSION['user_id'])) {

 // See if a login form was submitted with a username for login
 if (isset($_POST['username'])) {
 // Try and log the user in
 $username = mysql_real_escape_string(trim($_REQUEST['username']));
 $password = mysql_real_escape_string(trim($_REQUEST['password']));

 // Look up the user
 $query = sprintf("SELECT user_id, username FROM users " .
         " WHERE username = '%s' AND " .
         "    password = '%s';",
         $username, crypt($password, $username));

 $results = mysql_query($query);

 if (mysql_num_rows($results) == 1) {
  $result = mysql_fetch_array($results);
  $user_id = $result['user_id'];
  // No more setcookie
  $_SESSION['user_id'] = $user_id;
  $_SESSION['username'] = $username;
  header("Location: show_user.php");
 } else {
  // If user not found, issue an error
  $error_message = "Your username/password combination was invalid.";
 }
}
```

Now you use $_SESSION to both retrieve values from the session and insert values into the session. All the while, behind the scenes, all this information is stored on the server, rather than the client.

Sessions Must Be Restarted, Too

Here's something a little strange. Try to sign in by using a good user name/password combination. You're not going to see what you expect. Instead, you'll get the error about not being logged in that's illustrated in Figure 14-6.

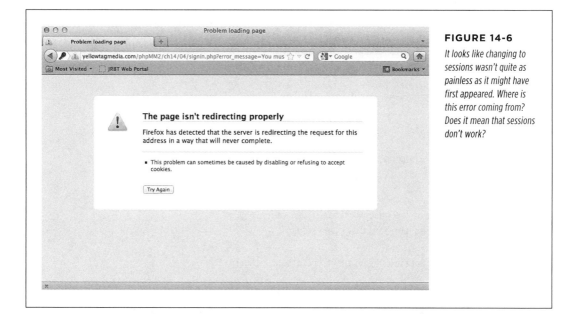

FIGURE 14-6

It looks like changing to sessions wasn't quite as painless as it might have first appeared. Where is this error coming from? Does it mean that sessions don't work?

What's going on? Think carefully; you might even want to search through *signin.php*. Is this an error related to sessions as well as the obvious cookie-related issue? Well, kind of, but it's generated by *show_user.php*, not *signin.php*. In fact, it's actually an issue in authorize_user, which resides in *authorize.php*; that function is called at the beginning of *show_user.php*:

```php
<?php

require '../scripts/authorize.php';
require '../scripts/database_connection.php';
require '../scripts/view.php';

// Authorize any user, as long as they're logged in
authorize_user();
```

When you think about it, it makes perfect sense that things aren't behaving. authorize_user (in *authorize.php*) is expecting to find a user ID in $_COOKIE:

```php
<?php

require_once 'database_connection.php';
require_once 'app_config.php';

function authorize_user($groups = NULL) {

  // No need to check groups if there aren't cookies set
  if ((!isset($_COOKIE['user_id'])) || (!strlen($_COOKIE['user_id']) > 0)) {
    header('Location: signin.php?' .
        'error_message=You must login to see this page.');
    exit();
  }
```

```
// And so on...
```

This is another easy change. $_COOKIE just has to become $_SESSION:

```php
<?php

require_once 'database_connection.php';
require_once 'app_config.php';

function authorize_user($groups = NULL) {

  // No need to check groups if there aren't cookies set
  if ((!isset($_SESSION['user_id'])) || (!strlen($_SESSION['user_id']) > 0)) {
    header('Location: signin.php?' .
        'error_message=You must login to see this page.');
    exit;
  }
```

```
// And so on...
```

Don't forget to make a similar change later in the function, when the query string used for group searching is constructed:

```php
// Set up the query string
$query_string =
  "SELECT ug.user_id" .
  " FROM user_groups ug, groups g" .
  " WHERE g.name = '%s'" .
  "   AND g.id = ug.group_id" .
  "   AND ug.user_id = " . mysql_real_escape_string($_SESSION['user_id']);
```

This looks better. Unfortunately, you're going to get the exact same result. Sign in again, and you'll get Figure 14-7, yet another error. What's going on now?

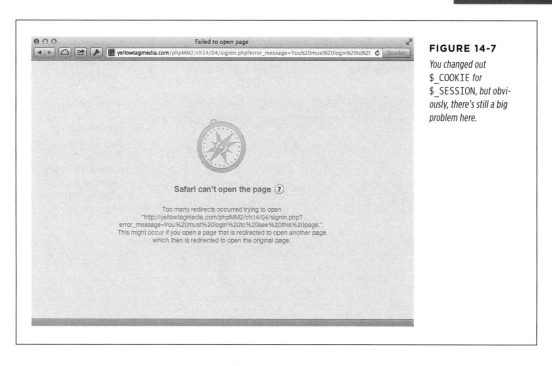

FIGURE 14-7

You changed out
$\$\_COOKIE$ *for*
$\$\_SESSION$, *but obviously, there's still a big problem here.*

> **NOTE** You might see a different response, depending on your browser. You might see a timeout, or your browser just might hang. In all these cases, it's not good.

The secret is in the rather poorly named session_start function. That function sounds like it starts a new session. In that case, you should call it once—as you did—in *signin.php*. However, PHP scripts each run on their own, without connection to any other script. As a result, when *show_user.php* is called, it has no idea that a session was started back in *signin.php*.

In fact, there's no connection at all between two scripts; they're just two calls from a browser out there somewhere, hooked to the Internet via Wi-Fi or an Ethernet cable. So, how do two scripts—or an entire application's worth of scripts—share this session data? The truth is a bit surprising: calling start_session actually creates a cookie on the client. Yes, you're back to cookies!

Unlike other cookies you've seen so far, though, this one holds a fairly cryptic value (see Figure 14-8). This value refers to where a particular user's data is stored on the server. It's a way to say, "Look up this code in all the server's session data. Whatever's there... that's mine."

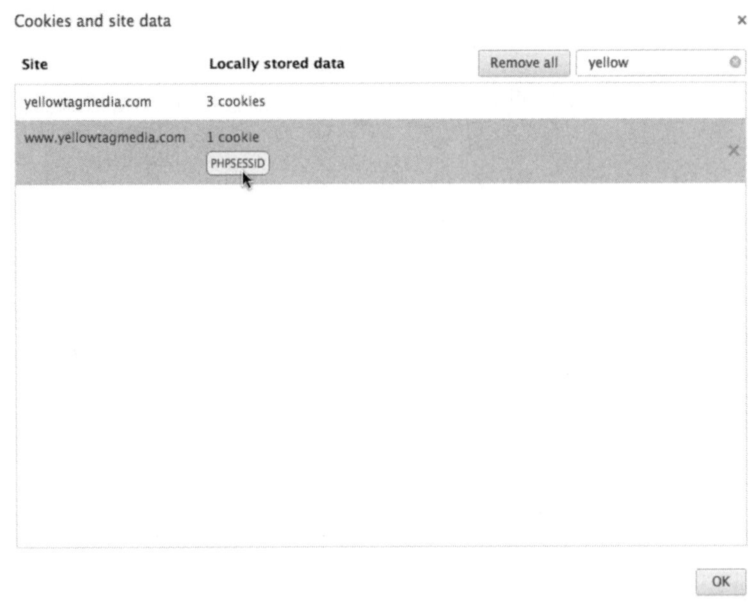

FIGURE 14-8

All the work you've been doing in this section to move away from cookies actually requires cookies. Still, you're avoiding any valuable information being stored on the client. The unique key isn't useful to anyone who doesn't have access to your server, and that's a good, secure thing.

What all of this means is that `session_start` does a lot more than start a one-time session. It looks up a user's cookie, and if it's there, *restarts* the session that ID references, so every script that wants to use `$_SESSION` has to call `session_start`.

Fixing the problem in *show_user.php* means two things: first, you need to call `session_start` in *authorize.php*, to ensure that session data is available to `authorize_user` and the other functions in *authorize.php*.

```php
<?php

require_once 'database_connection.php';
require_once 'app_config.php';

session_start();

function authorize_user($groups = NULL) {
  // an so on...
}
?>
```

Try this out, and you'll see an error pointing you to the second thing you've got to do. That error is a familiar one, and you can see it in Figure 14-9.

FIGURE 14-9

You've seen this a few times, such as on page 244. What's going on in this particular case? For some reason, the code that looks up the user's ID isn't working, and it's kicking the user out with this error about his information not being found.

$_REQUEST Doesn't Include $_SESSION

Here's the line in *show_user.php* that's causing the problem:

```
// Get the user ID of the user to show
$user_id = $_REQUEST['user_id'];
```

This worked when you were using cookies for authorization (page 424) because whether the user's ID was in $_REQUEST, $_GET, $_POST, or $_COOKIE didn't matter. All of these bubble up to $_REQUEST. Now, however, you're passing the user ID in a different superglobal, one not included in $_REQUEST: $_SESSION.

Not only that, you still have code in *show_users.php* that passes the user ID in a request parameter:

```
$user_row = sprintf(
 "<li><a href='show_user.php?user_id=%d'>%s %s</a> " .
 "(<a href='mailto:%s'>%s</a>) " .
 "<a href='javascript:delete_user(%d);'><img " .
  "class='delete_user' src='../images/delete.png' " .
  "width='15' /></a></li>",
 $user['user_id'], $user['first_name'], $user['last_name'],
 $user['email'], $user['email'], $user['user_id']);
echo $user_row;
```

NOTE This code is deep into the middle of *show_users.php.* Look for the `while` loop within the HTML and you'll find it.

Clearly, you can't just switch $_REQUEST to $_SESSION and call it a day. Instead, you need to check both $_SESSION and $_REQUEST to cover all your bases:

```php
<?php

require '../scripts/authorize.php';
require '../scripts/database_connection.php';
require '../scripts/view.php';

// Authorize any user, as long as they're logged in
authorize_user();

// Get the user ID of the user to show
$user_id = $_REQUEST['user_id'];

if (!isset($user_id)) {
 $user_id = $_SESSION['user_id'];
}

// Look up user using $user_id
```

Now, if there's no user ID found in $_REQUEST, the $_SESSION is checked. And then, last but not least, you need to call `session_start` before you can do any work with the session:

```php
<?php

require '../scripts/authorize.php';
require '../scripts/database_connection.php';
require '../scripts/view.php';

session_start();

// Authorize any user, as long as they're logged in
authorize_user();

// Get the user ID of the user to show
$user_id = $_REQUEST['user_id'];

if (!isset($user_id)) {
 $user_id = $_SESSION['user_id'];
}

// Look up user using $user_id
```

Finally, you can get back to viewing user profiles.

> **NOTE** You're actually now calling `session_start` twice in the *show_user.php* flow: once in *authorize .php*, pulled in through `require_once`; and a second time, in the body of *show_user.php*.
>
> Still, that extra call doesn't do much beyond causing PHP to issue a notice, and there's no guarantee that other scripts that bring in *authorize.php* will also call `session_start`. Thus, the duplicate in *show_user.php* won't always happen. It's a better bet to treat each script as self-contained. Use `session_start` *every time* you're working with sessions, even if it might have been called somewhere else.

Menu, Anyone?

All that's left is the menu that's created in *view.php*. It still uses $_COOKIE, but you know exactly what to do now. First, add the all-important call to session_start:

```php
<?php

require_once 'app_config.php';
require_once 'authorize.php';

define("SUCCESS_MESSAGE", "success");
define("ERROR_MESSAGE", "error");

session_start();

// And then functions follow...

?>
```

Then, replace $_COOKIE with $_SESSION in display_title:

```php
unction display_title($title, $success_msg = NULL, $error_msg = NULL) {
echo <<<EOD
 <body>
 <div id="header"><h1>PHP & MySQL: The Missing Manual</h1></div>
 <div id="example">$title</div>
 <div id="menu">
  <ul>
   <li><a href="index.html">Home</a></li>
EOD;
 if (isset($_SESSION['user_id'])) {
  echo "<li><a href='show_user.php'>My Profile</a>";
  if (user_in_group($_SESSION['user_id'], "Administrators")) {
   echo "<li><a href='show_users.php'>Manage Users</a></li>";
  }
  echo "<li><a href='signout.php'>Sign Out</a></li>";
 } else {
  echo "<li><a href='signin.php'>Sign In</a></li>";
```

```
  }
echo <<<EOD
  </ul>
  </div>
EOD;
  display_messages($success_msg, $error_msg);
}
```

Be sure to check your menu; when you're logged in, you should see Sign Out and My Profile. When you're signed out, you shouldn't.

And Then, Sign Out...

That leads you back to signing out. With cookies, you set the expiration value to a time in the past. With $_SESSION, you need to call unset on the session variable.

And, as odd as it might seem, you can't work with $_SESSION—even if that work is to unset values—without calling session_start. Here's what *signout.php* should look like:

```
<?php

session_start();

unset($_SESSION['user_id']);
unset($_SESSION['username']);

header('Location: signin.php');
?>
```

The cookies are gone, and once *signout.php* runs, so will your user's sessions variables.

And just like that, with less than 20 lines of code changed, you've moved out of cookies and into sessions. Nice work! Your security-conscious users will thank you for it.

■ Memory Lane: Remember That Phishing Problem?

There's just one little annoyance left to which you should attend. Remember the phishing problem back in Chapter 8 on page 236? It had to do with your use of error_message as a request parameter to *show_error.php*. *show_error.php* takes in the error message it displays from a request parameter:

```
if (isset($_REQUEST['error_message'])) {
  $error_message = preg_replace("/\\\\/", '', $_REQUEST['error_message']);
} else {
  $error_message = "something went wrong, and that's how you ended up here.";
}
```

NOTE This code is in *scripts/show_error.php*.

And you saw that a URL like this:

*http://yellowtagmedia.com/phpMM2/ch08/scripts/show_error.
php?error_message=%3Ca%20href=%22http://www.amctv.com/shows/
breaking-bad%22%3EClick%20Here%20To%20Report%20Your%20Error%3C/a%3E*

could create a page that looks like Figure 14-10. It seems safe, but it's not.

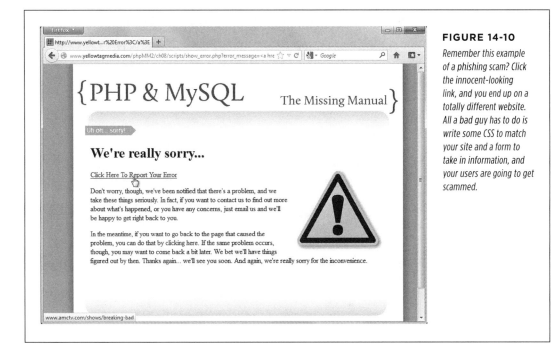

FIGURE 14-10

*Remember this example
of a phishing scam? Click
the innocent-looking
link, and you end up on a
totally different website.
All a bad guy has to do is
write some CSS to match
your site and a form to
take in information, and
your users are going to get
scammed.*

With sessions, you don't have to settle for this security hole. The security problem stemmed from the fact that you were letting a request parameter handle the error message payload. But now, with sessions, you can remove those errors from view. This way, a hacker can't possibly force-feed in a bad request parameter because you're no longer using those parameters for that purpose.

Hop back over to *scripts/app_config.php*, and look at handle_error:

```
function handle_error($user_error_message, $system_error_message) {
  header("Location: " . SITE_ROOT . "scripts/show_error.php?" .
    "error_message={$user_error_message}&" .
    "system_error_message={$system_error_message}");
  exit();
}
```

That's the code that turns a PHP-supplied error into a request parameter. But now, you can rework this code using sessions:

```php
function handle_error($user_error_message, $system_error_message) {
  session_start();
  $_SESSION['error_message'] = $user_error_message;
  $_SESSION['system_error_message'] = $system_error_message;
  header("Location: " . SITE_ROOT . "scripts/show_error.php");
  exit();
}
```

It's a simple change. In fact, it makes handle_error a lot clearer.

Open *show_error.php* and make the accompanying change to pull values from the session:

```php
<?php
require 'app_config.php';

session_start();

if (isset($_SESSION['error_message'])) {
  $error_message = preg_replace("/\\\\/", '', $_SESSION['error_message']);
} else {
  $error_message = "something went wrong, and that's how you ended up here.";
}

if (isset($_SESSION['system_error_message'])) {
  $system_error_message = preg_replace("/\\\\/", '',
                    $_SESSION['system_error_message']);
} else {
  $system_error_message = "No system-level error message was reported.";
}
?>
```

NOTE The HTML portion below the PHP stays exactly the same.

Next, update the problematic URL to reflect the new location of *show_user.php* (in your *scripts/* directory). So it might look something like this:

*http://yellowtagmedia.com/phpMM2/ch14/scripts/show_error.php?
error_message=%3Ca%20href=%22http://www.amctv.com/shows/
breaking-bad%22%3EClick%20Here%20To%20Report%20Your%20Error%3C/a%3E*

NOTE You should be able to replace the domain name and update the path but leave the file name and request parameters the same.

Now, visit that page in your browser. You should see a response like that shown in Figure 14-11.

FIGURE 14-11

Sessions protect you, and in many cases, actually simplify your code. A session is often a better choice for passing data between scripts, and it certainly beats using request parameters in most cases.

This time, that phishing message is gone. Because the error message is stored in the session, it's resistant to someone coming along and controlling the message via the URL. It's a tiny change with huge implications for your users.

■ Why Would You Ever Use Cookies?

It's easy to think that sessions are the answer for everything. They're not, though. Probably the biggest limitation with sessions is that when the browser closes, the session's over. There's no way to get around that limitation. If you want to offer users the ability to remain logged in across browser closings, sessions aren't an option. You've got to use cookies.

Second, just because cookies can be used poorly doesn't mean you *have* to use them poorly. You can expire your cookies more frequently. You can store only very small bits of information in your cookies. In addition, you can avoid storing much meaningful data in cookies. In fact, you might choose to do a few extra database lookups—even causing your app to run a little slower—to avoid storing much useful information on your users' computers.

Of course, like almost everything at this stage of the game, you're going to have to make a good decision for *your* application. But, that's no problem. You know what you're doing now, and you know the tools at your disposal. Use them wisely, play around...and most important, learn.

Appendixes

Installing PHP on Windows Without WAMP

I n Chapter 1, you installed 7 either MAMP for Mac OS X or WAMP for Windows. That collection of programs, all conveniently bundled together, gave you not just PHP but also MySQL, plus an Apache web server and a few other goodies like phpMyAdmin and SQLiteManager. It's easy to install and lets you control all your programs from a centralized manager.

On the other hand, convenience almost always costs you control. In the case of WAMP, you lose the ability to pick a specific version of PHP. In fact, you're often going to end up with a version of PHP that's several months behind the latest stable release, simply because that's the amount of time it takes the good folks at WAMP to update their bundle to that release. (For more information on releases, see the box on page 30.)

Most of the time, none of this is an issue. But, as you become more familiar with PHP (and more advanced) you might want to take back some of the control you gave up for the convenience of WAMP. If that's the case, then you'll want to install PHP manually, and this appendix instructs you how.

Release the Version Within

If you've never worked with software that comes in versions or releases, don't worry; it's easy. A software *version* or *release* is simply a program (or, more often than not, a package of programs that work together) that's ready to install on your computer.

Because software changes frequently, though, the folks that make software need a way to say, "Hey, our software has some new cool bells and whistles! There's a new package available!" Software companies use *version numbers* (or *release numbers*)

to do that. Generally, software starts out at version 1.0, and that number increments higher as the software adds new features. Thus, version 2.2 of PHP is newer than version 1.1, and probably will have some cool new features, too.

Sometimes, as on the PHP website, you'll see several different packages or downloads, each with a different version number. Most of the time, you want to download the most recent version. Most important, ensure that you're downloading the correct version for the operating system you're using.

■ Installing PHP from *www.php.net*

Open your favorite web browser and head to *www.php.net*. This website is the online home of PHP, and it's where you'll download your own version of the PHP language, along with all the tools you need to write and run PHP programs. Look along the right side of the PHP home page for the Stable Releases heading; you can see it on the right of Figure A-1.

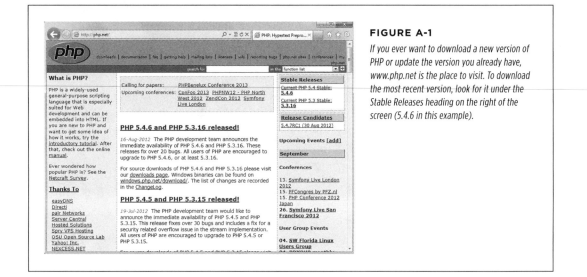

FIGURE A-1

If you ever want to download a new version of PHP or update the version you already have, www.php.net is the place to visit. To download the most recent version, look for it under the Stable Releases heading on the right of the screen (5.4.6 in this example).

Click the link for the version with the highest number.

Once you've chosen a PHP version link, you'll see a screen similar to Figure A-2, with links for the current version of PHP as well as at least one older version (which you can identify by the lower version number).

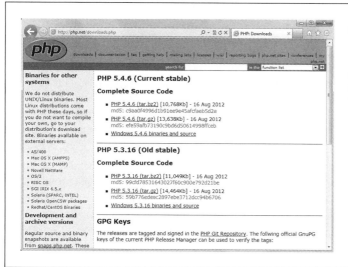

FIGURE A-2

The PHP site always has at least the latest stable version and the previous stable version available for download. Unless you've got a good reason to do otherwise, always go with the latest stable version, which is the one listed at the top.

Before you download PHP, though, look for a link called Windows Binaries; that's your ticket to getting PHP up and running on your Windows-based computer. Clicking this link takes you to another site, *http://windows.php.net/download/,* which should look something like Figure A-3.

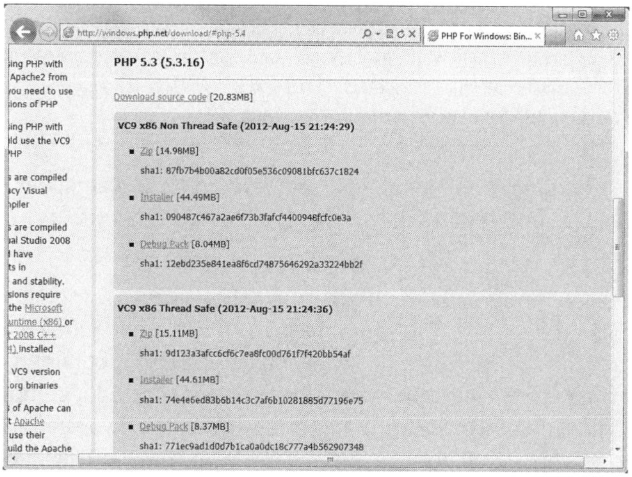

FIGURE A-3

PHP has a page dedicated to downloads for Windows-based computers. There are still a lot of options, but don't get distracted by all the choices. You're looking for a single word: Installer.

This page has options for the latest version and well as several older versions. For the newest version, there will be two big, gray blocks: the first for the Non Thread Safe version, and the second for the Thread Safe version. You want to download the Non Thread Safe version. To learn why, read the following box.

UNDER THE HOOD

PHP on Windows: Fast or Safe?

PHP first appeared in a Windows-friendly version back in 2000. In those early releases, PHP came in only one flavor: Thread Safe. Whereas Mac OS X and Unix/Linux systems use something called *processes* to run multiple things at one time, Windows systems use *threads*. Those Windows threads can interact with each other. To prevent them from messing one another up, PHP came in a version that was *thread safe*.

Unfortunately, keeping those threads out of each other's way takes a lot of time. Yes, thread-safe PHP on Windows is slow, and PHP programmers flocked away from Windows whenever possible. A few clever PHP programmers figured out ways to recycle threads, and a lot of web servers that run on Windows now come preinstalled with a PHP version that can recycle threads right from the start.

Still, not everyone likes installing PHP and then having to install a tweaked web server or make manual changes to PHP to get it running at tip-top speed. As a result, there's now a *non-thread safe* option. This option doesn't worry about other threads, and the result is a pretty significant performance increase, ranging anywhere from 10 to 40 percent, depending on your applications.

Chances are that if you don't have a strong opinion or idea about which version of the PHP binaries you need, you'll do great with the non-thread safe binaries, and you'll get a nice snappy performance. If you have real concerns about the non-thread safe version, you can certainly choose the thread-safe binaries and tweak your own installation as you see fit.

Just look for the Installer option and click the link. The download is usually large, but includes a nice Windows installer that will make getting PHP running a breeze. Click this link and then grab a cup of coffee while you're waiting for your download to complete.

NOTE If you're wondering whether you could have just gone directly to *http://windows.php.net/download*— you're right. You could have. Six months from now, you might forget that longer URL, but remember *www.php .net*. On top of that, a good old-fashioned Google search for PHP takes you to *www.php.net*, so it's a good idea to know how to get to the Windows installer from the main PHP home page.

Once your download is done, find the downloaded file and double-click it. Let Windows run the installer and then click Next on the pop-up screen to start the installation.

You have to accept a license agreement and then select an installation directory. Going with the suggested directory, *C:\Program Files\PHP*, is a good idea unless you have a specific reason not to. Next, the installer asks you about configuring a web server, as shown in Figure A-4. For now, you'll be using PHP on your computer to test programs and then upload those programs to a web server, so you can select "Do not setup a web server." If you want to add a web server later, you can always come back and add or change this option.

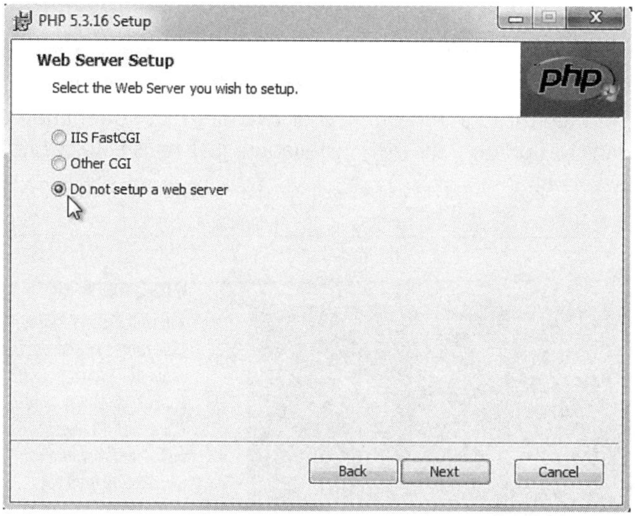

FIGURE A-4

If you want to install a local web server to test your entire web applications on your computer, in the Web Server Setup window, select the IIS FastCGI or Other CGI option. But for getting started, "Do not setup a web server" is the simplest option.

Next, you'll be prompted about which items to install. The default options shown in Figure A-5 are fine for now. Just click Next to go to the next screen.

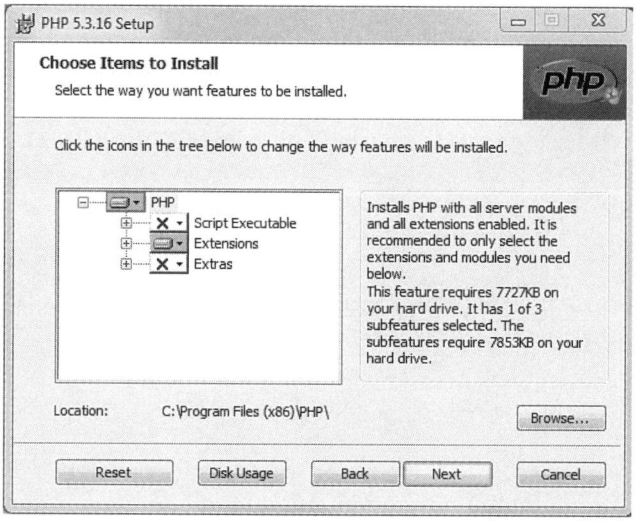

FIGURE A-5

The Windows installer comes with the basic PHP installation, but you can also add several extra by clicking the white + box next to Extras and selecting individual features.

Finally, click Install and then let your progress indicator march to full. That's it! You've got PHP running on your computer.

To check out PHP, open a command prompt and type **php_version**, as you see in Figure A-6.

Even though it doesn't look like much, that blank line and empty command prompt means PHP is installed correctly. Now, you're ready to get into your first program— or if you've already worked through this book, your twentieth...or your hundredth! And anytime you want to update your PHP installation, just revisit *www.php.net* and download a new version.

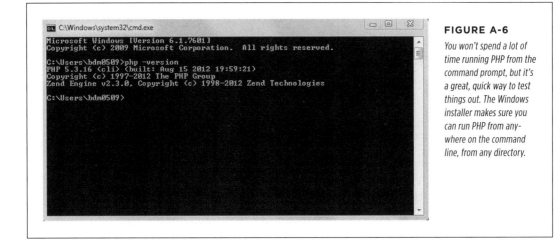

FIGURE A-6

You won't spend a lot of time running PHP from the command prompt, but it's a great, quick way to test things out. The Windows installer makes sure you can run PHP from any-where on the command line, from any directory.

Installing MySQL
Without MAMP or WAMP

J ust as you might find it useful to install PHP apart from the WAMP stack on a Windows-based computer as described in Appendix A, you might similarly find it useful to install MySQL without using WAMP (Windows) or MAMP (Mac OS X). By installing MySQL manually, you can control the versions you're using, the paths MySQL and related programs use, and all the MySQL-specific environment variables.

Of course, manual installation isn't for everyone. Avoiding MAMP or WAMP doesn't make MySQL work any better, per se; installing MySQL yourself is mostly an exercise in getting a better handle on what's going on with your system. On the other hand, that's a good goal in and of itself and can actually help you become a better programmer.

▉ Installing MySQL

The MySQL database is easy to get, easy to install, and easy to use, even without the convenience of WAMP and MAMP. The process is slightly different for Windows and Mac OS X, but the end result is the same: an installation of MySQL that's separate from the web server and from your computer's copy of PHP.

MySQL on Windows

Installing MySQL on Windows is straightforward. You just need to know one thing: whether your computer is running the 32-bit or 64-bit version of Windows. For example, in Windows 7 you can determine this by clicking your Start menu, right-clicking Computer, and then selecting Properties from the pop-up menu. You should see something like Figure B-1.

FIGURE B-1

The computer shown here is a 64-bit system, running Windows 7 Home Premium. Whether you have 32-bit or 64-bit is determined partly by the Windows version you have installed, but also by what your computer is capable of. Both 32-bit and 64-bit systems can run MySQL with no problems, so either works great.

Under the System section, Look for "System type." It will be either "32-bit Operating System" or "64-bit Operating System." Remember which one it is, because you'll need this information in a minute.

Next, start your web browser and visit *www.mysql.com*. A page opens, similar to in Figure B-2, showing you lots of introductory information about MySQL. You can skip all that and click the big "Downloads (GA)" tab to get right to the software. A page appears that presents information about a few different versions of MySQL. You want the first one—MySQL Community Server—so click the DOWNLOAD link under that option.

This page auto-detects that you're running Windows and presents you several choices (see Figure B-3). You want the version that offers you an MSI installer and matches your system type (32-bit or 64-bit). Select the correct version. You're then asked to register on the MySQL website. If you're worried that the MySQL folks might one day use your street address to stage a government coup, you can skip this option and go straight to the download servers.

FIGURE B-2

A few years back, MySQL moved from a completely open-source project to a company-backed project. The database is still free, but now there's a much more professional support system behind it. That's much of what www. mysql.com website offers: professional support and documentation.

FIGURE B-3

Just as with PHP, you have lots of choices about which version and release of MySQL to download. Generally, the best option is the MSI Installer that matches your system. The Zip archive options aren't packed up nearly so nicely.

Once your download is complete, you have a file called something like *mysql-5.5.27.2.msi*. Double-click this file to run the installer. The installation wizard prompts you to select "Install MySQL Products"; requires you to accept a license agreement; gives you a chance to fetch the latest components from the Internet, which you should do; and finally, lets you choose the setup type. Select Developer Default, and then let the installation process whir along.

Next, you must click through the installation of a secondary set of programs and then the installation will finish. When it's done, you see several Server Configuration options (Figure B-4). Take this opportunity to get your computer and MySQL playing nicely together.

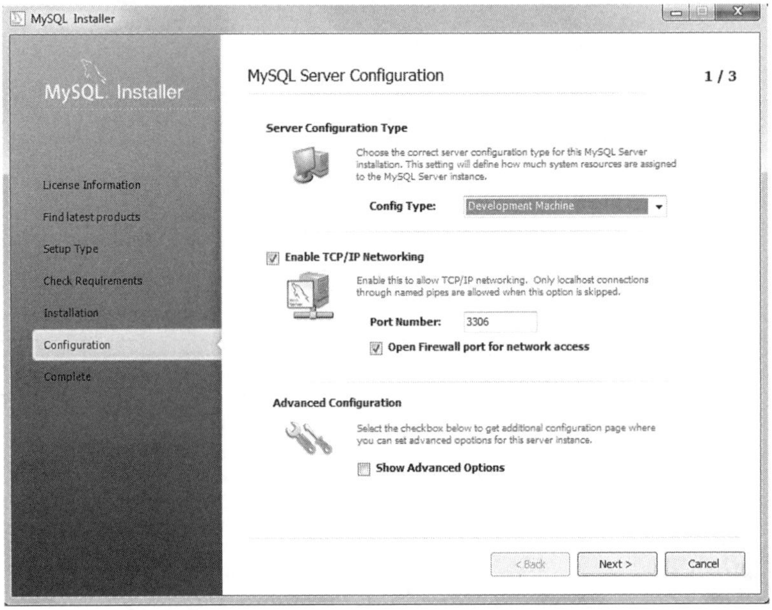

FIGURE B-4

MySQL is worth a thick book on its own. There are literally hundreds of options you can tweak to make it run better, faster, and with less strain on your system. For your purposes, though, these aren't the issue; you just want a local database in which you can store information.

In the configuration wizard, unless there's something specific about your system to change, accept the standard configuration. For the Config Type, though, choose Development Machine and then click Next.

Next, you must enter a *root password*, which is basically a master password. If this were a real database running on a server for, say, Amazon or Zappos, here's where you'd come up with some wild, 22-character password that the most powerful computer couldn't crack. Of course, you're just running MySQL on your own computer, so something a little less intimidating is fine; try `myqsl_root` if you're stumped.

You should also create at least one user who has MySQL access privileges. Figure B-5 shows a user called bdm0509, with a password and administrative privileges.

Then, be sure to let MySQL set itself up as a Windows service. This simply means that your Windows installation can access and control MySQL directly. Configure your setup so that MySQL starts automatically when your computer is turned on. Also, turn on the checkbox to add the MySQL bin directory to your Windows path (see Figure B-6), which means that when you start up a command prompt, you can run MySQL programs.

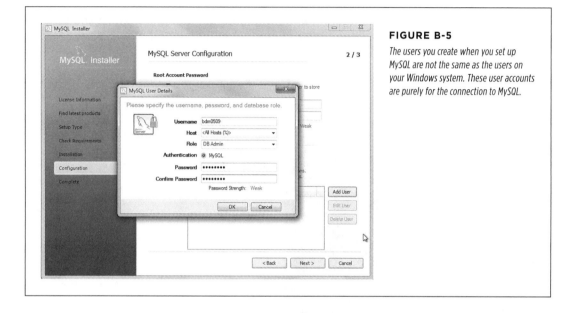

FIGURE B-5

The users you create when you set up MySQL are not the same as the users on your Windows system. These user accounts are purely for the connection to MySQL.

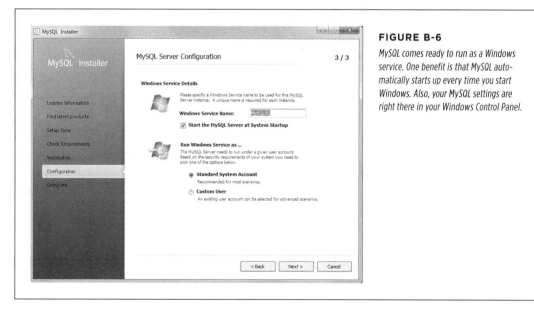

FIGURE B-6

MySQL comes ready to run as a Windows service. One benefit is that MySQL automatically starts up every time you start Windows. Also, your MySQL settings are right there in your Windows Control Panel.

At last, the MySQL installer is ready to execute your setup. Click Next and let the installer spin away.

NOTE You're starting to get a handle on why most of the programmers you might have met are impatient, a bit jittery, and drink a lot of coffee. There's a lot of waiting around when it comes to installing software, and a lot more waiting when it comes to running your programs and making sure they behave the way they're supposed to.

When the wizard closes, your MySQL database is installed. When you click the Start menu, you see a new program available, the MySQL Command Line Client, as shown in Figure B-7.

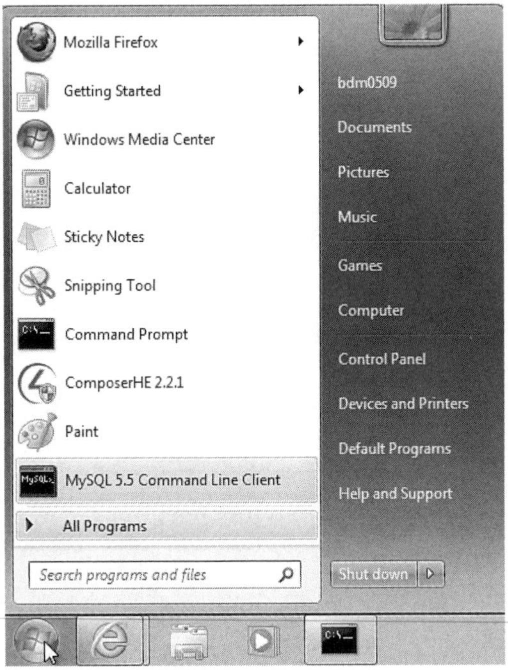

FIGURE B-7

*If you ever lose track of the MySQL command-line client, you can just open up a command prompt and type **mysql**. This command starts the command-line client, as long as you were careful to add the MySQL bin directory to your Windows PATH during installation of MySQL.*

Start the command-line client and enter your super-secret password. You should see something similar to Figure B-8.

That's it: if you can log into MySQL, you've got a running database, and you're ready to start working with that database and shoving information into it.

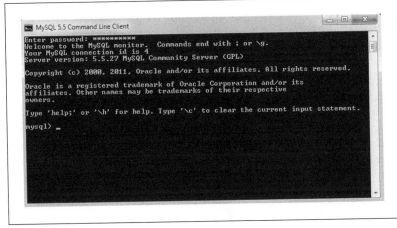

FIGURE B-8

The command-line program always starts by asking you for your password. That's not trivial; you can do everything from creating and deleting structures to messing around with MySQL's data from this command line. It's like a direct line of access to MySQL, which is exactly what you'll need for testing out the PHP code you'll be writing soon.

MySQL on Mac OS X

The MySQL installation process on Mac OS X is similar to the installation on Windows. Visit *www.mysql.com* and select the Downloads (GA) tab near the top of the page. Then, select the "MySQL Community Server" link to get to the downloads. The site should autodetect that you're on Mac OS X and present options like those shown in Figure B-9.

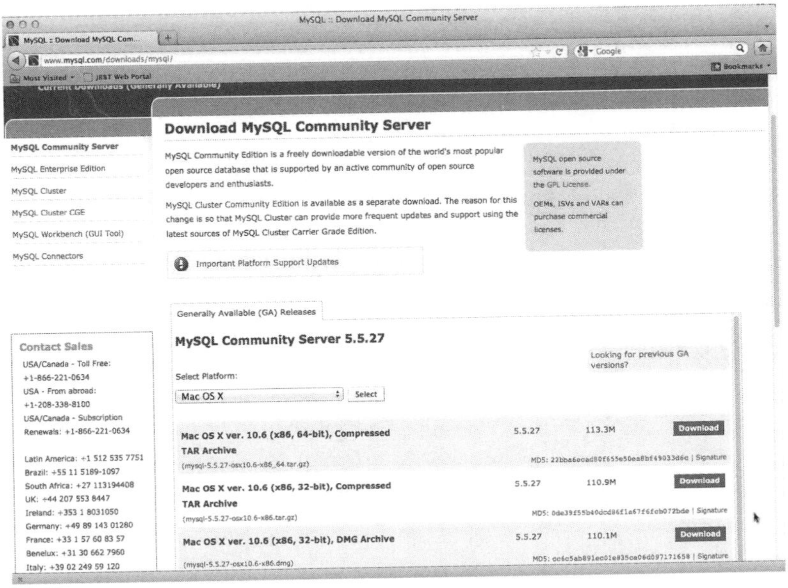

FIGURE B-9

As with the Windows versions, you have plenty of options from which to choose for Mac OS X. The developers that work on MySQL tend to favor the Compressed TAR Archive options, because those give you the actual MySQL code. Because you're not planning on working on the actual MySQL code, that's a lot more than you need.

Scroll down and find the DMG links. These are easy-to-install versions of MySQL that provide a (graphic user interface) and a nice setup. First, though, you must determine whether you have a 32-bit or 64-bit system. This is a multistep process on Macs.

First, choose →About This Mac. Click the "More Info" button, which opens a window like the one in Figure B-10. Look for the line that reads "Processor" or "Processor Name".

FIGURE B-10

There's no one-step process for figuring out whether your system is 32-bit or 64-bit on Macs. That's because that decision is based on your computer's processor, so you need to establish which type of processor your computer is using.

Look up your processor in Table B-1; this will let you know whether your Mac is 32-bit or 64-bit.

TABLE B-1 *Fortunately, you don't have to worry about tons of options. Macs have one choice (32-bit or 64-bit) for each processor.*

PROCESSOR NAME	32-BIT OR 64-BIT
Intel Core Solo	32-bit
Intel Core Duo	32-bit
Intel Core 2 Duo	64-bit
Intel Quad-Core Xeon	64-bit
Dual-Core Intel Xeon	64-bit
Quad-Core Intel Xeon	64-bit
Core i3	64-bit
Core i5	64-bit
Core i7	64-bit

Macs, PCs, are constantly coming out with new hardware. If you can't find your processor in Table B-1, visit *http://support.apple.com/kb/HT3696*, which usually has an updated list of processor names and whether they're 32-bit or 64-bit.

Now, select the DMG download for MySQL that matches your processor. You can then register (or skip registration), select a download site, and start your download.

Once the DMG is downloaded, it opens automatically. You should see several files, as shown in Figure B-11.

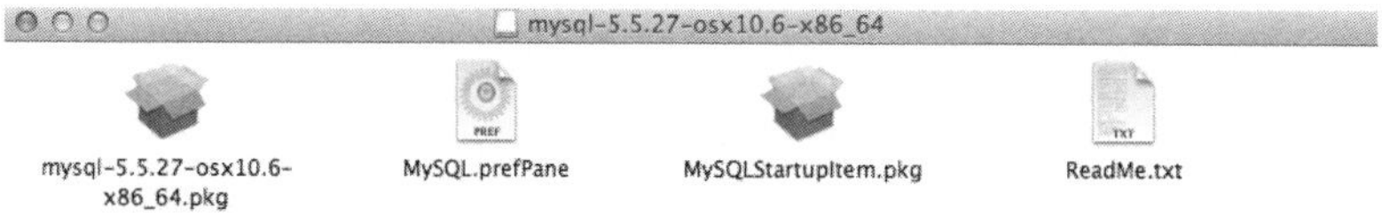

FIGURE B-11

Most DMGs have a single file and, if you're lucky, some poorly written instructions. MySQL is a little more heavyweight, though, so you get the core installation, a preference pane (which you'll install in a few minutes), a program to handle automatic startup, and a helpful ReadMe.txt file.

Select the main file, which is called something like *mysql-5.5.27-osx10.6-x86_64.pkg*.

NOTE On Mac OSX Mountain Lion, you must Control-click, click Open, and then click Open again in the resulting warning box. This procedure gets you past Mountain Lion's restrictions on opening files from an unidentified developer.

Double-click this file to begin installation. You'll have to agree to a license and select an installation location. You then must type an administrator password for your computer to launch the installation itself.

NOTE If you're on your own Mac, this password is most likely the password you normally use for login. Macs with only a single user set that user up as an administrator. Otherwise, go make some cookies and bribe the computer's owner to give you an admin account and let you turn her Mac OS X computer into a PHP and MySQL powerhouse.

Installation doesn't take long. While it's proceeding, you see a screen like the one in Figure B-12.

Don't get too excited, though. There are a few steps left. Go back to the DMG, double-click it to reopen it if necessary so that you can see its contents again (which you saw back in Figure B-11).

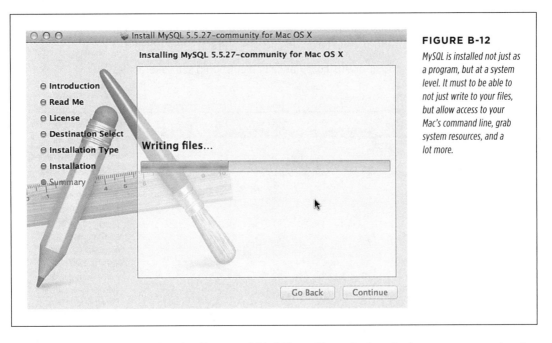

FIGURE B-12

MySQL is installed not just as a program, but at a system level. It must to be able to not just write to your files, but allow access to your Mac's command line, grab system resources, and a lot more.

Double-click the file named *MySQL.prefPane*. System Preferences opens, showing you a new pane just for controlling MySQL. It also asks you whether you want to install this pane for you alone, or all users. (You can probably keep the pane to yourself, unless there's a line behind you of other database-hungry users.)

Once the pane is installed, it's automatically opened, as shown in Figure B-13. Turn on the checkbox to have MySQL startup automatically and then enter your password one more time. When you're done, start up MySQL to verify that things are working as they should.

And with that, you have an installed, running database on your Mac. Now, start a new Terminal window (Applications→Utilities→Terminal). (If you haven't done so already, drag that Terminal icon into your dock where you can get to it easily.) In the Terminal window, type the following command:

```
$ /usr/local/mysql/bin/mysql
```

This command is a bit long, unfortunately. That's because one thing the installation *doesn't* do is set up your path so that you can easily call the MySQL tools and programs. Still, you'll probably do most of your MySQL work on your web server, so it isn't a huge deal.

This command starts the MySQL command prompt. You should see output like that shown in Figure B-14.

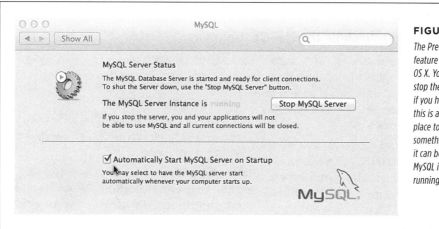

FIGURE B-13

The Preferences Pane is a feature of MySQL on Mac OS X. You can start and stop the database, and if you have problems, this is a quick convenient place to go figure out why something is going wrong: it can be as simple as your MySQL installation isn't running.

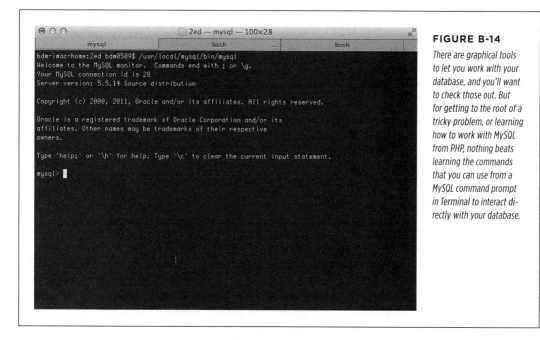

FIGURE B-14

There are graphical tools to let you work with your database, and you'll want to check those out. But for getting to the root of a tricky problem, or learning how to work with MySQL from PHP, nothing beats learning the commands that you can use from a MySQL command prompt in Terminal to interact directly with your database.

If you're seeing something similar on your Mac, you have a running installation of MySQL, and you're ready to start working with your database.

Update Your PATH to Include the MySQL Programs

It's a bit disappointing that after you went to all the trouble of downloading MySQL and installing it—including a handy Preferences pane—you still can't just type mysql at a Terminal window and get off to the races. Still, if you're not afraid of a little work, you can fix this problem yourself.

The secret to all these programs that run—and don't run—in your Terminal is your computer's PATH. That's a special variable (just like the variables discussed on page 52) that tells your computer where to look when you enter a command. When you type mysql, if your PATH includes */usr/local/mysql/bin*, your computer looks in that directory, sees a program called mysql, and runs it. Perfect!

But, what about when your PATH doesn't include a directory you want? You can update the PATH, but it involves editing a file that's normally hidden. First, go back to Terminal and enter these two commands:

```
$ defaults write com.apple.finder Apple-
ShowAllFiles TRUE
$ killall Finder
```

The first line instructs the Finder—the program that shows you directories on a Mac—to show hidden files, including the one you need to edit. The second line restarts Finder and puts this change into action. Next, open a Finder window and go to your home directory. You'll see a bit of a weird view of your normal directory window; it probably looks something like Figure B-15. You'll see tons of files that are light gray, and seem faded or nearly invisible. These files are normally hidden from your view, and you might notice that most of them begin with a dot (.), which is why they're hidden.

Scroll until you find a file called *.profile*, and open that file in a text editor like Mac OS X's TextEdit. If you've never worked with PATHs before, you might not have this file at all, and that's okay, too. Just open TextEdit to a new file.

You want to add two lines to this file:

```
MYSQL_HOME=/usr/local/mysql
export PATH=$MYSQL_HOME/bin:$PATH
```

If you're creating a new file, just make these the first lines. If you already have a *.profile*, add these lines at the very bottom of whatever else is in the file.

The first line creates a new variable called MYSQL_HOME, and sets it to where you installed MySQL. This way, if you ever change your MySQL installation location, you can just update this variable, just like you updated the $facebook_url variable in your PHP script. The second line then sets the PATH variable to be the current PATH, but it adds the *bin* directory under MYSQL_HOME to the beginning of that path. The export keyword instructs Mac OS X to make this updated PATH variable available to all the programs on your computer.

Finally, save your file. If you're creating a new file, be careful to name it correctly, beginning the file name with a dot (.). You also need to ensure that the file doesn't have an extension. If you accidentally save the file with an extension, just remove that extension in Finder.

When you're done, you should have a file in your home directory called *.profile*. It should be grayed out, too, because it's hidden. Now, you can open up a new Terminal window and type **mysql**. You should see the MySQL command line program open right up.

Finally, before you hang up your new system-editing ninja skills, set Finder to hide all those files again:

```
$ defaults write com.apple.finder Apple-
ShowAllFiles FALSE
$ killall Finder
```

You can always unhide them if you need to access them later.

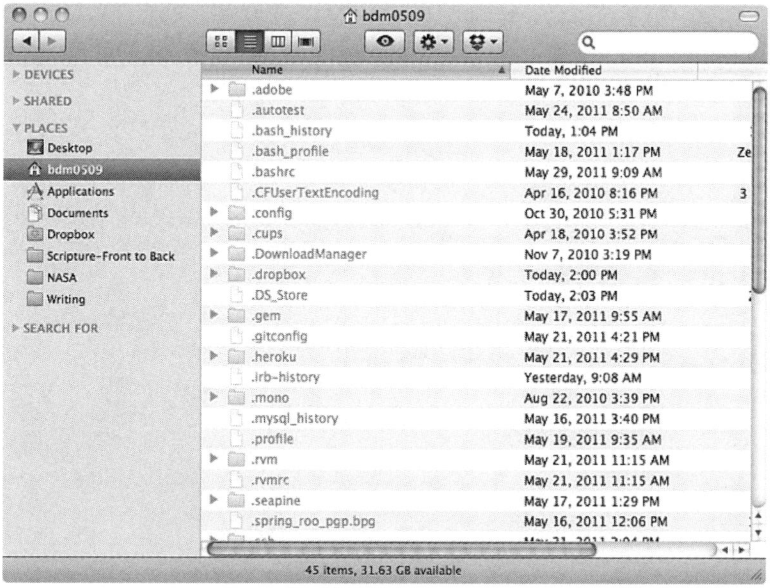

FIGURE B-15

Most programs that update and work on your system itself create hidden files, all starting with a dot (.). So, git, a version control system, creates .gitconfig, and DropBox, a popular file-sharing system, creates .dropbox.

Index

Symbols

0 (zero)
    arrays counting from, 84
    functions counting from, 76
    using in programming languages, 74
1:1 relationships, 458
1Password, 402
$ (dollar sign)
    in regular expressions, 162–163
    in variables, 53
< > (angle brackets), 78
=> (arrows), in arrays, 264
* (asterisk)
    using with \r and \n characters, 167
**\ (backslash), in escaping
    characters,** 158–159
^ (carat), in regular expressions,
    162–163
{ } (curly braces)
    in loops, 86
    in printing out constants, 137
    printing to strings inside, 297
    surrounding variables, 137
. (dot), adding constants using, 137
**== (double-equals sign), regular
    expressions and,** 163
|| (double-pipe), 154
" (double quotes)
    alternating single and, 78
    in regular expressions, 157
    using in searching text, 80
    using in web form, 70–71
    vs. single quotes ('), 158

**! (exclamation point), bang (negation)
    operator,** 127–128
/ (forward slash)
    in regular expressions, 157
    Root (Home) Directory, 56
-h option vs. --host option, 107
--host option vs. -h option, 107
<i> tags, HTML, 63
\n (line feed character), 166–167,
    216–217, 365
**@ operator, suppressing errors
    using,** 268–269
**.org and .com, mixing up in domain
    names,** 79
**( ) parentheses, mixing up square
    brackets ([ ]) and,** 266
--password option vs. -p option,
    106–107
. (period), in regular expressions, 159
<?php...?>, 78
.php file extension
    about, 46–47
    opening files in browsers, 49–51
| (pipe), in regular expressions, 159
**+ (plus) sign, in regular
    expressions,** 165
-p option
    in MAMP, 99
    vs. --password option, 107
<p> tags, HTML, 63
\r (carriage return), 166–167, 216–217
; (semicolon), in MySQL, 109

Z

zero (0)
arrays counting from, 84
functions counting from, 76
using in programming languages, 74

PHP & MySQL

THE MISSING CD

There's no
CD with this book;
you just saved $5.00.

Instead, every single Web address, practice file, and
piece of downloadable software mentioned in this
book is available at *missingmanuals.com*
(click the Missing CD icon).
There you'll find a tidy list of links,
organized by chapter.

Don't miss a thing!
Sign up for the free Missing
Manual email announcement
list at missingmanuals.com.
We'll let you know when we
release new titles, make
free sample chapters available,
and update the features and
articles on the Missing Manual
website.